DATE DUE

DEMCO 128-5046

SOMETHING ABOUT THE AUTHOR®

Something about
the Author *was named
an "Outstanding
Reference Source,"*
*the highest honor given
by the American
Library Association
Reference and Adult
Services Division.*

ISSN 0276-816X

SOMETHING ABOUT THE AUTHOR®

**Facts and Pictures about Authors
and Illustrators of Books for Young People**

EDITED BY
ALAN HEDBLAD

VOLUME 91

GALE

DETROIT · NEW YORK · TORONTO · LONDON

STAFF

Editor: Alan Hedblad
Managing Editor: Joyce Nakamura
Publisher: Hal May
Associate Editors: Joanna Brod, Sheryl Ciccarelli
Assistant Editor: Marilyn O'Connell Allen

Sketchwriters/Copyeditors: Linda R. Andres, Shelly Andrews,
Mary Gillis, Kevin S. Hile, Janet L. Hile, Laurie Hillstrom,
Motoko Fujishiro Huthwaite, David Johnson, J. Sydney Jones, Thomas F. McMahon,
Gerard J. Senick, Pamela L. Shelton, Diane Telgen, Michaela Swart, and Kathleen Witman

Research Manager: Victoria B. Cariappa
Project Coordinator: Cheryl L. Warnock
Research Associate: Laura C. Bissey
Research Assistant: Alfred A. Gardner

Permissions Manager: Marlene S. Hurst
Permissions Associate: Maureen A. Puhl
Permissions Assistants: Sarah Chesney and Kelly A. Quin

Production Director: Mary Beth Trimper
Production Assistant: Deborah Milliken

Macintosh Artist: Sherrell Hobbs
Image Database Supervisor: Randy Bassett
Imaging Specialists: Mikal Ansari and Robert Duncan
Photography Coordinator: Pamela A. Reed

Library of Congress Catalog Card Number 72-27107

ISBN 0-8103-9948-2 ISSN 0276-816X

Printed in the United States of America

10 9 8 7 6 5 4 3 2 1

Contents

Authors in Forthcoming Volumes viii
Introduction ix
Acknowledgments xi
Illustrations Index 223
Author Index 245

Authors in Forthcoming Volumes

Below are some of the authors and illustrators that will be featured in upcoming volumes of *SATA*. These include new entries on the swiftly rising stars of the field, as well as completely revised and updated entries (indicated with *) on some of the most notable and best-loved creators of books for children.

Jo Ellen Bogart: American/Canadian author Bogart has written a number of popular picture books for preschoolers and primary graders, including the well-received *Daniel's Dog, Sarah Saw a Blue Macaw,* and *Gifts,* the latter work having been shortlisted for two Canadian national book awards: the Mr. Christie's and the Ruth Schwartz Children's Book Award.

*Nancy White Carlstrom: Best known for her "Jesse Bear" books, Carlstrom has been praised as the author of simple, humorous picture and board books for young readers that address subjects ranging from counting and colors to more sophisticated topics like intergenerational and multi-cultural relationships.

*Arthur Geisert: A resident of the American midwest, author and illustrator Geisert has become somewhat of an expert on pigs, which figure prominently in several of his humorous, award-winning picture books. One of his most recent efforts, *Haystack,* was honored by *Parents' Choice, Time,* and *Boston Globe-Horn Book* in 1995.

Barbara Diamond Goldin: Goldin is the author of a variety of works for young people, including picture books, story collections, novels, and nonfiction, that emphasize her Jewish heritage through an exploration of community traditions, history, and folklore. Her *Passover Journey: A Seder Companion* was named an American Library Association notable book in 1995.

*Ronald Himler: A celebrated illustrator of scores of works by such noted children's authors as Eve Bunting and Arnold Adoff, Himler has most recently turned to projects that involve his area of greatest interest: the history of Native Americans and of the American West.

*Ron Koertge: Considered among the finest authors of fiction for young adults, Koertge has been praised for exploring concerns universal to adolescents with humor and insight.

Hilary McKay: English author McKay, whose works have been likened to those of Beverly Cleary and Lois Lowry, has been cited favorably for her strong characterizations, witty dialogue, and skillful evocation of place in such popular tales as *The Exiles* and *Dog Friday.*

*Colin McNaughton: Beloved English author and illustrator McNaughton has delighted countless children on both sides of the Atlantic with his lighthearted stories and cartoon-like drawings. One of his more recent efforts, *Here Come the Aliens!,* was shortlisted for the Kate Greenaway Medal in 1995.

Donna Jo Napoli: A professor of linguistics, Napoli employs both humor and skillful prose to craft stories of hope and inspiration for young readers. She has received scores of favorable assessments and honors for her works, among the most recent of which include *The Bravest Thing, Zel,* and *Song of the Magdalene.*

*Katherine Paterson: Two-time Newbery Medal winner Paterson continues to garner favorable notice with such critically acclaimed efforts as *The Flip-Flop Girl* and *Jip: His Story.*

Stewart Ross: A prolific author of nonfiction for young people, English writer Ross is perhaps best known for his highly regarded *Shakespeare and Macbeth: The Story Behind the Play,* which one reviewer described as a "dynamic gem."

Frances Thomas: Three-time Tir Na N'Og Award-winner Thomas, a native of Wales, is the author of a variety of works for young people of all ages, including picture books for children and historical, contemporary, and science fiction/fantasy stories for older readers.

Connie Nordhielm Wooldridge: *Wicked Jack,* Wooldridge's very successful debut picture book illustrated by Will Hillenbrand, has been described as "stunning."

Introduction

Something about the Author (*SATA*) is an ongoing reference series that deals with the lives and works of authors and illustrators of children's books. *SATA* includes not only well-known authors and illustrators whose books are widely read, but also less prominent individuals whose works are just coming to be recognized. This series is often the only readily available information source on emerging writers and artists. You'll find *SATA* informative and entertaining, whether you are a student, a librarian, an English teacher, a parent, or simply an adult who enjoys children's literature.

What's Inside SATA

SATA provides detailed information about authors and illustrators who span the full time range of children's literature, from early figures like John Newbery and L. Frank Baum to contemporary figures like Judy Blume and Richard Peck. Authors in the series represent primarily English-speaking countries, particularly the United States, Canada, and the United Kingdom. Also included, however, are authors from around the world whose works are available in English translation. The writings represented in *SATA* include those created intentionally for children and young adults as well as those written for a general audience and known to interest younger readers. These writings cover the entire spectrum of children's literature, including picture books, humor, folk and fairy tales, animal stories, mystery and adventure, science fiction and fantasy, historical fiction, poetry and nonsense verse, drama, biography, and nonfiction.

Obituaries are also included in *SATA* and are intended not only as death notices but also as concise overviews of people's lives and work. Additionally, each edition features newly revised and updated entries for a selection of *SATA* listees who remain of interest to today's readers and who have been active enough to require extensive revisions of their earlier biographies.

Two Convenient Indexes

In response to suggestions from librarians, *SATA* indexes no longer appear in every volume but are included in alternate (odd-numbered) volumes of the series, beginning with Volume 57.

SATA continues to include two indexes that cumulate with each alternate volume: the Illustrations Index, arranged by the name of the illustrator, gives the number of the volume and page where the illustrator's work appears in the current volume as well as all preceding volumes in the series; the Author Index gives the number of the volume in which a person's Biographical Sketch or Obituary appears in the current volume as well as all preceding volumes in the series.

These indexes also include references to authors and illustrators who appear in Gale's *Yesterday's Authors of Books for Children, Children's Literature Review,* and the *Something about the Author Autobiography Series.*

Easy-to-Use Entry Format

Whether you're already familiar with the *SATA* series or just getting acquainted, you will want to be aware of the kind of information that an entry provides. In every *SATA* entry the editors attempt to give as complete a picture of the person's life and work as possible. A typical entry in *SATA* includes the following clearly labeled information sections:

- *PERSONAL:* date and place of birth and death, parents' names and occupations, name of spouse, date of marriage, names of children, educational institutions attended, degrees received, religious and political affiliations, hobbies and other interests.

- *ADDRESSES:* complete home, office, electronic mail, and agent addresses, whenever available.

• *CAREER:* name of employer, position, and dates for each career post; art exhibitions; military service; memberships and offices held in professional and civic organizations.

• *AWARDS, HONORS:* literary and professional awards received.

• *WRITINGS:* title-by-title chronological bibliography of books written and/or illustrated, listed by genre when known; lists of other notable publications, such as plays, screenplays, and periodical contributions.

• *ADAPTATIONS:* a list of films, television programs, plays, CD-ROMs, recordings, and other media presentations that have been adapted from the author's work.

• *WORK IN PROGRESS:* description of projects in progress.

• *SIDELIGHTS:* a biographical portrait of the author or illustrator's development, either directly from the biographee—and often written specifically for the *SATA* entry—or gathered from diaries, letters, interviews, or other published sources.

• *FOR MORE INFORMATION SEE:* references for further reading.

• *EXTENSIVE ILLUSTRATIONS:* photographs, movie stills, book illustrations, and other interesting visual materials supplement the text.

How a SATA Entry Is Compiled

A *SATA* entry progresses through a series of steps. If the biographee is living, the *SATA* editors try to secure information directly from him or her through a questionnaire. From the information that the biographee supplies, the editors prepare an entry, filling in any essential missing details with research and/or telephone interviews. If possible, the author or illustrator is sent a copy of the entry to check for accuracy and completeness.

If the biographee is deceased or cannot be reached by questionnaire, the *SATA* editors examine a wide variety of published sources to gather information for an entry. Biographical and bibliographic sources are consulted, as are book reviews, feature articles, published interviews, and material sometimes obtained from the biographee's family, publishers, agent, or other associates.

Entries that have not been verified by the biographees or their representatives are marked with an asterisk (*).

Contact the Editor

We encourage our readers to examine the entire *SATA* series. Please write and tell us if we can make *SATA* even more helpful to you. Give your comments and suggestions to the editor:

BY MAIL: The Editor, *Something about the Author,* Gale Research, 835 Penobscot Bldg., 645 Griswold St., Detroit, MI 48226-4094.

BY TELEPHONE: (800) 347-GALE

BY FAX: (313) 961-6599

BY E-MAIL: CYA@Gale.com@Galesmtp

Acknowledgments

Grateful acknowledgment is made to the following publishers, authors, and artists whose works appear in this volume.

ABBAS, JAILAN. Portrait of Jailan Abbas. Reproduced by permission.

ALEXANDER, ELLEN. From an illustration in *Chaska and the Golden Doll* by Ellen Alexander. Arcade Publishing, 1994. Copyright © 1994 by Ellen Alexander. All rights reserved. Reproduced by permission. / Alexander, Ellen, photograph. Reproduced by permission.

AUEL, JEAN M. From a jacket of *The Plains of Passage* by Jean M. Auel. Crown Publishing, 1990. Reproduced by permission of Crown Publishers, a Division of Random House Inc.

AYME, MARCEL. Sendak, Maurice, illustrator. From *The Wonderful Farm* by Marcel Ayme. Translated by Norman Denny. HarperCollins Publishers, 1951. Copyright 1951 by Librarie Gallimard. Copyright renewed © 1979 by Librarie Gallimard. All rights reserved. Reproduced by permission of HarperCollins Publishers, Inc. / Sendak, Maurice, illustrator. From *The Magic Pictures: More about the Wonderful Farm* by Marcel Ayme. Translated by Norman Denny. Reproduced by permission of HarperCollins Publishers, Inc. / Ayme, Marcel, photograph by Jerry Bauer. Reproduced by permission.

BADT, KARIN L. From a cover of *Hair There and Everywhere* by Karin Luisa Badt. Children's Press, 1994. © Lawrence Migdale/Tony Stone Images; © Kennon Cooke/Valen. Reproduced by permission.

BALIAN, LORNA. From *Amelia's Nine Lives* by Lorna Balian. Abingdon Press, 1986. Copyright © 1996 by Lorna Balian. All rights reserved. Reproduced by permission. / Balian, Lorna, photograph. Reproduced by permission.

BIANCHI, JOHN. From *Spring Break at Pokeweed Public School* by John Bianchi. Bungalo Books, 1994. Reproduced by permission. / Bianchi, John, photograph. Reproduced by permission.

BIERHORST, JOHN. Brierley, Louise, illustrator. From a jacket of *Lightning Inside You and Other Native American Riddles*. Edited by John Bierhorst. Morrow, 1992. Jacket illustration © 1992 by Louise Brierley. All rights reserved. Reproduced by permission of William Morrow and Company, Inc. / Watson, Wendy, illustrator. From *Doctor Coyote* by John Bierhorst. Reprinted with the permission of Simon & Schuster Books for Young Readers, an imprint of Simon & Schuster Children's Publishing Division. Illustrations copyright © 1987 Wendy Watson. / Parker, Robert Andrew, illustrator. From *The Woman Who Fell from the Sky: The Iroquois Story of Creation* by John Bierhorst. Morrow, 1993. Illustrations copyright © 1993 by Robert Andrew Parker. All rights reserved. Reproduced by permission of William Morrow and Company, Inc. / Bierhorst, Jane Byers, jacket design, and Hansen-Sturm, Robert, photography. From a jacket of *The White Deer and Other Stories Told by the Lenape*. Edited by John Bierhorst. Morrow, 1994. Reproduced by permission of William Morrow and Company, Inc. / Bierhorst, John, photograph. Reproduced by permission.

BOULTON, JANE. Cooney, Barbara, illustrator. From *Only Opal: The Diary of a Young Girl* by Opal Whitely. Edited by Jane Boulton. Philomel Books, 1994. Illustrations copyright © 1994 by Barbara Cooney. All rights reserved. Reproduced by permission of Philomel Books.

BRADFIELD, CARL. Portrait of Carl Bradfield. Reproduced by permission.

BULLA, CLYDE ROBERT. Noonan, Julia, illustrator. From *A Place for Angels* by Clyde Robert Bulla. BridgeWater Books, 1995. Illustrations copyright © 1995 by Julia Noonan. All rights reserved. Reproduced by permission. / Magurn, Susan, illustrator. From *Singing Sam* by Clyde Robert Bulla. Random House, 1989. Illustrations copyright © 1989 by Susan Magurn. All rights reserved. Reproduced by permission of Random House, Inc. / Dorros, Arthur, illustrator. From a cover of *Charlie's House* by Clyde Robert Bulla. Thomas Y. Crowell, 1983. Jacket art © 1983 by Arthur Dorros. Reproduced by permission of HarperCollins Publishers, Inc. / Bulla, Clyde Robert, photograph. Reproduced by permission.

CAPOTE, TRUMAN. Peck, Beth, illustrator. From a jacket of *The Thanksgiving Visitor* by Truman Capote. Knopf, 1996. Jacket art copyright © by Beth Peck. Reproduced by permission of Alfred A. Knopf. / Peck, Beth, illustrator. From *A Christmas Memory* by Truman Capote. Knopf, 1986. Illustrations copyright © 1989 by Beth Peck. All rights reserved. Reproduced by permission of Alfred A. Knopf, Inc. / Capote, Truman, photograph.

CARTER, LIN. Vallejo, Boris, illustrator. From *Conan of the Isles* by L. Sprague de Camp and Lin Carter. Reproduced by permission of The Berkley Publishing Group. / Carter, Lin, photograph.

CEBULASH, MEL. Krych, Duane. From a cover of *Bat Boy* by Mel Cebulash. The Child's World, Inc., 1993. Reproduced by permission. / Sabin, Robert, illustrator. From a cover of *The Spring Street Boys Settle a Score* by Mel Cebulash. Scholastic Book

Services, 1981. Reproduced by permission. / Wyman, Cherie R., illustrator. From a cover of *Ruth Marini: World Series Star* by Mel Cebulash. Lerner Publications Company, 1985. Reproduced by permission. / Cebulash, Mel, photograph. Reproduced by permission.

CHASE, ANDRA. Portrait of Andra Chase. Reproduced by permission.

CONWAY, DIANA C. Portrait of Diana C. Conway. Reproduced by permission.

CREEDEN, SHARON. Portrait of Sharon Creeden.

DAVIDSON, DIANE. Portrait of Diane Davidson. Reproduced by permission.

DONER, KIM. Portrait of Kim Doner.

ECKERT, ALLAN W. Ayers, Alan, illustrator. From *That Dark and Bloody River* by Allan W. Eckert. Cover Art copyright © 1995 by Alan Ayers. All rights reserved. Reproduced by permission of Bantam Books, a division of Bantam Doubleday Dell Publishing Group, Inc. / Glanzman, Lou, illustrator. From *The Frontiersmen: A Narrative* by Allan W. Eckert. Cover art copyright © by Lou Glanzman. All rights reserved. Reproduced by permission of Bantam Books, a division of Bantam Doubleday Dell Publishing Group, Inc. / Gough, Alan, illustrator. From *A Sorrow in Our Heart: The Life of Tecumseh* by Allan W. Eckert. Bantam Books, 1992. Cover art copyright © 1992 by Alan Gough. All rights reserved. Reproduced by permission of Bantam Books, a division of Bantam Doubleday Dell Publishing Group, Inc. / Glanzman, Lou, illustrator. From *Twilight of Empire* by Allan W. Eckert. Cover art copyright © 1993 by Lou Glanzman. All rights reserved. Reproduced by permission of Bantam Books, a division of Bantam Doubleday Dell Publishing Group, Inc. / Schoenherr, John, illustrator. From *Incident at Hawk's Hill* by Allan W. Eckert. Bantam Books, 1987. Cover art copyright © 1987 by Bantam Books. All rights reserved. Reproduced by permission of Bantam Books, a division of Bantam Doubleday Dell Publishing Group, Inc. / Eckert, Allan W., photograph by Jay Paris. Reproduced by permission.

EDDINGS, DAVID. Schwinger, Laurence, illustrator. From a cover of *Castle of Wizardry* by David Eddings. Reproduced by permission of Ballantine Books, a division of Random House, Inc. / From a cover of *Sorceress of Darshiva* by David Eddings. Copyright © 1989 by David Eddings. All rights reserved. Reproduced by permission of Ballantine Books, a division of Random House, Inc. / Eddings, David, photograph by Richard Heinzen. Reproduced by permission.

EGAN, LORRAINE HOPPING. Portrait of Lorraine Hopping Egan. Reproduced by permission.

EPANYA, CHRISTIAN A. Portrait of Christian A. Epanya. Reproduced by permission.

ESTES, ELEANOR. From a jacket of *The Curious Adventures of Jimmy McGee* by Eleanor Estes, illustrations copyright © 1987 by John O'Brien, reproduced by permission of Harcourt Brace & Company. / From *The Moffat Museum,* copyright © 1983 by Eleanor Estes, reproduced by permission of Harcourt Brace & Company. / Ayer, Jacqueline, illustrator. From *The Lost Umbrella of Kim Chu* by Eleanor Estes. Reprinted with the permission of Margaret K. McElderry Books, an imprint of Simon & Schuster Children's Publishing Division. Illustrations copyright © 1978 by Jacqueline Ayer. / Estes, Eleanor, photograph by Jim Theologos. Reproduced by permission.

FONTENOT, MARY ALICE. Blazek, Scott R., illustrator. From *Clovis Crawfish and Bidon Box Turtle* by Mary Alice Fontenot. Pelican Publishing Company, 1996. Copyright © 1996 by Mary Alice Fontenot and Scott R. Blazek. All rights reserved. Reproduced by permission. / Fontenot, Mary Alice, photograph. Reproduced by permission.

FOURIE, CORLIA. Portrait of Corlia Fourie. Reproduced by permission.

GENTILE, PETRINA. Portrait of Petrina Gentile. Reproduced by permission.

GETZ, DAVID. From a cover of *Frozen Man* by David Getz. Copyright © 1994 by David Getz. Illustrations © 1994 by Peter McCarty. Reprinted by permission of Henry Holt & Co., Inc.

GILSON, JAMIE. deRosa, Dee, illustrator. From a jacket of *Soccer Circus* by Jamie Gilson. Lothrop, Lee & Shepard Books, 1993. Jacket art © 1993 by Dee deRosa. All rights reserved. Reproduced by permission of Lothrop, Lee & Shepard Books, a division of William Morrow Company, Inc. / Gilson, Jamie, photograph by Matthew Gilson. © 1996 by Matthew Gilson. All rights reserved. Reproduced by permission.

GREEN, TIMOTHY. Portrait of Timothy Green. Reproduced by permission.

HAAB, SHERRI. Portrait of Sherri Haab by Pete Fox. Reproduced by permission.

HARTMAN, VICTORIA. Alley, R. W., illustrator. From a jacket of *The Silliest Joke Book Ever* by Victoria Hartman. Lothrop, Lee & Shepard Books, 1993. Jacket illustrations © 1993 by R. W. Alley. All rights reserved. Reproduced by permission of Lothrop, Lee & Shepard Books, a division of William Morrow Company, Inc.

HAYES, GEOFFREY. From *The Night of the Circus Monsters* by Geoffrey Hayes. Random House, 1996. Copyright © 1996 by Geoffrey Hayes. All rights reserved. Reproduced by permission of Random House, Inc.

HILL, ANTHONY. Portrait of Anthony Hill by Sandy Spiers. Reproduced by permission.

HILLERT, MARGARET. Werner, Tom, illustrator. From a cover of *The Sky Is Not So Far Away* by Margaret Hillert. Boyds Mills Press, 1996. Reproduced by permission. / Hillert, Margaret, photograph by Kathleen Balkema. Reproduced by permission.

HOGARTH, GRACE ALLEN. Marriott, Pat, illustrator. From *A Sister for Helen* by Grace Hogarth. Andre Deutsch, 1976. Illustrations © 1976 by Pat Marriott. All rights reserved. Reproduced by permission of Andre Deutsch Ltd.

HOLLINGSWORTH, MARY. Portrait of Mary Hollingsworth. Reproduced by permission.

HOSTETLER, MARIAN. Portrait of Marian Hostetler. Reproduced by permission.

HUNT, IRENE. From a cover of *Up a Road Slowly* by Irene Hunt. Tempo Books, 1966. Copyright © 1966 by Irene Hunt. All rights reserved. Reprinted by permission of The Berkley Publishing Group. / From a cover of *Across Five Aprils* by Irene Hunt. Tempo Books, 1965. Copyright © 1964 by Irene Hunt. All rights reserved. Reprinted by permission of The Berkley Publishing Group. / Portrait of Irene Hunt. American Library Association. Reproduced by permission.

JACKSON, DAVE. Jackson, Julian, illustrator. From *Danger on the Flying Trapeze* by Dave Jackson and Neta Jackson. Illustrations copyright © 1995 Bethany House Publishers. All rights reserved. Reproduced by permission. / Jackson, Dave and Jackson, Neta, photograph by Jeff Slocomb. Reproduced by permission.

JACKSON, MIKE. Portrait of Mike Jackson. Reproduced by permission.

JACKSON, NETA. McLaughlin, Catherine Reishus, illustrator. From a cover of *Listen for the Whippoorwill* by Dave Jackson and Neta Jackson. Bethany House Publishers, 1993. Illustrations © 1993 Bethany House Publishers. All rights reserved. Reproduced by permission.

JOHNSON, LOIS WALFRID. Jorgenson, Andrea, illustrator. From a cover of *Disaster on Windy Hill* by Lois Walfrid Johnson. Bethany House Publishers, 1995. Reproduced by permission. / Jorgenson, Andrea, illustrator. From *Escape into the Night* by Lois Walfrid Johnson. Bethany House Publishers, 1995. Reproduced by permission. / Johnson, Lois Walfrid, photograph by Buz Swerkstrom. Reproduced by permission.

KELLER, BEVERLY L. Wimmer, Mike, illustrator. From a cover of *Fowl Play, Desdemona* by Beverly Keller. Copyright © 1991 by Mike Wimmer. All rights reserved. Reproduced by permission of HarperCollins Publishers, Inc. / Newsom, Tom, illustrator. From a cover of *Only Fiona* by Beverly Keller. Copyright © 1989 by Tom Newsom. All rights reserved. Reproduced by permission of HarperCollins Publishers, Inc. / Keller, Beverly, photograph. Reproduced by permission.

KUNTZ, J. L. Portrait of J. L. Kuntz. Reproduced by permission.

KURTZ, JANE. Cooper, Floyd, illustrator. From a jacket of *Pulling the Lion's Tail* by Jane Kurtz. Jacket illustration copyright © 1995 by Floyd Cooper. Reprinted with the permission of Simon & Schuster Books for Young Readers, an imprint of Simon & Schuster Children's Publishing Division. / Kurtz, Jane, photograph. Reproduced by permission.

LEHMAN, BOB. Lehman, Elaine. From a cover of *Petey the Peacock Breaks a Leg!* by Bob Lehman and Elaine Lehman. Scythe Publications, Inc., 1995. © 1995 by Bob Lehman and Elaine Lehman. All rights reserved. Reproduced by permission.

LIGHTBURN, RON. From *Waiting for the Whales* by Sheryl McFarlane. Philomel Books, 1991. Illustrations copyright © 1991 by Ron Lightburn. All rights reserved. Reproduced by permission of Philomel Books. / Lightburn, Ron, photograph by Jon Hoadley.

LIGHTBURN, SANDRA. Portrait of Sandra Lightburn by Ron Lightburn. Reproduced by permission.

LUTTRELL, IDA. Pretro, Korinna, illustrator. From *The Star Counters* by Ida Luttrell. Tambourine Books, 1994. Reproduced by permission. / Lewin, Betsy, illustrator. From *Mattie's Little Possum Pet* by Ida Luttrell. Illustrations copyright © 1993 by Betsy Lewin. Reprinted with the permission of Atheneum Books for Young Readers, an imprint of Simon & Schuster Children's Publishing Division.

MANN, KENNY. Leonard, Richard and Alcala, Alfredo, illustrators. From *"I Am Not Afraid!"* by Kenny Mann. Bantam Books, 1993, Cover and interior illustrations copyright © 1993 by Byron Preiss Visual Publications. All rights reserved. Reproduced by permission of Bantam Books, a division of Bantam Doubleday Dell Publishing Group, Inc. / Mann, Kenny, photograph. Reproduced by permission.

MANN, PAMELA. Portrait of Pamela Mann. Reproduced by permission.

MCCALLUM, STEPHEN. Portrait of Stephen McCallum. Reproduced by permission.

MCKINNEY, NADINE. Portrait of Nadine McKinney.

METCALF, DORIS H. Portrait of Doris H. Metcalf. Reproduced by permission.

MILLER, ROBERT H. Hanna, Cheryl, illustrator. From *The Story of Stagecoach Mary Fields* by Robert H. Miller. Silver Press, 1995. Illustrations copyright © 1995 Cheryl Hanna. All rights reserved. Reproduced by permission. / Miller, Robert H., photograph. Reproduced by permission.

MISHICA, CLARE. Portrait of Clare Mishica by Gary Mishica. Reproduced by permission.

SOMETHING ABOUT THE AUTHOR®

ABBAS, Jailan 1952-

■ Personal

Born March 11, 1952, in Cairo, Egypt; daughter of Mohamed Aly Abbas (an Egyptian Undersecretary of State for Finance) and Mariam A. Farid (a pharmacist); children: Mariam Bahi El Din. *Education:* Helwan University, B.A., 1972, M.A., 1988, Ph.D., 1996; Cairo University, postgraduate diploma (archaeology), 1978. *Religion:* Muslim.

■ Addresses

Home—24 Rd. 200 Degla, Maadi, Cairo, Egypt. *Office*—Cairo American College, P.O. Box 39, Maadi, Cairo 11431, Egypt.

■ Career

School of Tourism and Hotel Management, Helwan University, Cairo, professor of guiding methodology, 1979-93; Cairo American College, Cairo, Egypt, teacher of Egyptian culture, 1981—. Active in community volunteer activities. Guest lecturer on Egyptian history and culture in many cultural and educational institutions. *Member:* Women's Association of Egypt, Union of Arab Historians.

■ Writings

FOR CHILDREN

The Festivals of Egypt, Hoopoe Books (Egypt), 1995, AMIDEAST Publications (Washington, D.C.), 1995.

Abbas has also published two books in Arabic for adults: *Metals and Jewelry of Islamic Egypt,* Egyptian Information Department, 1987, and *The Monuments of Ancient Egypt as Seen by Middle Ages Travelers,* Egyptian-Lebanese Publishers, 1992. In addition, she writes a monthly column called "Dardashah" on Egyptian cultural and educational issues in the *Cairo-glyphics,* the newsletter of Cairo American College.

■ Work in Progress

Egypt Land and People, for children, in English; several books in Arabic for adults, including *Islamic Monuments of Egypt as seen by Middle Ages Travelers* and *Feasts and Festivals of Egypt and Their Historical Origins.*

■ Sidelights

"When I was a child, my teachers always complimented my compositions and essay writing in both English and Arabic," Egyptian writer Jailan Abbas told *SATA.* "In middle school and high school I started writing poems which I kept for myself. I never thought I would be an author until I was asked by the Information Department in Egypt to write a simple book in a series to introduce laymen to Islamic arts. My first book was *Metals and*

JAILAN ABBAS

Jewelry of Islamic Egypt; still I did not think of myself as an author. It was not until I finished my M.A. that I felt I wanted people to benefit from what I researched, and not just academic professionals. In 1992 my second book, *The Monuments of Ancient Egypt as Seen by Middle Ages Travelers,* was published, also in Arabic and also for adults. This book was greatly complimented and very well received by the media.

"Now, how did I start writing for children? I teach Egyptian culture at Cairo American College in the elementary school. When I started fifteen years ago we had no text books. As a matter of fact, I could not find one book to cover all of what I wanted to teach, so I started writing the material for children in grades 1-6. At that point I felt I would like children to know more about Egypt as I know it and feel it. I was very busy with my Ph.D. so I waited for a while. Coincidently, a friend of mine who knew the owner of children's book publisher Hoopoe mentioned my idea. *The Festivals of Egypt* was the result; the information in this book was part of the research I did for my Ph.D. thesis. The book was also very well received and eighteen months after its publication we are preparing the second edition.

"I will continue writing for children in both English and Arabic. I believe that children are the future, and that the best way to respect other people's cultures is to know one's own culture and be proud of it. I also believe that to learn about a country you need to learn about its people—not just history or political movements. I hope to write for Egyptian children in Arabic, a series about Egypt so they may establish a belief and pride in their own culture. I have one daughter; she is an excellent, talented writer of poems and short stories and she illustrates her writing. Since her early childhood I have encouraged her to read and to write. I wish she would become a writer one day."

■ For More Information See

PERIODICALS

Middle East Times (Egypt), May 21-27, 1995, p. 13.

* * *

ADAMS, Nicholas
See PINE, Nicholas

* * *

ALEXANDER, Ellen 1938-

■ Personal

Born October 1, 1938, in New York, NY; children: Lisa Cochran, Elaine, Kate. *Education:* State University of New York, Albany, B.A. (Spanish), M.A. (English); Syracuse University, M.F.A. (Illustration). *Hobbies and other interests:* Travel and study related to Native Peoples of the Americas.

■ Addresses

Home and office—110 Mesa Vista, Sante Fe, NM 87501.

■ Career

Author, reteller, and illustrator. Teacher and professor of Spanish, English, ESL, art, and silversmithing at high schools and colleges in New York and New Mexico. Self-employed as a painter and woodcarver. Member of arts councils and festival boards of directors in New York and New Mexico. Speaker about children's books and Latin America at schools, colleges, and community organizations. Activities director and Campfire Girls leader. *Member:* Society of Children's Book Writers and Illustrators.

■ Awards, Honors

Grant from the National Parks Foundation to write and illustrate *Pecos and Its People,* a history of Pecos, New Mexico, for middle-grade students.

■ Writings

(Self-illustrated) *Llama and the Great Flood: A Folktale from Peru,* Crowell, 1989; also reprinted in *Make a Splash,* a bilingual text/workbook in Spanish and English for third graders, Macmillan/McGraw-Hill, 1990.

(Self-illustrated) *Atsuki: A Young Traveler,* Unitarian Church, 1990.

(Self-illustrated) *Chaska and the Golden Doll,* Arcade, 1993.

(Self-illustrated) *Pecos and Its People,* 1996.

ILLUSTRATOR

Andrea Clardy, *Dusty Was My Friend,* Human Sciences Press, 1979.

Judy Hawes, *Fireflies in the Night,* HarperCollins, 1991; also reprinted by IBM as part of a computerized reading program.

■ Work in Progress

Where the Mockingbird Sang, a historical novel for middle graders that describes the coming of Don Juan de Onate to San Gabriel Pueblo in New Mexico in 1598 and uses the relationship of two ten year olds, a Spanish girl and a Pueblo Indian boy, to demonstrate cultural conflict; two picture book retellings: a Zapotec Indian legend from Mexico and a Carib Indian legend from the West Indies.

■ Sidelights

Ellen Alexander told *SATA:* "My lifelong interest in languages (my native language is German) has led to an interest in travel, and that has led to my fascination with other cultures. I think it is very important to make children aware of different cultures and how people

Wandering to the courtyard, Chaska found her mother and grandfather stripping maize. They pulled the golden kernels from the cobs and put them into bags to send to market.

While playing near her home in the Andes Mountains, Chaska unearths an ancient Incan idol made of gold. (From *Chaska and the Golden Doll,* written and illustrated by Ellen Alexander.)

everywhere share the same basic universal needs and desires.

"Through my travels in South America and my recent move to New Mexico, my interest has focused increasingly on Native American cultures. I live in an area rich in those cultures, including Pueblo, Navajo, and Apache. Each day I learn more about how these amazing people have suffered and survived the clash with non-native peoples. They have a lot to teach us, as do the other natives of the Americas."

Alexander's books for children reflect her fascination with native culture, especially its myths and legends. Her first book, *Llama and the Great Flood: A Folktale from Peru,* is a picture book inspired by a collection of myths from the northeastern region of that country and illustrated with watercolors outlined in pen. Paralleling the Bible story of Noah's Ark, the book describes how a llama, who dreams that the world is destroyed by a flood, saves himself, his master, and the man's family from destruction. When the party goes to the top of a mountain, they find themselves joined by all the animals and birds of the world; after staying on the mountain for five days, they come down and begin to start a new life. Ilene Cooper comments in *Booklist* that *Llama and the Great Flood* "should prove useful as a supplement to South American units, where folktales are in short supply, and as an interesting comparison to other great flood stories." Alexander's third book,

ELLEN ALEXANDER

Chaska and the Golden Doll, is the true story of a young girl living in a remote Andean village who finds an Inca idol among some ancient ruins. Influenced by an old tale her grandfather tells her in which the sweat of the Incan Sun God falls to earth as gold, Chaska thinks the treasure is a golden doll. After speaking to the elders of her village, she decides to sell the idol to a nearby history museum, an act which provides money for a schoolhouse big enough for all of the local children. *Chaska and the Golden Doll* is described by *Kirkus Reviews* as "a likeable, useful contribution," while *Publishers Weekly* notes that "its focus on Incan culture gives it some educational value."

"My stories and pictures," Alexander told *SATA,* "develop as I live in a place: I did *Llama* and *Chaska* in the Peruvian Andes, the Zapotec story in Mexico, and the Carib story while staying in the Carib Territory on the island of Dominica in the West Indies. The Onate story takes place at the San Gabriel-San Juan Pueblo ten minutes from my house, and I did a lot of writing and sketching for the Pecos story right in Pecos, sitting among the ruins of the ancient pueblo.

"Another thing that is very important to me is to work with the people I'm writing about. If I am to tell their story, it must be as *they* would want it told. And, of course, it is wonderful for me to be able to spend time talking with Quechua Indians in Peru, the Carib chief in Dominica, the elders of San Juan Pueblo, and the last remaining full-blooded Pecos Indian!"

■ Works Cited

Review of *Chaska and the Golden Doll, Kirkus Reviews,* June 1, 1994, p. 771.
Review of *Chaska and the Golden Doll, Publishers Weekly,* May 30, 1994, p. 56.
Cooper, Ilene, review of *Llama and the Great Flood: A Folktale from Peru, Booklist,* April 1, 1989, p. 1378.

*   *   *

ALLEN, Grace
See HOGARTH, Grace (Weston) Allen

*   *   *

ARLEY, Robert
See JACKSON, Mike

*   *   *

AUEL, Jean M(arie) 1936-

■ Personal

Surname pronounced "owl"; born February 18, 1936, in Chicago, IL; daughter of Neil S. (a painter and decorator) and Martha (Wirtanen) Untinen; married Ray B. Auel (an operations manager for an electrical firm), March 19, 1954; children: RaeAnn, Karen, Lenore,

Kendall, Marshall. *Education:* Attended Portland State University; University of Portland, M.B.A., 1976. *Politics:* Independent. *Hobbies and other interests:* Writing poetry, cooking, math, wine tasting, art collecting, archaeology, anthropology, science in general, traveling, giving lectures, and studying French.

■ Addresses

Office—c/o Crown Publishers, 201 E. 50th St., New York, NY 10022.

■ Career

Tektronix, Beaverton, OR, clerk, 1965-66, circuit board designer, 1966-73, technical writer, 1973-74, credit manager, 1974-76; writer. Lecturer at universities and museums, including Smithsonian Institution, American Museum of Natural History, Academy of Science, and Royal Ontario Museum; speaker at numerous conferences. Member of board, International Women's Forum. *Member:* Authors League of America, Authors Guild, PEN, Mensa, Oregon Writers Colony, Willamette Writers Club.

■ Awards, Honors

Pacific Northwest Booksellers Association, 1980, American Book Award nomination for best first novel, Award for Excellence in Writing, Vicki Penziner Matson Award, Friends of Literature, all 1981, all for *The Clan of the Cave Bear;* Golden Plate award, American Academy of Achievement, 1986; Cultural Resources Management Award, U.S. Department of the Interior, and Publieksprijs voor het Nederlandse Boek (Holland), both 1990; award from National Zoo, Washington, DC. D.L., University of Portland, 1983; D.H., University of Maine, 1985; D.H.L., Mt. Vernon College, 1985.

■ Writings

NOVELS; "EARTH'S CHILDREN" SERIES

The Clan of the Cave Bear, Crown, 1980.
The Valley of Horses, Crown, 1982.
The Mammoth Hunters, Crown, 1985.
The Plains of Passage, Crown, 1990.

OTHER

Contributor of poetry to *From Oregon with Love,* edited by Anne Hinds, Hern's Quill. Auel's works have been translated into eighteen languages, including Dutch, Finnish, Hebrew, Italian, Japanese, Portuguese, Serbo-Croatian, and Spanish.

■ Adaptations

The Clan of the Cave Bear was adapted into a motion picture and released by Warner Brothers in 1986; each of Auel's books is available on audiocassette.

■ Work in Progress

Further books in the "Earth's Children" series.

JEAN M. AUEL

■ Sidelights

Jean M. Auel is noted for bringing the world of prehistory alive in a series of exciting, fast-paced novels that includes *The Clan of the Cave Bear, The Valley of Horses,* and *The Mammoth Hunters.* Topping bestseller charts and earning their author many awards, these well-researched and entertaining epics follow the life of a young woman named Ayla. They have broken publishing convention by drawing many readers to a subject—cavemen—that has otherwise proven relatively unpopular. "Auel's evocation of a prehistoric landscape where aurochs and mammoths roamed at will, and of a primordial society bound in by talisman and taboo, is shiningly intense," wrote Barbara A. Bannon in a review of *The Valley of Horses* for *Publishers Weekly.* But Auel's triumph has been one of a personal as well as literary nature: "One publisher told me my story was too long, that no one would pay the money to buy such a long book by an unknown author," Auel admitted to Norma Libman in the *Chicago Tribune.* "But if you believe in what you're doing, you just don't give up."

One of five children born to a housepainter and his wife, Auel was raised in Chicago, Illinois. Her love for books developed early; "I cried after my first day in first grade because I hadn't learned to read yet," she once commented. "I expected it to happen instantly!" Devouring fairy tales, science fiction, and anything else that crossed

her path, Auel soon grew into a well-rounded reader. In 1954, eighteen-year-old Auel married a young man whom she had known since grade school; scarcely seven years later she found herself the mother of five children. Balancing many family-centered responsibilities with a part-time job as a data-entry clerk, Auel had little free time to indulge in hobbies like writing. By the mid-1960s, after her youngest child was school age, she decided to go back to school and pursue a college degree. She also began a full-time job at a local manufacturing company, where she was promoted from data-entry to typist, circuit board designer, and then to technical writer. Auel earned her master's degree in business administration in 1976.

By this time Auel was well established in her career, having been promoted to the position of credit manager. However, dissatisfaction with her current job prompted the forty-year-old manager to resign shortly after obtaining her M.B.A. With three children in college, she knew she needed to find some way to replace the substantial salary she had been making. While she was contemplating her next move, Auel began to formulate the idea behind "Earth's Children." Despite some early efforts at writing poetry, she had always counted herself among those who wished they were a writer but who could never find the time to translate their ideas into words. For the first time in years she suddenly found herself with the time to put pen to paper and let her story ideas flow freely. One idea in particular haunted Auel, and on a winter's night in 1977 she sat down at the typewriter and began to type. "I decided to write this story of a young woman who was living with people who were different," she explained of the short outline that would eventually take on mammoth proportions as a 450,000-word novel called *The Clan of the Cave Bear.*

Lots of research gave Auel the focus she needed for what had been only a rough idea when she first jotted it down that night in 1977. "The more I read, the more the story kept growing," she recalled to interviewer Libman in the *Chicago Tribune,* "and I'd read about something and think of something new to add to the story. And I got so fired up about it. I thought: 'Here's this whole world and it's fresh, it's green; you can write fiction that's never been written before. And it's not cave man, Hollywood-style. We're talking about people who were modern humans." In addition to library trips, Auel and her husband took part in a winter wilderness survival course, so she could better bring to life her protagonist's attempts to make shelter during the Ice Age. In addition, she traveled to many of the sites that provide the backdrop for her fiction.

After Auel researched and wrote the first draft of her novel, she read it and realized she didn't like it. She determined to rewrite the story, honing her writing skills in order to better express the passion she felt for her subject. "I knew that to make my story believable I would have to get in some depth of description," she told Roy Bongartz in *Publishers Weekly.* "Anyway, I hate a book that just says, 'They went out and got food and ate it.' How did they get it? Where did they get it?

How did they cook it? I want to know." During the rewriting process, the manuscript actually grew larger. Auel then realized that her story was too big for one novel. In fact, she had enough material for several books. "I can still remember telling my husband, 'I've got six books,'" Auel reminisced in *At the Field's End: Interviews with Twenty Pacific Northwest Writers.* Her husband was somewhat skeptical, however. "He said, 'You've never written a short story, and now you're going to write six books?'"

Any worries her husband may have had were soon put to rest; Auel worked furiously on her fiction. 1980's *The Clan of the Cave Bear* is the first installment in her "Earth's Children" series, which follows the character of Ayla as she searches for a permanent place in her prehistoric world. Set in the Black Sea region of Eastern Europe during the Upper Paleolithic period—between thirty-five and forty thousand years ago—*The Clan of the Cave Bear* focuses on the adventures of its young heroine, orphaned at age five after her Cro-Magnon parents are killed in an earthquake. Ayla is adopted by members of the Cave Bear clan—a tribe of Neanderthal hunter-gatherers who will eventually be replaced everywhere on earth by Cro-Magnon as the dominant human species. The young, blonde girl is first shunned by these silent, dark people because of her "strange" physical appearance and is known as one of the "Others." But she eventually finds a friend in the tribe's medicine woman, who adopts Ayla and teaches her the ways of the clan. Despite her independent, innovative, and sometimes defiant nature, Ayla brings the clan good fortune by using her higher intelligence—the Cro-Magnon brain was more highly developed than that of the Neanderthal—to improve their quality of life. She is eventually honored with a clan name—The Woman Who Hunts—and lives among the Cave Bear clan until a tragic event occurs. After reaching womanhood, Ayla is attacked and made pregnant by a clan leader who is threatened by her abilities; she bears his child and is then banished without her son. Ayla ventures into the unknown realizing that her physical differences will always set her apart from the Cave Bear tribe; she accepts her fate and resolves to search for her own people.

Earning its author a large readership, Auel's first novel was nominated for the prestigious American Book Award in 1981, and was followed the next year by *The Valley of Horses.* In this second "Earth's Children" novel, Ayla learns to be self-sufficient. Now cast out of her tribe, she must use her intelligence, resourcefulness, and strength to survive several cold winters. Hunting for food, taming and learning to ride a horse, fashioning tools, and raising a small lion cub are just a few of the things that she accomplishes over a period of three years. Then her path crosses that of two strangers, who turn out to be members of her own race of "Others." When they are attacked by her lion, one of the men is killed, but Ayla rescues his brother, a handsome Cro-Magnon hunter named Jondalar. She nurses the wounded hunter back to health, and getting to know the tall, blond, charismatic Jondalar is a turning point for Ayla.

His use of spoken rather than sign language and his sophistication in other areas broadens her outlook and her aspirations. The two ultimately fall in love and begin a journey west to Europe and the land of Jondalar's people.

After the publication of *The Valley of Horses,* Auel found a need for further research. Visits to several European and Russian archeological sites containing Ice Age remains—particularly the cave in Lascaux, France, that houses the most famous example of Paleolithic art yet discovered—inspired Auel's next book. Published in 1985, *The Mammoth Hunters* is the third installment of "Earth's Children." Again featuring Ayla, who is now almost twenty years old, *The Mammoth Hunters* focuses on the Cro-Magnon culture. Traveling with her lover Jondalar, Ayla reaches a tribe of mammoth hunters called the Mamutoi. Among the Mamutoi, distant cousins to Jondalar, the beautiful woman is first viewed with suspicion due to her varied abilities, her unusual dialect, her graceful manner, and the instinctive understanding of nature that she inherited from the clan of the Cave Bear. However, Ayla eventually wins the respect of this new tribe, and finds romance with one of its members. Meanwhile Jondalar becomes distant; he begins to have doubts about his beloved Ayla and fears

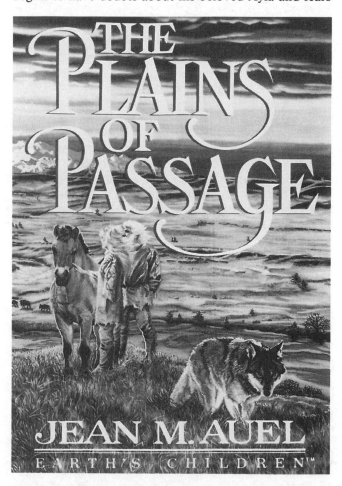

Auel's 1990 book from the "Earth's Children" series continues Ayla's difficult journey across prehistoric Europe in search of her own people.

she may not be accepted by his own people, the Zelandonii. However, he eventually reconfirms his love for her and the couple are reunited.

In *The Plains of Passage,* published in 1990, Ayla and Jondalar leave the Mamutoi and continue their journey to the lands of the Zelandonii tribe. Their travels take them across the grass-covered plains of Europe—what are now Hungary, Austria, and Germany—where their appearance is met with suspicion by people of lesser talents and skills. On their way to their destination in southwestern France, they are faced with several trials: floods and ice-flows, blizzards, a swarm of locusts, and battles with hostile peoples to whom they must prove themselves through their skill in healing the sick.

Auel's popularity continues to grow as new readers discover the series. While her Ice Age saga has won over countless readers, some critics have dismissed Auel's work as mere historic romance fiction containing unnecessarily graphic portrayals of sex. And her characters' use of twentieth-century speech and jargon has also been criticized. However, as Grover Sales notes in the *Los Angeles Times Book Review,* "One must admire the painstaking anthropological research Auel has poured into her [work] .... Even readers turned off by the gimmicky form ... may find fascination in the technique of human survival in the late Pleistocene Epoch."

One of the most common criticisms of the "Earth's Children" series concerns the character of Ayla, who has been dismissed as a modern-day feminist in prehistoric drag. However, by endowing Ayla with heroic characteristics, Auel deliberately attempted to counterbalance the overwhelmingly male heroes of the books from her own childhood. From the beginning, she resolved to create a female character possessing those same qualities: strength, intelligence, resourcefulness, even aggressiveness, and yet also compassion and caring. Throughout Auel's saga, Ayla survives her position as an outcast and actually makes several technological advancements. She is credited with developing a sling to hurl projectiles in self-defense, designing a sewing needle to draw cord through skins, the ability to coax fire from a piece of stone, and using plants to heal.

The research necessary to depict such human advances in a way that holds a reader's attention has won over many reviewers. Auel's books have also gained stature from their use as texts in college and university undergraduate archaeology classes. As Lindsy Van Gelder explains in *Ms.,* "We learn about the plants that an Ice Age medicine woman might use to cure different ills, how to build an earthlodge out of mammoth bones and skins, how to knap flint, how to use mashed animal brains and stale human urine to process soft, white leather, and much, much more." "There's an authenticity about the life styles and survival techniques of these cavemen that's deeply moving," adds Willard Simms in the *Los Angeles Times Book Review.* "When it's man against the elements, struggling to survive in a forbidding and hostile world he doesn't understand, the writing rings clear and true."

One of the most interesting aspects of Auel's interpretation of prehistoric life is her hypothesis as to why Cro-Magnon man survived over the Neanderthal; because of the scant physical evidence that remains, this is a question that continues to divide anthropologists. Ken Ringle explains in the *Washington Post* that Auel "decided to endow [the Neanderthal] with a dominant racial memory that wedded them to the past, while Cro-Magnon man's ability to learn and adapt better equipped him for the future. This melding of known fact with imagination," adds Ringle, "may be Auel's greatest achievement."

■ Works Cited

Auel, Jean M., interview with Roy Bongartz in *Publishers Weekly,* November 29, 1985, pp. 50-51.

Auel, Jean M., interview in *At the Field's End: Interviews with Twenty Pacific Northwest Writers,* edited by Nicholas O'Connell, Madronas Publishers, 1987, pp. 208-19.

Auel, Jean M., interview with Norma Libman in *Chicago Tribune,* December 16, 1990.

Bannon, Barbara A., review of *The Valley of Horses, Publishers Weekly,* July 30, 1982, p. 61.

Ringle, Ken, "Jean M. Auel: The Smashing Saga of the 'Cave' Woman; Ice Age Melodramas and Mammoth Success," *Washington Post,* February 13, 1982, p. D1.

Sales, Grover, "Primordial Passions of Pleistocene Times: The Flesh Is Willing but the Diction Is Weak," *Los Angeles Times Book Review,* September 12, 1982, p. 3.

Simms, Willard, "Neanderthal as a Dummy," *Los Angeles Times Book Review,* November 2, 1980, p. 4.

Van Gelder, Lindsy, "Lindsy Van Gelder on Jean Auel," *Ms.,* March, 1986, pp. 64, 70.

■ For More Information See

PERIODICALS

Booklist, July 15, 1980, p. 1638.

Boston Globe, January 14, 1986, pp. 59, 62.

Chicago Tribune, September 14, 1980; November 11, 1985; February 16, 1986; December 24, 1990.

Los Angeles Times, November 3, 1982; February 9, 1986.

New York Times, November 21, 1982; November 28, 1985.

New York Times Book Review, July 27, 1980; August 31, 1980, pp. 7, 20; October 26, 1980; November 24, 1985, p. 24; November 18, 1990, p. 29.

People, December 16, 1985, pp. 113-14, 117.

Publishers Weekly, August 24, 1990, p. 53.

School Library Journal, November, 1980, p. 91; February, 1983, p. 94; May, 1986; April, 1991, p. 153.

Tribune Books (Chicago), October 7, 1990.

Voice of Youth Advocates, December, 1982, p. 28.

Washington Post Book World, September 28, 1980, pp. 6, 10; December 15, 1985.*

AYME, Marcel (Andre) 1902-1967

■ Personal

Born March 28, 1902, in Joigny, France; died of pneumonia, October 14, 1967, in Paris, France; son of Joseph (a blacksmith) and Emma (Monamy) Ayme; married Marie-Antoinette Arnaud, 1932. *Education:* Studied medicine for one year.

■ Career

Novelist; author of short stories and children's books; playwright. Worked as office and bank clerk, insurance broker, movie extra, bricklayer, reporter, salesman, and accountant in the Paris bourse. *Military service:* Served in the French Army.

■ Awards, Honors

Theophraste Renaudot prize, 1929, for *La Table-aux-creves;* Prix Chanteclair, 1935, for *Les Contes du chat perche.* Numerous awards and honors refused, including membership in the Academie Francaise.

■ Writings

FOR YOUNG READERS; IN ENGLISH TRANSLATION

The Wonderful Farm, translated by Norman Denny, illustrations by Maurice Sendak, Harper, 1951 (originally published as *Les Contes du chat perche,* Gallimard, 1934).
The Magic Pictures: More about the Wonderful Farm, translated by Norman Denny, illustrations by Maurice Sendak, Harper, 1954 (originally published as *Autres contes du chat perche,* Gallimard, 1950).

FOR ADULTS; IN ENGLISH TRANSLATION

The Hollow Field, translated by Helen Waddell, Dodd, Mead, 1933 (originally published as *La Table-aux-creves,* Gallimard, 1929).
The Transient Hour, translated by Eric Sutton, A. A. Wyn, 1948 (originally published as *Le Chemin des ecoliers,* Gallimard, 1946).
The Fable and the Flesh, translated by Eric Sutton, Bodley Head, 1949 (originally published as *La Vouivre,* Gallimard, 1943).
The Walker through Walls and Other Stories, translated by Norman Denny, Berkley, 1950 (originally published as *Le Passe-muraille,* Gallimard, 1943).
Clerambard: A Comedy in Four Acts (play; first produced in Paris at Comedie des Champs-Elysees, 1950, produced Off-Broadway, 1957), translated by Norman Denny, Bodley Head, 1952 (originally published as *Clerambard,* Grasset, 1950).
The Barkeep of Blemont, translated by Norman Denny, Harper, 1950 (originally published as *Uranus,* Gallimard, 1948).
The Second Face, translated by Norman Denny, Harper, 1951, reprinted as *The Miraculous Barber,* translated by Eric Sutton, Harper, 1951 (originally published as *Travelingue,* Gallimard, 1941).

MARCEL AYME

The House of Men, translated by Norman Denny, Bodley Head, 1952 (originally published as *Maison basse,* Gallimard, 1935).
The Secret Stream, translated by Norman Denny, Harper, 1953 (originally published as *Le Moulin de la Sourdine,* Gallimard, 1936).
The Green Mare, translated by Norman Denny, Harper, 1955 (originally published as *La Jument verte,* Gallimard, 1933).
Moonbirds (play; first produced in Paris at Theater de l'Atelier, 1955), translated by John Parker, Hart Stenographic Bureau, 1959 (originally published as *Les Oiseaux de lune,* Gallimard, 1956).
Grand Seduction, Fawcett, 1958 (originally published as *La Belle Image,* Gallimard, 1941).
The Proverb and Other Stories, translated by Norman Denny, Atheneum, 1961.
The Conscience of Love, translated by Norman Denny, Atheneum, 1962 (originally published as *Les Tiroirs de l'inconnu,* Gallimard, 1960).
(With Antoine Blondin) *The Paris I Love* (nonfiction), translated by Jean-Paul Clebert, Tudor, 1963 (originally published as *Paris que j'aime,* Editions Sun, 1956).

FOR CHILDREN; IN FRENCH

Derniers du chat perche, Gallimard, 1958.
Les Contes bleus du chat perche, Gallimard, 1975.
Les Contes rouges du chat perche, Gallimard, 1978.

FOR ADULTS; IN FRENCH

Brulebois, Cahiers de France, 1926.
Aller retour, Gallimard, 1927.

Les Jumeaux du diable, Gallimard, 1928.
La Rue sans nom, Gallimard, 1930.
La Vaurien, Gallimard, 1931.
Le Puits aux images (short stories), Gallimard, 1932.
Le Nain (short stories), Gallimard, 1934.
Gustalin, Gallimard, 1937.
Derriere chez Martin (short stories), Gallimard, 1938.
Silhouette du scandale, Sagittaire, 1938.
Le Boeuf clandestin, Gallimard, 1939.
Vogue la galere (play), Grasset, 1944.
Lucienne et le boucher, Grasset, 1947.
Le Vin de Paris (short stories), Gallimard, 1947.
Le Confort intellectuel (nonfiction), Flammarion, 1949.
En arriere (selected works), Gallimard, 1950.
La Tete des autres (play; first produced in Paris at Theatre de l'Atelier, 1952), Grasset, 1952.
Le Quatre verites (play; first produced in Paris at Theatre de l'Atelier, 1954), Grasset, 1954.
La Mouche bleue (play; first produced in Paris at Comedie des Champs-Elysees, 1957), Gallimard, 1957.
Soties de la ville et des champs (short stories), Club de Libraires de France, 1958.
Louisiane (play; first produced in Paris at Theatre de la Renaissance, 1961), Gallimard, 1961.
Oscar et Erick, Gautier-Languereau, 1961.
Les Maxibules (play: first produced in Paris at Theatre des Bouffes Parisiens, 1961), Gallimard, 1962.
Le Minotaure, precede de La Convention Belzebir et de Consommation (plays; first produced in Paris at Theatre de l'Athenee, 1966), Gallimard, 1967.
Enjambees, Gallimard, 1967.
Oeuvres romanesques (collected works), six volumes, Flammarion, 1977.
L'Etrange, le merveilleux et le fantastique (selected works), Societe des Amis de Marcel Ayme, 1983-84.
La Fille du sherif, Gallimard, 1987.

OTHER

Ayme also wrote several screenplays, including *Papa, Mama, the Maid and Me; La Jument verte* (an adaptation of his novel); *Les Sorcieres de Salem* (an adaptation of the play *The Crucible* by Arthur Miller); *Vu du pont* (an adaptation of the play *View from the Bridge* by Arthur Miller); and *Desert vivant*, 1957 (an adaptation of *The Living Desert*, released by Walt Disney Productions).

■ Sidelights

Marcel Ayme was a prolific French author of plays, novels, and short stories. A fabulist who revelled in the use of animals or children as the innocent narrators of much of his fiction, the late Ayme composed stories that have been enjoyed by young readers and adults alike. Ayme is perhaps best known for his novel, *The Green Mare* (*La Jument verte*), and for his play, *Clerambard*, which was originally produced in the 1950s both in France and in New York and which had a successful revival in 1986. But arguably some of his best known works in translation are those for children, collected in *The Wonderful Farm* and *The Magic Pictures: More*

about the Wonderful Farm. Three further "Wonderful Farm" books are as yet untranslated.

Ayme was born in 1902 and spent much of his early life in rural France. His mother died when he was two; he was thereafter raised by his maternal grandparents and by an aunt. School was a torture for Ayme, who once admitted that "even today in my most horrible nightmares, I dream that I am in the classroom." On his own he discovered the poetry of Francois Villon with its earthy themes, as well as the realistic novels of Balzac, both of which were to have a profound effect on him. Upon graduation from the lycee, Ayme served for a time as a soldier in the French artillery. After this service, he worked at various jobs, including a position as a reporter for a newspaper; it was then that he discovered his love of writing. Later, while convalescing from an illness, he wrote his first novel, *Brulebois,* which was largely based on his childhood memories. When Ayme's fourth novel, *The Hollow Field* (*La Table-aux-creves*), won the Prix Theophraste Renaudot in 1929, the young writer from the provinces had finally begun to find his place in the French literary pantheon.

These early novels look at rural France and tell realistic stories of lusty peasants and small town intrigues. Then came *The Green Mare* which was, according to Dorothy Brodin in *Dictionary of Literary Biography,* Ayme's "masterpiece" and "earned him an international reputation." Told from the point of view of a green mare in a painting on a wall, the novel demonstrates Ayme's trademark blending of both the realistic and the surreal. Thereafter Ayme resided in Paris, and subsequent novels deal less with rural subjects and more with realistic portrayals of city life, skewering the Parisian middle classes as he had those of the villages of the Franche-Comte region where he had grown up. "In Ayme's writings the pretentious and self-righteous are constantly satirized," noted Brodin. "His treatment of naive and honest country people, of hard-working postmen, gendarmes, and clerks is always kind, albeit amusing." Some of Ayme's later novels, such as *The Fable and the Flesh* (*La Vouivre*) return to the countryside, to the tillers of the soil. As with *The Green Mare,* this later novel also has a fabulist element in the form of a woodland divinity who wanders about and seduces a young peasant who does not believe in the supernatural. Much of Ayme's later career was taken up with the theater, *Clerambard* being the best known of his plays. He also wrote screenplays, including work on the French version of Disney's *The Painted Desert.*

Ayme's short stories "contain some of his best and certainly most imaginative writing," according to Brodin, and among these are the "Wonderful Farm" series. The French title comes from a children's game of tag (*le chat-perche*), but also suggests the idea of an animal—*le chat,* or cat. The first of these books, *Les Contes du chat perche,* was published in 1934, at about the same time as *The Green Mare,* and introduces Marinette and Delphine, two very active and imaginative sisters who live on a farm with parents who are their exact opposites— thrifty and unimaginative. Their barn is filled with a

Illustrated by Maurice Sendak, *The Wonderful Farm* features the antics of two rambunctious sisters who live with their parents on an enchanted farm where all the animals talk. (From *The Wonderful Farm,* written by Ayme.)

variety of animals that are both anthropomorphic and capable of magical feats. Most of the stories revolve around the mischievous Marinette and Delphine disobeying their parents. The resolution of the predicaments that arise as a result of their disobedience is often brought about by animal magic. By the end of each story the farm returns to normal and lessons have been learned by the girls and animals alike: good deeds will be rewarded; punishment comes to those who transgress. The girls' pranks are often the result of their innocence rather than ill will. Genuinely concerned for the rights of the animals, the sisters try to protect them from being eaten or overworked, attempting to circumvent or undermine the laws of nature or the family's necessary farm procedures in the process. For instance, in the story "The Oxen" ("Les Boeufs"), the girls decide to educate the oxen because they have heard that education is good. They teach the animals to read, and so taken are some of the animals with this activity that they are no longer of any use on the farm. Lesson: good intentions are not always enough. One must also use good common sense. Ayme once said that he wrote these stories for children from "four to seventy-five."

"The Peacock" ("Le Paon"), another story in *The Wonderful Farm*, relates how a pig with delusions of grandeur goes on a diet so as to rival the peacock in beauty. In order to save him from anoretic death, the girls tell him that his diet has worked, and attempting to look over his shoulder the pig sees the reflection of a sudden rainbow on his back. Such a combination of human wonders and human frailties enchanted reviewers on both sides of the Atlantic. A *Junior Bookshelf* critic noted that in *The Wonderful Farm* "incidents are a happy blend of the fantastic and commonplace" and that many of the stories "reach heights of true imaginative power and insight." A *New York Herald Tribune Book Review* contributor commented that Ayme "has given us a very well written, most truly imaginative book ... full of sharp wit," and Alice S. Morris commented in *New York Times Book Review* that with *The Wonderful Farm* Ayme "demonstrates that the wit and feeling and intelligence that make him one of the distinguished modern writers of France can perform with delightful and apropos results on a juvenile level."

Ayme's second volume of translated children's stories, *The Magic Pictures: More about the Wonderful Farm*, has the sisters involved in morning painting sessions while the real life animals they draw subsequently take on attributes the girls give them in the paintings. There is a pig adorned with buzzard's wings, an evil wolf turned kind, and the girls themselves become a horse and a donkey and are almost sold by their parents. "Here as before," noted Alice S. Morris in another *New York Times Book Review* piece, "Mother and Father are abysmally addicted to common sense.... Delphine and Marinette are disarmingly naughty and nice, and the animals comfortably gifted with human speech." Maria Cimino, reviewing *The Magic Pictures* in *The Saturday Review*, concluded that "only a writer with a vein of poetry in him could have created this touching children's world," and a *New York Herald Tribune Book*

In his second volume of stories about two young French girls and their magical farm, Ayme creates fanciful tales about pigs with wings and kind-hearted wolves. (From *The Magic Pictures: More about the Wonderful Farm,* illustrated by Maurice Sendak.)

Review contributor commented that Ayme "gives us one delightful story after another, each proving the stern parents in the wrong, the clever animals right, and the little girls the anxious, busy age　s between the two.... The combination of stern realism and most original make-believe is wonderfully well done."

Ayme has often been compared to that other French writer of fables, La Fontane. According to Mark J. Temmer in *French Review,* Ayme's fables demonstrate a basic truth "that life triumphs over those who are victims of preconceived ideas about their destiny and instincts." Temmer also noted that Ayme is a "master at treating a natural interplay between the children and the denizens of the barnyard and surrounding fields.... And above all, Ayme, like La Fontane, is an acute observer of the human and animal kingdoms." In a study of Ayme's children's books in *Three Centuries of Children's Books in Europe,* Bettina Hurlimann concluded that *Les Contes du chat perche* "are a mixture of fable, fairy tale, and straight story and they have a popularity in France similar to that of King Babar among younger children. Since the appearance of the first story in 1934 they have become some of the most-read books of France." With illustrations by Maurice Sendak in the translated versions, the books have also become a staple for children in the United States.

Ayme died in 1967, somewhat disillusioned with the technological direction the modern world was taking. He left behind a body of work that was at times ironic, realistic, and surreal. As Brodin noted in *Dictionary of Literary Biography,* Ayme "was irreverent and quick to challenge heavy-handed and senseless authority. He detested posturing and sham but was ever kind in his treatment of simple and sincere creatures." These traits were all at play in his "Wonderful Farm" stories.

■ Works Cited

Brodin, Dorothy, "Marcel Ayme," *Dictionary of Literary Biography,* Volume 72: *French Novelists, 1930-1960,* Gale, 1988, pp. 32-41.

Cimino, Maria, review of *The Magic Pictures: More about the Wonderful Farm, The Saturday Review,* May 15, 1954, p. 60.

Hurlimann, Bettina, "Fantasy and Reality," *Three Centuries of Children's Books in Europe,* 2nd edition, edited and translated by Brian W. Alderson, Oxford University Press, 1967, pp. 76-92.

Review of *The Magic Pictures: More about the Wonderful Farm, New York Herald Tribune Book Review,* May 11, 1954, p. 10.

Morris, Alice S., "The Pig Had Delusions," *New York Times Book Review,* November 11, 1951, p. 26.

Morris, Alice S., "Eloquent Beasts," *New York Times Book Review,* May 2, 1954, p. 26.

Temmer, Mark J. "Marcel Ayme, Fabulist and Moralist," *French Review,* April, 1962, pp. 453-62.

Review of *The Wonderful Farm, Junior Bookshelf,* October, 1952, p. 158.

Review of *The Wonderful Farm, New York Herald Tribune Book Review,* November 11, 1951, p. 5.

■ For More Information See

BOOKS

Brodin, Dorothy, *The Comic World of Marcel Ayme,* Debresse, 1964.

Children's Literature Review, Volume 25, Gale, 1991.

Contemporary Literary Criticism, Volume 11, Gale, 1979.

Lord, Graham, *Marcel Ayme,* Lang, 1987.

Oxford Companion to Children's Literature, Oxford University Press, 1984.

Twentieth-Century Children's Writers, 4th edition, St. James Press, 1995.

PERIODICALS

Booklist, November 1, 1977, p. 486.

Kirkus Reviews, November 1, 1951, p. 633; February 15, 1954, p. 109.

Times Literary Supplement, March 6, 1953.

■ Obituaries

BOOKS

Obituaries on File, Facts on File, 1979.

PERIODICALS

Newsweek, October 30, 1967.

New York Times, October 15, 1967.*

—Sketch by J. Sydney Jones

B

BADT, Karin L(uisa) 1963-

■ Personal

Born December 1, 1963, in Utah; daughter of Milton, Jr. (an engineer/teacher) and Lucia (a homemaker; maiden name, Giacomini) Badt. *Education:* Brown University, B.A. (with honors), 1985; University of Chicago, M.A., 1986, Ph.D., 1994.

■ Addresses

Home—230, rue Marcadet, Porte 66, 75018 Paris, France. *Office*—American University of Paris, 31, avenue Bosquet, 75007 Paris, France.

■ Career

University of Chicago Continuing Education Program, Chicago, IL, basic program instructor, 1989-90, open program instructor, 1993-94; John Cabot University, lecturer, 1991-93; University of Rome, La Sapienza, Italy, lecturer, 1992; University of Chicago, lecturer, 1994-95; American University of Paris, Paris, France, assistant professor, 1995—; University of Paris, lecturer, 1995—; Science Po, Paris, lecturer, 1996—. Parsons School of Design (Paris), cinema instructor, summer, 1996.

■ Awards, Honors

Century Scholarship, 1986-90; Phoenix Fellowship, 1988; Overseas Dissertation Grant, 1990; Beznos Award, 1991.

■ Writings

The Mississippi Flood of 1993, Children's Press, 1993.
Charles Eastman: Sioux Physician and Author, Chelsea House, 1994.
The Underground Railroad (play), Discovery Enterprise, 1995.
(With Mira Bartok) *The Southeast Indians,* HarperCollins, 1995.

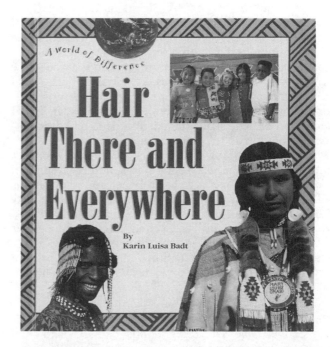

Karin L. Badt discusses how people around the world express their culture, religion, and even social status through intricate hairstyles.

Ohiyesa (play), Discovery Enterprise, 1996.
The Southwest Indians, Discovery Enterprise, 1996.

Contributor to *African American Review.*

"A WORLD OF DIFFERENCE" SERIES; PUBLISHED BY CHILDREN'S PRESS

Good Morning, Let's Eat, 1994.
Greetings, 1994.
Hair There and Everywhere, 1994.
Let's Go!, 1994.
On Your Feet!, 1994.
Pass the Bread!, 1994.

■ Work in Progress

The Teacher, a novel.

■ Sidelights

Karin L. Badt is the author of the young readers' multicultural series "A World of Difference," which focuses on common aspects of everyday life around the world. She has also written about other multicultural and historical topics for children, including works on Native Americans, the Underground Railroad, and the Mississippi Flood of 1993. Badt told *SATA,* "Writing is a means to learn about oneself and the world around one: what makes humanity tick. Whether I'm writing children's history books or fiction, I feel a sense of power, my personal engagement with the task of life."

The multicultural series "A World of Difference" explores cultural diversity by examining a number of basic, everyday objects, events, or needs that illustrate how common and yet diverse people from around the world truly are. Badt's focus reveals much about the individual or group's politics, religious beliefs, social status, and environment. *Hair There and Everywhere,* for example, stresses that the way a person wears his or her hair—curled, straightened, braided, or covered—speaks volumes about that person and his or her culture. *On Your Feet!* discusses the ways in which one's shoes indicate native customs, social status, and environment. Included in each book are brightly colored photographs with brief yet informative captions. "Badt's objectivity clearly reveals that regardless of a 'World of Difference,' we are all equally similar," stated Claudia Cooper for *School Library Journal.* About the series, Frances Bradburn, writing for *Booklist,* noted that it "will bring a world of information and fascination to library shelves."

While writing the "World of Difference" series, Badt also penned *The Mississippi Flood of 1993,* and then wrote the biography *Charles Eastman: Sioux Physician and Author. The Southeast Indians* and *The Southwest Indians* are two other titles written by Badt about Native Americans. In addition to these books, Badt has published two plays, *The Underground Railroad* and *Ohiyesa,* the story of the Native American leader.

"Writing history or anthropological books for children is for me a way to learn about and deeply explore subjects which interest me," Badt explained to *SATA.* "My aim is to convey to children the same enthusiasm and curiosity which led me to want to write the books in the first place. Children's books are an intellectual and artistic challenge: not only do I have to master the basic complex concepts germane to a given topic, but I must think of creative, fresh ways to make the narrative artful and exciting. Children are ideal readers: they are open to good stories and are natural critics of that which lacks passion and depth. I enjoy writing for such a mentally energetic audience."

■ Works Cited

Bradburn, Frances, review of *Hair There and Everywhere, Booklist,* January 1, 1995, p. 817.

Cooper, Claudia, review of *Hair There and Everywhere* and *On Your Feet!, School Library Journal,* January, 1995, p. 817.

*   *   *

BALIAN, Lorna 1929-

■ Personal

Surname rhymes with "stallion"; born December 14, 1929, in Milwaukee, WI; daughter of Henry W. (a telephone company employee) and Molly (Pope) Kohl; married John J. Balian (an industrial designer and artist), March 4, 1950; children: Heather, Japheth, Ivy, Aram, Lecia, Poppy. *Education:* Attended Layton School of Art, 1948-49. *Hobbies and other interests:* Gardening, cooking, sewing, painting.

■ Addresses

Office—Humbug Books, 202 West Main St., Watertown, WI 53094.

■ Career

Writer and illustrator. Freelance artist, 1948—; American Lace Co., Milwaukee, WI, artist, 1949-51. Has worked as an editor in residence for Atheneum Publishers. Teacher of crafts in adult vocational school. *Member:* Society of Children's Book Writers and Illustrators, Children's Cooperative Book Center, Children's Reading Round Table.

LORNA BALIAN

■ Awards, Honors

University of Wisconsin Little Archer Award; Colorado Children's Book Award; Georgia Children's Picture Book Award; Washington Children's Choice Picture Book Award; PIA Graphics Award; First-place award, Nashville Art Director's Club. The Lorna Balian Prize, an award offered by Abingdon that is presented to unpublished author-illustrator teams or individual creators of children's books, was named in her honor.

■ Writings

FOR CHILDREN; SELF-ILLUSTRATED

Humbug Witch, Abingdon, 1965.
I Love You, Mary Jane, Abingdon, 1967.
The Aminal, Abingdon, 1972.
Sometimes It's Turkey—Sometimes It's Feathers, Abingdon, 1973.
Where in the World Is Henry?, Bradbury, 1973.
Humbug Rabbit, Abingdon, 1974.
The Sweet Touch, Abingdon, 1976.
Bah! Humbug?, Abingdon, 1977.
A Sweetheart for Valentine, Abingdon, 1979.
Leprechauns Never Lie, Abingdon, 1980.
Mother's Mother's Day, Abingdon, 1982.
Humbug Potion: An A-B-Cipher, Abingdon, 1984.
A Garden for a Groundhog, Abingdon, 1985.
Amelia's Nine Lives, Abingdon, 1986.
The Socksnatchers, Abingdon, 1988.
Wilbur's Space Machine, Holiday House, 1990.

■ Adaptations

Humbug Handbook: The Lorna Balian Educational Activity Book, Humbug Books (Watertown, WI), 1994, adapted from the author's work by daughter, Poppy Balian, with illustrations by Poppy and Lecia Balian.

■ Sidelights

Author and illustrator Lorna Balian has brought a droll sense of humor and a childlike imagination to her picturebooks for young readers. Beginning her career as a children's author after reading countless stories to her own growing children, Balian created books which are noted for their entertaining illustrations and their imaginative settings. She insists upon including a "surprise" in her stories designed to captivate young readers and engage them in a lifelong love of reading.

Balian remembers growing up in both the city and the country: her father worked in the busy city of Milwaukee, but her summers were spent on the family farm in the town of Readfield in the Wisconsin countryside. She brings the best of both worlds to her books. In love with art as long as she can remember, Balian was strongly influenced by her grandmother, a lively, energetic, white-haired woman who inspired her young granddaughter with optimism and an ability to see the wonder in everyday things, and who would also serve as the model for many of the elderly characters in Balian's stories.

Balian's first book for children, *Humbug Witch,* was inspired by a local Halloween parade. Searching for a story on which to test her skill as an illustrator, Balian was struck by one of the children in the parade; memories of her own childhood experiments in which she dressed up in her Grandmother's clothing came back to her, and *Humbug Witch* was born. The story of a little witch whose magic does not quite power her would-be broomstick or bubble up her make-believe cauldron, Balian eventually reveals the witch to be a girl playing in a costume.

Humbug Witch was followed by several other books, many focusing on holiday themes, a need that Balian had felt keenly in her years as a mother looking for books appropriate for special occasions. *Humbug Rabbit,* for instance, humorously tells of confusion in the farmyard as one father rabbit finally convinces his offspring that he is NOT the Easter Bunny, only to find his burrow suddenly full to brimming with colored eggs after Barnaby the cat has pushed them down the rabbit hole. In Balian's *Bah! Humbug?,* Christmas finds Margie aiding her older brother in his attempt to prove Santa doesn't exist by setting a trap for the jolly old elf; when her brother falls asleep, Margie proves him wrong by witnessing the arrival of Father Christmas himself. Valentine's Day is the focus of *A Sweetheart for Valentine,* as a village works together to clothe and care for an abandoned giant-child. Eventually growing into a young giant-woman, Valentine, as she has been named by the citizens of the village of St. Valentine, finally finds a suitor and the town celebrates their marriage in a story that *Booklist* reviewer Barbara Elleman called "a heart-felt treat to make February 14 last all year long."

Mother's Mother's Day, published in 1982, finds six generations of mouse children going in search of their mothers to wish them a happy Mother's Day but finding no one home. The tables turn quickly when the oldest mother does an about face to flee from a hungry cat, meeting her daughter, her granddaughter, and each successive younger generation in turn, all of whom join her in her race to a safe burrow, where a true Mother's Day celebration is in order. Even Groundhog Day receives its due from Balian in *A Garden for a Groundhog,* as Mr. and Mrs. O'Leary plan to outwit the groundhog who comes out of hibernation early each year to check on the progress of their annual vegetable garden. "Sure to join other Balian titles as a much-read favorite," commented Sharron McElmeel, reviewing *A Garden for a Groundhog* in *School Library Journal.*

In addition to finding humorous stories in traditional holidays, Balian's amusing outlook also shines through in imaginative tales based on everyday events. In *The Sweet Touch,* Peggy's prize from a gumball machine calls forth a young, novice genie; when she wishes for everything she touches to turn into something sweet to eat, problems arise as the genie is unable to undo his spell and the two find themselves surrounded by a growing world of sugar. *Amelia's Nine Lives* is about a special black cat called Amelia who goes astray, causing its young owner Nora a great deal of distress. Friends

After little Nora's beloved feline Amelia disappears, family and friends bring her identical black cats one after another, only to be surprised when Amelia returns with four kittens of her own. (From *Amelia's Nine Lives,* written and illustrated by Balian.)

and relatives try to help by bringing black cats to replace Amelia, but Nora knows the difference, though the cats are all identical in appearance. Finally Amelia returns with four kittens in tow, and Nora and her family are overrun with black cats in a story that will cause readers to "bask in the affection that propels the search for an especially beloved pet," according to one *Kirkus Reviews* critic. Ilene Cooper of *Booklist* adds that, in addition to its humorous plot, "the rest of the story's charm comes from Balian's crisp, colorful pictures that are filled with funny little nuances and from the striking black cats that stand out against the snow-white pages." In *Wilbur's Space Machine,* an elderly couple who find their peaceful community disrupted by the clatter and noise of new neighbors—prime among them being a loudmouthed youngster called Googie—build a machine to bring back the "clean, peaceful space" they have lost. When the space that is created floats away, Wilbur catches it in balloons that his wife continues to attach to the outside of their home until they find themselves airborne. While some critics felt that having older people as protagonists would lessen the appeal for young readers, Deborah Abbott, in her review for *Booklist,* called *Wilbur's Space Machine* "a whimsical fantasy that is sure to fly."

Balian has also written a clever alphabet game book that challenges young readers to decipher a simple code that substitutes numbers for letters. *Humbug Potion: An A-B-Cipher* features a "homely witch" who mixes a secret coded formula in hopes of gaining beauty, but impatiently omits a vital ingredient as she finishes her task. "Droll pictures in spanking-fresh colors illustrate this clever story *cum* brain teaser," wrote a *Publishers*

Weekly reviewer. *School Library Journal* contributor Lee Bock noted that *Humbug Potion* would "challenge children's powers of observation," adding that "children will delight in the animated scurry and the well-illustrated clutter that accumulates at [the witch's] feet."

Working from a studio in an old country schoolhouse in Wisconsin that she and her husband have patiently restored, Balian creates her illustrations using the mediums of pen and ink, pencil, line drawing, and watercolor wash. Her own six children have often served as models for her drawings and have also provided ideas for stories. "My story ideas are often inspired by my childhood," Balian has asserted. Now the grandmother of more than a dozen grandchildren, she clearly recalls many of the incidents of her own childhood. "I have observed ... that feelings and interests of young children are universal and do not change. No matter how sophisticated or complex life may become later, the basic needs of the very young remain the same through the generations." Balian has spent most of her life in rural Wisconsin and notes that her Midwest surroundings have "provided me with a simple and tranquil perspective. I enjoy sharing my insights and feelings with children in amusing ways, through my stories and illustrations."

"Writing and illustrating books for children is something I love to do," Balian has commented. "My hope is that my books will help persuade children that reading is something *they* love to do. To free children's imaginations, and to compete with television, their books must be appealing and give pleasure.... I truly believe that one of the most important things we can do for children is to instill in them the love of books. They will benefit from this enrichment all of their lives."

■ Works Cited

Abbott, Deborah, review of *Wilbur's Space Machine, Booklist,* October 15, 1990, p. 445.

Review of *Amelia's Nine Lives, Kirkus Reviews,* November 15, 1986, p. 1720.

Bock, Lee, review of *Humbug Potion: An A-B-Cipher, School Library Journal,* September, 1984, p. 98.

Cooper, Ilene, review of *Amelia's Nine Lives, Booklist,* December 1, 1986, p. 572.

Elleman, Barbara, review of *A Sweetheart for Valentine, Booklist,* September 1, 1979, p. 38.

Review of *Humbug Potion: An A-B-Cipher, Publishers Weekly,* April 27, 1984, p. 87.

McElmeel, Sharron, review of *A Garden for a Groundhog, School Library Journal,* March, 1986, p. 142.

■ For More Information See

BOOKS

Authors of Books for Young People, 3rd edition, Scarecrow Press, 1990.

PERIODICALS

Bulletin of the Center for Children's Books, October, 1965, p. 26; January, 1973, p. 70; November, 1977;

January, 1980, p. 87; July-August, 1982; October, 1984, p. 19.

Chicago Tribune Book World, August 1, 1982.

Kirkus Reviews, September 15, 1972; June 15, 1974, p. 629; June 15, 1977, p. 623; August 15, 1980.

Library Journal, January 15, 1966, p. 417.

Publishers Weekly, July 29, 1974; April 12, 1976, p. 66; June 25, 1979, pp. 122-23.

School Library Journal, September, 1976, pp. 94-95; January, 1981, p. 46; February, 1987, p. 63; January, 1989, p. 60; February, 1991, p. 66.

*   *   *

BARRY, Sheila Anne

■ Personal

Born in New York, NY; daughter of Mark Henry (a lawyer) and Bertha (a lawyer; maiden name, Robinson) Shulman; married Paul Weissman, 1960 (divorced, 1974); children: Mark John, Lael Tiu Kimble. *Education:* Columbia University, B.F.A.; also attended Cornell University. *Hobbies and other interests:* Neurolinguistic programming, hypnosis.

■ Addresses

Office—Sterling Publishing Co., Inc., 387 Park Ave. S., New York, NY 10016.

■ Career

Editor, writer, publishing executive. Taplinger Publishing Co., New York City, senior editor, 1962-69; Sterling Publishing, New York City, acquisitions director, 1971—.

■ Writings

FOR CHILDREN

The Super-Colossal Book of Puzzles, Trick & Games, illustrated by Doug Anderson, Sterling, 1978.

Our New Home, Sterling, 1981.

Tricks and Stunts to Fool Your Friends, illustrated by Doug Anderson, Sterling, 1984.

Test Your Wits!, illustrated by Doug Anderson, Sterling, 1986.

The World's Best Party Games, illustrated by Doug Anderson, Sterling, 1987.

The World's Best Travel Games, illustrated by Doug Anderson, Sterling, 1987.

The World's Most Spine-Chilling True "Ghost Stories," illustrated by Jim Sharpe, Sterling, 1992.

The World's Best Card Games for One, illustrated by Myron Miller, Sterling, 1992.

(Editor) *Kids' Funniest Jokes,* illustrated by Jeff Sinclair, Sterling, 1993.

OTHER

(Compiler) Lady Wilde, *Irish Cures, Mystic Charms, and Superstitions,* illustrated by Marlene Ekman, Sterling, 1991.

(Compiler) Lady Wilde, *Ancient Legends of Ireland,* illustrated by Marlene Ekman, Sterling, 1996.

■ For More Information See

PERIODICALS

Booklist, October 15, 1978, p. 370; November 1, 1979, p. 458; January 1, 1985, p. 637; February 15, 1986, p. 875; August, 1987, p. 1740; January 15, 1988, p. 860.

Horn Book Guide, spring, 1993, p. 86.

Kliatt, fall, 1984, p. 72.

School Library Journal, February, 1979, p. 51.

*   *   *

BIANCHI, John 1947-

■ Personal

Born August 23, 1947, in Rochester, NY; son of Cosmo and Josephine Bianchi; married Margaret Cameron (a financial planner), December 15, 1978; children: Jessica, Sascha.

■ Addresses

Home—11674 North Cassiopeia Dr., Tucson, AZ 85737.

■ Career

Author and illustrator. Worked at various jobs, including janitor, playground supervisor, and construction worker; became professional artist; worked at a film studio, painting backgrounds for animated films and designing cartoon characters and storyboards; co-founded publishing company, Bungalo Books, with Frank B. Edwards, 1986.

■ Awards, Honors

Governor General's Award nomination, Canada Council, 1985, for *The Dingles,* written by Helen Levchuk; Juvenile Science Book Award, New York Academy of Sciences, 1989, for *Exploring the Night Sky,* written by Terence Dickinson.

■ Writings

FOR CHILDREN; SELF-ILLUSTRATED

The Bungalo Boys: Last of the Tree Ranchers, Bungalo Books, 1986.

The Bungalo Boys II: Bushmen Brouhaha, Bungalo Books, 1987.

Princess Frownsalot, Bungalo Books, 1987.

The Swine Snafu, Bungalo Books, 1988.

The Bungalo Boys III: Champions of Hockey, Bungalo Books, 1989.

Snowed In at Pokeweed Public School, Bungalo Books, 1991.

Penelope Penguin: The Incredibly Good Baby, Bungalo Books, 1992.

JOHN BIANCHI

The Artist, Bungalo Books, 1993.

The Bungalo Boys: Flight of the Space Quester, Bungalo Books, 1993.

Spring Break at Pokeweed Public School, Bungalo Books, 1994.

Three Stories High: The First Big Bungalo Boys Book, Bungalo Books, 1995.

The Toad Sleeps Over, Bungalo Books, 1995.

Welcome Back to Pokeweed Public School, Bungalo Books, 1996.

ILLUSTRATOR

Helen Levchuk, *The Dingles,* Groundwood, 1985.

Dennis Foon, *The Short Tree and the Bird That Could Not Sing,* Groundwood, 1986.

Terence Dickinson, *Exploring the Night Sky: The Equinox Astronomy Guide for Beginners,* Camden House Books, 1987.

Terence Dickinson, *Exploring the Sky by Day: The Equinox Guide to Weather and the Atmosphere,* Camden House Books, 1988.

Margaret Atwood, *For the Birds,* Douglas & McIntyre, 1990.

Frank B. Edwards, *Mortimer Mooner Stopped Taking a Bath,* Bungalo Books, 1990.

Helen Levchuk, *Doris Dingle's Crafty Cat Activity Book: Games, Toys, and Hobbies to Keep Your Cat's Mind Active,* Alaska Northwest Books, 1991.

Frank B. Edwards, *Melody Mooner Stayed Up All Night,* Bungalo Books, 1991.

Frank B. Edwards, *Grandma Mooner Lost Her Voice,* Bungalo Books, 1992.

Frank B. Edwards, *Snow: Learning for the Fun of It,* Bungalo Books, 1992.

Frank B. Edwards, *A Dog Called Dad,* Bungalo Books, 1994.

Frank B. Edwards, *Mortimer Mooner Makes Lunch,* Bungalo Books, 1995.

Frank B. Edwards, *Melody Mooner Takes Lessons,* Bungalo Books, 1996.

OTHER

Also creator of CD-ROM *The Bungalo Boys: The Big Fish Wish,* 1996. Contributed to Terence Dickinson's *Other Worlds: A Beginner's Guide to Planets and Moons,* 1995.

■ Work in Progress

The Lab Rats of Doctor Eclair.

■ Sidelights

Author and illustrator John Bianchi has enjoyed drawing, especially cartoons, since he was a boy. "I could always impress my friends with a quick rendering of Mickey Mouse or Pluto," he recalled for *SATA.* "My parents encouraged my creativity and I always did well in art class. But it wasn't until I turned twenty that I decided to make my living as an artist." At first Bianchi worked at odd jobs to support himself and painted at night, reading books about art to refine his technique, but eventually he became successful enough to earn a living as an artist.

For a time Bianchi put his artistic talents to work at a film studio, painting backgrounds for animated movies. Before long his duties expanded to include creating cartoon characters and storyboards. One of his most popular efforts was the original *Raccoons Christmas Special,* which aired on CBC Television in Canada. After his marriage in 1978, Bianchi left the city for a home in the country. "Life was different out there," he explained to *SATA.* "Lots of funny things happened to us—like the time the cows wandered into the cabbage, or when I thought it might be fun to keep bees. I couldn't resist doing cartoons about all these funny experiences. I even started writing short stories for magazines."

After illustrating his first picture book in 1985, Bianchi tried without success to find a publisher for some of his own stories. At the suggestion of a friend, magazine editor Frank B. Edwards, he agreed to start a publishing company, Bungalo Books. The company's motto is "Reading for the Fun of It!" Since its inception, Bungalo Books has published over twenty titles that have sold more than one million copies.

This year, as always, we neatly packed a few odds and ends and gathered in the school parking lot. Then, under the expert supervision of Ms. Mudwortz and Principal Slugmeyer, we all boarded the bus and headed off for . . .

While on spring break at Lake Weegonnahaha, the clever students from Pokeweed Public School solve the mystery of the swamp monster Ogopokeweed. (From *Spring Break at Pokeweed Public School,* written and illustrated by Bianchi.)

The first book for children that Bianchi published with his new company was *The Bungalo Boys: Last of the Tree Ranchers,* which he both wrote and illustrated. The story follows the adventures of the Bungalo brothers, four goofy cowboys who spend their time saddling, roping, feeding, and watering a herd of trees. When a gang of rustlers, the Beavers, come along to make trouble, the Bungalos take many silly steps to protect their herd. A reviewer for *Canadian Children's Literature* called the book, which is full of puns and cowboy cliches, "a fun book for all ages."

Bianchi continued the adventures of the Bungalo brothers in several sequels, including *The Bungalo Boys III: Champions of Hockey,* published in 1989, and *Flight of the Space Quester,* published in 1993. In the first book, the brothers form a hockey team—along with their secret weapon, Projectile the Wonder Dog—to play for the ultimate trophy: the Bungalo Birdbath. Their opponents at the local pond are three mixed-up penguins and three enormous bears. Though some reviewers wondered whether Bianchi's word-play and puns might be too complex for younger readers, Linda Holeman, writing in *Canadian Materials,* noted that "tiny details in the lively, brightly colored drawings will amuse both older readers and younger listeners." In the 1993 book, the brothers make hilarious preparations to embark on a journey into outer space. Before long, however, it becomes clear that they are actually about to go on a carnival ride.

In 1988 Bianchi published *The Swine Snafu,* another humorous animal-centered tale, but with a serious message behind it. In the story, two neighbor families, the wild Boars and the sedate Pigs, are each preparing for the birth of a baby. The families are so different, however, that a great deal of animosity grows between them. As the babies grow up, after being born in the

same hospital on the same day, the mothers begin to suspect that they have taken home the wrong child. But Mrs. Pig soon learns that what she fears are tusks in her baby's mouth are actually just crooked teeth, and the families begin to overcome their differences and become friends. "The implication of *The Swine Snafu* is that you cannot avoid people with differences so you should learn to live with them," according to a reviewer for *Canadian Children's Literature.* Bianchi addresses a similar theme in *The Toad Sleeps Over,* a tale humorously relating a fieldmouse's apprehension over his son's non-mouse friend. When Tony the Toad uses his instinctive defenses to wondrous effect in scaring off a hungry coyote, father fieldmouse comes to a better appreciation of the value of being different.

Another of Bianchi's series of books for young readers involves the animal students at Pokeweed Public School. In *Spring Break at Pokeweed Public School,* published in 1994, the kids spend their school break at a camp on Lake Weegonnahaha. They have a number of comical adventures as they put up tents, go canoeing, and roast marshmallows over a campfire. When the school principal tells the children a story about Ogopokeweed, the monster who lives in the lake and steals campers' food, they become determined to capture it on film. Amusingly, what they end up with is a suspicious picture of the principal's hat. In a review for *Quill and Quire,* Kit Pearson commented that "the bright, cartoony, zany pictures are up to Bianchi's usual high standards."

Bianchi has noted that he spends between six and eight hours per day writing and illustrating works for Bungalo Books. "Ideas for stories come to me all the time—driving with the family, jogging, biking, visiting schools, talking with young students, playing with my children. Whenever I have an idea for a book, I write it down on a note pad, or a scrap of paper, or an old receipt, or the back of a parking ticket," he explained to *SATA*. "A good idea is worth holding on to."

■ Works Cited

Review of *The Bungalo Boys: Last of the Tree Ranchers, Canadian Children's Literature*, Number 45, 1987, pp. 94-95.

Holeman, Linda, review of *The Bungalo Boys III: Champions of Hockey, Canadian Materials*, January, 1990, p. 11.

Pearson, Kit, review of *Spring Break at Pokeweed Public School, Quill and Quire*, April, 1994, p. 38.

Review of *The Swine Snafu, Canadian Children's Literature*, Number 51, 1988, p. 100.

■ For More Information See

PERIODICALS

Appraisal: Science Books for Young People, spring/summer, 1993, p. 11.

Canadian Children's Literature, Number 59, 1990, p. 106; Number 63, 1991, p. 89.

Canadian Materials, January, 1989, p. 33; September, 1992, p. 207.

Quill and Quire, December, 1989, p. 22; December, 1992, p. 28; April, 1993, p. 35.

School Library Journal, November, 1987, p. 86; May, 1989, p. 77; May, 1991, p. 77; May, 1995, p. 84.

* * *

BIERHORST, John (William) 1936-

■ Personal

Born September 2, 1936, in Boston, MA; son of John William, Jr. (a mechanical engineer) and Sadie Belle (Knott) Bierhorst (a commercial artist); married Jane Elizabeth Byers (a graphic designer), June 25, 1965; children: Alice Byers. *Education:* Cornell University, B.A., 1958.

■ Addresses

Home—Box 10, West Shokan, NY 12494.

■ Career

Writer. Former concert pianist. *Member:* American Folklore Society, American Anthropological Association.

■ Awards, Honors

Grants from Center for Inter-American Relations, 1972 and 1979, National Endowment for the Humanities, 1979 and 1986, and National Endowment for the Arts, 1986; named a May Hill Arbuthnot Honor Lecturer, Association for Library Service to Children of the American Library Association, 1988. American Library Association notable book citations for *In the Trail of the Wind: American Indian Poems and Ritual Orations, Black Rainbow: Legends of the Incas and Myths of Ancient Peru, The Girl Who Married a Ghost: Tales from the North American Indian, A Cry from the Earth: Music of the North American Indians, The Whistling Skeleton: American Indian Tales of the Supernatural, The Sacred Path: Spells, Prayers, and Power Songs of the American Indians, Spirit Child: A Story of the Nativity*, and *The Naked Bear: Folktales of the Iroquois*.

■ Writings

FOR CHILDREN

A Cry from the Earth: Music of the North American Indians, Four Winds (Bristol, FL), 1979.

The Mythology of North America, Morrow, 1985.

The Mythology of South America, Morrow, 1988.

The Mythology of Mexico and Central America, Morrow, 1990.

The Way of the Earth: Native America and the Environment, Morrow, 1994.

FOR CHILDREN; EDITOR AND TRANSLATOR

The Fire Plume: Legends of the American Indians, Dial, 1969.

The Ring in the Prairie: A Shawnee Legend, Dial, 1970.

In the Trail of the Wind: American Indian Poems and Ritual Orations, Farrar, Straus, 1971.

Songs of the Chippewa, Farrar, Straus, 1974.

Black Rainbow: Legends of the Incas and Myths of Ancient Peru, Farrar, Straus, 1976.

The Girl Who Married a Ghost: Tales from the North American Indian, Four Winds, 1978.

The Glass Slipper: Charles Perrault's Tales of Times Past, Four Winds, 1981.

The Whistling Skeleton: American Indian Tales of the Supernatural, Four Winds, 1982.

JOHN BIERHORST

The Sacred Path: Spells, Prayers, and Power Songs of the American Indians, Morrow, 1983.

The Hungry Woman: Myths and Legends of the Aztecs, Morrow, 1984.

Spirit Child: A Story of the Nativity, Morrow, 1984.

The Monkey's Haircut and Other Stories Told by the Maya, Morrow, 1986.

The Naked Bear: Folktales of the Iroquois, Morrow, 1987.

Doctor Coyote: A Native American Aesop's Fables, Macmillan, 1987.

Lightning Inside You and Other Native American Riddles, Morrow, 1992.

The Woman Who Fell from the Sky: The Iroquois Story of Creation, Morrow, 1993.

On the Road of Stars: Native American Night Poems and Sleep Charms, Macmillan, 1994.

The White Deer and Other Stories Told by the Lenape, Morrow, 1995.

FOR ADULTS

A Nahuatl-English Dictionary, Stanford University Press (Stanford, CA), 1985.

Codex Chimalpopoca: The Text in Nahuatl with a Glossary and Grammatical Notes, University of Arizona Press (Tucson), 1992.

The Ashokan Catskills: A Natural History, Purple Mountain Press (Fleischmanns, NY), 1995.

Mythology of the Lenape: Guide and Texts, University of Arizona Press, 1995.

FOR ADULTS; EDITOR AND TRANSLATOR

Four Masterworks of American Indian Literature: "Quetzalcoatl," "The Ritual of Condolence," "Cuceb," "The Night Chant," Farrar, Straus, 1974.

The Red Swan: Myths and Tales of the American Indians, Farrar, Straus, 1976.

Cantares Mexicanos: Songs of the Aztecs, Stanford University Press, 1985.

History and Mythology of the Aztecs: The Codex Chimalpopoca, University of Arizona Press, 1992.

OTHER

Also editorial advisor for the Smithsonian Series of Studies in Native American Literatures, 1990—; editorial associate for *The Norton Anthology of World Masterpieces, Expanded Edition,* edited by Maynard Mack, Norton, 1995.

■ Work in Progress

A collection of arctic folktales; a book of Native American stories about little people.

■ Sidelights

A specialist in the language of the Aztecs, John Bierhorst is the author of many works focusing on the customs, traditions, and stories that Native Americans have passed on for centuries, although he once said in a *Something about the Author Autobiography Series* (*SAAS*) essay, "I've never been sure what an 'author' is. Like physicians who call themselves 'doctors,' and

Based on sixteenth century manuscripts, Bierhorst retells Aztec versions of Aesop's Fables which include a favorite Native American trickster, the coyote. (From *Doctor Coyote: A Native American Aesop's Fables,* retold by Bierhorst, illustrated by Wendy Watson.)

lawyers who call themselves 'attorneys,' writers appreciate being called authors. It's more of an honorific title than a word that tells what you actually do.... But in my own mind, I am a translator, specializing in one thing: the native literature of the Americas."

Bierhorst says that his "serious work" with the Aztec language started when he and his wife, Jane, visited the Museum of Anthropology in Mexico City. While there, he was moved by an Aztec poem translated into Spanish that someone had engraved into a stone wall centuries ago. Interested in the source of the poem, Bierhorst located the manuscript of Aztec poetry from which the poem had been taken and began translating his first book of Aztec verse. While he was at work on the project, Bierhorst also discovered two Aztec texts that he thought perfect for translating into children's picture books, one of which became *Spirit Child: A Story of the Nativity,* and the other *Doctor Coyote: A Native American Aesop's Fables.*

Doctor Coyote, published in 1987, is a collection of Aztec adaptations of Latin and Greek fables that were brought over to the New World by the Spaniards in the sixteenth century. The Aztecs took these stories and blended them with their own traditional tales, including stories of a trickster coyote who appears as the main character in all of the fables. Although some of the stories are recognizable, a reviewer in *Booklist* observed

In his unique collection of Native American riddles, Bierhorst challenges young readers to solve riddles translated from over twenty different Indian languages. (Cover illustration by Louise Brierley.)

that "many of these, especially with their Aztec veneer, will seem new to listeners." In *School Library Journal,* Karen Zimmerman applauded the "unique" book "because of its Native American flavor" and suggested libraries purchase the compilation as an alternative to traditional versions of Aesop's tales.

Bierhorst said in his *SAAS* essay that "people often ask me why I do what I do. 'How did you get started in this?' they say. Or, less tactfully, 'How did you *ever* get started in this?'

"I try to have a different answer ready, but it comes out differently each time. Sometimes I just say that Jane got me started in books. Which is true enough . . . .

"One time I gave an elaborate explanation about being in the mountains in Peru and hearing the *quena* (a kind of flute) played at twilight . . . .

"Another explanation is that there were virtually no books of Indian stories or Indian poetry for young readers when I was a child, and I wanted to help change that."

Bierhorst began to strive toward that goal of making more books about Native Americans available for

children as he edited his first book of Indian tales, *The Fire Plume: Legends of the American Indians* (1969). Gathered from the collection of Henry Rowe Schoolcraft, who recorded stories told by his Chippewa wife, *The Fire Plume* contains seven Chippewa legends retold to children in a much simpler style than Schoolcraft's version. In the *New York Times Book Review,* George F. Scheer praised Bierhorst's amendments, stating that the author has "produce[d] a most pleasing collection of wonder tales and legends."

Seven years later, Bierhorst concentrated his efforts on the native peoples of South America and produced a compilation of folk tales from the Incas. *Black Rainbow: Legends of the Incas and Myths of Ancient Peru* is full of myths, legends, and fables teaching children about Incan customs, interpersonal relations, and forms of punishment. Appreciating the "erudite and informative introduction," a reviewer in the *Bulletin of the Center for Children's Books* lauded Bierhorst's selective choices of stories which are "retold with skill." In *Horn Book,* Virginia Haviland also complimented Bierhorst on his faithful translations and "meticulous documentation of the source of each narrative."

Beginning in 1985, Bierhorst extended his research of Native American stories by editing three volumes of myths from Indians in North, South, and Central America. *The Mythology of North America, The Mythology of South America* and *The Mythology of Mexico and Central America* are full of photographs, maps, and Indian drawings, complimenting a diverse selection of legends. Unlike some of his earlier collections which featured entire stories, this series on New World mythology takes more of an anthropological approach, comparing and contrasting myths between regions, identifying recurring themes, and summarizing traditional tales. Commenting on *The Mythology of North America* in *Kirkus Reviews,* a critic praised the "compelling imagery" with which Bierhorst writes, as well as his "impressively knowledgeable and flexibly eclectic" commentary. Writing in the *New York Times Book Review* about *The Mythology of North America,* Ursula K. Le Guin described Bierhorst's myths as "moving and fascinating," going on to say that his "descriptions of the background and history, the connections and crossovers, of the myths and mythologies, and his glimpses of the world views of the various peoples and regions, are varied and thoughtful."

The Mythology of South America and *The Mythology of Mexico and Central America* also received favorable reviews. In a *School Library Journal* review of *The Mythology of Mexico and Central America,* Ann Welton called Bierhorst's handling of the material "sophisticated" and said his "intelligent writing and impeccable scholarship . . . is hard to beat." A critic in *Booklist* noted that "scholarship, not entertainment, is the ultimate objective" of *The Mythology of South America,* "and Bierhorst accomplishes that admirably."

Moving to a much lighter, but still educational subject, Bierhorst collected over one hundred riddles told by

Native Indians in North, South, and Central America. Remarkably, *Lightning Inside You and Other Native American Riddles* is the first compilation of Indian riddles ever published. Previously, scholars did not believe riddling was a traditional aspect of Native American culture. Bierhorst also provides important information about the tribes from which the riddles came, where these tribes were located, and the role riddles played in tribal beliefs. While some of the answers are not obvious, in *Horn Book,* Maeve Visser Knoth credited Bierhorst for making children "chang[e] their thought patterns to solve riddles about a world that may be foreign to them." Although she called the book "important for Native American folklore collections," in *School Library Journal,* Patricia Dooley remarked that some of the jokes lacked a snappy punch line and were "straightforward as a catechism."

After publishing two scholarly books about the history of the Aztec language and the Aztec creation epic, Bierhorst once again returned to children's literature in 1993 with a retelling of the Iroquois legend of creation. *The Woman Who Fell from the Sky: The Iroquois Story of Creation* explains the Iroquois belief that when pushed by her jealous husband, sky woman fell to the

THE WHITE DEER
and Other Stories Told by the Lenape
EDITED BY **JOHN BIERHORST**

In this work, Bierhorst compiles twenty-five creation, hero, and animal tales told by the original inhabitants of the Hudson and Delaware valleys.

earth with her children, Sapling and Flint. As she fell, all the sea animals helped cushion her fall, building a giant mud pile on a turtle's back. When the sky woman landed, her magical life-giving powers turned the soft mud to earth. Growing up on this new world, Sapling created everything gentle and soft, while Flint made all things hard and difficult. Once the earth was finished and humans formed, the two took to the sky and went their separate ways, and the Iroquois believe their paths still stretch across the sky every night as the Milky Way appears. Calling the story "simple, but dramatically retold," a critic in *Kirkus Reviews* said that *The Woman Who Fell from the Sky* is "most satisfying to look at, to read aloud, or to hear."

After writing so many books about Native Americans in other areas, Bierhorst realized that little of the native literature from the Indians near his own home was ever preserved in print. In *The White Deer and Other Stories Told by the Lenape,* Bierhorst recorded many stories from the Delaware, or Lenape as they call themselves, the original inhabitants of New Jersey, southeastern New York, and eastern Pennsylvania. The collection features twenty-five stories, including origin myths, trickster tales, prophecies, and dog stories. Each tale is kept in its original form, which according to Carolyn Polese in *School Library Journal,* "retains the sense of oral tradition." Describing *The White Deer and Other Stories Told by the Lenape* as "a rich collection," Betsy Hearne wrote in the *Bulletin of the Center for Children's Books* that "Bierhorst should be getting more attention for his folklore collections."

Bierhorst's obvious love for the rich culture, traditions, and language of Native Americans is evident in all of the works he has painstakingly assembled. In his *SAAS* essay, Bierhorst said, "What I really want is for readers to appreciate not my own writing but the poetry, myths, and stories of the American Indians. This has come to be an important idea for me. Really, it is a political idea. It means that I identify with the struggle of Native Americans for more land and more control over their lives. And it means that I believe literature, like art and music, is part of a people's strength."

■ Works Cited

Bierhorst, John, essay in *Something about the Author Autobiography Series,* Volume 10, Gale, 1990, pp. 21-35.

Review of *Black Rainbow: Legends of the Incas and Myths of Ancient Peru, Bulletin of the Center for Children's Books,* March, 1977, p. 101.

Review of *Doctor Coyote: A Native American Aesop's Fables, Booklist,* March 15, 1987, p. 1123.

Dooley, Patricia, review of *Lightning inside You and Other Native American Riddles, School Library Journal,* July, 1992, p. 79.

Haviland, Virginia, review of *Black Rainbow: Legends of the Incas and Myths of Ancient Peru, Horn Book,* February, 1977, pp. 46-7.

Illustrated with delicate watercolors by Robert Andrew Parker, Bierhorst's retelling *The Woman Who Fell from the Sky: The Iroquois Story of Creation* explains the ancient Indian belief of how a woman and her two sons create the earth and give life to all of its inhabitants.

Hearne, Betsy, review of *The White Deer and Other Stories Told by the Lenape, Bulletin of the Center for Children's Books,* July/August, p. 377.

Knoth, Maeve Visser, review of *Lightning inside You and Other Native American Riddles, Horn Book,* September/October, 1992, pp. 590-91.

Le Guin, Ursula K., *Loon Woman in the Long Ago, New York Times Book Review,* September 1, 1985, p. 7.

Review of *The Mythology of North America, Kirkus Reviews,* May 15, 1985, p. 46.

Review of *The Mythology of South America, Booklist,* September 15, 1988, p. 145.

Polese, Carolyn, review of *The White Deer and Other Stories Told by the Lenape, School Library Journal,* September, 1995, p. 204.

Scheer, George F., review of the *Fire Plume: Legends of the American Indians, New York Times Book Review,* July 27, 1969, p. 18.

Welton, Ann, review of *The Mythology of Mexico and Central America, School Library Journal,* November 11, 1990, p. 142.

Review of *The Woman Who Fell from the Sky, Kirkus Reviews,* February 15, 1993, p. 222.

Zimmerman, Karen, review of *Doctor Coyote: A Native American Aesop's Fables, School Library Journal,* May, 1987, p. 81.

■ For More Information See

PERIODICALS

Booklist, September 15, 1971, p. 99; October 15, 1972, p. 177; December 15, 1973, p. 601; September 1, 1974, p. 38; September 15, 1974, p. 65; February 1, 1977, p. 804; June 1, 1979, p. 1488; July, 1983, p. 1397; June 1, 1984, p. 1399; June 15, 1985, p. 1445; July, 1986, p. 1615; August, 1987, p. 1750; September 1, 1987, p. 79; September 15, 1988, p. 145; October 15, 1991, p. 375; June 15, 1992, p. 1832; March 15, 1993, p. 1322; April 15, 1994, p. 1537; May 15, 1994, p. 1672; June 1, 1995, p. 1742.

Bulletin of the Center for Children's Books, January, 1972, p. 71; December, 1974, p. 58; July, 1979, p. 186; July, 1983, p. 203; July, 1984, p. 200; March, 1986, p. 122; March, 1987, p. 122; June, 1988, p. 198; July, 1992, p. 289; May, 1993, p. 278; March, 1994, p. 216; April, 1994, p. 252.

Horn Book, August, 1971, p. 378; October, 1974, p. 145; June, 1979, p. 315; August, 1983, p. 459; August, 1984, p. 481; September, 1986, p. 602; May, 1987, p. 348; September, 1987, p. 621; November, 1988, p. 794; July, 1994, p. 477; September, 1994, p. 604; September, 1995, p. 611.

Kirkus Reviews, April 15, 1970, p. 443; April 15, 1971, p. 444; July 1, 1974, p. 682; July 15, 1976, p. 800; November 1, 1976, p. 1176; April 15, 1979, p. 458; April 15, 1983, p. 463; May 1, 1984, p. 55; July 1, 1986, p. 1015; February 15, 1987, p. 300; March 1, 1987, p. 370; May 1, 1988, p. 689; June 1, 1992, p. 715; April 1, 1994, p. 477; May 15, 1994, p. 695.

Library Journal, November 15, 1969, p. 4280; May 15, 1971, p. 1809; August, 1974, p. 1951; November 15, 1974, p. 3043.

New York Times Book Review, June 14, 1970, p. 22; October 3, 1971, p. 8; January 31, 1982; October 19, 1986, p. 44; November 22, 1987, p. 44; October 2, 1988, p. 35; August 23, 1992, p. 26; June 17, 1993, p. 21; July 17, 1994, p. 18.

Publishers Weekly, July 7, 1969, p. 71; April 5, 1971, p. 55; June 24, 1974, p. 56; July 5, 1985, p. 67; March 13, 1987, p. 84; April 24, 1987, p. 73; June 15, 1992, p. 103; February 15, 1993, p. 239; March 7, 1994, p. 72.

School Library Journal, February, 1977, p. 70; May, 1979, p. 58; September, 1983, p. 118; August, 1984, p. 82; August, 1985, p. 71; August, 1986, p. 90; June, 1987, p. 92; May, 1988, p. 114; April, 1993, p. 104; May, 1994, pp. 106, 136.

Voice of Youth Advocates, June, 1988, p. 99; October, 1994, p. 228; October, 1995, p. 262.

BOULTON, Jane 1921-

■ Personal

Born September 25, 1921, in Indianapolis, IN; daughter of John and Martha (Morris) Balch; married Peter Boulton (divorced, 1980); married DeWitt Whittlesey (deceased, 1992); children: Ann, Michael Dorn, Celeinne Ysunza. *Education:* Rollins College, B.A. *Politics:* Democrat.

■ Addresses

Home—649 University Ave., H 441, Palo Alto, CA 94301-2032. *Agent*—Laurie Harper, Sebastian Agency, 333 Kearny St., No. 708, San Francisco, CA 94108.

■ Career

Poet and children's author.

■ Writings

Opal, Macmillan, 1976.
Opal: The Journal of an Understanding Heart, Tigoa (Palo Alto, CA), 1984.
Only Opal: The Diary of a Young Girl, illustrated by Barbara Cooney, Philomel, 1994.

■ Work in Progress

A novel, *Journey within a Journey.*

■ Sidelights

Jane Boulton is the author of *Only Opal: The Diary of a Young Girl,* a poetical biography of a young pioneer girl in late eighteenth-century Oregon. Orphaned at five, Opal Whitely spent her remaining childhood with a foster family, following the logging family as they worked at nineteen different lumber camps. Calling her foster mother "the mama where I live," Whitely escapes the harsh treatment of her adoptive family by keeping a diary of her "fifth and sixth year." Boulton has gathered parts of this diary she originally collected in *Opal* and arranged them like a poem for this picture book. In the journal, young Opal writes of her pets, favorite tree, and deceased parents in the uncomplicated prose of a child.

A critic writing in *Kirkus Reviews* calls the colorfully illustrated work "a touching, fascinating portrait" and in *Horn Book,* Mary M. Burns applauds the book's "ingenious quality which speaks directly to the emotions." *School Library Journal* contributor Martha Rosen notes that some of Whitely's wording is "awkward," but she insists "readers will respond positively to this glimpse of history." However, Ann Banks questions the authenticity of the poetical text in the *New York Times Book Review.* While calling *Only Opal* "intense, poetic, and quaintly ungrammatical in places," Banks tells of skeptics who believe Whitely wrote the diary as an adult and how one of Whitely's own relatives claims that

Jane Boulton masterfully sets to poetry the diary of Opal Whiteley, a young orphan adjusting to her new life with a logging family in Oregon. (From *Only Opal: The Diary of a Young Girl,* selected by Boulton and illustrated by Barbara Cooney.)

Whitely's so-called foster family was indeed her own birth family.

■ Works Cited

Banks, Ann, review of *Only Opal: The Diary of a Young Girl, New York Times Book Review,* May 22, 1994, p. 20.
Burns, Mary M., review of *Only Opal: The Diary of a Young Girl, Horn Book,* May/June, 1994, p. 338.
Review of *Only Opal: The Diary of a Young Girl, Kirkus Reviews,* February 15, 1994, p. 235.
Rosen, Martha, review of *Only Opal: The Diary of a Young Girl, School Library Journal,* May, 1994, p. 106.

■ For More Information See

PERIODICALS

Booklist, March 15, 1994, p. 1348.
Bulletin of the Center for Children's Books, June, 1994, p. 338.
Children's Book Review Service, March, 1994, p. 90.
Children's Book Watch, May, 1994, p. 4.
Horn Book Guide, fall, 1994, p. 387.
Quill & Quire, May, 1994, p. 38; February, 1995, p. 35.

Reading Time, October, 1994, p. 167.

* * *

BRADFIELD, Carl 1942-

■ Personal

Born April 5, 1942, in Baltimore, MD; son of Leonard Daniel and Dorothy Eunice Bradfield; divorced, May 1982; former wife's name, Myrna; children: Sandra Lynn. *Education:* Attended Poly Techn., 1957-59, Towson State University, 1969-72, Essex Community College, and Charminade College. *Politics:* None. *Religion:* "Servant of the Lord Jesus Christ."

■ Addresses

Office—ASDA Publishing, 904 Forest Lake Dr., Lakeland, FL 33809.

■ Career

Has been self-employed as a trucker, martial arts instructor, publisher, and playwright. Has been a Christian youth leader in two churches, 1980-90. *Military service:* U.S. Army, 1963-69, served in South Korea and Vietnam; received Combat Infantryman's Badge, two battle stars, NDB, VCB. *Member:* Society of 1st Infantry Division, U.S. Navy Memorial, 26th Infantry Regiment Association (Blue Spaders).

CARL BRADFIELD

■ Writings

The Blue Spaders-Vietnam: A Private's Account, 1-26th Inf., 1965-1966, ASDA Publishing (Lakeland, FL), 1992.
U-Turn, U.S.A.: The Wendells Family, ASDA Publishing, 1993.
Getting in Shape with Wendell and Myrtle: The Wendells Family, at It Again, ASDA Publishing, 1994.
Tecumseh's Trail: The Appalachian Trail, Then & Now, Northwest (Salt Lake City, UT), 1996.

Also author of one-act plays *Wendell and Myrtle Meet Mr. Peanut* and *Cleopatra ... Long Distance!* Regular columnist for *U.S. Veterans Magazine.*

■ Work in Progress

Hawaii Calls Wendell & Myrtle: The Wendells Family Make It to the Big Island, and "my best work," *The Sullivans of Little Horsepen Creek,* both due from ASDA Publishing. Research ongoing for *The Sullivans,* a sequel set in the colonial period.

■ Sidelights

Carl Bradfield told *SATA:* "I am a Vietnam combat veteran who looked into the eyes of the Vietcong that I killed just paces away—I can never change that. But my genre is family humor/children's comedy. I am probably the only combat war veteran in the country (and maybe others) who considers himself a comedy writer for kids (they don't start wars). All of my writings except the *Blue Spaders-Vietnam* are family humor and historical novels where the children are the protagonists—the heroes. Kids (of all ages) love to have fun, and so do I. Completed, I have written six novels and two plays where kids are projected as the protagonists. But of all my writings, I would like to be remembered for my work *The Sullivans of Little Horsepen Creek.* It is my best, most researched work to-date, with a sequel planned.

"I am an acquaintance of James A. Michener and Tom Clancy (a brother in Baltimore) and other famous writers, but writing for the family is something they don't do. I was Mister Peanut in the first two Disney World parades in Florida in 1971. I haunted a heap of houses on Halloween, took plenty of kids on theme park rides (I won't get on those rides because I crashed twice in helicopters in Vietnam), and guided hundreds of high-steppers through March of Dimes walk-a-thons.

"If there's one thing I hope to be remembered for it's treating kids like they were people, too."

* * *

BULLA, Clyde Robert 1914-

■ Personal

Born January 9, 1914, in King City, MO; son of Julian W. (a farmer) and Sarah Ann (a homemaker; maiden

name, Henson) Bulla. *Education:* Attended King City
High School for one year. *Hobbies and other interests:*
Music, theater, travel.

■ **Addresses**

Home—Los Angeles, CA. *Agent*—Curtis Brown, LTD,
10 Astor Place, New York, NY 10003.

■ **Career**

Farmer until 1942; *Tri-County News,* linotype operator
and columnist, King City, MO, 1942-47; writer, 1947—.
Member: Authors Guild, Authors League of America,
Society of Children's Book Writers and Illustrators.

■ **Awards, Honors**

Authors Club of Los Angeles award for outstanding
juvenile book by Southern California author, 1961, for
Benito; Southern California Council on Children's Literature award, 1962, for distinguished contribution to
field of children's literature, 1976, for *Shoeshine Girl,*
and 1987, for outstanding contribution of lasting value
in a body of work; Commonwealth Club of California
Silver medal, 1970, for *Jonah and the Great Fish;*
Christopher Award, 1971, for *Pocahontas and the
Strangers; Noah and the Rainbow: An Ancient Story* was
selected as a Children's Book Showcase title, 1973;
Charlie May Simon Award, 1978, Sequoyah Children's
Book Award, 1978, and South Carolina Children's Book
Award, 1980, all for *Shoeshine Girl; A Lion to Guard Us*
was selected as a Notable Children's Trade Book in
Social Studies, 1982.

■ **Writings**

FICTION

The Donkey Cart, illustrated by Lois Lenski, Crowell,
  1946.
Riding the Pony Express, illustrated by Grace Paull,
  Crowell, 1948.
The Secret Valley, illustrated by Grace Paull, Crowell,
  1949.
Surprise for a Cowboy, illustrated by Grace Paull,
  Crowell, 1950.
A Ranch for Danny, illustrated by Grace Paull, Crowell,
  1951.
Johnny Hong of Chinatown, illustrated by Dong King-
  man, Crowell, 1952.
Song of St. Francis, illustrated by Valenti Angelo,
  Crowell, 1952.
Star of Wild Horse Canyon, illustrated by Grace Paull,
  Crowell, 1953.
Eagle Feather, illustrated by Tom Two Arrows, Crowell,
  1953.
Squanto, Friend of the White Men, illustrated by Peter
  Burchard, Crowell, 1954, reprinted as *Squanto,
  Friend of the Pilgrims,* 1969.
Down the Mississippi, illustrated by Peter Burchard,
  Crowell, 1954.
A Dog Named Penny, illustrated by Kate Seredy, Ginn
  (Boston), 1955.

CLYDE ROBERT BULLA

White Sails to China, illustrated by Robert Henneber-
  ger, Crowell, 1955.
The Poppy Seeds, illustrated by Jean Charlot, Crowell,
  1955.
John Billington, Friend of Squanto, illustrated by Peter
  Burchard, Crowell, 1956.
The Sword in the Tree, illustrated by Paul Galdone,
  Crowell, 1956.
Old Charlie, illustrated by Paul Galdone, Crowell, 1957.
Ghost Town Treasure, illustrated by Don Freeman,
  Crowell, 1957.
Pirate's Promise, illustrated by Peter Burchard, Crowell,
  1958.
The Valentine Cat, illustrated by Leonard Weisgard,
  Crowell, 1959.
Three-Dollar Mule, illustrated by Paul Lantz, Crowell,
  1960.
The Sugar Pear Tree, illustrated by Taro Yashima,
  Crowell, 1961.
Benito, illustrated by Valenti Angelo, Crowell, 1961.
Viking Adventure, illustrated by Douglas Gorsline, Cro-
  well, 1963.
Indian Hill, illustrated by James Spanfeller, Crowell,
  1963.
White Bird, illustrated by Leonard Weisgard, Crowell,
  1966.
The Ghost of Windy Hill, illustrated by Don Bolognese,
  Crowell, 1968.
Mika's Apple Tree: A Story of Finland, illustrated by Des
  Asmussen, Crowell, 1968.
The Moon Singer, illustrated by Trina Schart Hyman,
  Crowell, 1969.
New Boy in Dublin: A Story of Ireland, illustrated by Jo
  Polseno, Crowell, 1969.
Pocahontas and the Strangers, illustrated by Peter
  Burchard, Crowell, 1971.
Open the Door and See All the People, illustrated by
  Wendy Watson, Crowell, 1972.

Dexter, illustrated by Glo Coalson, Crowell, 1973.

The Wish at the Top, illustrated by Chris Conover, Crowell, 1974.

Shoeshine Girl, illustrated by Leigh Grant, Crowell, 1975.

Marco Moonlight, illustrated by Julia Noonan, Crowell, 1976.

The Beast of Lor, illustrated by Ruth Sanderson, Crowell, 1977.

Keep Running, Allen!, illustrated by Satomi Ichikawa, Crowell, 1978.

(With Michael Syson) *Conquista!,* illustrated by Ronald Himler, Crowell, 1978.

Last Look, illustrated by Emily McCully, Crowell, 1979.

Daniel's Duck, illustrated by Joan Sandin, Harper, 1979.

The Stubborn Old Woman, illustrated by Anne Rockwell, Crowell, 1980.

My Friend the Monster, illustrated by Michele Chessare, Crowell, 1980.

A Lion to Guard Us, illustrated by Michele Chessare, Crowell, 1981.

Almost a Hero, illustrated by Ben Stahl, Dutton, 1981.

Poor Boy, Rich Boy, illustrated by Marcia Sewall, Harper, 1982.

Dandelion Hill, illustrated by Bruce Degen, Dutton, 1982.

Charlie's House, illustrated by Arthur Dorros, Crowell, 1983.

The Cardboard Crown, illustrated by Michele Chessare, Crowell, 1984.

The Chalk Box Kid, illustrated by Thomas B. Allen, Random House, 1987.

Singing Sam, illustrated by Susan Magurn, Random House, 1989.

The Christmas Coat, illustrated by Sylvie Wickstrom, Knopf, 1990.

A Place for Angels, illustrated by Julia Noonan, Troll, 1995.

NONFICTION

Stories of Favorite Operas, illustrated by Robert Galster, Crowell, 1959.

A Tree Is a Plant, illustrated by Lois Lignell, Crowell, 1960.

What Makes a Shadow?, illustrated by Adrienne Adams, Crowell, 1962, second edition, illustrated by June Otani, HarperCollins, 1994.

The Ring and the Fire: Stories from Wagner's Niebelung Operas, illustrated by Clare and John Ross, Crowell, 1962.

St. Valentine's Day, illustrated by Valenti Angelo, Crowell, 1965.

More Stories of Favorite Operas, illustrated by Joseph Low, Crowell, 1965.

Lincoln's Birthday, illustrated by Ernest Crichlow, Crowell, 1966.

Washington's Birthday, illustrated by Don Bolognese, Crowell, 1967.

Flowerpot Gardens, illustrated by Henry Evans, Crowell, 1967.

Stories of Gilbert and Sullivan Operas, illustrated by James and Ruth McCrea, Crowell, 1968.

Jonah and the Great Fish, illustrated by Helga Aichinger, Crowell, 1970.

Joseph the Dreamer, illustrated by Gordon Laite, Crowell, 1971.

(Translator) Max Bollinger, *Noah and the Rainbow: An Ancient Story,* illustrated by Helga Aichinger, Crowell, 1972.

A Grain of Wheat: A Writer Begins, Godine (Boston), 1985.

OTHER

(Adult fiction) *These Bright Young Dreams,* Penn (Philadelphia), 1941.

Manuscript collections: Kerlan Collection, University of Minnesota, Minneapolis; University of Oregon Library, Eugene; de Grummond Collection, University of Southern Mississippi, Hattiesburg; Ophelia Gilbert Collection, Missouri State University, Warrensburg.

COMPOSER OF MUSIC FOR SONG BOOKS, WITH LYRICS BY LOIS LENSKI

Cotton in My Sack, Lippincott, 1949.

I Like Winter, Walck, 1950.

Twelve-year-old Charlie Brig sets sail for the New World, unaware that he will arrive in the American colonies as an indentured servant. (Cover illustration by Arthur Dorros.)

Prairie School, Lippincott, 1951.
We Are Thy Children, Crowell, 1952.
Mamma Hattie's Girl, Lippincott, 1953.
On a Summer Day, Walck, 1953.
Corn-Farm Boy, Lippincott, 1954.
Songs of Mr. Small, Oxford University Press, 1954.
A Dog Came to School, Oxford University Press, 1955.
Songs of the City, Edward B. Marks Music Corp., 1956.
Up to Six: Book I, Hansen Music, 1956.
Flood Friday, Lippincott, 1956.
Davy and Dog, Walck, 1957.
I Went for a Walk, Walck, 1958.
At Our House, Walck, 1959.
When I Grow Up, Walck, 1960.

Also a composer of incidental music for plays *The Bean-Pickers,* 1952; *A Change of Heart,* 1952; and *Strangers in a Strange Land,* 1952, all by Lois Lenski; composer of librettos for two unproduced operas.

■ **Adaptations**

The Moon Singer was adapted for orchestra, with music by William Winstead, first performed at the Academy of Music, Philadelphia, PA, by the Philadelphia Orchestra, 1972; *Shoeshine Girl* was adapted as a film, Learning Corporation of America, 1980.

■ **Work in Progress**

A children's novel tentatively called *The Stranger Upstairs,* a story of the Great Depression.

■ **Sidelights**

Clyde Robert Bulla is an award-winning and prolific children's author whose works demonstrate that he has not forgotten what it's like to be a child. Jane Yolen once declared in the *New York Times Book Review* that Bulla is "one writer who has always had the talent to see the beautiful in the homey and even with a simple vocabulary can lift the ordinary into something special." His confident tone, simple language, and quick-paced plots appeal to young readers, as does his subject matter, including historical fiction, the retelling of Old Testament stories and opera plots, and stories set in contemporary America and foreign lands.

Raised on a farm near King City, Missouri, Bulla was the youngest of four children. He attended a nearby one-room country school run by one of his sisters. As a child, Bulla had a strong desire to become a writer. "By the time I was seven or eight, I was enamored of words," Bulla told *SATA.* "I announced that I was going to be a writer. My family and everyone else I knew told me that this was not likely to happen. We lived in a farming community where no one had ever seen a writer." At age ten, however, Bulla entered a writing contest in which he won a small prize. Winning this contest convinced Bulla that he was a writer, despite what his friends or family may have thought.

After her father's death, Claudine finds comfort in his collection of magnificently sculptured angels. (From *A Place for Angels,* written by Bulla and illustrated by Julia Noonan.)

Bulla continued to attend school with great enthusiasm. As a teenager, he became interested in opera and taught himself how to play piano. After attending only a year of high school, however, Bulla dropped out to help his family on the farm, finishing his education by correspondence. To improve his writing skills, Bulla read popular magazines—patterning stories on what he read—and writers' magazines as well. He explained to *SATA,* "Late at night, when the house was quiet, I sat up and wrote as long as I could stay awake. I sent my stories out to magazines. They all came back, and every rejection plunged me into deep, dark despair. To this day, I don't accept rejections gracefully."

Finally, in 1934 Bulla sold his first story—a love story to a woman's magazine. "I had learned about pulp magazines, and that first story was sold to one of them," Bulla recalled to *SATA.* "There were dozens of pulp magazines then. I sold other stories to them, and the sales helped my family and me during the depression. Then almost overnight, the pulp magazine empires crumbled and disappeared." During this time, Bulla joined a group of writers from various areas of the country who exchanged manuscripts and critiqued one another's work. Through this group, Bulla met Emma

Thibodaux, an elementary school teacher and published children's writer who became a close friend to Bulla and an important influence on his career.

When his first—and only—adult novel, *These Bright Young Dreams,* was published in 1941, Bulla felt he had at last found a measure of success. Unfortunately, the publishing company went bankrupt before paying Bulla his promised royalties. A few years later Bulla's mother became ill, which prompted the family to move to King City. There, the struggling writer worked as a typesetter and columnist for the town's weekly newspaper, the *Tri-County News.* Bulla told *SATA,* "In spare time I wrote. I tried various kinds of writing—short stories, poetry, novels." Bulla still corresponded regularly with Thibodaux, who persistently suggested that Bulla write something for children. "I hadn't much liked the children's stories I'd read as a child," Bulla admitted. "This was a field that didn't interest me. I told my friend I had no feeling for it, had no ideas."

Bulla, however, finally agreed, and with an idea suggested by Thibodaux he wrote a story that was eventually published as *The Donkey Cart.* "It was about two impossibly good children and their mild little adventures on a farm," Bulla described to *SATA.* Convinced that children wouldn't be interested in the story, Bulla went back to writing adult magazine stories. To his surprise his editor asked him to write another book. "No editor had ever asked me for anything before," Bulla exclaimed to *SATA.* "I started another story. The book was published. It was *Riding The Pony Express.* It fell far short of my hopes, but it was a beginning."

After *Riding the Pony Express* Bulla began writing a book or two per year. His other books on historical subjects include *Lincoln's Birthday, Washington's Birthday, A Lion to Guard Us,* and *Charlie's House. A Lion to Guard Us* is about Amanda Freebold, a young English maid living in seventeenth-century London with her mother and younger brother and sister. After their mother dies the children set out for America to find their father in Jamestown, Virginia. Based on the historical records of a rescue mission from Plymouth to the ailing Virginia colony in 1609, the work describes the children's harsh journey, which includes shipwreck, and the poor conditions in which they find their father. *Charlie's House* also presents a difficult journey from England to America. In this story, however, a bondsman tricks twelve-year-old Charlie Brig into becoming an indentured servant in eighteenth-century colonial America. Reviewing *Charlie's House* in the *New York Times Book Review,* Janet Taylor Lisle noted that the book "is a fine historical adventure story that confronts harsh truths in simple prose."

In addition to these titles are a number of historical books that focus on Native Americans, including *Squanto, Friend of the Pilgrims, Pocahontas and the Strangers,* and *Conquista!.* The award-winning *Pocahontas and the Strangers* describes the life of this famous Native American heroine who aided John Smith and the English during the early seventeenth century. Zena

When Sam and his new owner Amy become famous as a piano playing and singing duet, Rob demands that Amy return the dog he once rejected. (From *Singing Sam,* written by Bulla and illustrated by Susan Magurn.)

Sutherland of the *Bulletin of the Center for Children's Books* appreciated Bulla's "balanced and objective picture of the motivations and actions of the Indians and the white men." *Conquista!,* adapted from the film of the same name, is set in 1541 and tells the story of Little Wolf—a young Native American who encounters a horse for the first time.

Books featuring contemporary young male and female protagonists include *Shoeshine Girl, Keep Running, Allen!, The Chalkbox Kid,* and *A Place for Angels.* Gregory is *The Chalk Box Kid.* When his father loses his job and the family must move, Gregory has to share his room with Uncle Max, an unlikable man. Gregory has no place of his own, but finds his escape in an abandoned building where he creates a fanciful chalk garden on the walls. At school, where his imagination and artistic ability are recognized and appreciated, Gregory finds that life need not be so grim. *A Place for Angels* features Claudine, a young girl who must live with her overbearing aunt after her father dies. Against her aunt's wishes, Claudine takes along angels she and her father made together after her mother died. Unable to live with her aunt any longer, Claudine finds a new home filled with a loving family and friends. Lucinda Snyder Whitehurst, commenting in *School Library Journal,* viewed the book as "a simple, sweet selection that lacks lasting impact." However, Carolyn Phelan, writing for *Booklist,* noted that "the cogency and simplicity of style make it accessible to a wide age range."

Inspired by the many places he has visited around the world, Bulla has written many books set abroad, including *The Sword in the Tree, Mika's Apple Tree, New Boy in Dublin: A Story of Ireland,* and *The Beast of Lor.* Filled with detail and historical content, *The Beast of Lor* is set in Britain near the time of the Roman invasion. It features the outcast Lud who meets a runaway elephant previously brought to Britain by the Romans. The two travel together and eventually help rid a village of its evil rulers. "Despite a wealth of unusual detail, the story of the lonely boy and the displaced animal is simply told," noted Charlotte W. Draper in her *Horn Book* review.

Also reflected in Bulla's work is his interest in music. He included songs in some of his early works but stopped after he received negative comments from critics. Yet Bulla continued to write songs for children, and he also set lyrics by children's author Lois Lenski to music. In an effort to introduce children to opera, Bulla wrote *Stories of Favorite Operas, The Ring and the Fire: Stories from Wagner's Niebelung Operas, More Stories of Favorite Operas,* and *Stories of Gilbert and Sullivan Operas,* which retell the stories of these famous works in Bulla's simple and straightforward style.

Reflecting on how he developed his writing style, Bulla told *SATA,* "Remembering the heavy weather most of my schoolmates had made of reading, I tried to keep the writing simple and easy-to-read." Sticking with what works, Bulla employs the same method of writing today that he used when writing his second book *Riding the Pony Express.* Since 1981 Bulla has traveled less but continues to write stories for young readers.

■ Works Cited

Draper, Charlotte, W., review of *The Beast of Lor, Horn Book,* February, 1978, p. 43.

Lisle, Janet Taylor, review of *Charlie's House, New York Times Book Review,* July 11, 1993, p. 27.

Phelan, Carolyn, review of *A Place for Angels, Booklist,* January 1, 1996, p. 832.

Sutherland, Zena, review of *Pocahontas and the Strangers, Bulletin of the Center for Children's Books,* July-August, 1972, p. 166.

Whitehurst, Lucinda Snyder, review of *A Place for Angels, School Library Journal,* December, 1995, p. 102.

Yolen, Jane, "Easy and Early," *New York Times Book Review,* November 11, 1979, pp. 55, 60.

■ For More Information See

BOOKS

Bulla, Clyde Robert, *A Grain of Wheat: A Writer Begins,* Godine, 1985.

Hopkins, Lee Bennett, *Books Are by People,* Citation Press, 1969.

PERIODICALS

Booklist, July, 1984, p. 1547; December 1, 1987, p. 628; June 1, 1989, p. 1728; March 15, 1994, p. 1366.

Bulletin of the Center for Children's Books, April, 1978, p. 123; February, 1979, p. 95; July-August, 1983, p. 204.

Horn Book, October, 1971, p. 474; August, 1980, p. 393; August, 1981, p. 420; April, 1984, p. 194.

Kirkus Reviews, September 15, 1971, p. 1016; November 15, 1978, p. 1246; June 15, 1980, p. 774; April 1, 1981, p. 432; October 15, 1995, p. 1488.

Publishers Weekly, July 1, 1983, p. 102; March 29, 1993, p. 56.

School Library Journal, December, 1987, p. 71; April, 1994, p. 117.

—Sketch by Kathleen L. Witman

C

CAPOTE, Truman 1924-1984

■ Personal

Born Truman Streckfus Persons; name changed legally; born September 30, 1924, in New Orleans, LA; died August 25, 1984, of liver disease complicated by phlebitis and multiple drug intoxication, in Los Angeles, CA; son of Archulus Persons (a nonpracticing lawyer) and Lillie Mae (Faulk) Persons Capote; adopted by Joseph G. Capote. *Education:* Attended Trinity School and St. John's Academy, both New York City, and public schools in Greenwich, CT.

■ Career

Writer. Worked for *New Yorker* magazine as a newspaper clipper and cartoon cataloguer, c. 1943-44; also moonlighted as a filmscript reader and freelance writer of anecdotes for a digest magazine. Appeared in motion picture comedy *Murder by Death*, Columbia, 1976.

■ Awards, Honors

Won first literary prize at age ten in *Mobile Press Register* contest, for short story "Old Mr. Busybody"; O. Henry Award, Doubleday & Co., 1946, for "Miriam," 1948, for "Shut a Final Door," and 1951; National Institute of Arts and Letters creative writing award, 1959; Edgar Award, Mystery Writers of America, 1966, and National Book Award nomination, 1967, both for *In Cold Blood;* Emmy Award, 1967, for television adaptation *A Christmas Memory.*

■ Writings

FOR CHILDREN AND ADULTS

A Christmas Memory (first published in *Mademoiselle,* December, 1956), Random House, 1968, reprinted with illustrations by Beth Peck and including cassette, Knopf, 1989.

The Thanksgiving Visitor (first published in *McCall's*), Random House, 1968, reprinted with illustrations by Beth Peck, Knopf, 1996.

Miriam (first published in *Mademoiselle*), illustrated by Sandra Higashi, Creative Education, 1982.

One Christmas (first published in *Ladies Home Journal*), Random House, 1983.

I Remember Grandpa (first published in *Redbook*), illustrations by Barry Moser, Peachtree, 1987.

FOR ADULTS

Other Voices, Other Rooms (novel), Random House, 1948, reprinted with an introduction by the author, 1968.

A Tree of Night, and Other Stories, Random House, 1949.

The Grass Harp (novel), Random House, 1950.

The Grass Harp, and A Tree of Night, and Other Stories, New American Library, 1956.

The Muses Are Heard: An Account (first published in *New Yorker*), Random House, 1956, published in England as *The Muses Are Heard: An Account of the Porgy and Bess Visit to Leningrad,* Heinemann, 1957.

Breakfast at Tiffany's: A Short Novel and Three Stories, Random House, 1958, published in England as *Breakfast at Tiffany's,* Hamish Hamilton, 1959.

(Author of commentary) Richard Avedon, *Observations,* Simon & Schuster, 1959.

Selected Writings, introduction by Mark Schorer, Random House, 1963.

In Cold Blood: A True Account of a Multiple Murder and Its Consequences (nonfiction novel; first serialized in *New Yorker*), Random House, 1966.

The Dogs Bark: Public People and Private Places, Random House, 1973.

Music for Chameleons: New Writing, Random House, 1983.

Answered Prayers: The Partial Manuscript (first serialized in *Esquire*), edited by Joseph Fox, Random House, 1986.

PLAYS

The Grass Harp: A Play (based on his novel of the same title; first produced on Broadway at Martin Beck Theatre, 1952; produced as a musical on Broadway

TRUMAN CAPOTE

at Martin Beck Theatre, 1971), Random House, 1952.

(With Harold Arlen) *The House of Flowers* (libretto; based on his short story of the same title; first produced on Broadway at Alvin Theatre, 1954; rewritten version first produced Off-Broadway at Theater de Lys, 1968), Random House, 1968.

FILMSCRIPTS

(With John Huston) *Beat the Devil*, United Artists, 1954.

The Innocents (based on Henry James's novel of the same title), Twentieth Century-Fox, 1961.

(With Eleanor Perry) *Trilogy* (adapted from his stories *Miriam*, "Among the Paths to Eden," and *A Christmas Memory*), Allied Artists, 1969.

TELEVISION SCRIPTS

A Christmas Memory (based on his book of the same title), first broadcast on American Broadcasting Co. (ABC-TV), 1966.

The Thanksgiving Visitor (based on his book of the same title), first broadcast on ABC-TV, 1968.

Also author of television play *Among the Paths of Eden* (adapted from his story of the same title), first produced in 1967.

OTHER

(Author of introduction) *The Collected Works of Jane Bowles*, Farrar, Straus, 1966.

(With E. Perry and Frank Perry) *Trilogy: An Experiment in Multimedia*, Macmillan, 1969.

Also author of *Then It All Came Down: Criminal Justice Today Discussed by Police, Criminals, and Correction Officers, with Comments by Truman Capote*, 1976. Contributor to numerous anthologies, including *Five Modern American Short Stories*, edited by Helmut Tischler, M. Diesterweg, 1962. Many of Capote's books have been translated into foreign languages, including French, German, Spanish, and Italian. Author of column, "Observations," *Esquire*, beginning March, 1983. Contributor to magazines, including *Vogue, Mademoiselle, Ladies Home Journal, Esquire*, and *New Yorker.*

■ Adaptations

Capote made a sound recording of his short story "Children on Their Birthdays" for Columbia in the 1950s; *Breakfast at Tiffany's* was filmed by Paramount in 1961 and starred Audrey Hepburn and George Peppard; *In Cold Blood* was filmed by Columbia Pictures in 1967; "Handcarved Coffins" was sold to Lester Persky Productions, 1980.

Inspired by his childhood holiday experiences, Capote creates a warm story about a seven-year-old boy's annual ritual of baking fruitcakes with his eccentric cousin during the Depression. (From *A Christmas Memory,* illustrated by Beth Peck.)

■ Sidelights

A masterful stylist who took great pride in his writing, Truman Capote was also a well-known television personality who was openly obsessed with fame. In addition to literary recognition, the flamboyant, Southern-born writer sought social privilege and public celebrity, objectives he achieved in 1948 with the appearance of his first novel, *Other Voices, Other Rooms.* Capote is perhaps best known for works like *Breakfast at Tiffany's,* the story of a Manhattan playgirl that was later adapted into a popular film of the same title, and *In Cold Blood,* a novel based on the true story of two murderers who were executed for killing an entire family. Capote spent years researching this "nonfiction novel," a genre he invented, and the stress of the project is sometimes blamed for his addiction to tranquilizers. In addition to these famous works, Capote also wrote several childhood reminiscences appropriate for young readers, including his classic story *A Christmas Memory.*

Born Truman Streckfus Persons in New Orleans, Louisiana, Capote had a childhood that, by all accounts, was difficult. His mother, a former Miss Alabama who later committed suicide, considered herself temperamentally unsuited to motherhood and sent her son off to be raised by relatives in Monroeville, a small Alabama town. When he was four, his parents ended their marriage in a bitter divorce: his mother went north to New York, his father moved south to New Orleans, and young Truman

was neglected by both. Though he frequently summered with his father, traveling up and down the Mississippi on the family-owned Streckfus Steam Boat Line, the two were never close, and Capote never thought highly of him. Capote's closest friends at this time were his elderly cousin, Miss Sook Faulk, and a neighborhood tomboy, Harper Lee, who would become the author of *To Kill a Mockingbird.*

After Capote's mother married a Cuban-born New York businessman named Joe Capote, she had several miscarriages. Realizing she would never have any more children, she sent for Truman, who was then nine years old. Legally adopted by his stepfather, the young Capote attended school in Manhattan, then enrolled at Trinity School, and, at thirteen, was sent to live at St. John's Academy, a military boarding school. Capote hated school. Lonely and emotionally neglected by his parents, he received such low grades that it was feared he was mentally disabled. Capote proved that idea wrong, however, when he took an IQ test and scored 215, over twice the IQ of the average person. Although he finished high school, Capote had no inclination to attend college, and so he found a menial job working at the *New Yorker.* Shortly after leaving this job, he published his short story "Miriam" in *Mademoiselle.* In 1946 "Miriam" earned the author his first of three O. Henry awards.

After enduring months of torment from a school yard bully, Buddy acts on his cousin's idea to invite Odd Henderson to share Thanksgiving Dinner with them. (Cover illustration by Beth Peck.)

Capote wrote many short stories during his lifetime, which were published in magazines such as *Vogue, Mademoiselle, Ladies Home Journal, Esquire,* and *New Yorker.* Some of these stories are appropriate for young readers, the best known of these being his classic, *A Christmas Memory,* for which Capote would later win an Emmy award for his 1967 television adaptation. *A Christmas Memory,* set during the Depression, is a tender reminiscence of the last Christmas that Capote spent with his beloved elderly cousin, Sook Faulk. The two are best friends in every sense of the word, doing everything together and comforting one another when the other relatives in the house yell at them. The seven-year-old boy's cousin calls him "Buddy," after the name of a dear friend she knew when she was a child and who died back in the 1880s. As Christmas approaches, the two friends bake fruitcakes together, which they generously share with perfect strangers. When the boy's cousin, who is slightly eccentric, allows him to drink some of the whiskey she uses in the cakes, the relatives in the house denounce her as a terrible influence, making the old woman cry. The boy comforts her, and together they decide to go out and cut down a tree, which they decorate with paper ornaments they have created. For Christmas, they make kites to give to each other, and on Christmas Day they fly them together. It is a memory the boy never forgets, one that he recalls vividly when, years later while he is in military school, he receives word that his beloved cousin has died.

A Christmas Memory is considered a classic by many for its poignant and heartfelt description of a very special and rare friendship that crosses the generations. Originally published in *Mademoiselle* magazine, it was reprinted in 1989 as a children's book with illustrations by Beth Peck. One *School Library Journal* reviewer described the work as a "tiny gem of a holiday story," and of the new edition, *Horn Book* contributor Nancy Vasilakis said the work "has been given new life in this beautifully illustrated volume which is certain to occupy a treasured place among the read-aloud favorites." Capote also wrote other reminiscences set during the holidays, including *The Thanksgiving Visitor* and *One Christmas.*

After Capote's death in 1984, his aunt, Marie Rudisill, discovered a manuscript that would later be published, with illustrations by Barry Moser, as *I Remember Grandpa.* It is a somber story in some ways reminiscent of *A Christmas Memory.* Set on a West Virginia farm, it tells of the day a boy named Bobby must move to the city with his parents and say farewell to his grandparents. Bobby's grandmother soon dies, and, after only sending one letter to him, his grandfather dies as well. Later, Bobby receives a package full of photographs that remind him of his time on the farm and how he longs to return there. A biographical note published with the story explains that the tale was written by Capote in memory of his uncle.

"When he died just over a month short of his sixtieth birthday," wrote Craig Goad in the *Concise Dictionary of American Literary Biography,* "Truman Capote left

Born and raised in West Virginia farm country, Bobby has trouble adjusting to a new life in the city without his beloved grandparents. (From *I Remember Grandpa,* written by Capote and illustrated by Barry Moser.)

behind a substantial fortune, a legacy of literary success and controversy, and a sense of incompleteness, of promise unfulfilled." Capote's short story reminiscences invoke a similar feeling, a longing for something irretrievably lost.

■ Works Cited

Review of *A Christmas Memory, School Library Journal,* December, 1989, p. 98.

Goad, Craig, "Truman Capote," *Concise Dictionary of American Literary Biography,* Gale, 1987, pp. 128-39.

Vasilakis, Nancy, review of *A Christmas Memory, Horn Book,* March/April, 1990, pp. 198-99.

■ For More Information See

PERIODICALS

Booklist, October 15, 1983, p. 323; June 1, 1993, p. 1864; October 1, 1993, p. 334.

Kirkus Reviews, September 15, 1968, p. 1071; July 1, 1987, p. 966.

Library Journal, October 15, 1983, p. 1958.

Newsweek, December 4, 1989, p. 76.

New York Times, November 17, 1966, p. 49M.

New York Times Book Review, November 13, 1983, p. 19.

Publishers Weekly, September 9, 1968, p. 56; July 17, 1987, p. 51; September 30, 1996, p. 86.

School Library Journal, March, 1983, pp. 188-89.

Times Literary Supplement, January 1, 1970, p. 15.*

*   *   *

CARTER, Lin(wood Vrooman) 1930-1988

■ Personal

Born June 9, 1930, in St. Petersburg, FL; died of cardiac arrest brought on by chronic emphysema, in Montclair, NJ, February 7, 1988; son of Raymond Linwood and Lucy (Vrooman) Carter; married Judith Ellen Hershkowitz, 1958 (divorced, 1959); married Noel Vreeland, August 19, 1964 (divorced, 1975). *Education:* Attended Columbia University, 1953-54. *Religion:* "None, but anti-all."

■ Career

Copywriter for advertising agencies and book publishers, including Prentice-Hall and Albert Frank-Guenther Law Agency, 1957-69; full-time free-lance writer of science fiction and heroic fantasy, 1969-88. Editorial consultant, Ballantine Books, Inc. Originator and funder of Gandalf Award for Grand Master of Fantasy, World Science Fiction Convention, 1976. *Military service:* U.S. Army, infantry, 1951-53; served in Korea.

■ Awards, Honors

Nova award, 1972.

■ Writings

The Star Magicians (bound with *The Off-Worlders,* by Howard Hunt), Ace Books, 1966.

The Flame of Iridar (bound with *Peril of the Starmen,* by Kris Neville), Belmont, 1967.

(With David Grinnell) *Destination: Saturn* (bound with *Invader on My Back,* by Philip E. High), Ace Books, 1967.

The Thief of Thoth (bound with *And Others Shall Be Born,* by Frank Belknap Long), Belmont, 1968.

Tower at the Edge of Time, Belmont, 1968.

Giant of World's End, Belmont, 1969.

The Purloined Planet (bound with *The Evil That Men Do,* by John Brunner), Belmont, 1969.

Lost World of Time, New American Library, 1969.

Tower of the Medusa, Ace Books, 1969.

The Quest of Kadji, Belmont, 1972.

The Black Star, Dell, 1973.

The Man Who Loved Mars, Fawcett, 1973.

The Valley Where Time Stood Still, Doubleday, 1974.

Time War, Dell, 1974.

The City outside the World, Berkley, 1977.

The Wizard of Zao, DAW Books, 1978.

LIN CARTER

Journey to the Underground World, DAW Books, 1979.

Tara of the Twilight, Zebra, 1979.

Zanthodon (sequel to *Journey to the Underground World*), DAW Books, 1980.

Darya of the Bronze Age, DAW Books, 1981.

Hurok of the Stone Age, DAW Books, 1981.

Eric of Zanthodon, DAW Books, 1982.

Kellory the Warlock, Doubleday, 1984.

Down to a Sunless Sea, DAW Books, 1984.

Found Wanting, DAW Books, 1985.

Horror Wears Blue, Doubleday, 1987.

"CALLISTO" SERIES

Black Legion of Callisto, Dell, 1972.

Jandar of Callisto, Dell, 1972.

Sky Pirates of Callisto, Dell, 1973.

Mad Empress of Callisto, Dell, 1975.

Mind Wizards of Callisto, Dell, 1975.

Lankar of Callisto, Dell, 1975.

Ylana of Callisto, Dell, 1977.

Renegade of Callisto, Dell, 1978.

"CONAN" SERIES

(With Robert E. Howard and L. Sprague de Camp) *Conan,* Ace Books, 1967.

(With Robert E. Howard and L. Sprague de Camp) *Conan the Wanderer,* Lancer, 1968.

(With L. Sprague de Camp) *Conan of the Isles,* Lancer, 1968.

(With Robert E. Howard and L. Sprague de Camp) *Conan of Cimmeria*, Lancer, 1969.

(With L. Sprague de Camp) *Conan the Buccaneer*, Lancer, 1971.

(With L. Sprague de Camp) *Conan of Aquilonia*, Lancer, 1971.

(With L. Sprague de Camp, Catherine Crook de Camp, and Bjorn Nyberg) *Conan the Swordsman*, Bantam, 1978.

(With L. Sprague de Camp and Catherine Crook de Camp) *Conan the Liberator*, Bantam, 1979.

(With L. Sprague de Camp and Catherine Crook de Camp) *Conan the Barbarian* (screenplay novelization), Bantam, 1982.

"GREAT IMPERIUM" SERIES

The Man without a Planet (bound with *Time to Live*, by John Rackham), Ace Books, 1966.

Star Rogue, Lancer, 1970.

Outworlder, Lancer, 1971.

"GREEN STAR SAGA" SERIES

Under the Green Star, DAW Books, 1972.

When the Green Star Calls, DAW Books, 1973.

By the Light of the Green Star, DAW Books, 1974.

As the Green Star Rises, DAW Books, 1975.

In the Green Star's Glow, DAW Books, 1976.

"GONDWANE EPIC" SERIES

The Warrior of World's End, DAW Books, 1974.

The Enchantress of World's End, DAW Books, 1975.

The Immortal of World's End, DAW Books, 1976.

The Barbarian of World's End, DAW Books, 1977.

The Pirate of World's End, DAW Books, 1978.

"THONGOR" SERIES

The Wizard of Lemuria, Ace Books, 1965, revised edition published as *Thongor and the Wizard of Lemuria*, Berkley, 1969.

Thongor of Lemuria, Ace Books, 1966, revised edition published as *Thongor and the Dragon City*, Berkley, 1970.

Thongor against the Gods, Paperback Library, 1967.

Thongor at the End of Time, Paperback Library, 1968.

Thongor in the City of Magicians, Paperback Library, 1968.

Thongor Fights the Pirates of Tarakus, Berkley, 1970 (published in England as *Thongor and the Pirates of Tarakus*, Tandem, 1971).

"TERRA MAGICA" SERIES

Kesrick, DAW Books, 1982.

Dragonrouge: Further Adventures in Terra Magica, DAW Books, 1984.

Mandricardo: New Adventures in Terra Magica, DAW Books, 1987.

Callipygia, DAW Books, 1988.

"ZARKON, LORD OF THE UNKNOWN" SERIES

The Nemesis of Evil, Doubleday, 1975.

Invisible Death, Doubleday, 1975.

The Volcano Ogre, Doubleday, 1976.

The Earth-Shaker, Doubleday, 1982.

EDITOR

Dragons, Elves, and Heroes, Ballantine, 1969.

The Young Magicians, Ballantine, 1969.

Golden Cities, Far, Ballantine, 1970.

The Magic of Atlantis, Lancer, 1970.

H. P. Lovecraft, *The Dream-Quest of Unknown Kadath*, Ballantine, 1970.

Clark Ashton Smith, *Zothique*, Ballantine, 1970.

Lord Dunsany, *At the Edge of the World*, Ballantine, 1970.

Clark Ashton Smith, *Hyperborea*, Ballantine, 1971.

New Worlds for Old, Ballantine, 1971.

The Spawn of Cthulhu, Ballantine, 1971.

Discoveries in Fantasy, Ballantine, 1972.

Lord Dunsany, *Beyond the Fields We Know*, Ballantine, 1972.

George MacDonald, *Evenor*, Ballantine, 1972.

Clark Ashton Smith, *Xiccarph*, Ballantine, 1972.

Great Short Novels of Adult Fantasy, two volumes, Ballantine, 1972-73.

Clark Ashton Smith, *Poseidonis*, Ballantine, 1973.

(And contributor) *Flashing Swords!*, three volumes, Doubleday, 1973-77; two volumes, Dell, 1976-81.

Lord Dunsany, *Over the Hills and Far Away*, Ballantine, 1974.

(And contributor) *The Year's Best Fantasy Stories*, six volumes, DAW Books, 1975-80.

Realms of Wizardry, Doubleday, 1976.

(And contributor) *Kingdoms of Sorcery*, Doubleday, 1976.

Warriors and Wizards, Dell, 1976.

Realms of Wizardry, Doubleday, 1976.

Barbarians and Black Magicians, Doubleday, 1977.

(And contributor) *Weird Tales*, four volumes, Zebra, 1981-83.

OTHER

Sandalwood and Jade (verse), Sign of the Centaur, 1951.

(With Robert E. Howard) *King Kull* (short stories), Lancer, 1967.

Tolkien: A Look behind "The Lord of the Rings" (criticism; excerpts published in *Xero*, 1961-67), Ballantine, 1969.

Beyond the Gates of Dream (short stories), Belmont, 1969.

Lovecraft: A Look behind the "Cthulhu Mythos" (criticism), Ballantine, 1972, second edition, 1996.

Imaginary Worlds: The Art of Fantasy, Ballantine, 1973.

Dreams from R'lyeh (verse; originally published in *Amra*), introduction by L. Sprague de Camp, Arkham House, 1975.

(Author of text) David Wenzel, *Middle-Earth: The World of Tolkien*, illustrated by David Wenzel, Centaur, 1977.

Lost Worlds (anthology), DAW Books, 1980.

Editor and author of introductions for "Ballantine Adult Fantasy Series," Ballantine Books, 1969-73; editor of "Lin Carter Fantasy Selections," for Zebra Books. Contributor to books, including *Dark Things, Nameless Places, The Disciples of Cthulhu*, and *The DAW Science Fiction Reader*, as well as the "Call of Cthulhu" series, which includes *The Shub-Niggurath Cycle: 15 Horror*

Tales Involving Shub-Niggurath and Her Thousand Young and *The Azathoth Cycle: 16 Horror Tales Concerning the Ultimate Chaos.* Contributor of short stories, poems, and criticism to periodicals, including *Amra, Canadian Fandom, Fantastic, Inside, Magazine of Fantasy and Science Fiction,* and *Xero.* Editor and publisher of fan magazines, including *Spaceteer, The Saturday Evening Toad,* and *Spectrum.*

■ Adaptations

A folk-rock musical, *Thongor in the City of Magicians,* loosely based on Carter's book of the same title, was produced in London in the late 1960s.

■ Sidelights

Lin Carter's name, declared Bill Crider in the *Dictionary of Literary Biography Yearbook 1981,* was "one of the most prominent ... in the field of fantasy." Besides editing the significant "Ballantine Adult Fantasy" series that reintroduced works of fantasy by major authors, Carter produced major works of criticism on the genre, wrote stories in the style of 1930s pulp magazines, and helped spark the revolution in fantasy publishing of the 1960s and 1970s. Also, for over twenty years, wrote Catherine Crook and L. Sprague de Camp in *Locus,* Carter "was an active producer of heroic fantasy and sword-and-planet tales," authoring more than one hundred science fantasy and fantasy stories.

Fantasy was Carter's great passion. An early devotee to L. Frank Baum's Oz books, Robert E. Howard's stories of Conan the Barbarian, and Edgar Rice Burroughs' Martian tales and stories of Tarzan, Carter began publishing stories, articles, and reviews in fan magazines while he was still in high school. In his "Author's Note" to his own novel *Under the Green Star,* Carter said that when he started reading Burroughs' book, he was "a helpless captive from the first page on," and much of his writing reflects a strong Burroughs influence. A review of *Hurok of the Stone Age* in *Kliatt* mentioned how the story is "another of Carter's seemingly endless series in the SF pastorals in the tradition of E. R. Burroughs, with strong overtones of Robert E. Howard and Rider Haggard showing through."

Carter's enthusiasm for Howard's work led L. Sprague de Camp, who was working on a series of stories about Conan the Barbarian for Howard's estate, to invite Carter to collaborate with him on the stories. Carter and de Camp completed several Conan stories that Howard had left unfinished and then wrote a number of original Conan tales at the behest of the Howard heirs. "Although opinions differ as to the success of these collaborations," the de Camps explained, "the readers thus introduced to Conan clamored for more, until there were twelve volumes of stories about the Great Barbarian."

While some reviewers appreciated Carter's work in and enthusiasm for the sword-and-sorcery and fantasy genres, other reviewers found Carter's style unappeal-

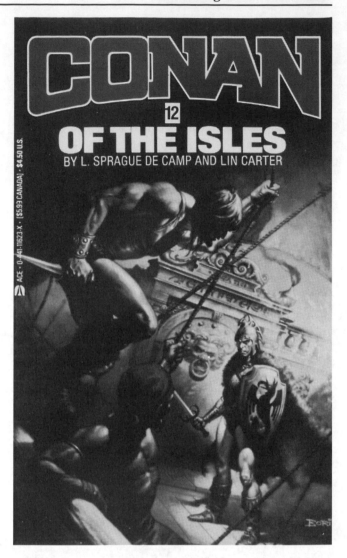

Carter, along with co-author L. Sprague de Camp, kept alive Robert E. Howard's popular "Conan" series after Howard's death. (Cover illustration by Boris Vallejo.)

ing; William M. Schuyler, Jr., wrote in *Fantasy Review* of *Down to a Sunless Sea,* "Even on pain of death do not read this book," and in the same periodical Paul M. Lloyd exclaimed about *Kellory the Warlock,* "Alas, my heart was grieved within me when I thought of how many innocent trees gave their lives that this tome might live." But others recognized the value of his fiction: "One should not overlook the entertainment value of Carter's work," warned Crider, who added, "It might also be pointed out that the theme of much Sword & Sorcery literature, including Carter's, that of Order versus Chaos, is not an ignoble one."

Carter attempted to define his own fascination with fantasy in *Imaginary Worlds,* his history of fantastic literature. "Why do we who love fantasy read it with such delight and gusto, returning to it again and again over the years as to a source of entertainment that is inexhaustible?" he asked. "We read fantasy because we love it; we love it because we find it a source of the marvel and mystery and wonder and joy that we can find nowhere else.... Why do I read fantasy? I really don't know; I really don't care. All I know is that something within me wakes and thrills and responds to phrases like 'the splendid city of Celephais, in the Valley of Ooth-Nargai, beyond the Tanarian Hills,' where galleys 'sail up the river Oukranos past the gilded spires of Thran,' and 'elephant caravans tramp through perfumed jungles in Kled,' where 'forgotten palaces with veined ivory columns sleep lovely and unbroken under the moon.' Such phrases, such sequences of gorgeous imagery, touch something that is within most of us, really. I believe that a hunger of the fabulous is common to the human condition.... But whatever it is that sings within me to such imagery," he concluded, "I am happy that it is there."

Carter's professional nonfiction began in 1969 with *Tolkien: A Look behind "The Lord of the Rings,"* which stemmed from some of the articles he had written in high school. In this work Carter briefly discusses Tolkien's life, gives a summary of the "Lord of the Rings" trilogy and *The Hobbit,* investigates Tolkien's sources, and gives a concise history of fantasy literature. His next major work of nonfiction, *Lovecraft: A Look behind the "Cthulhu Mythos"* (1972), is a study of the invented myths used over a period of years by H. P. Lovecraft. It also includes a complete bibliography of Cthulhu Mythos stories (written by Lovecraft and others between 1921 and 1971) and an appendix comparing the differing opinions of various Lovecraft scholars and fans regarding the Mythos. The *Lovecraft* book in particular has been criticized for its subjectivity and its informal, chatty style. Carter himself admitted that many of his value judgments were personal opinion, but the book remains a repository of valuable information for anyone interested in Lovecraft's work or its influence on later writers.

It was on the basis of his Tolkien study that Carter was asked to edit Ballantine Books' adult fantasy series. In his capacity as general editor Carter performed some of his most influential work, stated Crider, reprinting relatively unknown books by authors such as Evangeline Walton, Poul Anderson, William Morris, Lord Dunsany, H. Rider Haggard, and George MacDonald, anthologizing fantastic episodes from varied sources of world literature ranging from *The Kalevala* and *The Volsung Saga* to the poetry of Browning and Tennyson, and publishing works by new authors such as Katherine Kurtz and Joy Chant.

Throughout his long and industrious career, stated Crider, Lin Carter "established himself as a figure of the first importance in the field of fantasy. He [had] the ability to entertain and the ability to inform, and he ... preserved and caused to be published volumes of importance to any scholar interested in the fantastic in literature." Carter himself was something of a fantasy figure: "Despite his many virtues," reported the de Camps, "... Lin was a living embodiment of Peter Pan. His view of the world and his relation to it was totally unrealistic." His heavy smoking, and his refusal to seek medical attention for the mouth cancer that developed because of it, led to a disfiguring operation in 1985 and

to his death three years later. Perhaps the fullest revelation of Carter's commitment to the genre, however, is revealed in the dedication to his *Imaginary Worlds;* he inscribed the volume "to the fantasy writers of tomorrow, to those men and women not yet born, whom I shall never know, whose books I shall not live to read, but whose dreams I have shared and whose visions would not be strange or alien to me."

■ Works Cited

Carter, Lin, *Under the Green Star,* DAW Books, 1972.
Carter, Lin, *Imaginary Worlds: The Art of Fantasy,* Ballantine, 1973.
Crider, Bill, *Dictionary of Literary Biography Yearbook: 1981,* Gale, 1982.
de Camp, L. Sprague, and Catherine Crook de Camp, "Remembering Lin Carter," *Locus,* March, 1988, p. 70.
Review of *Hurok of the Stone Age, Kliatt,* spring, 1981, p. 17.
Lloyd, Paul M., review of *Kellory the Warlock, Fantasy Review,* September, 1994, p. 26.
Schuyler, William M., Jr., review of *Down to a Sunless Sea, Fantasy Review,* October, 1984, p. 25.

■ For More Information See

BOOKS

Price, Robert M., *Lin Carter: A Look behind His Imaginary Worlds,* Borgo Press, 1991.
Schweitzer, Darrell, *Science Fiction Voices #5,* Borgo Press, 1981.
Searles, Baird, Martin Last, Beth Meacham, and Michael Franklin, *A Reader's Guide to Science Fiction,* Avon, 1979.
Searles, Baird, Beth Meacham, and Michael Franklin, *A Reader's Guide to Fantasy,* Avon, 1982.

PERIODICALS

Fantasy Review, January, 1985; March, 1987.
Kliatt, April, 1987; April, 1988.
Locus, October, 1992.
Los Angeles Times Book Review, February 6, 1983.
Magazine of Fantasy and Science Fiction, March, 1976.
Science Fiction and Fantasy Book Review, October, 1982.
Science Fiction Chronicle, May, 1985.
Voice of Youth Advocates, February, 1983; June, 1987; April, 1988; October, 1988.*

*   *   *

CEBULASH, Mel 1937-
(Ben Farrell, Glen Harlan, Jared Jansen, Jeanette Mara)

■ Personal

Surname is pronounced "*seb*-yu-lash"; born August 24, 1937, in Jersey City, NJ; son of Jack (a mailman) and Jeanette (Duthie) Cebulash; married Deanna Penn, August 19, 1962 (divorced); married Dolly Hasinbiller,

MEL CEBULASH

June 19, 1977; children: (first marriage) Glen Harlan, Benjamin Farrell, Jeanette Mara; (second marriage) Patchin Hasinbiller. *Education:* Jersey City State College, B.A., 1962, M.A., 1964; University of South Carolina, graduate study, 1964-65. *Religion:* Jewish. *Hobbies and other interests:* Literature and popular music of the 1930s, the works of James T. Farrell ("a friend and inspiration"), handicapping horses and prize fights.

■ Addresses

Home—11820 North 112th St., Scottsdale, AZ 85259. *Office*—11811 North Tatum Blvd., Suite 1081, Phoenix, AZ 85028.

■ Career

Junior high school teacher of reading, Teaneck, NJ, 1962-64; Fairleigh Dickinson University, Rutherford, NJ, instructor in reading clinic, 1965-67; Scholastic Magazines, Inc., New York City, editor for language arts, 1966-76; Bowmar/Noble Publishing Co., Los Angeles, CA, editor in chief, 1976-80; Cebulash Associates, Phoenix, AZ (formerly Pasadena, CA), publisher, 1980-83, 1986—; Fearon Educational (imprint of Simon & Schuster), publisher, 1983-86. *Military service:* U.S. Army, 1955-58. *Member:* Authors Guild, Authors League of America, Mystery Writers of America (regional vice president, Southern California chapter, 1981-82).

■ Awards, Honors

Author Award, New Jersey Association of Teachers of English, 1969, for *Through Basic Training with Walter Young;* New Jersey Institute of Technology award, 1972, for *The Ball That Wouldn't Bounce, Benny's Nose,* and *Dic-tion-ar-y Skilz,* 1983, for *Ruth Marini—Dodger Ace*

and *Ruth Marini of the Dodgers;* Children's Choice Award, International Reading Association (IRA), 1975, for *Football Players Do Amazing Things,* and 1976, for *Basketball Players Do Amazing Things;* Children's Book of the Year, Child Study Association, Bank Street College, 1977, for *Basketball Players Do Amazing Things;* IRA Young Adult Choice Award, 1987, for *Ruth Marini—World Series Star;* Public Library Association (PLA) Certificate of Merit, 1994, for "Great Sports of the 20th Century" series and "Sully Gomez Mystery" series.

■ Writings

FICTION

The Ball That Wouldn't Bounce, illustrated by Tom Eaton, Scholastic, 1972.

Benny's Nose, illustrated by Ib Ohlsson, Scholastic, 1972.

(Under pseudonym Ben Farrell) *Nancy and Jeff,* Scholastic, 1972.

(Under pseudonym Jared Jansen) *Penny the Poodle,* Scholastic, 1972.

(Under pseudonym Glen Harlan) *Petey the Pup,* Scholastic, 1972.

The See-Saw, Scholastic, 1972.

The Grossest Book of World Records, Pocket Books, 1977.

The Grossest Book of World Records II, Pocket Books, 1978.

Blackouts, Scholastic, 1979.

The Champion's Jacket, Creative Education, 1979.

Ruth Marini of the Dodgers, Lerner Publications, 1983.

Ruth Marini—Dodger Ace, Lerner Publications, 1983.

The Face That Stopped Time, Pitman Learning, 1984.

Ruth Marini—World Series Star, Lerner Publications, 1985.

Hot Like the Sun: A Terry Tyndale Mystery, Lerner Publications, 1986.

Campground Caper, Fawcett, 1990.

Carly and Company, Fawcett, 1990.

Part-Time Shadow, Fawcett, 1990.

(Under pseudonym Ben Farrell) *Dad Saves the Day,* Silver Burdett/Ginn, 1991.

(Under pseudonym Jared Jansen) *Showtime,* Silver Burdett/Ginn, 1991.

Batboy, illustrated by Duane Krych, Child's World, 1993.

Catnapper, illustrated by Duane Krych, Child's World, 1993.

Flipper's Boy, illustrated by Duane Krych, Child's World, 1993.

Muscle Bound, illustrated by Duane Krych, Child's World, 1993.

Rattler, illustrated by Duane Krych, Child's World, 1993.

Snooperman, illustrated by Duane Krych, Child's World, 1993.

Willie's Wonderful Pet, Scholastic, 1993.

Scared Silly, Trumpet Book Club, 1995.

(Under pseudonym Ben Farrell) *My Family Band,* Harcourt, 1996.

(Under pseudonym Glen Harlan) *Play Ball!*, Harcourt, 1996.
(Under pseudonym Ben Farrell) *Let's Visit the Moon*, Harcourt, 1996.
(Under pseudonym Ben Farrell) *One More Time*, Harcourt, 1996.
(Under pseudonym Ben Farrell) *What a Shower!*, Harcourt, 1996.

NONFICTION

Through Basic Training with Walter Young, Scholastic, 1968.
Man in a Green Beret and Other Medal of Honor Winners, Scholastic, 1969.
Baseball Players Do Amazing Things, Random House, 1973.
Dic-tion-ar-y Skilz, Scholastic, 1974.
Football Players Do Amazing Things, Random House, 1975.
Basketball Players Do Amazing Things, Random House, 1976.
Math Zingo, Bowmar/Noble, 1978.
Reading Zingo, Bowmar/Noble, 1978.
Big League Baseball Reading Kit, Bowmar/Noble, 1979.
Crosswinds Reading Program, Bowmar/Noble, 1979.
Spanish Math Zingo, Bowmar/Noble, 1979.
The 1,000 Point Pro Sports Quiz Book: Football, Random House, 1979.
The 1,000 Point Pro Sports Quiz Book: Basketball, Random House, 1979.
The 1,000 Point Pro Sports Quiz Book: Baseball, Random House, 1980.
A Horse to Remember, Bowmar/Noble, 1980.
I'm an Expert: Motivating Independent Study Projects for Grades 4-6, Scott, Foresman, 1982.

"SPRING STREET BOYS" SERIES; PUBLISHED BY SCHOLASTIC

The Spring Street Boys Team Up, 1982.
The Spring Street Boys Settle a Score, 1982.
The Spring Street Boys Hit the Road, 1982.
The Spring Street Boys Go for Broke, 1982.

"CARLY AND COMPANY" SERIES; PUBLISHED BY FAWCETT

Carly and Company, 1990.
Campground Caper, 1990.
Part-time Shadow, 1990.

"GREAT SPORTS OF THE 20TH CENTURY" SERIES; PUBLISHED BY NEW READERS PRESS

Bases Loaded: Great Baseball of the 20th Century, 1993.
Fast Break: Great Basketball of the 20th Century, 1993.
Lights Out: Great Fights of the 20th Century, 1993.
Third and Goal: Great Football of the 20th Century, 1993.

"SULLY GOMEZ MYSTERY" SERIES; PUBLISHED BY NEW READERS PRESS

Dirty Money, 1993.
Knockout Punch, 1993.
Set to Explode, 1993.
A Sucker for Redheads, 1993.

SCREENPLAY NOVELIZATIONS

Monkeys, Go Home, Scholastic, 1967.
The Love Bug, Scholastic, 1969.
The Boatniks, Scholastic, 1970.
Herbie Rides Again, Scholastic, 1974.
The Strongest Man in the World, Scholastic, 1975.
Ghostdad, Berkley, 1990.

OTHER

Editor, "ACTION Reading Kit" series, Scholastic, 1970. Contributor, sometimes under pseudonyms Ben Farrell and Jeanette Mara, of short stories to university literary journals. Contributing editor, *Scholastic Scope*.

■ Work in Progress

California Listing, an adult mystery about the high-stakes textbook adoption business; *Freak Times*, a humorous juvenile title.

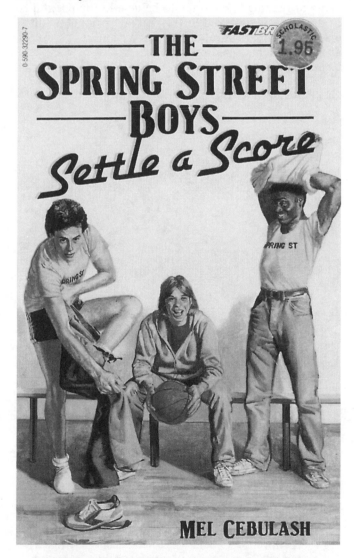

When thugs from a different neighborhood terrorize their friend Tiny, the Spring Street Boys come up with a plan to get even.

■ Sidelights

Educator Mel Cebulash has written over sixty books for children, young adults, and adults. Most of his books deal with high-interest subjects—such as sports, mysteries, and movies—and are intended to encourage reluctant young people to read. During what he has described as an ordinary childhood in Union City, New Jersey, Cebulash developed a lifelong appreciation for the way that reading can open young minds. "My mother's deep respect for books led me to a library at a very early age, and reading allowed me to entertain all sorts of dreams and to become all sorts of people," he once told *SATA*. "I still believe that reading is the most important subject taught in school."

After teaching junior high school for a few years, Cebulash "left teaching and moved into writing and editing as a full-time activity," he recalled for *SATA*. "My parents and friends looked upon the move as the foolish pursuit of a far-fetched dream. Fortunately, years of reading had led me to believe in the possibility of dreams." He worked for several educational publishers, developing high-interest materials and programs for at-risk students, before starting his own company, Cebulash Associates, in 1980.

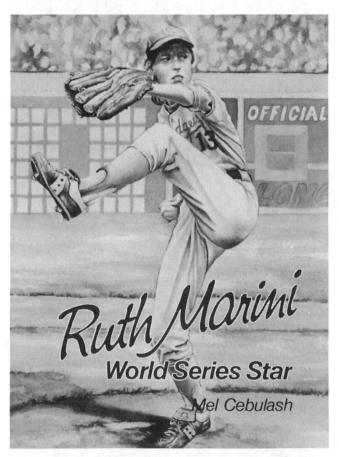

In the third of Cebulash's books about a fictional female professional baseball player, pitching sensation Ruth Marini returns from a serious injury to lead her Los Angeles Dodgers in the World Series. (Cover illustration by Cherie R. Wyman.)

One of Cebulash's well-received series of books for reluctant readers includes the titles *Baseball Players Do Amazing Things,* published in 1973, and *Football Players Do Amazing Things,* published in 1975. The first book features thirteen short chapters, each describing an interesting story or event from baseball history. For example, one chapter recalls the time that the great power hitter Babe Ruth pointed to the spot in the grandstand where he predicted he would hit his next home run, and another discusses the career of Eddie Gaedel, who at three feet, seven inches was the shortest man ever to play professional baseball. Similarly, *Football Players Do Amazing Things* contains eleven chapters about famous football players and their feats. It tells the story of a 1948 game between the Chicago Cardinals and the Philadelphia Eagles that took place in a blinding blizzard, and describes the time that Viking player Jim Marshall ran sixty yards to score a touchdown in the opposition's end zone. Each book is illustrated with numerous black-and-white photographs. A reviewer for *Booklist* praised Cebulash's "smooth, down-to-earth style" and noted that the books "will impress and amuse readers."

In 1982 Cebulash published a series of four fictional works about the Spring Street Boys, a group of high school students who live in the same neighborhood and share many sports-related adventures. In *The Spring Street Boys Settle a Score,* the boys set out to avenge Tiny, a younger kid who was injured by a car when he ran into the street to retrieve his ball. Just before the accident, two mean older boys had been teasing Tiny and had thrown his ball into the street. The Spring Street Boys find out who the two boys are and get even with them, even though they end up losing an important game in the process. In a review for *The High-Low Report,* Thetis Powers Reeves commented that Cebulash's "kids are real and likeable and his complex plots fast paced and fun. The Spring Street Boys are well worth knowing."

In *Ruth Marini of the Dodgers,* published in 1983, as well as two sequels, Cebulash tells the fictional story of the first woman to break the gender barrier and play major league baseball. Ruth is a star pitcher on her high school baseball team, but she believes that her career is over after graduation. She initially takes an office job, but then she is thrilled to be invited to attend training camp for the Los Angeles Dodgers. As a rookie assigned to the Dodgers' minor league system, Ruth must face the sexist attitudes of some of her fellow players and fans as well as the hardships of playing frequently and living on the road. She also struggles to find a place in her life for a romantic relationship.

In the first sequel, *Ruth Marini—Dodger Ace,* Ruth makes it to the big leagues but is injured during the season. She also meets her father, who had left her family many years earlier. The final book in the series, *Ruth Marini—World Series Star,* follows Ruth as she recovers from her injury in time to help her team defeat the New York Yankees for the world championship. A reviewer for *School Library Journal* called Ruth "a

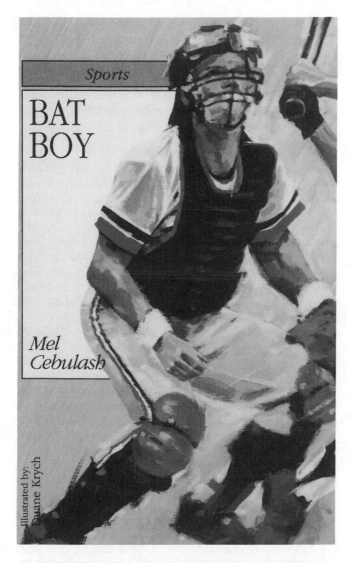

Sports

BAT
BOY

*Mel
Cebulash*

Illustrated by:
Duane Krych

**Mike convinces everyone to allow four-feet, six-inch-
tall Elliot to join the baseball team.** (Cover illustration
by Duane Krych.)

winning character and a convincing one," while a writer
for *Bulletin of the Center for Children's Books* added
that the series has "plenty of action, an appealing idea,
and baseball sequences that are well written."

In a writing career spanning thirty years, Cebulash has
motivated many at-risk students to read with his
entertaining, high-interest books. In addition to his
sports-related stories, he has written book-length adaptations of several popular movies—such as *The Love
Bug, The Strongest Man in the World,* and *Ghostdad*—
as well as books of study projects and quizzes for
students. "I've been pleased by the sales of my books,
but my real joy in writing has come from the letters I've
received from young people," Cebulash explained to
SATA. "When I think I'm all alone with a computer, I
remind myself of the many friends I've made through
writing."

■ **Works Cited**

Review of *Football Players Do Amazing Things, Book-
list,* November 15, 1975, p. 459.
Reeves, Thetis Powers, review of *The Spring Street Boys
Settle a Score, The High-Low Report,* February,
1982.
Review of *Ruth Marini—Dodger Ace, School Library
Journal,* May, 1983, p. 95.
Review of *Ruth Marini—World Series Star, Bulletin of
the Center for Children's Books,* September, 1985, p.
3.

■ **For More Information See**

PERIODICALS

Booklist, August, 1983, p. 1483; January 15, 1990, p.
990.
Bulletin of the Center for Children's Books, November,
1973; May, 1983; July-August, 1983; July-August,
1986.
Childhood Education, November-December, 1983, p.
136.
Kirkus Reviews, October 1, 1975.
Library Journal, October 15, 1973.
Publishers Weekly, March 4, 1983, p. 99.
Reading Teacher, May, 1983, p. 950.
School Library Journal, August, 1983; January, 1994, p.
112.

*   *   *

CHAPMAN, Walker
    See SILVERBERG, Robert

*   *   *

CHASE, Andra 1942-

■ **Personal**

Born May 5, 1942, in New Orleans, LA; daughter of
Alexander (a home builder and millwork foreman) and
Ada (a horticulturalist; maiden name, Sullwold) de
Monsabert; married John Churchill Chase, August 22,
1964; children: Alyssa Chase, Katrina C. Motsinger.
Education: Attended John McCrady Art School at
Louisiana State University, 1960-65, and Johnson City
Community College, 1974-77 (studied art and art histo-
ry). *Politics:* "Independent (Republican)." *Religion:*
Catholic. *Hobbies and other interests:* Gardening, out-
door activities, fishing, and painting.

■ **Addresses**

Home—5900 West 89 Ter., Overland Park, KS 66207.

■ **Career**

Artist for L. M. Berry & Co., 1960-61; Swiftway Inc.,
New Orleans, LA, artist, 1961; Walther Brothers Inc.,
New Orleans, artist, 1962; Maison Blanche Department

ANDRA CHASE

Store, New Orleans, fashion illustrator, 1962-64; D. H. Holmes and Co., New Orleans, fashion illustrator, 1964-67, part-time artist, 1967-73; freelance artist in Kansas City, MO, 1978-83; freelance artist, 1982-90. Children's book illustrator, 1990—. *Exhibitions:* Has participated in numerous solo and juried shows in Kansas, Missouri, Oklahoma, and Louisiana, 1980—. *Member:* Society of Children's Book Writers and Illustrators, Kansas Watercolor Society, Kansas City Artists' Coalition.

■ **Awards, Honors**

First place, Heritage Art Show, 1979; Purchase Award, New Orleans Watercolor art show, 1982; Patron Purchase Award, Kansas Watercolor art show, 1990; Purchase Award, Art in the Woods art show, 1991.

■ **Illustrator**

J. Bowden, *Where Does Our Garbage Go?*, Bantam, 1992.
Theresa Hayes, *Celebrate the Birth of Jesus Poster Book*, Standard Publishing (Cincinnati, OH), 1992.
Ruth S. Odor, *God Keeps His Promises*, Standard Publishing, 1992.
Sylvia Tester, *Where Are We Going Today?*, Standard Publishing, 1992.
Elizabeth Happy, *Kiki and the Cuckoo*, Marsh Media (Shawnee Mission, Kansas), 1992.
Marion Duckworth, *B. J. Bernard Grows Up*, Standard Publishing, 1993.
Alyssa Chase, *Jomo and Mata*, Marsh Media, 1993.

Elizabeth Happy, *Bailey's Birthday*, Marsh Media, 1994.
Jami Parkinson, *Inger's Promise*, Marsh Media, 1996.

■ **Work in Progress**

Another book for Marsh Media.

■ **Sidelights**

"Being a book illustrator is something I've aspired to for a long time, but eased into gradually while pursuing a commercial art career," Andra Chase told *SATA*. "One thing led to another, a client recommended me to a publisher, and finally I am here. This work is very meaningful and enjoyable to me because some of my books are used as a vehicle in education, have a certain longevity, and possibly bring a little art appreciation to the young mind while offering the child a deeper insight into the author's tale and the emotions of the character.

"When illustrating a book such as *Bailey's Christmas,* the dog characters were developed first and then the family and friends. Extensive research of New York City followed. I used my own photos from a prior trip to New York and Brooklyn and then asked a young writer/editor who lived in New York to take specific photos of scenes in the story. My own dog was a model for Bailey's expressions and other dogs were photographed for research on Claudia the Basset Hound. My local library and librarian were a great help. All this information was gathered before any page layouts were started.

"I recommend that aspiring authors and illustrators research the children's department in book stores, libraries, etc., even though it can be mind-boggling and intimidating. Doing so keeps you attuned to trends and competition. This is something I do a few times a year to keep current, however I try not to let myself be influenced by other artists. Finding my own solutions to composition and style are the things that keep me interested and searching for excellence."

■ **For More Information See**

PERIODICALS

Publishers Weekly, March 28, 1994, p. 96.
School Library Journal, November 1994, p. 81.*

*   *   *

COLEMAN, Andrew
  See PINE, Nicholas

*   *   *

CONWAY, Diana C(ohen) 1943-

■ **Personal**

Born May 29, 1943, in Marshall, MO; daughter of Joseph (an actor and teacher) and Sara Roe (a secretary)

Cohen (name later changed to Conway); married Herbert Berkowitz, May 22, 1966 (divorced 1980); children: Andrew, Jason. *Education:* University of California, Los Angeles, B.A., 1964; New York University, M.A., 1965, Ph.D., 1970. *Politics:* "Bleeding-heart liberal." *Religion:* "I describe myself as a 'cultural Jew.'" *Hobbies and other interests:* "I'm fluent in Spanish and can get by in French and Chinese. I play the guitar (folk songs), have made five quilts all by hand, and love to bake bread. We live a semi-subsistence lifestyle."

■ Addresses

Home and office—Box 6461, Halibut Cove, AK 99603-6461.

■ Career

Anchorage Community College, Anchorage, AK, Spanish teacher, 1971-87; University of Alaska, Anchorage, professor of Spanish, 1987-89.

■ Writings

Northern Lights: A Hanukkah Story, illustrated by Shelly O. Haas, Kar-Ben Copies (Rockville, MD), 1994.

DIANA C. CONWAY

A story, "Little Swallow," was published in *Ranger Rick* and anthologized in *It's Up to You,* by Prentice Hall, 1996. Has published other fiction in *Cricket, Spider, Highlights, Skipping Stones,* and *Pockets* magazines. Contributor of a bi-monthly column to *We Alaskans,* the Sunday supplement to the *Anchorage Daily News,* and book reviews to the *Homer News.*

■ Work in Progress

A children's book about the Holocaust, based in part on memories from an in-law who escaped from a death-train.

■ Sidelights

Diana C. Conway told *SATA:* "I don't have great ambitions to make a career as a children's writer. I just want to write one really good book, the kind of book someone reads to you when you're very young and that you never forget. You'll be walking along a city street and pass a bookstore, and there it is! The illustration on the cover just the way you remember it. The emotions inside as powerful as the first time you opened the book.

"There are perhaps half a dozen books from before the time I learned to read that have stayed with me that way. All of them are still in print, which proves that quality endures and that children know quality when they see it.

"Perhaps today's children are too overwhelmed by TV and movies to experience the same sensual joy from books that I recall from my childhood, but I don't think so. That's why I concentrate on picture stories for the youngest readers.

"I live what many people would consider an idyllic life on an island in south-central Alaska with only twenty-five year-round residents. My longtime companion and I eat mostly fish we've caught ourselves, vegetables from our own garden, and homemade bread. I'm very aware of the gifts life has given me and distraught over the conditions in which children live all over the world and in our own inner cities. In our writings all of us need to speak for love, social justice, and a better tomorrow."

*   *   *

COOK, Roy
See SILVERBERG, Robert

*   *   *

CREEDEN, Sharon 1938-

■ Personal

Born November 4, 1938; married Will Creeden (a pilot); children: three. *Education:* Washburn University, B.A., 1964; Seattle University School of Law, J.D., 1980.

SHARON CREEDEN

■ Addresses

Office—2536 Alki S.W., Seattle, WA 98116-2270.

■ Career

Storyteller, 1983-95. Served as a deputy prosecuting attorney. *Member:* National Storytelling Association, Seattle Storytellers Guild, Arizona Tellers of Tales.

■ Awards, Honors

Aesop Prize, Children's Folklore Section, American Folklore Society, 1995.

■ Writings

Fair Is Fair: World Folktales of Justice, August House, 1995.

■ Work in Progress

In Full Bloom: Folktales of Women in Their Prime.

■ Sidelights

After spending a few years as a deputy prosecuting attorney, Sharon Creeden decided to switch careers and become a storyteller. In 1995, she combined her legal training with her storytelling skills and produced *Fair Is Fair: World Folktales of Justice,* a collection of stories about how justice is served around the world. Comparing traditional folktales with modern legal decisions, Creeden teaches children about justice by telling stories

rather than by lecturing about right and wrong. Describing the book as "interesting and easy-to-read," Judy Sokoll in *School Library Journal* says that *Fair Is Fair* is "a fine example of stories serving both to entertain and to educate." In *Booklist,* reviewer Mary Carroll notes that Creeden's folktales are useful in "remind[ing] lawyers and nonlawyers alike that justice is a universal, demanding human ideal."

■ Works Cited

Carroll, Mary, review of *Fair Is Fair, Booklist,* May 15, 1995, p. 1615.
Sokoll, Judy, review of *Fair Is Fair, School Library Journal,* October, 1995, p. 169.

■ For More Information See

PERIODICALS

Library Journal, April 1, 1995, p. 102.

*   *   *

CUNNINGHAM, Dru

■ Personal

Born in Hanford, WA; daughter of John (an electrician and farmer) and Helen (Smith) Pohl; married Spencer V. Cunningham (a photographer and teacher), July 21, 1968; children: Anika Dru, Kristoff Spencer. *Education:* Attended Ohio State University, Lima; Bluffton College, Bluffton, OH, B.S. (elementary education), 1966. *Religion:* Mennonite. *Hobbies and other interests:* "I love doing things with my family: biking, exploring nature, visiting museums and exhibits, camping, travel, music festivals—I like it ALL!"

■ Addresses

Home—418 North Main St., Bowling Green, OH 43402.

■ Career

Author, journalist, and teacher. Celina School System, Celina, OH, and Bellefontaine School System, Bellefontaine, OH, elementary teacher, c. 1970s; Bowling Green Christian Academy, Bowling Green, OH, elementary teacher, 1992—.

■ Writings

It's Fun to Choose, illustrated by Richard Hackney, Stanford Publishing, 1988.
The Most Wonderful Place to Live, Winston-Derek (Nashville, TN), 1995.

Also contributor of interviews, articles, and poems to numerous magazines and newspapers.

■ Work in Progress

Researching information on the wife of an early Christian martyr.

■ Sidelights

"Ever since I was a young child I wanted to be a teacher and an author," Dru Cunningham told *SATA*. "God has really blessed me as I have been able to get to do both of my choices. Getting to be a 'Mom' besides has been the interesting surprise.

"Growing up on a farm in Northwest Ohio was the best of everything! Nature all around, a pony of my own, and a wonderful family that loved me sounds too good to be true these days, but I really got to have what could be a child's dream. I came to know and experience the reality of God at that point in time.

"So many of my ideas have come from incidents and activities that have happened with my own children or something that comes to me through the children that I teach. I've always loved poetry and have done a lot of rhyming even as a child. When some of my poetry was published in our church paper, I was pleased. I never thought of getting my work published professionally until after I taught school for a while, but I never stopped writing, although what I wrote was not being done with that objective in mind. My first professional break came when I got an article published in *American Legion Magazine* about an interesting war mural. One thing has led to another ever since. I don't write constantly, yet I'm always writing or thinking about it. I think that when I use the gifts that God has given me, I can give something meaningful to the children or various other readers whose lives help to create the myriad of memories, emotions, and experience that we know as 'Life.'"*

*   *   *

CURTIS, Wade
See POURNELLE, Jerry (Eugene)

D

DAVIDSON, (Marie) Diane 1924-

■ Personal

Born March 6, 1924, in Los Angeles, CA; daughter of Charles C. (in the U.S. Cavalry) and Stella Ruth (a writer and art critic; maiden name, Bateman) Winnia; married William E. Davidson (a U.S. artillery captain), February 27, 1948 (divorced); children: David William, Ronald M. *Education:* University of California, Berkeley, A.B., 1943, teaching credential, 1944; Sacramento State University, M.A., 1959. *Politics:* Democrat. *Religion:* Episcopalian. *Hobbies and other interests:* Gardening, photography, writing.

DIANE DAVIDSON

■ Addresses

Agent—Swan Books, P.O. Box 2498, Fair Oaks, CA 95628.

■ Career

Actress in U.S.O. Camp Shows' Far East circuit, 1946-47; Kurokamiyama School, Nara, Japan, teacher and principal, 1947-49; El Camino High School, Sacramento, CA, teacher, 1954-84; Swan Books, Fair Oaks, CA, writer and publisher, 1979—. *Member:* National Education Association, Authors Guild, Authors League of America, PEN, Actor's Equity, National Association of Teachers of English, California Association of Teachers of English, California Writers Club, Phi Beta Kappa, Pi Lambda Theta.

■ Writings

Feversham (novel), Crown (New York City), 1969.
Shakespeare on Stage (eight volumes), Swan Books (Fair Oaks, CA), 1979-85.
Shakespeare for Young People (nine volumes), Swan Books, 1986-94.
History of Trinity Episcopal Church, Folsom, 1856-1994, Trinity (Folsom, CA), 1996.

■ Work in Progress

Additional volumes in *Shakespeare for Young People,* including *Twelfth Night for Young People;* a novel entitled *A Very Likely Story.*

■ Sidelights

"My major works are the two series *Shakespeare on Stage* and *Shakespeare for Young People,* a total of seventeen books so far," Diane Davidson told *SATA.* "They are easy-to-read editions of Shakespeare's plays without changing the words. The two series arose quite naturally from elements in my life: a background that includes a Phi Beta Kappa key in dramatic literature, professional acting, and an M.A. in playwriting, plus a career of teaching high school for thirty-five years.

"After years of teaching Shakespeare, I still marvelled that some intelligent college-prep students found the plays difficult. Why? Over and over, I would interrupt and explain the line till I felt like a robot. So I began to experiment by putting the plays on mimeograph with the explanations added in parentheses. The students approved. Then I typed new editions on dittos with the dialogue in modern running style, as an actor never uses an artificial end-of-line pause every ten syllables. Also, like a theatre director, I cut the slow parts. Better and better. I added descriptions of fights and flirtations, modern style, so the students could visualize the plays easier. They asked for more explanations, and I rewrote endlessly. Finally I abolished my pet peeve—footnotes, with the attendant eye-jumps that cause a reader to lose his place and interrupt his concentration. Instead, I inserted headnotes in italics, giving explanations *before* a hard part. Much better! The last script in xerox was quite readable, and it moved so swiftly that the reader felt the full momentum of the play. The whole process had taken only eight years.

"What had happened was that I put Shakespeare's plays into modern playwriting format. To test my point that format caused the difficulty, I taped a sequence of *Magnum, P.I.* and typed it in sixteenth-century format with ten syllables per line, no stage direction, and no explanations. The seniors could not read even *Magnum, P.I.* in this style. Format was the key to intelligibility!

"After fifty-six rejections by professional publishers, I took out a second mortgage on my old house and became my own publisher of Swan Books. The eight original high school plays became the *Shakespeare on Stage* series. Then teachers at conventions asked me to do shorter editions for middle school. Thus emerged the forty-minute adaptations known as *Shakespeare for Young People,* nine playlets that proved even more popular than the high school series. My latest is *Twelfth Night for Young People.* All are endorsed by educators at the University of California, Berkeley, Folger Shakespeare Library, and the Ashland Shakespeare Festival.

"So far as I know, no one else has stumbled on this simple method for presenting the world's best writer so that he can be enjoyed in print."

■ For More Information See

PERIODICALS

Kliatt, spring, 1980, p. 22.

*   *   *

DeBRY, Roger K. 1942-

■ Personal

Born October 17, 1942, in Idaho Falls, ID; son of James and Winnifred (Jensen) DeBry; married Patricia Spenc-

er; children: Todd, Jennifer Lacanienta, Peter, Elizabeth. *Education:* University of Utah, B.S., 1964, M.S., 1967, Ph.D. (computer science), 1972. *Religion:* Church of Jesus Christ of Latter-Day Saints.

■ Addresses

Home—3214 Lakeview Circle, Longmont, CO 80503.

■ Career

IBM Corporation, Boulder, CO, senior technical staff member, 1972—. Instructor in technology management program, Denver University. *Member:* Association for Computing Machinery.

■ Writings

FOR CHILDREN

Bartholomew's Christmas Adventure: A Bear's Tale, Roberts Rinehart (Niwot, CO), 1995.

OTHER

Communicating with Display Terminals, McGraw-Hill, 1985.

Contributor of numerous technical articles to journals.

*   *   *

DONER, Kim 1955-

■ Personal

Born July 21, 1955, in Tulsa, OK; daughter of Otto (a sales engineer) and Elizabeth Jane (Hamilton) Doner; married John L. Wieczorek, June 15, 1974 (divorced 1987); children: Sophie Alison Wieczorek, Lucy Amanda Wieczorek. *Education:* University of Tulsa, B.A. (medical illustration), 1976, and graduate study. *Religion:* Non-denominational.

■ Addresses

Office—P.O. Box 702724, Tulsa, OK 74170-2724.

■ Career

Portraitist, beginning 1984, then illustrator, 1992—; Philbrook Museum, Tulsa, OK, instructor, 1995—; Tulsa Junior College, computer graphics instructor, 1995—. Member of "I'd Sooner Read" Literacy Task Force; speaker on the arts, Arts and Humanities Council, Tulsa, beginning 1993. *Member:* Society of Children's Book Writers and Illustrators, Oklahoma Writers Federation, Tuesday Writers Group (Tulsa, OK).

■ Awards, Honors

Oklahoma Book Award for best illustrated book, Center for the Book, 1995, for *Green Snake Ceremony.*

KIM DONER

■ Illustrator

Sherrin Watkins, *White Bead Ceremony,* Council Oak Books (Tulsa, OK), 1994.

Sherrin Watkins, *Green Snake Ceremony,* Council Oak Books, 1995.

Molly Levite Griffis, *The Buffalo in the Mall,* Eakin Press (Austin, TX), 1996.

■ Work in Progress

Writing and illustrating *Buffalo Dreams,* about a child who brings a gift in honor of the white buffalo that was born in Wisconsin in 1995; several other books.

■ Sidelights

"Many acquaintances in my life have teased me about 'What do you want to be when you grow up?,'" illustrator Kim Doner told *SATA,* "and I have had a question in return: 'Can't I just BE when I grown up?' It has only been in the past few years that I've realized I don't have to grow up. I can immerse myself in my favorite profession (art), my favorite pastime (stories), my favorite people (kids, including those who still think like them), and my favorite hobby (communication in all forms), and have the whole enchilada. What a deal!

"I've studied art my whole life, and three years ago was approached by Council Oak Books to illustrate their first children's book, *White Bead Ceremony.* As I began to learn about publishing, I wondered if the people I ultimately work for would be interested, too—do kids want to know how publishing works? So I adopted a neighborhood school (they were thrilled) and shared each stage of the process. This became a cross between a performance, speech, and demonstration, which snowballed through Oklahoma schools. Now I illustrate and write (which satisfies the solitary side of me) and tour school systems to present the process of publishing (which keeps my extrovert side quite happy).

"A large part of my presentation has to do with the development of the illustrations for the second book, *Green Snake Ceremony. Green Snake Ceremony* is the story of a Shawnee family searching for a green snake to use in an empowering ceremony they perform for their children. Part of the ceremony involves putting the snake in the mouth of a child. The family never finds a green snake—they buy a garter snake and wrap it in green cloth to use. The snake is later released at a nearby nature center. The little girl misinterprets the description of the ceremony and (of course) doesn't want a snake in her mouth. When I read the story, I thought, 'I wouldn't want to be *her ... or* the snake.' Then I thought, 'What if there is a green snake? What if he lives under the house, and hears they are looking for him? And what if he manages to never get caught?' A whole second, humorous story was added through illustrations of this mythical little guy avoiding capture. It was a blast to do, and received the award of Best Illustrated Book of 1995 in Oklahoma.

"I work every day with such a variety of jobs that it's hard to say how many hours and where: I draw, paint, write, do scheduling, plan tours, balance the books, research, do presentations, and teach. My vision of my work is broad: I hope that each and every book enriches as many lives as possible through humor or meaning or education or entertainment. My advice: If you *know* you have found what you love, DON'T EVER QUIT. Join critique groups, work hard, stay disciplined, ask questions, volunteer services, stay open, and nurture your dreams. Life is too short to sink into a 'life of quiet desperation,' and creating is tantamount to breathing.

"I've found a secret to all of this, too. I am no longer aging. Through connecting with imagination and humor and creativity and kids, I am 'younging'. Sometime next year, I'll probably turn ten years old and get to start trick or treating again. Watch out!"

*   *   *

DORFLINGER, Carolyn 1953-

■ Personal

Born November 26, 1953, in Montclair, NJ; daughter of William (a chemical engineer) and Betty (a homemaker) Heffner; married Ernest Dorflinger (a doctor in pharmaceutical research), December 23, 1978; children: Eric, Lindsey. *Education:* Douglass College, B.A., 1975.

■ Addresses

Home—17 Elmwood Ave., Chatham, NJ 07928.

■ Career

Spanish and French teacher at Branchburg Central School, Branchburg, NJ, 1975-80, Shenendehowa Schools, Clifton Park, NY, 1988-89, and Harding Township School, New Vernon, NJ, 1995—. Writer. *Member:* Society of Children's Book Writers and Illustrators.

■ Awards, Honors

"Celebrating Womanhood" Essay Contest winner, New Jersey Women's Festival, 1992.

■ Writings

Tomorrow Is Mom's Birthday, illustrated by Iza Trapani, Whispering Coyote Press, 1994.

Also contributor to *Guideposts for Kids.*

■ For More Information See

PERIODICALS

Booklist, May 1, 1994, p. 1607.*

* * *

DRUMMOND, Walter
See SILVERBERG, Robert

E

ECKERT, Allan W. 1931-

■ Personal

Born January 30, 1931, in Buffalo, NY; son of Edward Russell (an inventor) and Ruth Rose (a registered nurse; maiden name, Roth) Eckert; married Joan Dowling, May 14, 1955 (divorced 1975); married Gail Ann Hagemann, April, 1976 (divorced 1978); married Nancy Cross Dent (a writer and literary agent), June 19, 1978; children: (first marriage) Joseph Matthew, Julie Anne. *Education:* Attended University of Dayton, 1951-52, and Ohio State University, 1953-54. *Politics:* "Uncommitted." *Religion:* Agnostic. *Hobbies and other interests:* Exploring uncharted areas of jungle or wilderness; collecting butterflies, moths, beetles, and other insects (collection includes over twenty-five thousand specimens), as well as fossils, mineral specimens, and other nature objects; collecting rare books (collection exceeds fifteen thousand volumes); observing nature; fishing.

■ Addresses

Home and office—Bellefontaine, OH. *Agent*—Virginia Kidd, Virginia Kidd Agency, Arrowhead, 538 East Harford St., P.O. Box 278, Milford, PA 18337.

■ Career

Writer. Prior to 1955, worked as postman, private detective, fireman, plastics technician, cook, dishwasher, laundryman, salesman, chemist's assistant, trapper, commercial artist, draftsman, factory worker, and farmer; National Cash Resister Co., Dayton, OH, associate editor of *NRC Factory News,* 1955-56; *Dayton Journal-Herald,* Dayton, outdoor editor, nature editor, police reporter, columnist, and feature writer, 1957-60. Member of board of trustees, Dayton Museum of Natural History, 1963-65; founder and board chairperson of Lemon Bay Conservancy (now Allan W. Eckert Conservancy), Englewood, FL; member of board of directors, Charlotte County (FL) Civic Association. Consultant to LaSalle University, Chicago, and Writer's Digest, Inc., Cincinnati, OH. *Military service:* U.S. Air Force, 1948-

ALLAN W. ECKERT

52; became staff sergeant. *Member:* Outdoor Writers Association (board member, 1962-64), Dayton Museum of Natural History (life member), Society of Magazine Writers, Authors League of America, Authors Guild, American Society of Gem Cutters, Mazon Creek Project of Paleontology.

■ Awards, Honors

Pulitzer Prize nominations, 1964, 1965, 1967, 1968, 1970, 1992, and 1994; Ohioana Book Award, 1968, for *The Frontiersmen;* Friends of American Writers Awards, 1968, for *Wild Season* and *The Frontiersmen;* Emmy Award, outstanding program achievement, National Academy of Television Arts and Sciences, 1968-69, for *Wild Kingdom;* Newbery Honor Book, American Library Association, 1972, Recognition of Merit, George C. Stone Center for Children's Books, 1975, and Austrian Juvenile Book of the Year Award, 1977, all for *Incident at Hawk's Hill;* Second Annual Silver Arrow Humanitarian Award, Scioto Society, 1987; finalist, Western Writers of America Spur Award for Best Western Nonfiction—historical, 1995, for *That Dark and Bloody River.* Honorary Ph.D., Bowling Green State University, 1985; commissioned as Kentucky Colonel, Governor of the State of Kentucky, 1987.

■ Writings

FOR CHILDREN

Bayou Backwaters (novel), illustrated by Joseph Cellini, Doubleday, 1967.

The Dreaming Tree (novel), Little, Brown, 1968.

The Crossbreed, illustrated by Karl E. Karalus, Little, Brown, 1968.

The King Snake (novel), illustrated by Franz Altschuler, Little, Brown, 1968.

Blue Jacket: War Chief of the Shawnees (biographical fiction), Little, Brown, 1968.

In Search of a Whale (novel), illustrated by Joseph Cellini, Doubleday, 1969.

Incident at Hawk's Hill (novel), illustrated by John Schoenherr, Little, Brown, 1971.

Savage Journey (novel), Little, Brown, 1979.

Song of the Wild (novel), Little, Brown, 1980.

Johnny Logan: Shawnee Spy, Little, Brown, 1983.

The Dark Green Tunnel ("Mesmerian Annals" series), illustrated by David Wiesner, Little, Brown, 1984.

The Wand: The Return to Mesmeria ("Mesmerian Annals" series), illustrated by David Wiesner, Little, Brown, 1985.

DOCUMENTARY FICTION

The Great Auk, Little, Brown, 1963, published as *The Last Great Auk,* Goodchild Publishers, 1984.

The Silent Sky: The Incredible Extinction of the Passenger Pigeon, Little, Brown, 1965.

Wild Season, Little, Brown, 1967.

The Court-Martial of Daniel Boone, Little, Brown, 1973.

HISTORICAL NARRATIVES

A Time of Terror: The Great Dayton Flood, Little, Brown, 1965.

A Sorrow in Our Heart: The Life of Tecumseh, Bantam, 1992, limited edition published as *Sorrow of the Heart: The Life of Tecumseh,* 1992.

Men at War: Tecumseh, Smithmark Publishers, 1994.

That Dark and Bloody River: Chronicles of the Ohio River Valley, Bantam, 1995.

"WINNING OF AMERICA" SERIES

The Frontiersmen, Little, Brown, 1967.

Wilderness Empire, Little, Brown, 1968.

The Conquerors, Little, Brown, 1970.

The Wilderness War, Little, Brown, 1978.

Gateway to Empire, Little, Brown, 1982.

Twilight of Empire: A Narrative, Little, Brown, 1988.

NONFICTION

The Writer's Digest Course in Article Writing, Writer's Digest, 1962.

The Writer's Digest Course in Short Story Writing, Writer's Digest, 1965.

The Owls of North America: All the Species and Subspecies Described and Illustrated, illustrated by Karl E. Karalus, Doubleday, 1973, new edition, 1975, reprinted as *The Owls of North America, North of Mexico: All the Species and Subspecies Illustrated in Color and Fully Described,* Weathervane, 1987.

The Wading Birds of North America: All the Species and Subspecies Described and Illustrated, illustrated by Karl E. Karalus, Doubleday, 1979, published as *The Wading Birds of North America (North of Mexico),* Weathervane, 1987.

Earth Treasures: Where to Collect Minerals, Rocks, and Fossils in the United States, Volume 1: *The Northeastern Quadrant,* Volume 2: *The Southeastern Quadrant,* Volume 3: *The Northwestern Quadrant,* Volume 4: *The Southwestern Quadrant,* Harper, 1985-87.

The World of Opals, Wiley & Sons, 1997.

OTHER

Tecumseh! (play), Little, Brown, 1974.

The HAB Theory (science fiction), Little, Brown, 1976.

Whattizzit? Nature Pun Quizzes (humor), Landfall Press, 1981.

The Scarlet Mansion (novel), Little, Brown, 1985.

Also author of more than 200 television scripts for the series *Wild Kingdom* and of screenplays, including *The Legend of Koo-Tan,* 1971, *Wild Journey,* 1972, *The Kentucky Pioneers,* 1972, and *George Rogers Clark,* 1973. Contributor of more than 200 articles to periodicals, including *Field & Stream, Reader's Digest,* and *Saturday Evening Post.* Eckert's works have been translated into thirteen languages. The Allan W. Eckert Collection was established at Mugar Memorial Library, Boston University, 1965; another Allan W. Eckert Collection, containing historical documents, manuscripts, and other pieces, was established at the Filson Historical Society Club, Louisville, KY, 1994.

■ Adaptations

Incident at Hawk's Hill was adapted into a two-part television movie by Walt Disney Productions.

■ Work in Progress

Two more novels in the "Mesmerian Annals" series, *The Phantom Crystal* and *The Witching Well; The Green Conspiracy,* a large contemporary novel concerning the exploitation of Amazon tribes and resources; *Return to Hawk's Hill* (tentative title; sequel to *Incident at Hawk's Hill*).

■ Sidelights

Combining thorough research and factual details with literary techniques such as dialogue and narration, Allan

W. Eckert brings to life the world of nature in his documentary fiction and recreates the adventures and people of the past in his historical narratives. Eckert's enthusiasm for his subjects makes for well-told stories that both entertain and inform his readers. These same qualities are evident in his juvenile novels, which include *Blue Jacket: War Chief of the Shawnees, Incident at Hawk's Hill,* and *Savage Journey,* as well as the "Mesmerian Annals" nature and ecology series of fantasy novels. Having written such a variety of books, Eckert sees still more opportunities in the future: "I fully anticipate that some other wonderfully interesting thing will have captured my attention," he has related in an autobiographical essay for *Something about the Author Autobiography Series (SAAS).* "It may be something entirely apart from anything I have ever attempted before—the chances are good, in fact, that it *will* be—and once more I'll be off and running on the research

NARRATIVES OF AMERICA ■ BOOK I

In his 1967 historical narrative, Eckert blends fast-paced action with multi-dimensional characters to create a fascinating account of American settler Simon Kenton and his bitter battle against the great Shawnee leader Tecumseh. (Cover illustration by Lou Glanzman.)

trail as I attempt to track down all the information I can find or experience about it."

Although he was born in Buffalo, New York, Eckert spent the majority of his childhood in the Chicago area. His family was poor, but though he lived in the slums Eckert did not feel deprived; he had known no other way of life. "I was a child with an intense love of nature, which is rather strange, since the Chicago slums was hardly a place for developing an interest in wildlife," he explains in *SAAS.* "Yet, I remember crawling about in the gangways between buildings or in vacant lots, overturning boards and pieces of tin and other debris and studying the creatures I found beneath—mice, worms, spiders, centipedes, etc."

The financial situation became worse for Eckert and his family when his father died shortly after his sixth birthday. "My mother had a difficult time providing for my brother and me, but even though we did not have much more than the bare necessities for survival, she instilled in us good manners and morals and gave us plenty of love and care," he remembers in *SAAS.* Eckert's mother later met and married Austin Rexroat, and her family moved to Rexroat's house in the country outside of Chicago. At Eckert's new home were all kinds of insects, birds, mammals, and other creatures for him to examine. His stepfather gave him his first rifle for a birthday present, and taught him how to use it safely.

All of this nature study gave Eckert a desire to see the rest of the country and the many wonders it had to offer. "The notion grew on me that I wanted to see a lot more of the United States, especially areas that differed from where we lived, and so I began to pester my mother to allow me to go off on my own, as soon as school finished for the summer, and hitchhike to distant places," recalls Eckert in his autobiographical essay. Hitchhiking was much safer at this time, and although Eckert's mother first said no, he was finally allowed to go after a lot of begging and a promise to send a postcard every other day; he also had to be back in time for the new school year. "I packed a duffle bag, a few changes of clothes, a few books to read, some writing materials, my fishing rod, and my little single-shot .22 rifle and started to hitchhike toward the northwest—toward Canada," writes Eckert in *SAAS.* "My mother had stuck a five-dollar bill to my stomach with adhesive tape for emergency use, if necessary. I was nine years old."

This first trip brought only good experiences for Eckert: all the people who picked him up were kind and interested in his adventure, he slept in old barns or made a little camp in the woods, and he ate roots and herbs with the fish he caught and the little animals he shot down. Reaching the Lake of the Woods region in Manitoba, Canada, he decided to spend his summer there. "I spent my days wandering about, mostly away from anywhere that people were, watching wildlife and studying the ways of nature," he describes in *SAAS.* "I caught plenty of fish to eat, and I was quite good with my rifle, so I rarely went hungry that whole summer long. It was a wonderful time, and I had many interesting adventures and learned a great deal about nature and survival." Having ignited a wanderlust spirit within himself during this first trip, Eckert continued to spend his summers this way all the way through high school. By the time he graduated he had traveled through the then forty-eight states of the United States, all of the lower provinces of Canada, and the northern part of Mexico.

"The many different people I met and the closeness I shared with nature gave me a very good foundation for what I would eventually become—a writer—even though that goal was not firmly fixed in my mind at the time," Eckert asserts in his autobiographical essay. It was not until he was a junior in high school that Eckert even realized that people actually made money and supported themselves as writers. "I guess, when you come right down to it, I always wanted to be a writer," he continues in *SAAS*. "I loved to write, but I didn't realize one could actually make a living at it; to me, writing was simply great fun and a way of expressing myself and my ideas better than I could in conversation." Once he knew he could make money doing something he loved to do, "the die was cast and I decided I would really become a professional writer. I started writing in earnest, with the idea of selling what I wrote, and began submitting my manuscripts to publishers everywhere."

Eckert's early interests in nature and animals became the main focus of these many writings. The writers that influenced him were those who dealt with similar subject matter—Ernest Thompson Seton, a self-taught naturalist who learned from observation, and William Beebe, a scientist who brought natural history subjects to life in his writings. "So, with these authors to influence me, little wonder that I decided to become a writer, with the emphasis on nature," Eckert relates in *SAAS*. "And so I wrote ... and wrote ... and wrote. Unfortunately, though I by then had a substantial background for writing pieces on nature, I had no actual training in the mechanics of writing and how best to direct my writing.... I simply wrote and submitted ... and received rejection after rejection. It was often quite discouraging but, fortunately, I had a very stubborn streak and would not give up, feeling that somehow, some way, someday I would make it as a writer."

By the time Eckert finished high school he had been writing for two years without selling anything. The family was still too poor to send him to college, so he enlisted in the United States Air Force in hopes of attending college with funds from the GI Bill. During the next four years Eckert continued his writing during his off-duty hours, often under difficult circumstances. "At night, when the barracks lights would have to be turned off, I would go to the latrine, where a single 60-watt bare bulb hung from the ceiling, but at least it was light," he recalls in *SAAS*. "There I would sit on a toilet and continue to write, often until the wee hours of the morning." Taking his discharge while stationed in Dayton, Ohio, Eckert enrolled at Ohio State University in Columbus, trying to stay close to a woman he was

THE MOVING AND TRIUMPHANT TALE OF A BOY'S SURVIVAL IN THE WILD

Eckert's popular Newbery Honor book tells the heartwarming story of a six-year-old boy who spends the summer in the care of a badger who adopts him as her own.

dating. Instead of enrolling in courses to further his writing career, though, Eckert decided to become a veterinarian. For two years he worked and went to school full time while trying to continue writing. Experiencing difficulty in some of the required veterinarian courses and becoming extremely burned out, Eckert quit school at the end of these two years and moved to Dayton to be with his fiancee.

While living in Dayton Eckert went through a series of jobs, including private detective, fireman, artist and illustrator, taxicab driver, stockman, and dishwasher. "Each new job I undertook held my interest only for so long as it took to learn the ropes, and then the very routine of the work would become overpoweringly boring and I would resign and move on to another field," explains Eckert in *SAAS*. Finally landing a job at the *Dayton Journal-Herald* daily newspaper, Eckert was able to write for a living, but he also continued his own writing, adding to his shoe boxes full of rejection slips. Realizing that he should have published something by this point, Eckert finally decided to look at his own writing from an objective standpoint. When he did, he found that it was lacking in direction. He had only been writing for himself. He began to examine the short stories and articles that were being published in magazines with regard to construction and audience. "Those writings were very specifically aimed at a certain readership; my own writing had been directionless and thus never quite made it for any particular periodical," Eckert points out in *SAAS*. "I guess I wasn't too bright; it had only taken me a dozen years to learn to be critical of my own writing."

With this insight, Eckert went back to his manuscripts and rewrote them with a specific audience in mind, giving his writing the slant it needed. "My first sale, after having received 1,147 rejections over the preceding twelve years, came in 1958—a full-length article bought by *Field & Stream*," Eckert recalls in *SAAS*. The following two years brought more of the same—sales of articles, short stories, and poetry to several major periodicals. "I continued revising and rewriting all those so-often-rejected pieces and wound up selling them as well. Every last one of them!" By 1960, Eckert was earning as much in freelance sales as he earned in a year at the newspaper, so he quit his job and began freelance writing full time. Despite the fact that he continued to sell a steady stream of pieces to magazines, money began to dwindle; most of the magazines Eckert sold to paid on publication instead of on acceptance. "Gradually the money began coming in and financial matters eased," he relates in *SAAS*. "It was becoming fun, not only to research and write new pieces, but to rewrite the old ones and make them salable."

There was one short story in particular, though, that Eckert could not sell. Entitled "The Valiant Migration," the story described the final migration of a flock of great auks (a penguin-like bird) just before they became extinct. "This short story had been rejected by over thirty magazines, although almost without exception the rejection, instead of a standard printed form, would arrive as a personal letter from the editor who would say how much he or she enjoyed the story, but just couldn't make it fit into their magazine's format," observes Eckert in *SAAS*. At this point, in early 1963, Eckert decided to turn the story into a short book that followed the life of the last great auk on earth. It took him only five days to expand his story into *The Great Auk*, which begins with the hatching of the last great auk, follows it into adulthood, describing its natural history, and ends with the final migration and the great auk's death.

Eckert sent the manuscript to a literary agent with whom he had previously corresponded, and it was first sold to *Reader's Digest* as a condensed book and then to Little, Brown. Published in 1963, *The Great Auk* was well-received; *Christian Science Monitor* reviewer Marian Sorenson maintained that Eckert, "in a beautifully written book, personally involves the reader in the tragedy of the extinction of a whole species." This first success prompted Little, Brown to ask Eckert for another book along the same lines, which he provided in *The Silent Sky*, an account of the life and history of the passenger pigeon. When asked for yet another work similar to these first two, however, Eckert feared that he would become categorized and instead offered a book on the great 1913 flood of Dayton, Ohio. *A Time of Terror* chronicles that natural disaster by focusing on both the historical facts and the people involved; "the result is a vividness and immediacy that will capture and hold readers of all ages," asserted Robert H. Donahugh in *Library Journal*. *A Time of Terror* was subsequently nominated for a Pulitzer Prize, the first of seven such nominations for Eckert.

With his newfound success as an author of books, Eckert began to devote less time to the writing of magazine articles and short stories. One of his earlier articles, however, gave him the idea for a book that both created a new genre and raised controversial questions among historians. Envisioned as a historical novel, *The Frontiersmen* soon grew into a biography focusing on Simon Kenton, an adventurous member of the American

The sixth book in Eckert's "Winning of America" series follows the incredible life of the legendary Indian chief Black Hawk and his heroic fight to preserve his ancestral land. (Cover illustration by Lou Glanzman.)

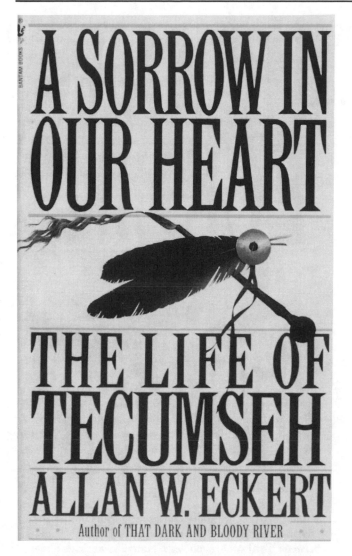

Eckert recounts the inspiring story of Tecumseh, the great Indian orator, warrior, and diplomat who led his fellow Native Americans in an unprecedented unified force against American and European invaders. (Cover illustration by Alan Gough.)

frontier, and Kenton's main adversary, the Shawnee Indian leader Tecumseh. History was a dull subject to Eckert as a child, but as he researched his topics he found information that was exciting and interesting. "I wondered why historians seemed to think it necessary to make history such a dull subject," he explains in *SAAS.* "I decided I wouldn't do that; that I would write in a narrative style, trying to embody all the better qualities of the novel form while at the same time retaining the veracity of straight historical writing."

In his attempt to blend these two forms of writing, Eckert filled *The Frontiersmen* with dialogue, as well as the thoughts and emotions of the characters, all founded in fact, as the historical events unfolded. "I termed this form of writing 'historical narrative' and wrote it chronologically, with no forecasting of events to come, in such a manner that, by utilizing the better elements of the novel form for excitement, pace, and continuity, while at the same time striving to remain reliable as an

accurate depiction of the history it embraces, the reader might, as with a good novel, feel himself drawn into the current events and be able to identify closely with the characters," Eckert explains in *SAAS.* The dialogue he gives these characters is what he terms reconstituted dialogue—it is found in original documents written as straight commentary. "But in the straight documentation are couched the keywords that legitimately allow such information, if the effort is made, to be returned to vibrant and meaningful dialogue that remains accurate to the intent and direction of what is occurring at any given time to the character of the individual making the utterance," Eckert asserts.

Eckert's first historical narrative was criticized by some historians because of his use of dialogue and other narrative techniques, but the book's success in making history more interesting and accessible paved the way for Eckert to publish five more such works and create the "Winning of America" series. In a review of the second book in the series, *Wilderness Empire, Christian Science Monitor* contributor James Nelson Goodsell wrote that the book is "readable and fascinating," concluding: "History need not be dull as Mr. Eckert proves. But whether such an approach is ideal is open to question." In a later review of the next book in the series, *The Conquerors,* Goodsell praised this same approach, stating that "the use of 'hidden dialogue' enhances the story and one puts the book down feeling that this concession to the novel has not hurt the story one whit." *Twilight of Empire,* the sixth work in the series, deals with the Black Hawk War of 1832, in which the whites won upper Mississippi Valley farmland from the Native people. In a review of this book, a *Publishers Weekly* commentator asserted: "Reading Eckert is like listening to a master storyteller: he presents his materials in vivid detail, using the novelist's technique to enhance dramatic events."

A Sorrow in Our Heart: The Life of Tecumseh, published in 1992, tells the story of the Shawnee chief who struggled against the white pioneers for the land along the Ohio River valley, and eventually established a short-lived confederacy of tribal nations. As in his other historical narratives, the author provides extensive historical detail using novelist techniques, recreating his subject's thoughts and conversations based on his research. A *Publishers Weekly* reviewer commented that Eckert's "colorful evocation of this seminal American figure will be more broadly accessible than are drier more factual accounts." In 1995 Eckert published the historical narrative *That Dark and Bloody River: Chronicles of the Ohio River Valley.* This work recounts the various battles for possession of the rich Ohio River Valley area, through which numerous settlers passed on their journey west. First the Native American tribes battled among themselves, with the Shawnees eventually winning out. This was followed by the Shawnees' struggle against the French and British, and finally the French and British fighting one another. Using letters, diaries, and government documents to recreate historical characters including George Washington and Daniel Boone, the author brings to life the tumultuous period of the French and Indian War and the American Revolution. *Booklist* writer Jay Freeman sums up *That Dark and Bloody River* as "an eloquent and often heartrending portrayal of a fascinating and pivotal epoch in American history."

While his career was branching into a variety of different genres, Eckert also began focusing on books directed toward young readers. About a year after the publication of *The Great Auk,* he was approached by the producers of the television series *Wild Kingdom* to write two juvenile novels based on previous episodes. The first, *Bayou Backwaters,* tells the story of the wildlife and plants that coexist through the balance of nature in the swampy bayou country of Louisiana. Because of Eckert's "eye for detail, his sense of the rhythms of the natural world, his feeling for its beauty and balance, *Bayou Backwaters* is a celebration of life in all its forms," observes Robert Berkvist in the *New York Times Book Review. In Search of a Whale* is similar to Eckert's adult nature stories, following the voyage of a scientific ship as it sets out to capture a young pilot whale for further study. A *Science Books* contributor lauded *In Search of a Whale* as "a well-written action narrative with plenty of excitement."

Following the progression of his adult book career, Eckert moved from nature novels to historical stories for his young audience. A character that first appeared in *The Frontiersmen* is, in fact, the main focus of Eckert's 1968 novel *Blue Jacket: War Chief of the Shawnees.* The greatest war chief of his tribe, Blue Jacket was actually part of a family of settlers on the Virginia frontier before being captured by the Shawnees. Adopted by the tribe, Blue Jacket slowly rose in power as his courage and intelligence developed. He eventually became the tribe's war chief and led his people into battle against the white people. Jane Manthorne, writing in *Horn Book,* described Eckert's documentary novel *Blue Jacket* as maintaining "a precise fidelity to the facts of history," adding that the story is "terse, brooding in its revelation of white man's greed."

At this point, Eckert's varied career took another unexpected turn when he was asked to write a few episodes for *Wild Kingdom.* These scripts were so well-liked that Eckert was asked to write the rest of the scripts for the season. "Though I wasn't really keen about writing more television scripts, the money was so good that it didn't take a great deal of coaxing to make me agree to do more," Eckert relates in *SAAS.* "The upshot was that even though I was continuing to write my own books, for the next ten years I also wrote all the *Wild Kingdom* shows, plus scattered others in subsequent years, until eventually, when new productions were finally halted, I had written well over two hundred *Wild Kingdom* half-hour scripts."

Among the novels Eckert wrote while busy with *Wild Kingdom* is his Newbery Honor-winning young adult novel *Incident at Hawk's Hill.* Published in 1971, this nature tale brought Eckert a new following of younger readers. He relates in *SAAS:* "I have received literally

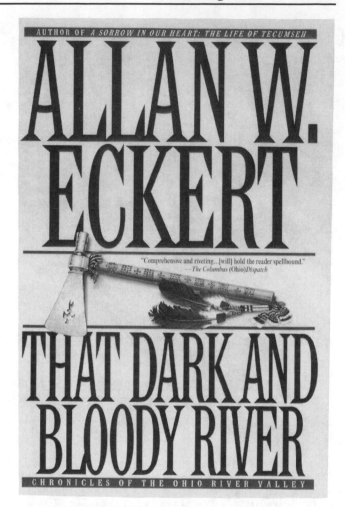

Taking material from old diaries, historical documents, and personal letters, Eckert brings to life the struggle between British, French, and Native American forces over control of the Ohio River Valley. (Cover illustration by Alan Ayers.)

thousands of letters over the years from children who are enthralled with the story of the little six-year-old boy who becomes lost in the vast prairies of Manitoba and is adopted by a badger who has just lost her litter of pups." Twenty-five years after *Incident at Hawk's Hill* was published, Eckert has given in to the hundreds of requests for a sequel, and work on the tentatively titled *Return to Hawk's Hill* is well underway. In another young adult nature novel, *Savage Journey,* Eckert tells the story of thirteen-year-old Sarah Francis as she accompanies her father on an archeological dig in the Amazon jungle. When her father is killed in an accident, Sarah must brave the jungle alone as she attempts to return to civilization.

"Having so much enjoyed writing various books for young readers," Eckert states in *SAAS,* "I then began a projected series of a dozen children's fantasies patterned after *The Chronicles of Narnia* by C. S. Lewis, except mine were set in modern times in the United States and, instead of being religious allegories, there were allegories of nature and ecology." The first two books of the "Mesmerian Annals" series, *The Dark Green Tunnel*

(1984) and *The Wand: The Return to Mesmeria* (1985), feature twins Barnaby and Lara as they first come across the land of Mesmeria while visiting their cousin William in the Florida Everglades. When the three children enter this new land they encounter evil King Thorkin, who killed their father and who fears that they will bring about the end of his rule. By the conclusion of the resulting struggle, Barnaby and Lara have become rulers of the kingdom. The twins return to their own world, but they find themselves transported back to Mesmeria when they lose their way in an airport. In the second installment, the evil sorcerer Krumpp has become ruler of Mesmeria. The twins set off on a dangerous journey to free their Mesmerian friends who have been locked up by Krumpp and to win back the kingdom that is rightfully theirs. Along the way, Lara receives a magic wand and becomes a sorceress. With the help of a dwarf, three hawk-people, and other creatures, the twins succeed in their quest.

In a review of *The Dark Green Tunnel*, a *Booklist* contributor observes that "Eckert's nature descriptions, strange characters, and fast-paced adventure contribute much to the fantasy, which, although quite scary in parts, ends with the children safe and secure." And Deborah Felder, writing in the *New York Times Book Review*, maintains that *The Wand* "is a satisfying fantasy," adding: "It has just about everything a good fantasy ought to have: bright, enterprising, likable children; noble, heroic adults; all manner of exotic, imaginatively named creatures ... and a plot of high adventure culminating in eventual triumph for the forces of good."

The adventures of Eckert's characters continue; so does his writing career. "If I were a youngster again, knowing what I know now, would I enter another profession? Absolutely not," Eckert reflected in *SAAS*. "I know of no other profession where one has such complete freedom to go wherever one wishes, live wherever one cares to, experience whatever one wishes to experience, and which can so frequently and delightfully change direction and interests; nor do I know of any other profession that, in the end result, is so fully and completely gratifying in the knowledge that one has left something of value behind, contributed something that may continue to benefit the world long after one is gone. What greater sense of fulfillment in one's life could there be?"

■ Works Cited

Berkvist, Robert, review of *Bayou Backwaters, New York Times Book Review*, June 30, 1968, p. 26.

Review of *The Dark Green Tunnel, Booklist*, April 1, 1984, pp. 1114-15.

Donahugh, Robert H., review of *A Time of Terror, Library Journal*, March 15, 1965, p. 1319.

Eckert, Allan W., essay in *Something about the Author Autobiography Series*, Volume 21, Gale, 1995, pp. 103-20.

Felder, Deborah, review of *The Wand: The Return to Mesmeria, New York Times Book Review*, January 19, 1986, p. 29.

Freeman, Jay, review of *That Dark and Bloody River: Chronicles of the Ohio River Valley, Booklist*, January 1, 1996, p. 780.

Goodsell, James Nelson, "Should History Read Like Fiction?," *Christian Science Monitor*, October 23, 1969, p. 15.

Goodsell, James Nelson, "In Living History: How the Wilderness Was Won," *Christian Science Monitor*, May 13, 1971, p. 11.

Review of *In Search of a Whale, Science Books*, May, 1970, p. 53.

Manthorne, Jane, "Red, Black, and White," *Horn Book*, April, 1969, p. 193.

Sorenson, Marian, "Noble Bird," *Christian Science Monitor*, October 31, 1963, p. 7.

Review of *A Sorrow in Our Heart: The Life of Tecumseh, Publishers Weekly*, January 1, 1992, p. 42.

Review of *Twilight of Empire, Publishers Weekly*, August 26, 1988, p. 71.

■ For More Information See

BOOKS

Contemporary Literary Criticism, Volume 17, Gale, 1981.

PERIODICALS

Booklist, March 1, 1992, p. 1193.

Kirkus Reviews, September 15, 1995, p. 1321.

Library Journal, February 15, 1992, p. 178; November 1, 1995.

Publishers Weekly, June 15, 1984, p. 83; October 9, 1995, p. 72.

School Library Journal, January, 1986, p. 66.

*   *   *

EDDINGS, David (Carroll) 1931-

■ Personal

Born July 7, 1931, in Spokane, WA; son of George Wayne and Theone (Berge) Eddings; married Judith Leigh Schall, October 27, 1962. *Education:* Reed College, B.A., 1954; University of Washington, Seattle, M.A., 1961. *Politics:* "Unaffiliated." *Religion:* "Unaffiliated."

■ Addresses

Agent—Eleanor Wood, Spectrum Literary Agency, 111 Eighth Ave., Suite 1501, New York, NY 10011.

■ Career

Writer; worked variously for Boeing Co., Seattle, WA, as a buyer; for a grocery store as a manager; and as a college English teacher. *Military service:* U.S. Army, 1954-56.

DAVID EDDINGS

■ Writings

"BELGARIAD" FANTASY SERIES; PUBLISHED BY DEL REY

Pawn of Prophecy, 1982.
Queen of Sorcery, 1982.
Magician's Gambit, 1984.
Castle of Wizardry, 1984.
Enchanter's Endgame, 1984.

"MALLOREON" FANTASY SERIES; PUBLISHED BY DEL REY

Guardians of the West, 1987.
King of the Murgos, 1988.
Demon Lord of Karanda, 1988.
Sorceress of Darshiva, 1989.
The Seeress of Kell, 1991.

"ELENIUM" FANTASY SERIES; PUBLISHED BY DEL REY

The Diamond Throne, 1989.
The Ruby Knight, 1990.
The Sapphire Rose, 1991.

"TAMULI" FANTASY SERIES; PUBLISHED BY DEL REY

Domes of Fire, 1993.
The Shining Ones, 1993.
The Hidden City, 1994.

OTHER

High Hunt, Putnam, 1973.
The Losers, Fawcett Columbine, 1992.

(With wife, Leigh Eddings) *Belgarath the Sorcerer,* Ballantine Books, 1995.

■ Sidelights

David Eddings is a prolific and widely read fantasy writer whose books offer winning characters, persuasive dialogue, and plenty of humor. His well-plotted stories featuring war, politics, and intrigue have earned him a loyal readership. Eddings once stated: "I have devoted the majority of my life to writing," adding that his approach to fiction has been "broadly ecumenical."

Born in Spokane, Washington, Eddings graduated from Reed College and received his M.A. at the University of Washington. His first book was *High Hunt,* an adventure set in the present. While working at a series of jobs that included teaching college English, working in a grocery store, and a stint as a buyer for Boeing aircraft company, Eddings continued to write. As he once commented, "I have tried my hand at a wide variety of subgenres with more interest in the technical problems presented by each type than in commercial success." His advice to aspiring writers is blunt: "Never be afraid to discard a day's work—or a month's, or even a year's. Attachment to one's own brilliance is the worst form of juvenile self-indulgence."

Eddings's second novel, *Pawn of Prophecy,* which appeared nine years after *High Hunt,* was the first to have a fantasy setting. The book's success allowed Eddings to write full-time and launched both the "Belgariad" and "Malloreon" series. These series chronicle the adventures of Garion, a young orphan who gradually recognizes his own magic abilities as extraordinary events begin to overtake the ordinary occurrences of his world. By accepting his own powers, Garion is able to enlist the aid of warriors and sorcerers to combat the followers of the evil god Torak. A *Publishers Weekly* reviewer remarked that *Pawn of Prophecy* was "obviously part of a longer work," and noted that Eddings's ability to avoid getting "bogged down in cliches and archaic language" made this first volume "a promising start." In *Castle of Wizardry,* the fourth book in the "Belgariad" series, Garion achieves his goal of being named Belgarion, receiving a talisman and a princess fiancee in the bargain. The series concludes with *Enchanter's Endgame,* in which Garion finally goes head to head with his nemesis.

Like *Pawn of Prophecy, Guardians of the West,* the first book in the "Malloreon" series, was well-received. In this book, Garion is Overlord of the West. He becomes locked in battle with the sorceress Zandramas, who kidnaps the king's young son to use in a ritual that will give Zandramas the power of the evil god Torak whom Garion killed. Dale F. Martin, writing in *Fantasy Review,* found that "the real interest is in the characters, who are skillfully presented and deftly developed"; Martin also commended the "wry humor and ... credible dialogue." As Garion journeys toward the Place Which Is No More in pursuit of Zandramas and his son in *King of the Murgos,* he encounters the queen of

Nyissa, who reveals that Zandramas may be a dragon. The quest continues in *Demon Lord of Karanda,* as the characters approach the final confrontation between the Child of the Light (Belgarion) and the Child of the Dark, encountering obstacles including captivity, plague, and demons. *Voice of Youth Advocates* contributor Judy Druse asserted that in *Demon Lord of Karanda* "Eddings has constructed a believable world peopled with engaging, fallible characters." Of the fourth book in the series, *The Sorceress of Darshiva,* a *Publishers Weekly* reviewer stated that "Eddings depicts a complex, believable and colorful society filled with nobles, rogues, and common people, the latter characters ringing particularly true." In the series finale, *The Seeress of Kell,* Eddings's title character is the only one who knows where the confrontation between Garion and Zandramas, which will determine the fate of the universe, must take place. "This story is allegory and adventure," according to Lesa M. Holstine in *Voice of Youth Advocates.* Reviewing the series as a whole, however, *Twentieth-Century Science-Fiction Writers* contributor Michael Cule finds that "there are few fresh characters" and "both plot and incident repeat themselves."

Critics have pointed out that Eddings's fantasy worlds and plots are fairly standard: parallels to Imperial Romans, ancient Egyptians, and Vikings are readily apparent. For his part, Eddings stresses the credibility factor in any story. His "basic formula" for believable fantasy, as he once stated, is to "take a bit of magic, mix well with a few open-ended Jungian archetypal myths, make your people sweat and smell and get hungry at inopportune moments, throw in a ponderous prehistory, and let nature take its course."

His third series, the "Elenium" books, was hailed by *Booklist* reviewer Roland Green for its "well-wrought world" and "originality." The trilogy depicts the adventures of Sparhawk, a knight on the quest for the jewel Bhelliom, whose powers will save Queen Ehlana, who is encased in crystal. A *Publishers Weekly* commentator championed Eddings's "graceful, fluid style of storytelling rare in fantasy writing" in a review of *The Diamond Throne.* In *The Ruby Knight,* Sparhawk attempts to save his queen by retrieving Bhelliom, a sapphire rose lost five hundred years earlier. A *Publishers Weekly* reviewer commented, "Eddings's delightful style propels the reader along a well-crafted and carefully unfolding course." Sparhawk succeeds in breaking the spell and attempts to fend off the many enemies his powers attract in *The Sapphire Rose.* Reviewing this last book in the series, a *Publishers Weekly* critic noted that Eddings "adroitly mixes the exalted with the mundane in a tale that should satisfy his many fans." Cule commented that this series "is designed to be shorter ... and is written with a greater emphasis on action.... Again the nature of magic and of the gods is a focus of interest, and destiny hangs heavy in the background, waiting to guide events."

Rather than embarking on another series, Eddings took a different direction with his next novel, *The Losers.* The novel's protagonist, Raphael Taylor, is a present-

day senior at Reed College in Portland, Oregon. Under the influence of his wealthy, reckless roommate, Damon Flood, Taylor plummets from the summit of academic and athletic success to an unhappy affair with an older woman and a lot of drinking. Taylor winds up in an automobile accident that results in an amputated leg. Dropping out of school and moving to Spokane, Washington, Taylor recuperates and watches the "losers" of his economically depressed neighborhood, passing judgment on them. Flood comes back into his life, but this time his former roommate's destructiveness is clear to Taylor, who recognizes Flood for the "loser" he is.

Eddings found little favor among critics for his foray into realistic fiction. Writing in *Voice of Youth Advocates,* Cecilia Swanson warned that readers looking for more of Eddings's "wonderful fantasies" would be disappointed and that the book was "basically a variation on good vs. evil," although she praised *The Losers* for being "well written." *Library Journal* contributor Jackie Cassada commented that, "stripped of their

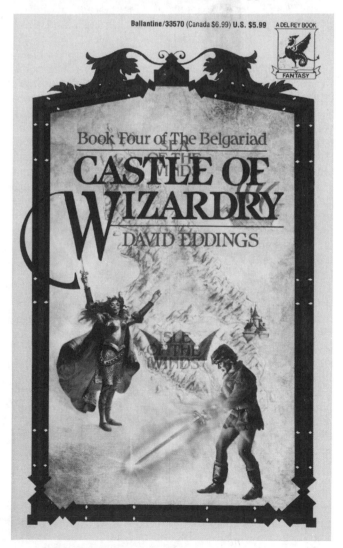

In this fourth book in the "Belgariad" series, Garion realizes his destiny is just beginning to unfold during his quest to reclaim the Orb. (Cover illustration by Laurence Schwinger.)

fantasy trappings, the author's opinions assume a heavy-handedness that verges on the polemic," and a critic for *Publishers Weekly* found that the "simplistic, fable-like quality ... patronizes its audiences."

Eddings responded to his critics' remarks for *SATA:* "Despite its gritty background, *The Losers* wasn't intended to be realistic. It was supposed to be an allegory. To be honest about it, I personally thought it was too obviously so.

"*The Losers* was one of those books that decided to write itself, and it totally rejected my personal philosophical orientation. I found myself writing very fast just to find out how the silly thing ended. The thing baffled me at every turn, but it *seemed* so right! Everything about it seemed so true that I was stuck with it. Some of that may have derived from the fact that I personally knew most of the characters. I even went so far as to briefly include myself.

"Call *The Losers* an existential allegory that missed its mark," the author concluded. "Next time I'll adjust my sights and drill it right between the eyes."

Eddings returned to fantasy for his next work, *Belgarath the Sorcerer,* coauthored with his wife, Leigh Eddings. This prequel to the "Belgariad" and "Malloreon" series essentially consists of the wizard Belgarath's memoirs of warring among gods, supernatural creatures, and human magicians. We learn in *Belgarath the Sorcerer* of the evil god Torak, who tore the world apart, and the good god Aldur, whose followers, including Belgarath, were appointed to fix things over the course of seven thousand years. "This rousing precursor to two five-book sagas is probably best read after them because of Belgarath's digressions into his own present," *Booklist* reviewer Sally Estes contended, adding "but make no mistake—the sagas' many fans will definitely relish it."

Eddings's "Tamuli" series begins with his 1993 work *Domes of Fire,* in which Sir Sparhawk and Queen Ehlana of the "Elenium" series reappear. Receiving a cry for help from the Tamul Empire, Sparhawk sets off on the long journey with his wife Ehlana and their daughter in tow. Along the way, they have several experiences that lead Sparhawk to suspect magical or godly opposition to his cause—that of ending a plot against the Emperor. A *Publishers Weekly* reviewer welcomed Eddings's "likable, spirited characters," which he felt reflected an "original touch." In the second book of the series, *The Shining Ones,* Eddings threw yet another obstacle in the way of Sparhawk and his entourage. The Shining Ones of the title seem human and friendly, but the knight strongly suspects that they are true to the Bhelliom stone rather than to himself and his mission. *Booklist* contributor Candace Smith highlighted the "well-drawn, likable characters" and "complex but not unwieldy plots" of the story. A *Publishers Weekly* reviewer called *The Shining Ones* "vintage Eddings." The final installment of the "Tamuli" books is entitled *The Hidden City.* In this work, Sir Sparhawk must rescue Queen Ehlana, now captive of the followers

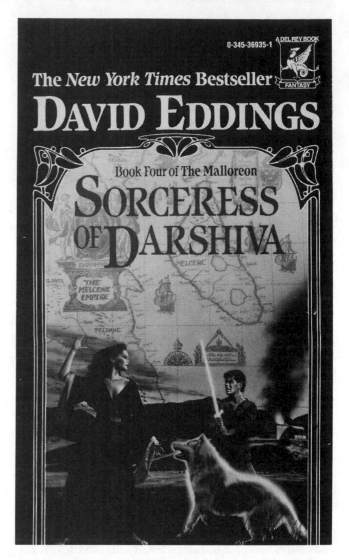

Reigning as Overlord of the West, Garion must rescue his kidnapped son from the evil Zandramas, sorceress of the Dark Destiny.

of the demented god Cyrgon, who plan to force Sparhawk to relinquish the jewel of power. Along the way Sparhawk battles a monster who is intent on destroying the world. A *Publishers Weekly* reviewer observed a "new note of introspection" which gives "a fuller dimension to Eddings's rousing adventure."

Eddings has emphasized the need for total credibility in fantasy writing. As he once explained, "My magic is at best a kind of pragmatic cop-out. Many of my explanations of how magic is supposed to work are absurdities—*but* my characters all accept these explanations ... and if the characters believe, then the readers seem also to believe." By combining the realities of the everyday world with the possibilities of a "world that never was," Eddings appears to have hit upon a magic formula that keeps his readers turning the pages and asking for more.

■ Works Cited

Cassada, Jackie, review of *The Losers, Library Journal,* June 15, 1992, p. 100.

Cule, Michael, "David Eddings," *Twentieth-Century Science-Fiction Writers,* edited by Noelle Watson and Paul E. Schellinger, St. James Press, 1991.

Review of *Domes of Fire, Publishers Weekly,* October 19, 1992, p. 62.

Druse, Judy, review of *Demon Lord of Karanda, Voice of Youth Advocates,* April, 1989, p. 40.

Estes, Sally, review of *Belgarath the Sorcerer, Booklist,* July, 1995, p. 1835.

Green, Roland, review of *The Sapphire Rose, Booklist,* December 1, 1991, p. 659.

Review of *The Hidden City, Publishers Weekly,* August 29, 1994, p. 65.

Holstine, Lesa M., review of *The Seeress of Kell, Voice of Youth Advocates,* December, 1991, p. 321.

Review of *The Losers, Publishers Weekly,* May 18, 1992, pp. 59-60.

Martin, Dale F., "New Series Begins," *Fantasy Review,* June, 1987, pp. 35-36.

Review of *Pawn of Prophecy, Publishers Weekly,* March 19, 1982, p. 69.

Review of *The Sapphire Rose, Publishers Weekly,* October 25, 1991, p. 49.

Review of *The Shining Ones, Publishers Weekly,* August 2, 1993, p. 66.

Smith, Candace, review of *Domes of Fire, Booklist,* October 15, 1992, p. 379.

Smith, Candace, review of *The Shining Ones, Booklist,* August, 1993, p. 2012.

Review of *The Sorceress of Darshiva, Publishers Weekly,* October 27, 1989.

Review of *The Diamond Throne, Publishers Weekly,* March 24, 1989.

Review of *The Ruby Knight, Publishers Weekly,* November 30, 1990, p. 61.

Swanson, Cecilia, review of *The Losers, Voice of Youth Advocates,* February, 1993, p. 348.

■ For More Information See

PERIODICALS

Booklist, May 1, 1984, p. 1226; June 15, 1988, p. 1689; June, 1994, p. 1724.

Kirkus Reviews, February 15, 1987, p. 259; February 15, 1988, p. 250; August 1, 1988, p. 1104; October 15, 1989, p. 1505; November 1, 1992; June 15, 1994; June 15, 1995, p. 820.

Library Journal, December, 1992, p. 191; September 15, 1993, p. 109; May 1, 1994; August, 1994, p. 139; April 1, 1995; August, 1995, p. 122.

Publishers Weekly, February 27, 1987, p. 154; August 29, 1994, p. 65.

Voice of Youth Advocates, June, 1985, p. 138; June, 1991, p. 107; June, 1992, p. 108; June, 1993, p. 102; February, 1994, p. 380; February, 1995, p. 346.

EGAN, Lorraine Hopping 1960-

■ Personal

Born October 1, 1960, in Detroit, MI. *Education:* Kalamazoo College, B.A. (cum laude; English and French), 1982; l'Universite de Caen, Normandy, France, certificate in French, 1980; also attended New York University continuing education program, 1990.

■ Addresses

Home—5606 North Dixboro Rd., Ann Arbor, MI 48105.

■ Career

Reporter for *Electronic Learning,* 1982-83; associate editor for *Teaching and Computers,* 1983-86; Scholastic, Inc., New York City, magazine editor of *Futures,* 1988, acting editor of *DynaMath,* 1988, editor of *SuperScience Blue,* 1988-91; Aristoplay, Ltd, Ann Arbor, MI, product development director, 1991-96; Hall of Fame Sports Books, Ann Arbor, owner, 1993-95. Freelance writer, 1986—. Has served as an advisor for the Learning Advantage Advisory Board, 1986; *Science & Technology Week,* National Science Foundation, 1992; Sundance Publishing Co. Elementary Science Series, 1992; American Association for the Advancement of Science's "Kinetic City Super Crew" Radio Show, 1992-94; and Learning Resources Power of Science Kit Series, 1993-94.

LORRAINE HOPPING EGAN

■ Writings

NONFICTION

(Coauthor and coeditor) *The Computer Ideabook,* Scholastic, 1985.

(Coauthor and coeditor) *Holiday Computer Activities,* Scholastic, 1985.

Micro Puzzles (for children), Scholastic, 1986.

(Coauthor and coeditor) *The Computer Ideabook II,* Scholastic, 1988.

The Kid's Book of Skateboarding (for young adults), Parachute Press, 1988.

(With others) *Explorer: Man Eaters* (for young adults), Parachute Press, 1988.

Wild Weather: Tornadoes (for young adults), Scholastic, 1994.

(With others) *My First Book of Animals A to Z* (for children), Scholastic, 1994.

Wild Weather: Hurricanes (for young adults), Scholastic, 1995.

Also contributor to *Classworks!* (workbook series for children), Scholastic, 1987-88; *Teacher's Guide to Modern American Literature,* CPI, 1988; *The Stock Market and You* (for young adults), New York Stock Exchange, 1988; *AIDS and Your World* (for children), Scholastic, 1988.

Also author of computer software and online materials, including teaching guide for four "Magic School Bus" CD-ROMs, Microsoft, 1994-96. Creator of games, card decks, and puzzles for companies such as Aristoplay. Contributor of articles to periodicals, including *Kids Today, Teaching and Computers, Kids Discover, Dyna-Math, Dynamite!, Forecast,* and *Math.* Author of educational materials. Editor, *Kinetic City Express Journal,* 1995. Contributor of four drama scripts to radio program *Kinetic City Super Crew,* 1994; author of scripts for audiocassettes *Lynne's Secret; or, How I Got the Friends Home,* Aristoplay, 1992, and *Music Maestro Parade,* Aristoplay, 1992.

*   *   *

ELIOT, Dan
See SILVERBERG, Robert

*   *   *

ELLIOTT, Don
See SILVERBERG, Robert

*   *   *

EPANYA, Christian A(rthur Kingue) 1956-

■ Personal

Born June 3, 1956, in Douala, Cameroon; son of Theodorien Epanya Ekambi and Francoise Ekalle Epanya (a homemaker); married Evelyne Abadie (a nurse), October 3, 1992; children: Francoise Cleopatre Ekalle,

CHRISTIAN A. EPANYA

Marthe Oho. *Education:* Lycee du Manengouba, Baccalaureat D; Ecole Emile Cohl, Graphic Arts Certificate. *Religion:* Protestant. *Hobbies:* Reading, tennis.

■ Addresses

Home and office—246, Avenue du plateau, 69009 Lyon, France.

■ Career

Author and illustrator. Elf Cameroon (an oil company), Douala, Cameroon, loading master, 1983-90.

■ Awards, Honors

UNICEF Bologna Illustrator of the Year, 1993.

■ Writings

(With Corlia Fourie and Madeleine van Biljon; self-illustrated) *Ganekwane and the Green Dragon: Four Stories from Africa,* edited by Christy Grant, Albert Whitman & Co., 1994.

ILLUSTRATOR

Charles Mungoshi, *Der sprechende kurbis,* Nagel & Kimche, 1993.

Agnes Bertron, *L'enfant, le singe et la petite fille,* Editions Bayard, 1994.

Amadou Hampate Ba, *Le petit frere d'Amkoullel,* Editions Syros, 1994.

Cristina Kessler, *Why the Chameleon Never Hurries,* Boyds Mills Press, 1997.

■ **Work in Progress**

Folk Tales of Guinea Bissau, for Editora Escolar.

■ **Sidelights**

Christian A. Epanya told *SATA:* "I was born on 3 June 1956 at Douala-Cameroon. I have lived in Foumban, Nkongsamba and Yaounde (Cameroon) and in Libreville (Gabon). I grew up in Douala and enjoyed drawing (reproducing comics covers). In the beginning my parents discouraged me to draw but as I kept drawing they finally accepted and began encouraging me. My favourite books were Bugs Bunny, Rodeo, Akim Strange from Marvel Comics, and the fairy tale books of Grimm, Andersen, and Perrault.

"I started drawing at age six, trying to reproduce my dad's bike. Ulises Wensell has influenced my work for the atmosphere present in his illustrations.

"I now live in Lyon (France). I am married and have two daughters. I intend to illustrate children's books for Editora Escolar, a Guinean publishing house in Guinea Bissau."

*   *   *

ELEANOR ESTES

ESTES, Eleanor 1906-1988

■ **Personal**

Born May 9, 1906, in West Haven, CT; died of a stroke, July 15, 1988, in Hamden, CT; buried at Oak Grove Cemetery, West Haven; daughter of Louis and Caroline (Gewecke) Rosenfeld; married Rice Estes (a library administrator), December 8, 1932; children: Helena. *Education:* Attended Pratt Institute, Brooklyn, NY, 1931-32. *Politics:* Democrat. *Religion:* Episcopalian.

■ **Career**

Author and illustrator. Free Public Library, New Haven, CT, children's librarian, 1924-31; New York Public Library, New York City, children's librarian, 1932-40.

■ **Awards, Honors**

Newbery Honor Book, American Library Association (ALA), 1943, for *The Middle Moffat,* 1944, for *Rufus M.,* and 1945, for *The Hundred Dresses;* Spring Book Festival Award, New York *Herald Tribune,* 1951, and Newbery Medal, 1952, both for *Ginger Pye;* Lewis Carroll Shelf Award, 1961, for *The Moffats;* Supervision and Curriculum Development Award, New York State Association, 1961, for outstanding contributions to children's literature; Pratt Institute Alumni Medal, 1968.

■ **Writings**

"THE MOFFATS" SERIES

The Moffats, illustrated by Louis Slobodkin, Harcourt, 1941.
The Middle Moffat, illustrated by Louis Slobodkin, Harcourt, 1942.
Rufus M., illustrated by Louis Slobodkin, Harcourt, 1943.
(Self-illustrated) *The Moffat Museum,* Harcourt, 1983.

FICTION FOR CHILDREN

The Sun and the Wind and Mr. Todd, illustrated by Louis Slobodkin, Harcourt, 1943.
The Hundred Dresses, illustrated by Louis Slobodkin, Harcourt, 1944.
(Self-illustrated) *The Sleeping Giant and Other Stories,* Harcourt, 1948.
(Self-illustrated) *Ginger Pye,* Harcourt, 1951.
(Self-illustrated) *A Little Oven,* Harcourt, 1955.
Pinky Pye, illustrated by Edward Ardizzone, Harcourt, 1958.
The Witch Family, illustrated by Edward Ardizzone, Harcourt, 1960.
The Alley, illustrated by Edward Ardizzone, Harcourt, 1964.
Miranda the Great, illustrated by Edward Ardizzone, Harcourt, 1967.
The Tunnel of Hugsy Goode, illustrated by Edward Ardizzone, Harcourt, 1972.

The Coat-Hanger Christmas Tree, illustrated by Susanne Suba, Atheneum, 1973.

The Lost Umbrella of Kim Chu, illustrated by Jacqueline Ayer, Atheneum, 1978.

The Curious Adventures of Jimmy McGee, illustrated by John O'Brien, Harcourt, 1987.

OTHER

The Echoing Green (adult novel), Macmillan, 1947.

(Self-illustrated) *The Lollipop Princess: A Play for Paper Dolls* (play for children), Harcourt, 1967.

Contributor to numerous magazines. Estes's books have been translated into many foreign languages. Manuscript collection housed in the Kerlan Collection at the University of Minnesota.

■ Adaptations

Ginger Pye (filmstrip and audio cassette), Miller-Brody; *Rufus M., Try Again* (filmstrip adapted from *Rufus M.*), produced by Martha Moran.

■ Sidelights

Eleanor Estes is considered among the most beloved twentieth-century American creators of juvenile literature. The author of eighteen books for the young, she wrote realistic fiction, fantasy, and works that combine the two; she also provided the pictures for several of her books. Presented with a Newbery Medal and three honor book designations, Estes is perhaps best known as the creator of the Moffats and the Pyes, families who live in the fictional city of Cranbury, Connecticut, and who appear in four and two books respectively. Her stories about the Moffats are a fictionalization of Estes's own childhood, with the town of Cranbury representing the author's native West Haven in the early part of this century. Estes characteristically uses a direct prose style to describe episodic, loosely connected events punctuated with the joys, sorrows, and defining moments of childhood. Praised for her rounded characterizations, evocative language, strong sense of place, and accurate depictions of the thoughts and speech of children, she is recognized as a writer who never lost touch with her young audience. "Eleanor Estes's most exceptional feat...," notes Carolyn Shute in *Twentieth-Century Children's Writers,* "was her ability to distill the very essence of childhood.... Estes wrote as a child writing for children, not as an adult writing for children, capturing with keen insight and sharp observation the vibrancy and vitality of that which is 'long ago and far away' for many adults, but everyday reality for the child." In his essay in *Children's Literature Association Quarterly,* David L. Russell comments that Estes has an implicit trust in the child's viewpoint "to speak faithfully and honestly for itself. Therein lies much of her success." Frances Clarke Sayers similarly notes in her essay in *Horn Book* that Estes's books "seem to be the product of some miracle child writing of the contemporary scene and the affairs of childhood with the skill and selectivity of the mature writer."

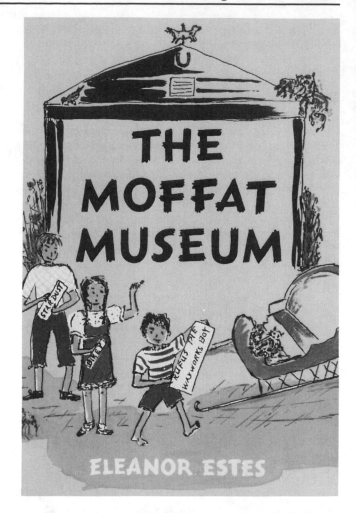

In this self-illustrated addition to her popular series of "Moffat" books, Estes relates the spirited adventures of the Moffat children as they try to establish the only museum in their hometown of Cranbury.

Like her character Jane Moffat, Estes was the daughter of a widowed dressmaker, the middle child in a family of four. Born Eleanor Rosenfeld in West Haven, Connecticut, Estes once told *SATA* that West Haven "had everything a child could want, great vacant fields with daisies in clover and buttercups and an occasional peaceful cow. There were marvelous trees to climb, fishing and clamming in the summertime, ice and snow and sliding down hills in the wintertime. My first four years of school were spent in the small wooden school that is a scene for a chapter in *The Moffats.* The remaining years were spent in a pretty ivy-covered brick school. In one of those classrooms the hero dog of *Ginger Pye,* the book which won the Newbery Medal, appeared in the window with a pencil in his mouth, earning the nickname of 'intellectual dog.'" Estes's parents, especially her mother, were influential in her becoming a lover of books. Her mother recited poetry to Estes and her siblings and also knew many folktales. "She had an inexhaustible supply of songs, stories, and anecdotes, fictitious and remembered ones, with which she entertained us as she went about her housework," Estes recounted in the *Junior Book of Authors.* Her mother regularly supplied Estes, her sister, and their two brothers with animated accounts of New York City, where she was born and raised. Years later, when Estes herself came to live in New York, "the sensation was rather like that of coming to my other home, my childhood and early days in West Haven seeming like a long holiday in the country," she noted in her *Junior Book of Authors* essay.

Before she began her writing career, Estes worked for many years as a children's librarian. After graduating from high school in 1924, she was employed in the children's department of New Haven's Free Public Library, and four years later was promoted to head of the department. After winning the Caroline M. Hewins scholarship for children's librarians in 1931, she was able to attend the library school at Pratt Institute in Brooklyn, New York, where she met Rice Estes, also a student of library science; the couple were married in 1932. In the same year, Estes began working at the New York Public Library, where she would serve as children's librarian until becoming a full-time writer after the publication of her first book, *The Moffats,* in 1941.

With *The Moffats,* Estes introduced her readers to the lives of the Moffat family as well as to their neighbors and several of Cranbury's prominent residents. Modeled after composites of children Estes had known throughout her life, the young main characters—Sylvie, Joe, Janey, and Rufus—range in age from five to fifteen and live with their widowed mother on New Dollar Street; Estes later featured Janey as the central character in *The Middle Moffat* and Rufus as the focal point of *Rufus M.* Estes, who set her stories in the years 1916 to 1918, wrote the first three books in the early 1940s, adding *The Moffat Museum* to the series nearly forty years later. In all of these works, the author describes the variety of childhood experiences, both pleasant and painful, that lead to the growing awareness of her protagonists. The novels are typically more episodic than tightly structured: *The Moffats,* for example, is loosely organized by the passing of one year, from the time the family's house is put up for sale until their move to a new neighborhood. The individual chapters, however, deal with a specific event in each of the children's lives—Jane's joy and guilt over finding a nickel and spending it on herself, Joe's horror at having to perform in a dance recital—and can almost be read as short stories. An ongoing theme in the books is the family's financial difficulty; they are depicted as poorer than most of the residents of Cranbury. In spite of this, the tone of the series is generally humorous and bright. "The Moffats are not poor in spirit, and they squeeze the last drop of fun and excitement out of every day," writes a reviewer in the *Times Literary Supplement.*

Estes was also acknowledged for her detailed portrayal of Cranbury. The *Times Literary Supplement* reviewer continues, "[The Moffats] live in a community, and it is a particular charm ... that the reader is allowed to explore Cranbury thoroughly, to know its topography and its inhabitants." As the series progresses, Estes subtly describes the personal development of her characters; the family remains closely knit even as the

children's experiences lead them to a greater understanding of life. In his essay in *Children's Literature Association Quarterly,* Russell comments that "the reader's ultimate interest is in the growth and maturation of the characters, the nuances of their personalities, and their commentaries on life itself. It is easy to confuse which Moffat episodes belong to which book, but it is impossible to forget the exhilarating characters themselves, just as it is impossible to avoid a strong and affectionate attachment to them." Frances Clarke Sayers adds that the Moffat books "are destined to become part of that glad heritage which parents share with children, remembered from childhood, through adulthood, and returned to childhood again through one's children, and their children's children."

A new family—the Pyes, also residents of Cranbury—is featured in Estes's Newbery Award-winning book *Ginger Pye* and its sequel *Pinky Pye.* Family stories that are generally thought to share the warmth, humor, and authenticity of the Moffats series, the Pye stories revolve around the family's love for animals. In *Ginger Pye,* Jerry and Rachel Pye spend months searching for their new puppy, Ginger, after she disappears on Thanksgiving Day. Ginger's loss and return serve as a

ELEANOR ESTES
The Curious Adventures of Jimmy McGee

Illustrated by John O'Brien

Readers meet Amy and Clarissa as they embark on an incredible journey with an eccentric plumber, Jimmy McGee, to find Amy's lost doll.

springboard for Rachel's imaginative reveries, which form the substance of the book. In her essay in *Dictionary of Literary Biography,* Virginia L. Wolf explains that "*Ginger Pye* differs most markedly from Estes's earlier books in its use of Rachel Pye's point of view.... Free of Janey [Moffat]'s financial worries and other family problems, Rachel is a child whose imagination colors all of the details of daily life with radiance. And because Rachel's point of view so controls *Ginger Pye,* the reader participates in a child's world that is so big and so full of the exciting and the mysterious that every instant is loaded with possibilities." In *Pinky Pye,* Estes blends the realistic and the fantastic to describe the black kitten that, after being adopted by the Pyes, learns to type on Mr. Pye's typewriter.

Although she gained popularity and critical acclaim for her Moffat and Pye books, Estes's other works show her diversity as a writer. For example, *The Hundred Dresses,* a novel published is 1944, deals with prejudice and its results. The story focuses on Wanda, a schoolgirl who has immigrated to the United States from Poland. After Wanda tells her classmates that the faded dress she wears every day is one of a hundred that she has at home, she is ridiculed and teased so incessantly that she drops out of school and her family moves away; at the end of the story, Wanda's guilt-ridden tormentors learn a hard lesson about compassion. In *Twentieth-Century Children's Writers,* Shute describes *The Hundred Dresses* as "a tribute to the invincibility of the human spirit," and Margaret K. McElderry notes in *Publishers Weekly* that it is "still among the most poignant and moving indictments of prejudice that exists in literature for children." Another of Estes's popular stories is *The Witch Family,* a fantasy filled with humor, adventure, and wordplay. In this work, which Shute describes as "a salute to the transforming power of a child's imagination," best friends Amy and Clarissa draw pictures that magically conjure up three witches as well as a bee that can spell. Estes's last book, *The Curious Adventures of Jimmy McGee,* published the year before her death, is a sequel to *The Witch Family* that features another creation of the two little girls, a magical plumber who wears a stovepipe hat. Estes's only adult novel, *The Echoing Green,* explores the implications of hardship on children more seriously and darkly than in the Moffats series. Although the book was reviewed favorably, Estes never made another contribution to adult literature.

Described as a "celebrant of childhood" by Shute, Estes is regarded as a writer whose direct connection with what appeals to children keeps her books fresh and immediate. Russell notes that her reputation "may rely upon a relatively small handful of works, but that reputation is unquestionably solid," and Wolf comments that among Estes's lasting contributions to children's literature are her "emphasis on the positive, her celebration of the child's spirit, her faith in the family, her fondness for small daily events and details, [and] her wonder over the miraculous tricks life plays." Estes once told *SATA,* "I like to feel that I am holding up a mirror and I hope that what is reflected in it is a true image of childhood." Her success in this goal is affirmed by

Nine-year-old Kim Chu begins an exciting journey through the streets of New York, chasing after the thief who stole her father's umbrella.

Sayers, who declares that "the vitality of Eleanor Estes derives from the fact that she sees childhood whole—its zest, its dilemmas, its cruelties and compassions," and adds that her creations have become "so close to the minds and hearts of present-day people—children and adults alike—that one can hardly imagine what life was like without them."

■ Works Cited

Estes, Eleanor, *Junior Book of Authors,* 2nd edition, edited by Stanley Kunitz and Howard Haycraft, H. W. Wilson, 1951, pp. 114-15.

McElderry, Margaret K., "Eleanor Estes, 1906-1988," *Publishers Weekly,* August 20, 1988, p. 60.

Review of *The Moffats, Times Literary Supplement,* May 29, 1959, p. xvii.

Russell, David L., "Stability and Change in the Family Saga: Eleanor Estes's Moffat Series," *Children's Literature Association Quarterly,* winter, 1989, pp. 171-74.

Sayers, Frances Clarke, "The Books of Eleanor Estes," *Horn Book,* August, 1952, pp. 257-70.

Shute, Carolyn, "Eleanor Estes," *Twentieth-Century Children's Writers,* 4th edition, St. James Press, 1995, pp. 324-25.

Wolf, Virginia L., "Eleanor Estes," *Dictionary of Literary Biography,* Volume 22: *American Writers for Children, 1900-1960,* Gale, 1983.

■ For More Information See

BOOKS

Arbuthnot, May Hill, *Children's Reading in the Home,* Scott, Foresman, 1969.

Cameron, Eleanor, *The Green and Burning Tree: On the Writing and Enjoyment of Children's Books,* Little, Brown, 1969.

Children's Literature Review, Gale, Volume 2, 1976.

Ellis, Anne W., *The Family Story in the 1960s,* Clive Bingley, 1970.

Field, Elinor W., *Horn Book Reflections,* Horn Book, 1969.

Fisher, Margery, *Who's Who in Children's Books: A Treasury of the Familiar Characters of Childhood,* Holt, 1975.

Hopkins, Lee Bennett, *More Books by More People,* Citation, 1974.

Lanes, Selma G., *Down the Rabbit Hole,* Atheneum, 1971.

Meigs, Cornelia, editor, *A Critical History of Children's Literature,* Macmillan, 1969.

Sutherland, Zena, and May Hill Arbuthnot, *Children and Books,* 8th edition, HarperCollins, 1991.

Townsend, John Rowe, *A Sense of Story: Essays on Contemporary Writers for Children,* Lippincott, 1971.

PERIODICALS

Bulletin of the Center for Children's Books, November, 1973; March, 1979; November, 1983; May, 1987.

Christian Science Monitor, December 22, 1960; June 28, 1965.

Cricket, February, 1974.

Growing Point, September, 1975.

Horn Book, May, 1951; August, 1955; October, 1960; April, 1967; December, 1967; April, 1972; December, 1973; November, 1991.

New York Times Book Review, November 30, 1947; April 22, 1951; November 1, 1964; April 23, 1972.

Saturday Review, November 12, 1960; November 7, 1964; November 11, 1967.

Times Literary Supplement, May 20, 1960; November 25, 1960; December 1, 1961; June 1, 1962.

■ Obituaries

PERIODICALS

New York Times, July 19, 1988.*

—Sketch by Gerard J. Senick

F–G

FARRELL, Ben
See CEBULASH, Mel

* * *

FONTENOT, Mary Alice 1910-

■ Personal

Surname is pronounced *fon*-te-no; born April 16, 1910, in Eunice, LA; daughter of Elias Valrie and Kate (King) Barras; married Sidney J. Fontenot, September 6, 1925 (died, 1963); married Vincent L. Riehl, Sr., November 14, 1966; children: (first marriage) Edith Ziegler, R. D. (deceased), Julie Landry. *Education:* Attended school in Eunice, LA. *Religion:* Roman Catholic.

■ Addresses

Home—1107 East 7th St., No. 4, Crowley, LA 70526. *Office*—Crowley Post-Signal, 602 North Parkerson Ave., Crowley, LA 70526-4354.

■ Career

New Era, Eunice, LA, reporter, columnist, and women's news writer, 1946-50; *Eunice News,* Eunice, editor, 1950-53; *Daily World,* Opelousas, LA, columnist, 1953-71, area editor, 1962-69; *Daily Advertiser,* Lafayette, LA, women's news reporter, 1958-60; *Rayne Tribune,* Rayne, LA, editor, 1960-62; *Crowley Post-Signal,* Crowley, LA, columnist and feature writer, 1977—. *Member:* League of American Pen Women, Louisiana Press Women.

■ Awards, Honors

First Prize from National Press Women, 1966; Louisiana Literary Award, Louisiana Library Association, 1976, for *Acadia Parish, La.,* Volume 1: *A History to 1900;* Children's Choice Award, 1984, for *Clovis Crawfish and the Orphan Zo-Zo.*

MARY ALICE FONTENOT

■ Writings

FOR CHILDREN

The Ghost of Bayou Tigre, Claitors, 1964.
The Star Seed: A Story of the First Christmas, illustrated by Nannette Cregan, Pelican, 1983.
Mardi Gras in the Country, illustrated by Patrick Soper, Pelican, 1995.
Tah-Tye, the Last 'Possum in the Pouch, illustrated by Scott R. Blazek, Blue Huron Press, 1996.

"CLOVIS CRAWFISH" SERIES

Clovis Crawfish and His Friends, Claitors, 1962, revised edition, illustrated by Keith Graves, Pelican, 1985.

Clovis Crawfish and the Big Betail, Claitors, 1963, reprinted, Pelican, 1988.

Clovis Crawfish and the Singing Cigales, Claitors, 1964, reprinted, illustrated by Eric Vincent, Pelican, 1981.

Clovis Crawfish and Petit Papillon, Claitors, 1966, reprinted, illustrated by Keith Graves, Pelican, 1985.

Clovis Crawfish and the Spinning Spider, Claitors, 1968, reprinted, illustrated by Christine Kidder, Pelican, 1987.

Clovis Crawfish and the Curious Craupaud, Claitors, 1970, reprinted, illustrated by Christine Kidder, Pelican, 1986.

Clovis Crawfish and Michelle Mantis, Claitors, 1976, reprinted, illustrated by Scott R. Blazek, Pelican, 1989.

Clovis Crawfish and Etienne Escargot, illustrated by Eric Vincent, Acadian Press, 1979, reprinted, illustrated by Scott R. Blazek, Pelican, 1992.

Clovis Crawfish and the Orphan Zo-Zo, illustrated by Eric Vincent, Pelican, 1983.

Clovis Crawfish and Simeon Suce-Fleur, illustrated by Scott R. Blazek, Pelican, 1990.

Clovis Crawfish and Bertile's Bon Voyage, illustrated by Scott R. Blazek, Pelican, 1991.

Clovis Crawfish and Batiste Bete Puante, illustrated by Scott R. Blazek, Pelican, 1993.

Clovis Crawfish and Bidon Box Turtle, illustrated by Scott R. Blazek, Pelican, 1996.

Several of Fontenot's "Clovis Crawfish" books have been translated into French by her daughter, Julie Landry.

FOR ADULTS

(Editor) *Quelque Chose Douce* (cookbook), Claitors, 1964.

(Editor) *Quelque Chose Piquante* (cookbook), Claitors, 1966.

(With husband, Vincent L. Riehl, Sr.) *The Cat and St. Landry* (biography), Claitors, 1972.

(Editor with Mercedes Vidrine) *Beaucoup Bon* (cookbook), Claitors, 1973.

(With Fran Dardeau and Cacky Riehl) *Cajun Accent* (cookbook), Cajun Classics Press, 1979.

Acadia Parish, La., Volume 1 (with Paul B. Freedland): *A History to 1900,* 1976, Volume 2: *A History to 1920,* Claitors, 1979.

Fontenot shares her love of the Cajun language and culture in her books about Clovis Crawfish and his unique bayou friends. (From *Clovis Crawfish and Bidon Box Turtle,* illustrated by Scott R. Blazek.)

(With daughter, Julie Landry) *The Louisiana Experience: An Introduction to the Culture of the Bayou State,* Claitors, 1983.

(With daughter, Edith Ziegler) *The Tensas Story,* Claitors, 1987.

■ Work in Progress

Clovis Crawfish and Paillasse Poule d'Eau; Clovis Crawfish and Fedora Field Mouse; Clovis Crawfish and Raoul Raccoon.

■ Sidelights

A newspaper journalist and former kindergarten teacher, Louisiana-born writer Mary Alice Fontenot once told *SATA* how she began writing children's books: "Three hours a day with thirty five-year-olds for two years is what led me into writing for children. This kindergarten teaching experience coincided with the start of the movement in south Louisiana to preserve the Acadian heritage and to restore the state to its former bilingual status. This revival of the French-Acadian culture strongly influenced my newspaper writings as well as the books I have written for children and adults."

One of Fontenot's most beloved creatures is the small Cajun-speaking crustacean named Clovis Crawfish. The central character of thirteen children's books, Clovis and his bayou friends teach children the value of cooperation and the importance of preserving the wetlands environment of southern Louisiana. Fontenot weaves Cajun words and songs into her text, giving children a taste of the Acadian culture. In a review of *Clovis Crawfish and the Singing Cigales,* a critic writing in *Publishers Weekly* applauds the tale about Clovis saving a young cicada from M'sieu Blue Jay, saying, "The story has suspense, lessons in nature lore, in French and plenty of fun."

■ Works Cited

Review of *Clovis Crawfish and the Singing Cigales, Publishers Weekly,* January 1, 1982, p. 51.

■ For More Information See

PERIODICALS

Children's Book Watch, December, 1993, p. 2.
Horn Book Guide, July, 1990, p. 58; spring, 1992, p. 32; spring, 1993, p. 28; spring, 1994, p. 33; fall, 1995, p. 291.
Reading Time, December, 1982, p. 265.
School Library Journal, August, 1982, p. 96; December, 1983, p. 54.

FOURIE, Corlia 1944-

■ Personal

Born December 11, 1944, in South Africa; daughter of C. H. Kuehn (an author) and Ora Kuehn; married Frans Fourie (an editor); children: Marianne, Carina. *Education:* University of Stellenbosch, B.A., 1965. *Hobbies and other interests:* Reading, photography, walking, music.

■ Addresses

Home—P.O. Box 1330, Rooseveltpark, 2129, South Africa.

■ Career

Journalist and writer, 1965—.

■ Writings

Ganekwane and the Green Dragon: Four Stories from Africa, translated by Madeleine van Biljon, illustrated by Christian Arthur Kingue Epanya, Albert Whitman (Morton Grove, IL), 1994.

Also author of short stories, plays, and books for children published in Afrikaans; author of *Tintinyane,*

CORLIA FOURIE

the Girl Who Sang like a Magic Bird and *The Magic Pouch and Other Stories,* both translated into English.

■ Work in Progress

Two new children's books in Afrikaans; a novel.

■ Adaptations

Tintinyane, the Girl Who Sang like a Magic Bird was adapted into a musical production by composer Peter Klatzow.

■ Sidelights

Corlia Fourie is a South African writer who has followed in her father's footsteps. Her father, C. H. Kuehn, was a well-known Afrikaans author who wrote under the pseudonym Mikro. Fourie writes short stories, plays, radio plays, and children's books in Afrikaans. She has received various literary prizes, including awards for her children's books. Three such works, *Tintinyane, the Girl Who Sang like a Magic Bird, Ganekwane and the Green Dragon,* and *The Magic Pouch and Other Stories,* have been translated into English, the latter by Fourie herself. *Ganekwane and the Green Dragon* has also been published in the United States.

Fourie's stories for children are usually fantasy tales set in prehistoric Africa. The characters are mythical African people—they do not belong to any particular tribe—who in fairy-tale fashion have to fight against dangerous forces. As a child, Fourie loved stories with active female characters, and all the tales in *Ganekwane* have young girls as heroes, saving themselves and others from dangerous situations. With these African tales she also tries to build bridges between African and European story traditions so that children from all cultures may enjoy them. For instance, the first tale in *Ganekwane and the Green Dragon,* according to *School Library Journal* contributor Susan Scheps, features a "girl reminiscent of Red Riding Hood" who must similarly confront a wild beast of the forest. Scheps called Fourie's stories "an inviting collection," and *Booklist* reviewer Julie Corsaro also commented favorably on Fourie's work, maintaining that "the style is simple and brisk, the tone is gentle, and the heroines are thoughtful."

■ Works Cited

Corsaro, Julie, review of *Ganekwane and the Green Dragon: Four Stories from Africa, Booklist,* October 15, 1994, p. 426.
Scheps, Susan, review of *Ganekwane and the Green Dragon: Four Stories from Africa, School Library Journal,* December, 1994, p. 108.

*   *   *

GAY, Amelia
See HOGARTH, Grace (Weston) Allen

PETRINA GENTILE

GENTILE, Petrina 1969-

■ Personal

Born October 27, 1969, in St. Catharines, Ontario, Canada; daughter of Petito (a construction worker and farmer) and Giovanna (a chef; maiden name, Sicuranza) Gentile. *Education:* University of Waterloo, B.A. (with honors), 1993; Carleton University, M.A. (journalism), 1996.

■ Addresses

Agent—Crabtree Publishing, Box 898, Niagara-on-the-Lake, ONT, Canada, L0S 1J0.

■ Career

Crabtree Publishing Co., Niagara-on-the-Lake, Ontario, editor and writer, 1993—.

■ Writings

WITH BOBBIE KALMAN AND DAVID SCHIMPKY

Settler Sayings, Crabtree Publishing (Niagara-on-the-Lake, Ontario), 1993.
Wings, Wheels, and Sails, Crabtree Publishing, 1994.
Homes around the World, Crabtree Publishing, 1994.

WITH BOBBIE KALMAN

Dirt Movers, Crabtree Publishing, 1994.
Ballet School, Crabtree Publishing, 1994.

(And with Tammy Everts) *Gymnastics,* Crabtree Publishing, 1996.

Big Wheels, Crabtree Publishing, 1997.

OTHER

Also creator of "Watching You," a thirty-minute television documentary on the effectiveness of anti-stalking legislation in Canada.

■ Sidelights

"While in University, I worked in the children's division of Houghton Mifflin Publishing Company," Petrina Gentile explained to *SATA.* "In four months I bought over one hundred books for children—everything from the *Chronicles of Narnia* to books of poetry and limericks. A little bewildered, my colleagues would ask, 'Why are you buying so many books? Are you planning to open a children's bookstore on the side?' I would turn away, a little embarrassed, and say, 'Well, actually, they're gifts for my nieces and nephews. I have eight of them!' Even though I did intend to give away some of those books as presents, when it came down to it I just couldn't part with any of them. So, I stored them away in cardboard boxes under my bed, in the back of my closet, and in the upstairs attic. Until one day my niece Danielle asked me to read her a story. At the time, she was four and old enough to appreciate a story from my 'private collection.' I'll never forget the expression on her face, the sparkle in her eyes, and the way she tried to recite the story of Anansi the spider after I finished reading it to her. From that day on, I displayed my collection of books. So, whenever Tommas, Kayla, Peter, Jordan, or Michael want to read a book, there is always one within reach.

"I love reading and writing ... especially children's books. I love being part of the educational process, and providing children with the materials they need to learn about life. I also love learning about everything from the capybara, the world's largest rodent, to life in a ballet school. Education is extremely important to me [too]. I went on a leave of absence from Crabtree Publishing to study journalism in graduate school. But I'll get back to the books ... children's books, that is. And I CAN'T WAIT!"

■ For More Information See

PERIODICALS

Kirkus Reviews, December 15, 1994.

*   *   *

GETZ, David 1957-

■ Personal

Born May 31, 1957, in New York, NY; son of Ed and Adriane Getz; married Jacqui (a teacher), November 1, 1986; children; Maxine. *Education:* State University of New York, Binghamton; Teacher's College, Columbia University. *Religion:* Jewish.

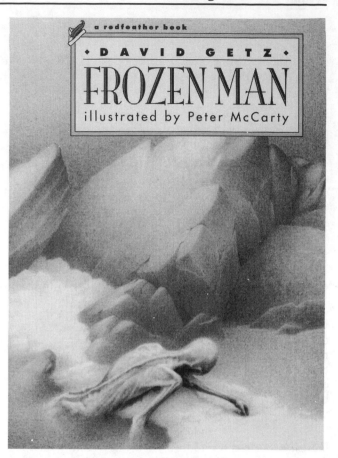

David Getz's 1994 book details the discovery of a well-preserved human body found frozen in the Austrian Alps.

■ Addresses

Home—375 Riverside Dr., Apt. 9D, New York, NY 10025.

■ Career

Author. New York City Board of Education, New York City, teacher, 1984—.

■ Writings

Thin Air (fiction), Holt, 1990.

Almost Famous (fiction), Holt, 1992.

Frozen Man (nonfiction), illustrated by Peter McCarty, Holt, 1994.

Floating Home (picture book), illustrated by Michael Rex, Holt, 1997.

Life on Mars (nonfiction), illustrated by Peter McCarty, Holt, 1997.

■ Sidelights

David Getz told *SATA:* "I started writing as a nine-year-old with the goal of making my fellow fourth-graders laugh. As I got older my writing and audience aged proportionately, though my goal remained the same. I continued to write to amuse my friends. When I was seventeen, I was writing for *Seventeen* magazine. In college, I wrote for my college paper. I expected this growth to continue well into the retirement home, where I would probably be dictating jokes to some attendant nurse.

"But then, at the age of twenty-seven in 1984, I became a fourth-grade teacher. Without missing a beat, I was back to making nine-year-olds laugh. During that year one of my students read *The Cat Ate My Gymsuit,* then wrote to the book's author, Paula Danziger. As it turned out, Paula lived around the corner from us and soon became a frequent visitor to our class and a friend. Paula also seemed to have no other goal than to make nine-year-olds laugh. Sometime that year I decided to write a book for children. Naturally, it would be a book about a funny kid in fourth grade. Henry Holt published *Thin Air* in 1990."

In her *Booklist* review of *Thin Air,* Hazel Rochman calls Getz's first novel "a very different story of a strong disabled boy." Sixth-grader Jacob Katz, a severe asthmatic, is determined to attend a regular school rather than the one for children with chronic illnesses that his overprotective parents have chosen for him. After becoming part of the regular school and attempting to pass himself off as healthy, Jacob runs away when he discovers that his teacher has told the truth about his problem to the class. When his reaction to a classmate's pistachios lands him in the hospital, Jacob receives a promise from his father to help him remain in the regular classroom. While respecting the seriousness of Jacob's disability, Getz invests *Thin Air* with what Hazel Rochman calls "sophisticated humor" and *School Library Journal* reviewer Joyce Adams Burner dubs "wry insight."

Getz's next novel, *Almost Famous,* features ten-year-old Maxine, who wants to be a famous inventor and to appear on the "Phil Donahue Show"; mostly, however, she wants to invent something to help her beloved five-year-old brother, who has a heart murmur. When Maxine receives an application to enter a contest for child inventors, she thinks it is from Phil Donahue and feels "almost famous." However, she needs a partner in order to qualify, and the only appropriate person in her class is Toni, a math whiz who wants nothing to do with the clever but aggressive Maxine. At the end of the story, the girls, who have decided to work together, come up with an invention that helps both Maxine's brother and Toni's problems at home. Writing in *Booklist,* Stephanie Zvirin says that "Getz's rapid-fire dialogue [is] just the way lonely, enthusiastic children caught up in ideas make themselves heard." A reviewer in *Publishers Weekly* notes that Maxine's "spirited ambition ... may hearten readers and convey to them the tenacity needed in pursuing goals," while a critic in *Kirkus Reviews* concludes that "Maxine is a pip."

With his next book, *Frozen Man,* Getz made his first contribution to the genre of nonfiction. As he explained to *SATA:* "It was during my first few years as a teacher that my only other goal as a writer emerged. As an adult,

I developed an interest in science. Not science facts, but the way scientists approach problems; the way they question, research, test, and discover. The way scientists think. I thought it would be fun to write for kids in a way that brought them along with scientists. I set out to write stories that would place my readers next to scientists as they did their work. I wrote *Frozen Man,* about the discovery of a frozen body in the Alps, as a vehicle to carry children along for a scientific investigation. It was published by Holt in 1994." Directed to middle-grade readers, *Frozen Man* describes the discovery of the Ice Man, a five-thousand-year-old mummified shepherd whose body was found in the Alps mountain system between Austria and Italy in 1991. Getz outlines both the recovery and the study of the Ice Man, who at the time was the oldest and most well-preserved specimen of Stone Age life in existence. In his review in *School Library Journal,* Joel Shoemaker writes that "young readers should find the book fascinating" and that Getz's text is "clear, concise, and interesting." Chris Sherman observes in *Booklist* that *Frozen Man* is "as smoothly written as Getz's fiction" and that it addresses questions that will keep young readers "interested till the very last page."

■ Works Cited

Review of *Almost Famous, Kirkus Reviews,* December 1, 1992, p. 1502.

Review of *Almost Famous, Publishers Weekly,* December 14, 1992, p. 57.

Burner, Joyce Adams, review of *Thin Air, School Library Journal,* January, 1991, p. 90.

Rochman, Hazel, review of *Thin Air, Booklist,* October 15, 1990, p. 442.

Sherman, Chris, review of *Frozen Man, Booklist,* November 15, 1994, p. 595.

Shoemaker, Joel, review of *Frozen Man, School Library Journal,* December, 1994, p. 122.

Zvirin, Stephanie, review of *Almost Famous, Booklist,* December 15, 1992, p. 730.

■ For More Information See

PERIODICALS

Appraisal: Science Books for Young People, Winter, 1995, p. 25.

Books for Keeps, November, 1993, p. 13.

Junior Bookshelf, December, 1992, p. 255.

Kirkus Reviews, November 15, 1994, p. 1529.

School Library Journal, February, 1993, p. 93.

*   *   *

GIFFORD, Kerri 1961-

■ Personal

Born October 2, 1961, in Provo, UT; daughter of Gerald Ray Gifford (a military dentist), Josephine K. Gifford (in dosimetry and radiation therapy), and Emiko Gifford (stepmother); lives with partner Daniel Miller (a sculptor and artist); children: Anthony, Ashton, Nathan.

Education: Attended Brigham Young University for three years. *Hobbies and other interests:* Studying metaphysics, physics, and psychology; camping, hiking, and exploring nature.

■ Addresses

Home—1706 South West Temple, Salt Lake City, UT 84115.

■ Career

Illustrator and teacher. WICAT Systems, Orem, UT, illustrator of children's educational and testing software, 1983-88; Utah Valley State College, Orem, computer graphics teacher, 1988; Barron's Educational Series, Hauppauge, NY, illustrator, 1990-96; Adventure Learning Software, Orem, illustrator of children's educational software, 1992-93.

■ Awards, Honors

First Place Honors, Fort Polk Annual Art Contest, dependent drawing division, 1978; art scholarship, Brigham Young University, 1981; Second Place Honors, Utah County Fair Art Show, professional graphics division, 1991.

■ Illustrator

"GET READY, GET SET, READ!" SERIES, WRITTEN BY KELLI C. FOSTER AND GINA C. ERICKSON; PUBLISHED BY BARRON'S EDUCATIONAL SERIES

The Bug Club, 1991.
A Mop for Pop, 1991.
Sometimes I Wish, 1991.
The Sled Surprise, 1991.
Find Nat, 1991.
Bub and Chub, 1992.
Frog Knows Best, 1992.
The Best Pets Yet, 1992.
Bat's Surprise, 1992.
What a Day for Flying!, 1992.
Whiptail of Blackshale Trail, 1993.
Jake and the Snake, 1993.
Pip and Kip, 1993.
The Tan Can, 1993.
Dwight and the Trilobite, 1994.
Pink and Blue, 1994.
What Rose Doesn't Know, 1994.
Two Fine Swine, 1994.
Jeepers Creepers, 1994.
What a Trip!, 1994.
Tall and Small, 1994.
Matthew's Brew, 1994.
By the Light of the Moon, 1995.
Colleen and the Bean, 1995.
Where Is the Treasure?, 1995.
The Pancake Day, 1995.
Hide and Seek, 1995.
The Old Man and the Moat, 1995.
Let's Play Ball, 1996.
Snow in July, 1996.
Night Light, 1996.
The Crossing, 1996.
How to Catch a Butterfly, 1996.
Bounder's Sound, 1996.
Ludlow Grows Up, 1996.

OTHER

Kelli C. Foster and Gina C. Erickson, *A Valentine that Shines: A First Book, Second Reading Level,* Forest House, 1994.

Also illustrator of *Alphabet Tails* (coloring book), by Gina C. Erickson and Kelli C. Foster, OnTrack, 1989; illustrator of educational software created by Adventure Learning Software, including *Daisy Quest,* Great Wave Software, 1992, and *Daisy's Castle,* Great Wave Software, 1993.

■ Work in Progress

A collection of fine-art erotic images using traditional and computer graphics media; research for the writing and illustration of a book about a fictional creature whose deformity is the source of her greatest misery and becomes the source of her deepest joy.

■ Sidelights

Kerri Gifford told *SATA:* "As long as I can remember I wanted to be an 'artist.' When I was about twelve years old, I began to specifically think about creating either fashion illustration or children's books. I wanted to freelance, so I could invest my primary time and interests in 'mommying.' It was strange when I realized one day that I was doing exactly what I had imagined I wanted as a child.

"So far, my work has been the product of someone else's dream. The work has had my heart however and I have been fortunate to almost completely control my creative process. I have grown from all of these projects. I hope to not only illustrate but write some of my own work for children of all ages. I would like to offer some of the tidbits of wisdom and beauty I have run across in my life. I would like to see my work enriching the lives of children and their parents by presenting some often overlooked wonders in our world and encouraging inquiry into ideas and beliefs we rarely question.

"Usually I am presented with very sketchy ideas about what I am to illustrate. Often, all I know is the sketch of a story. Depending on how intrigued I am by the idea, I will stew and meditate over visual images in my mind. I am generally very clear about what I want to produce before I ever pick up a tool. My mind work often forces what media I will use. If the media has been specified in advance, I love the challenge of pushing its limits.

"I haven't been influenced by any one illustrator. I try to find something positive about every piece of work I experience. I try to expose myself to as many different illustrators as I can. I figure this is one way I can continue my education. I have a great deal of respect for my contemporary illustrators. I can appreciate the blood, sweat, and passion that produces their work. In turn, I hope that same sort of blood, sweat and passion will fuel the development of my skills to a degree that words will only act as accents to what my images already communicate."*

*   *   *

GILSON, Jamie 1933-

■ Personal

Born July 4, 1933, in Beardstown, IL; daughter of James Noyce (a flour miller) and Sallie (a teacher; maiden name, Wilkinson) Chisam; married Jerome Gilson (a lawyer), June 19, 1955; children: Tom, Matthew, Anne. *Education:* Attended University of Missouri, 1951-52; Northwestern University, B.S., 1955.

■ Addresses

Home—Wilmette, IL.

■ Career

Thacker Junior High School, Des Plaines, IL, speech and English teacher, 1955-56; writer and producer for radio and television division of public school system in Chicago, IL, 1956-59; WFMT-Radio, Chicago, continuity director, 1959-63; Encyclopaedia Britannica, Chicago, writer in film division, 1963-65. Lecturer and writing workshop teacher, Wilmette Public Schools, 1974-90. *Member:* Society of Children's Book Writers

JAMIE GILSON

and Illustrators, Children's Reading Round Table, Society of Midland Authors, PEN American Center, Authors Guild, Authors League of America.

■ Awards, Honors

Merit Award, Friends of American Writers, 1979, for *Harvey, the Beer Can King;* Carl Sandburg Award, Friends of the Chicago Public Library, 1981, and Charlie May Simon Award, Arkansas Elementary School Council, 1983, both for *Do Bananas Chew Gum?;* Dallas Market Center Gift Editorial Award, 1983, for column "The Goods"; Sequoyah Award and Pacific Northwest Young Readers Choice Award, both 1985, Land of Enchantment Award, 1986, Buckeye Award and Sunshine Award, both 1987, all for *Thirteen Ways to Sink a Sub;* Children's Reading Round Table Award, 1992; *Do Bananas Chew Gum?* and *Can't Catch Me, I'm the Gingerbread Man* were Junior Literary Guild selections.

■ Writings

FOR CHILDREN

Harvey, the Beer Can King, illustrated by John Wallner, Lothrop, 1978.
Dial Leroi Rupert, D.J., illustrated by John Wallner, Lothrop, 1979.
Do Bananas Chew Gum?, Lothrop, 1980.
Can't Catch Me, I'm the Gingerbread Man, Lothrop, 1981.
Thirteen Ways to Sink a Sub, illustrated by Linda Strauss Edwards, Lothrop, 1982.
4-B Goes Wild, illustrated by Linda Straus Edwards, Lothrop, 1983.
Hello, My Name Is Scrambled Eggs, illustrated by John Wallner, 1985.
Hobie Hanson, You're Weird, illustrated by Elise Primavera, 1987.
Double Dog Dare, illustrated by Elise Primavera, Lothrop, 1988.
Hobie Hanson: Greatest Hero of the Mall, illustrated by Anita Riggio, Lothrop, 1989.
Itchy Richard, illustrated by Diane de Groat, Clarion, 1991.
Sticks and Stones and Skeleton Bones, illustrated by Dee DeRosa, Lothrop, 1991.
You Cheat!, illustrated by Maxine Chambliss, Bradbury Press, 1992.
Soccer Circus, illustrated by Dee DeRosa, Lothrop, 1993.
It Goes Eeeeeeeeeeeee!, illustrated by Diane de Groat, Clarion, 1994.
Wagon Train 911, Lothrop, 1996.

OTHER

Author of *Chicago Magazine* column "The Goods," 1977-87. Contributor of articles to *WFMT Guide* and *Perspective* magazine.

■ Sidelights

Jamie Gilson's humorous books for middle-grade readers, all written in first-person from the perspective of an adolescent, demonstrate her keen understanding of the priorities and concerns of younger teens. "Before writing books for children, all of my professional writing had been for the voice—radio, TV, films—so that my books, too, are *told*, as a child would tell them," Gilson once related to *SATA*. "To keep that voice genuine, I work with children a good deal, speaking to them about my writing, teaching writing to sixth graders, sitting in with classes, going with a fifth grade class on a nature study overnight.... My research is a joy."

One of the early books to grow out of Gilson's experience with children is *Do Bananas Chew Gum?*, published in 1980. Gilson got the idea for the story from an assignment she had as a reporter for *Chicago Magazine*, covering an archaeological dig in southern Illinois. "I discovered the real excitement that comes from finding broken arrowheads and shards of once-used clay pots," she recalled for *SATA*. "Sam Mott in *Bananas* shares that enthusiasm." Sam is a sixth-grader who has become the subject of his classmates' unkind jokes because he reads at a second-grade level. His reading difficulties make him feel stupid, so he tries to hide them from his family and friends. As the story progresses Sam receives encouragement and motivation to overcome his problem from a young archaeologist who shares her love of history with him, as well as from the kind woman for whom he baby-sits and from one of his classmates. He agrees to a series of tests and learns that he is not stupid after all—he has a learning disability. By working with an understanding teacher, Sam is not only able to read better, but also improves his confidence and outlook on life. "Told with humor and subtle compassion, this is a story that leaves you feeling good," reviewer Jane VanWiemokly commented in *Voice of Youth Advocates*. "I hope that children will not only find *Bananas* fun to read, but also revealing of the difficulties that a learning-disabled child faces," Gilson told *SATA*.

Gilson introduced one of her most popular characters, Hobie Hanson, in *Thirteen Ways to Sink a Sub*, published in 1982. In this story, Hobie and his fourth-grade classmates are surprised to find a substitute teacher, Miss Svetlana Ivanovich, taking over their lessons for the day. The boys and the girls quickly face off to see which team can be the first to "sink the sub," or upset her to the point of tears. Some of their antics include switching names, pretending not to speak English, and faking the loss of a contact lens. Miss Ivanovich remains pleasant and good-natured throughout the contest, which eventually makes the class like her too much to continue trying to "sink" her. Barbara Elleman of *Booklist* praised Gilson's book for its "crisp, inventive plot that is top drawer in the contemporary fiction genre for this age group."

Gilson rejoined Hobie and his friends in 1987's *Hobie Hanson, You're Weird*. When Hobie's best friend, Nick Rossi, goes away to computer camp for the summer,

Hobie is left on his own. At first he is annoyed when his classroom rival, Molly Bosco, begins following him around, but before long they find out how much they have in common and share some entertaining adventures. Writing in *School Library Journal*, Julie Cummins noted that "with dialogue right on target for the age, Gilson writes with humor and appeal for kids." A *Booklist* reviewer praised Gilson's "bulls-eye wit and ease with the written word" and claimed that "kids will be attracted to this like steel to a magnet."

Hobie has a harrowing adventure in *Hobie Hanson: Greatest Hero of the Mall*, published in 1989. In this story, heavy rains cause the nearby Hawk River to overflow its banks and flood much of Hobie's hometown. He tries to be a hero, but instead Molly Bosco floats by on an inflatable giraffe and rescues him and the little boy he is baby-sitting. Since the elementary school was damaged in the flood, Hobie and his friends learn that school will be held temporarily in an empty department store at the local mall. In this unusual educational setting, the class finds a variety of new ways to make hilarious mischief. Hobie finally does become a hero by finding some diamond earrings that were lost in the flood and returning them to their owner, and he is

Trouble seems to follow Gilson's popular protagonist Hobie Hanson, on and off the soccer field. (Cover illustration by Dee deRosa.)

only slightly less pleased with himself when he learns that the diamonds are fake. Denise Wilms, writing in *Booklist,* stated that the story "has action, humor, and a protagonist familiar enough to be the boy next door," and predicted that "Hobie's fans will be quick to line up for this one."

Gilson explores the relationship between two young brothers in 1992's *You Cheat!* Active, six-year-old Nathan longs to show up his video-game loving older brother, Hank. When he can't beat Hank at cards, Nathan challenges his brother to go fishing with him and see who can land the biggest fish. Since Hank thinks worms are gross and fishing is boring, Nathan convinces him to accept the challenge by promising to kiss every fish Hank catches on the mouth. Deciding that the prospect of Nathan kissing a fish is too good an opportunity to pass up, Hank agrees to the contest and makes Nathan deliver on his promise. In a review for *School Library Journal,* Maggie McEwen called *You Cheat!* "an excellent beginning chapter book" and noted that the "simple adventure will appeal to early readers."

Some of Gilson's remaining books for young readers deal with subjects like head lice (*Itchy Richard*), bats (*It Goes Eeeeeeeeeeeee!*), and ways to settle disputes peacefully (*Sticks and Stones and Skeleton Bones*). Hobie Hanson and friends are again featured at their temporary school in the mall in *Sticks and Stones and Skeleton Bones.* In this tale, Hobie and classmates Nick Rossi and Molly Bosco become embroiled in an accelerating cycle of practical jokes, misunderstandings, and retaliation, until all three end up in the school's new conflict management program, where they—and readers—learn that there are two sides to every story. Reviewing *Sticks and Stones and Skeleton Bones* for *Booklist,* Deborah Abbott maintained that Gilson "paints her characters with a refined brush, showing in an uncanny fashion the intricacies and nuances of the world of fifth-graders." *Itchy Richard* addresses a problem common to many grade schoolers: head lice. Someone in Mrs. Zookey's second-grade class has them, and rumors begin to fly among the children when the head nurse comes in to check each of their scalps. As the students exchange exaggerated ideas about these bugs and what they do, central protagonist Richard begins to feel kind of itchy himself. Mrs. Zookey settles everyone down with a simple explanation of head lice and how they are treated. "Loaded with kid-appealing humor and personalities straight out of a grade-school classroom," asserted Stephanie Zvirin for *Booklist,* "Gilson's sensitive story takes a fairly common elementary school problem and makes it seem, if no less 'yucky,' at least less scary." A reviewer for *Publishers Weekly* added that in *Itchy Richard* "Gilson displays the same snappy dialogue and brisk humor that have made her Hobie Hanson novels so popular with youngsters."

Richard and his friends from Mrs. Zookey's class return in *It Goes Eeeeeeeeeeeee!*, a story supplying a palatable dose of information about bats to again clear up the young students' misconceptions and fears. In her review of this tale in *Booklist,* Stephanie Zvirin noted that

Gilson "feeds the facts smoothly and memorably into the fictional format." Other commentators cited Gilson's trademark warmth, humor, and first-person narration, while appreciatively underscoring her remarkable understanding of the world of grade school students.

■ Works Cited

Abbott, Deborah, review of *Sticks and Stones and Skeleton Bones, Booklist,* March 1, 1991, p. 1392.

Cummins, Julie, review of *Hobie Hanson, You're Weird, School Library Journal,* June, 1987, p. 95.

Elleman, Barbara, review of *Thirteen Ways to Sink a Sub, Booklist,* October 1, 1982, p. 244.

Review of *Hobie Hanson, You're Weird, Booklist,* June 15, 1987, p. 1601.

Review of *Itchy Richard, Publishers Weekly,* September 20, 1991, p. 134.

McEwen, Maggie, review of *You Cheat!, School Library Journal,* September, 1992, p. 203.

VanWiemokly, Jane, review of *Do Bananas Chew Gum?, Voice of Youth Advocates,* April, 1981, p. 34.

Wilms, Denise, review of *Hobie Hanson: Greatest Hero of the Mall, Booklist,* September 1, 1989, p. 71.

Zvirin, Stephanie, review of *Itchy Richard, Booklist,* September 15, 1991, p. 150.

Zvirin, Stephanie, review of *It Goes Eeeeeeeeeeeee!, Booklist,* April 1, 1994, p. 1446.

■ For More Information See

BOOKS

Sixth Book of Junior Authors and Illustrators, edited by Sally Holmes Holtze, H. W. Wilson, 1989.

PERIODICALS

Booklist, September 1, 1983, p. 85; September 1, 1988, p. 76; August, 1992, p. 2011; April 1, 1993, p. 1431.

Bulletin of the Center for Children's Books, November, 1978, p. 43; March, 1981, p. 133; June, 1981, p. 171; December, 1982, p. 67; October, 1983, p. 27.

Kirkus Reviews, May 1, 1978, p. 497; December 15, 1980, p. 1570; July 15, 1981, p. 872; September 1, 1983, p. 161; March 1, 1985, p. 11; October 15, 1991, p. 1353; August 15, 1992, p. 1061; May 1, 1994, p. 629.

Publishers Weekly, June 24, 1988, p. 114; July 28, 1989, p. 222; January 18, 1991, p. 58; March 8, 1993, pp. 79-80.

School Library Journal, September, 1981, p. 124; January, 1983, p. 75; August, 1985, p. 64; September, 1988, p. 183; October, 1989, p. 118; March, 1991, p. 193; December, 1991, p. 90; June, 1993, p. 106; June, 1994, p. 100.

*   *   *

GOETZ, Delia 1898-1996

OBITUARY NOTICE—See index for *SATA* sketch: Born in June, 1898, near Wesley, IA; died June 26, 1996, in Washington, DC. Educator and author. Goetz gained prominence as the author of numerous children's books. After graduating from Iowa State Teachers' College in 1922, she left the United States to teach in Cuba, Guatemala, and Panama. In 1946, Goetz accepted a post with the U.S. Office of Education in Central America, a position she held until 1961. Her first book for children, *The Good Neighbors: The Story of the Two Americas,* was published in 1939. In all, Goetz wrote thirty books, mostly for children, with topics ranging from education to geology and daily life in Central America. Her works include *The Hidden Burro, Tropical Rain Forests, Half a Hemisphere: The Story of Latin America, Panchita, a Little Girl of Guatemala, Valleys,* and *Education in Panama.*

OBITUARIES AND OTHER SOURCES:

PERIODICALS

New York Times, July 14, 1996, p. 32.

*   *   *

GOODALL, John S(trickland) 1908-1996

OBITUARY NOTICE—See index for *SATA* sketch: Born June 7, 1908, in Heacham, Norfolk, England; died June 3, 1996, in London, England. Artist, illustrator, author. Goodall studied painting at the Royal Academy School of Art in London. He gained prominence as the author and illustrator of more than twenty children's books, including his popular *Paddy Pork* series centering on the humorous escapades of a gentlemanly Victorian pig. Regarded among the most skillful creators of wordless picture and pop-up books for primary graders, Goodall has also been praised as a storyteller and social historian whose animal fantasies and visual English histories are noted for their excellence of content and design. As an illustrator, Goodall has been celebrated as a superior draftsman whose precise line drawings and watercolor paintings in a representational style, featuring panoramic spreads that reflect both his use of deep, rich hues and more subtle shadings, are well composed and filled with interesting, accurate details. Also a successful landscape and portrait painter whose works have been exhibited internationally, Goodall listed among his credits for illustration an edition of Lewis Carroll's *Alice in Wonderland,* Barbara Ker Wilson's *Fairy Tales of England,* and several stories by Edith N. Blands, including *Phoenix and the Carpet.* His own self-illustrated children's stories include *Naughty Nancy Goes to School, The Midnight Adventures of Kelly, Dot, and Esmerelda,* and *Edwardian Entertainments,* as well as adaptations of *Puss in Boots* and *Little Red Riding Hood. The Adventures of Paddy Pork* won the *Boston Globe-Horn Book Award* for illustration in 1969. Named a Freeman of the City of London, Goodall also received several awards for his paintings.

OBITUARIES AND OTHER SOURCES:

PERIODICALS

Los Angeles Times, June 29, 1996, p. A22.

GREEN, Timothy 1953-

■ Personal

Born November 28, 1953; son of Buddy (an appliance repairman) and Virginia (a small business owner; maiden name, Scharrer) Green; married Kristine Hill (an education consultant), December 12, 1979; children: Dazhoni, Shundiin (daughters). *Education:* Moorhead State University, B.A.; University of North Dakota, M.F.A.; additional study at University of Phoenix.

■ Addresses

Home—P.O. Box 1966, Kaibeto, AZ 86053-1966.

■ Career

Bureau of Indian Affairs, junior high school English teacher on Navajo reservation in Arizona, 1989—. Has also taught art at Denver School for Gifted and Talented Students and for North Dakota Artist-in-Residence Program.

■ Awards, Honors

National Endowment for the Arts grants.

■ Writings

(Self-illustrated) *Mystery of Navajo Moon,* Northland Publishing (Flagstaff, AZ), 1991.
(Self-illustrated) *Mystery of Coyote Canyon* (young adult novel), Ancient City Press (Santa Fe, NM), 1993.
Twilight Boy (young adult novel), Northland Publishing, 1997.

Timothy Green and friends.

Also illustrator of cover, *There Still Are Buffalo,* by Ann Nolan Clark, Ancient City Press, 1993.

■ Work in Progress

The Ransom for Rebecca, an adult novel, expected 1998.

■ Sidelights

Timothy Green told *SATA:* "Living on the Navajo reservation in northern Arizona has provided me with a unique opportunity of experiencing Navajo culture firsthand, daily discovering the fascinating dynamics of this remote and brooding land. I enjoy hiking and exploring the countless canyons and mesas that surround my home, where I often encounter telltale signs of civilizations from the past: an ancient potsherd, an arrowhead, a cryptic petroglyph carved into rock, a crumbling wall of an Anasazi ruin. Needless to say, my hikes have inspired numerous settings and plots that were later hatched in my stories.

"Personally, my favorite time for writing is during the graveyard hours: between 5 and 7 A.M. For years I've clambered out of bed and over to my desk and pen during these early hours.

"As a teacher, I encourage aspiring young authors to write with complete unrestraint, dipping their pens into the deep and unsettled waters of their imagination. I emphasize the importance of rewriting. Rewrite and then rewrite some more. I stress that few sentences come out right the first time, or the second, or even the third time. Writing, like any art form, takes years of commitment and work to perfect. Henri Matisse once said: 'I have worked for years in order that people might say, "It seems so easy to do.'"

"I believe refinement marks the difference between novice and master, and fortunately, refinement can be cultivated."

■ For More Information See

PERIODICALS

School Library Journal, May, 1992, p. 88.

H

SHERRI HAAB

HAAB, Sherri 1964-

■ Personal

Born November 7, 1964, in Idaho Falls, ID; daughter of James R. (a data technician) and Shirley (maiden name, Gray; a loan officer) Hofmann; married Dan Haab (an electrical engineer), May 1, 1986; children: Rachel, Michelle, David. *Education:* Attending Brigham Young University. *Religion:* Church of Jesus Christ of Latter-Day Saints.

■ Addresses

Home—948 South 2350 E., Springville, UT 84663.

■ Career

Freelance illustrator, Springville, UT; jewelry and craft designer.

■ Writings

(And illustrator) *The Incredible Clay Book: How to Make and Bake a Million-and-One Clay Creations,* Klutz Press, 1994.

ILLUSTRATOR

(With others) *Kids Travel,* Klutz Press, 1994.
(With others) Nancy Cassidy, *Hullabaloo,* Klutz Press, 1995.

■ Work in Progress

Clay illustrations for *Klutz Sticker Book* and *Klutz Recipe Book; Kids' Nailpainting Book,* Klutz Press, due 1997.

■ Sidelights

Author and illustrator Sherri Haab told *SATA:* "I was raised in Seattle, Washington. My sister and I spent a lot of time making things when we were young. I guess it's because of the rainy days Seattle provides—that and the fact that our Mom took us to fabric and craft stores with her. I always found great enjoyment from art; it was my favorite subject in school. I was always the one kid so excited about working on a project that I was standing at my desk working while other kids were sitting. I was interested in anything made of clay: ceramics, bread dough, plasticine, even Play-Doh and homemade clays. I think that 3-D illustrations are one of the most interesting forms of art, especially in children's literature.

"For the first few years of my marriage I worked in a business office to support our family while my husband finished his degree. After he graduated I started my own business making jewelry out of clay. I didn't make very much money and worked very long hours to fill orders. Although it seemed like a failed business at the time, it gave me the experience that I needed to refine my art. My work led to a book that teaches children how to use the same clay I use in my own studio ... polymer clay. It comes in a wide range of colors and can be cured in a regular oven. It is easily manipulated and holds detail very well. Clay can be made to look like many other materials, depending on the surface treatments used. I find it more versatile than other mediums. You can create any scene with any tone you desire; the sky is the limit!

"When I work it feels like I'm ten years old again; it's like playing on the job. I get a kick out of the creativity of the children around me—they aren't the least bit afraid to try something new. They are the ones who inspire me. My husband and I now live in a small town in Utah, with our three children, a cat named Susie, and a few assorted fish. Most of the day revolves around helping children with school, getting them to piano lessons, softball, or gymnastics. I always stay up late to have time to work on current projects. I believe it is important to do what you love and find balance in all areas of your life."

*   *   *

HAMILTON, Franklin
See SILVERBERG, Robert

*   *   *

HARLAN, Glen
See CEBULASH, Mel

*   *   *

HARRIS, Aurand 1915-1996

OBITUARY NOTICE—See index for *SATA* sketch: Born July 4, 1915, in Jamesport, MO; died of cancer, May 6, 1996, in Manhattan, NY. Playwright. Harris is remembered as a prolific children's playwright and the author of the classic, *Androcles and the Lion.* Harris began his forty-year career as an author of children's plays in 1945, while teaching drama at William Woods College in Fulton, Missouri. His first children's work, *Once Upon a Clothesline,* a four-act play, was produced in Fulton. Between 1946 and 1977, Harris served as a drama instructor at Grace Church School, New York City. His fifty-some plays have been translated into twenty languages. He has received many honors, including a creative writing fellowship from the National Endowment for the Arts. Harris's other works include *Peter Rabbit and Me, Monkey Magic, The Orphan Train,* and *The Pinballs.* Harris also contributed to and served as editor for the anthologies *Short Plays of Theatre Classics* and *Plays Children Love.*

OBITUARIES AND OTHER SOURCES:

BOOKS

Who's Who in America, 51st edition, Marquis, 1996.
PERIODICALS

Chicago Tribune, May 10, 1996, section 3, p. 9.
Los Angeles Times, May 9, 1996, p. A31.
New York Times, May 8, 1996, p. D21.
Washington Post, May 13, 1996, p. D6.

*   *   *

HARTMAN, Victoria 1942-

■ Personal

Born July 8, 1942, in New York, NY; daughter of Leo (with the Department of Welfare) and Doris (a nursery school director; maiden name, Eichler) Hartman; married Joseph Gomez (an elementary school teacher), June 20, 1965 (divorced, August, 1983). *Education:* Cooper Union, B.F.A., 1964. *Hobbies and other interests:* Painting, choral singing, gardening, travel.

■ Addresses

Home—164 Halsey St., Southampton, NY 11968.

Victoria Hartman teams with illustrator R. W. Alley in this joke book for young people featuring whimsical riddles on a wide variety of subjects.

Career

Lothrop, Lee & Shepard (publishing house), New York City, art director, 1967-74; freelance book designer, 1974—. *Member:* Authors Guild, Authors League of America, Graphic Artists Guild.

Writings

The Silly Jokebook, Scholastic, 1987.
Westward Ho Ho Ho!: Jokes from the Wild West, illustrated by G. Brian Karas, Penguin, 1992.
The Silliest Jokebook Ever, illustrated by R. W. Alley, Lothrop, 1993.
Too Cool: Jokes for School, illustrated by Terry Koval-cik, Troll Communications, 1996.

Sidelights

Victoria Hartman told *SATA,* "I grew up in a word-loving family and have always enjoyed making puns, riddles, and jokes. Just can't help it."

For More Information See

PERIODICALS

Booklist, May 1, 1992, p. 1596; May 1, 1993, p. 1598.
Bulletin of the Center for Children's Books, April, 1993, p. 250.
Horn Book Guide, fall, 1992, p. 317; fall, 1993, p. 363.
School Library Journal, July, 1992, p. 69; October, 1993, p. 118.

*   *   *

HARWICK, B. L.
See KELLER, Beverly L(ou)

*   *   *

HAYES, Geoffrey 1947-

Personal

Born December 3, 1947, in Pasadena, CA; son of Philip Dutton (a waiter) and Juliette (a secretary; maiden name, Dante) Hayes. *Education:* Attended John O'Connell Institute, San Francisco Academy of Art, New York School of Visual Arts, and Hunter College.

Addresses

Home—338 Bocana St., San Francisco, CA 94110. *Agent*—Edite Kroll, 12 Grayhurst Park, Portland, ME 04102.

Career

Marling, Marx & Seidman (advertising agency), New York City, worked in art department, 1972-73; Kajima International, New York City, interior designer, 1973-75; Harper & Row Publishers, Inc., New York City,

artist and designer, 1975-1984; writer and illustrator, 1984—; Vanguard Public Foundation, San Francisco, grants associate, 1994—.

■ Awards, Honors

When the Wind Blew (written by Margaret Wise Brown) was chosen by the *New York Times* as one of the ten best illustrated books of 1977.

■ Writings

FOR CHILDREN; SELF-ILLUSTRATED

Bear by Himself, Harper, 1976.
The Alligator and His Uncle Tooth: A Novel of the Sea, Harper, 1977.
Patrick Comes to Puttyville and Other Stories, Harper, 1978.
The Secret Inside, Harper, 1980.
Elroy and the Witch's Child, Harper, 1982.
Patrick and Ted, Four Winds, 1984.
Patrick Buys a Coat, Knopf, 1985.
Patrick Eats His Dinner, Knopf, 1985.
Patrick Takes a Bath, Knopf, 1985.
Patrick Goes to Bed, Knopf, 1985.
The Mystery of the Pirate Ghost: An Otto and Uncle Tooth Adventure, Random House, 1985.
Christmas in Puttyville, Random House, 1985.
Patrick and His Grandpa, Random House, 1986.
The Lantern Keeper's Bedtime Book, Random House, 1986.
Patrick and Ted at the Beach, Random House, 1987.
Patrick and Ted Ride the Train, Random House, 1988.
The Secret of Foghorn Island, Random House, 1988.
The Treasure of the Lost Lagoon, Random House, 1991.
The Curse of the Cobweb Queen, Random House, 1994.
The Night of the Circus Monsters, Random House, 1996.
Swamp of the Hideous Zombies, Random House, 1996.
House of the Horrible Ghosts, Random House, 1997.

ILLUSTRATOR

Margaret Wise Brown, *When the Wind Blew,* Harper, 1977.
Joan Lowery Nixon, *Muffie Mouse and the Busy Birthday,* Seabury, 1978.
Fran Manushkin, *Moon Dragon,* Macmillan, 1980.
Fran Manushkin, *Hocus & Pocus at the Circus,* Harper, 1981.

■ Work in Progress

Valley of the Vicious Ducks, for Random House.

■ Sidelights

Author and illustrator Geoffrey Hayes has written several books for beginning readers that feature animal duos such as the young bears Patrick and Ted and amateur alligator sleuths Otto and the crusty Uncle Tooth. Through his whimsical watercolor illustrations of these and a menagerie of other animal characters, Hayes both entertains and educates young readers with

When Dr. Ocular's Sea Monster Circus comes to
Boogle Bay, the question of whether or not the sea
monsters are real is put to the test. (From *The Night of
the Circus Monsters,* written and illustrated by
Geoffrey Hayes.)

books geared both to reluctant readers and those seeking
more sophisticated material.

Readers are first introduced to Patrick in *Patrick Comes
to Puttyville and Other Stories.* In this collection, the
young bear moves with his family to a new house in a
small town, where Patrick makes new friends—including Ted—and has several real-life adventures with
which young children can identify. In *Patrick and Ted
Ride the Train,* the two take a day trip on the Skitter &
Scoo Railway to visit an elderly relative; fortunately
armed with squirt guns, they make short work of a gang
of annoying weasels.

The Alligator and His Uncle Tooth: A Novel of the Sea
introduces readers to an entirely different community of
animal characters, from young Corduroy Alligator and
Captain Poopdeck, to the roving adventurer Uncle
Tooth and the woebegone Ducky Doodle. Uncle Tooth
is joined by young Otto in mystery stories that include
*The Treasure of the Lost Lagoon, Swamp of the Hideous
Zombies,* and *The Curse of the Cobweb Queen.* Whether
encountering treasure ships, mermaids, suspicious for-

tune tellers, a gang of dastardly rats, or a sinister, pearl-
snatching witch, the long-jawed duo manage to save the
day in the town of Boogle Bay. And in *Elroy and the
Witch's Child* an orphaned kitten seeking his fortune
encounters a witch and a little girl, with whom he travels
after some misunderstandings and confused introductions. "Hayes's new romp, cause for rejoicing, sparkles
with his recital of nonsense and the gaudy hues in the
cartoons," noted a *Publishers Weekly* reviewer.

"Writing and drawing have always come naturally to
me," Hayes once told *SATA.* "My brother and I, being
only two years apart, channeled our creative energies
into stories and books which we gave to one another. All
the writing I do now is an extension and development of
those early works. Many authors relive their past in
their fiction, but while some (such as Proust) do so in
autobiographical novels, I find fantasy not only the best
form for expressing my feelings, but as viable as any
literary genre."

In addition to writing and illustrating books for young
people, the multi-talented Hayes designs and builds
custom, hand-painted furniture and is a member of a
San Francisco dance troupe that performs locally. He is
also involved in working for Vanguard Public Foundation, a non-profit organization that funds grassroots
organizations in northern California. As the author/
illustrator noted, "I find dealing with a diverse group of
people to be a nice compliment to the rather solitary act
of writing."

■ Works Cited

Review of *Elroy and the Witch's Child, Publishers
   Weekly,* September 10, 1982, p. 76.

■ For More Information See

PERIODICALS

Booklist, September 1, 1976, p. 38; May 15, 1977, p.
   1420; November 15, 1978, p. 546; January 15,
   1981, p. 1352; February 15, 1982, p. 762; June 15,
   1984, p. 1483; June 15, 1985, p. 1457; October 1,
   1988, p. 330; February 1, 1989, p. 935.
Bulletin of the Center for Children's Books, September,
   1977; October, 1977, p. 33; March, 1979, p. 117.
Horn Book, August, 1977, p. 441.
Junior Bookshelf, April, 1978, p. 88.
Kirkus Reviews, June 15, 1976, p. 680; April 1, 1977, p.
   350; December 15, 1978, p. 1357; May 15, 1980, p.
   642; July 15, 1982, p. 795.
New York Times Book Review, November 14, 1976, p.
   26; May 1, 1977, p. 47.
Publishers Weekly, May 2, 1980, p. 76; January 21,
   1983, p. 85; March 16, 1984, p. 87; April 25, 1986,
   p. 78; December, 1986, p. 55; June 12, 1987, p. 83;
   December 22, 1989, p. 57.
School Library Journal, October, 1976, p. 98; September, 1977, p. 109; October, 1978, p. 145; May, 1980,
   p. 58; September, 1982, p. 108; October, 1984, p.
   147; November, 1985, p. 72; December, 1986, p.
   80; December, 1988, p. 87; April, 1992, p. 92.

HERNDON, Ernest

■ Personal

Born in Memphis, TN; married; wife's name, Angelyn. *Education:* University of Memphis, M.A. *Hobbies and other interests:* World travel.

■ Addresses

Office—c/o Enterprise-Journal, P.O. Box 910, McComb, MS 39648.

■ Career

Enterprise-Journal, McComb, MS, reporter, 1979—; freelance writer.

■ Awards, Honors

Numerous journalism awards from Louisiana-Mississippi Associated Press, Mississippi Sportswriters Association, Southeastern Outdoor Press Association, and Mississippi Press Association Better Newspaper Contest; Mississippi Humanities Council/Mississippi Press Association Newspaper Project honoraria; Special Merit Award, Mississippi Wildlife Federation, 1995.

■ Writings

FOR CHILDREN; PUBLISHED BY ZONDERVAN

The Secret of Lizard Island, 1994.
Double-Crossed in Gator Country, 1994.
Night of the Jungle Cat, 1994.
Smugglers on Grizzly Mountain, 1994.
Sisters of the Wolf, 1996.
Trouble at Bamboo Bay, 1996.
Death Bird of Paradise, 1997.
Little People of the Lost Coast, 1997.

OTHER

In the Hearts of Wild Men, Enterprise-Journal (McComb, MS), 1987.
(With Dr. Tom Seabourne) *Self-Defense: A Body-Mind Approach* (textbook), Gorsuch-Scarisbrick (Dubuque, IA), 1987.
Morning Morning True: A Novel of Intrigue in New Guinea, Zondervan, 1988.
Island Quarry: A Novel of Suspense, Zondervan, 1990.
Backwater Blues: A Novel of Faith and Fury, Zondervan, 1991.

Contributor to anthologies, including *From behind the Magnolia Curtain: Voices of Mississippi,* Mississippi Press Association/Mississippi Humanities Council, 1988; *The Magnolia Club: Fine Times with Nature's Finest,* Mississippi Wildlife Federation, 1990. Contributor to numerous periodicals, including *Black Belt, Bowhunter, Canoe & Kayak, Frets, Mississippi Wildlife, Paddler,* and *Sports Afield.*

■ For More Information See

PERIODICALS

Booklist, September 1, 1994, p. 41; January 1, 1995, p. 830.
Voice of Youth Advocates, April, 1992, p. 29.

*　　*　　*

HILL, Anthony R(obert) 1942-

■ Personal

Born May 24, 1942, in Melbourne, Australia; son of Alan Eric (a draftsman) and Elizabeth Lilian (a florist; maiden name, Wardlaw) Hill; married Gillian Mann (an administrator), October 15, 1965; children: Jane Louise. *Education:* Attended Melbourne University, 1960-63. *Politics:* "Swinging voter." *Religion:* Protestant. *Hobbies and other interests:* Music, Scottish dancing, antique collecting, golf.

■ Addresses

Office—c/o Penguin Books, P.O. Box 257, Ringwood, Victoria 3134, Australia.

ANTHONY R. HILL

■ Career

Melbourne Herald, Melbourne, Victoria, Australia, journalist, 1960-75; *Australian Financial Review,* Canberra, Australia, journalist, 1976-77; self-employed antique dealer in New South Wales, Australia, 1977-82; freelance speech writer and author, 1982—. *Member:* Australian Society of Authors, Australian Journalists Association, Australiana Society, Royal Scottish Country Dancing Society.

■ Awards, Honors

Christian Children's Book of the Year and Children's Book Council of Australia honor book, both 1995, both for *The Burnt Stick.*

■ Writings

FOR CHILDREN

Birdsong, Oxford (Australia), 1988.
The Burnt Stick, illustrated by Mark Sofilas, Viking (Australia), 1994, Houghton Mifflin, 1995.
Spindrift, Puffin (Australia), 1996.
The Grandfather Clock, Lothian Books (Australia), 1996.

OTHER

The Bunburyists, Penguin (Australia), 1985.
Antique Furniture in Australia, Viking, 1985.

■ Work in Progress

Twenty-one, for Puffin (Australia).

■ Sidelights

Australian author Anthony Hill told *SATA,* "If there is a theme in my writing, it is a wish to explore and expand the imaginative powers of young readers. In my first children's book, *Birdsong,* the conversations young Samuel has with his pet cockatoo are certainly from the world of pretend, but they are also a way for him to express his growing sensitivity to nature and the human predicament. In *The Grandfather Clock* Constance has to undertake a dream journey through Time. The fact that she overcomes the obstacles in her way is entirely due to her courage, her wit, and—above all—to her imagination.

"I don't mean by this that I write escapist literature. On the contrary, I am concerned to portray the cruelties, the complexities, and the comedies of life in a realistic and unflinching manner. *The Burnt Stick* deals with the former practice of taking Aboriginal children away from their mothers. *Spindrift* is about the death of a loved grandmother and coming to terms with it. I am presently working on a novel, *Twenty-one,* which concerns war and betrayal."

Of his works thus far, *The Burnt Stick* has earned Hill the most praise. This short story of about fifty pages tells of John Jagamarra, a boy whose experiences represent what happened to many children of mixed parentage in pre-1960s Australia. Because his father is white, John is taken from his Aboriginal mother by officials from the government welfare office to attend a white mission school and learn English. (His mother tries to prevent this by concealing her son's light skin with charcoal from a burnt stick.) Although young John is not treated harshly, he has lost some of his freedom and is stripped of his heritage and traditions, not to mention the love of his mother. Years later, John returns with his son to the aboriginal camp where he was born, only to find that it has been abandoned. "This simple story will serve as a poignant reminder of the insensitivity with which white colonists have often dealt with native cultures," declared Nancy Menaldi-Scanlan in a *School Library Journal* review. *Horn Book* reviewer Maeve Visser Knoth called *The Burnt Stick* "an exceptional and very emotional novel," noting that it offers a powerful reminder "of the evil that can be done anywhere when governments make decisions about race and family." In a *Magpies* review of the same work, contributor Kevin Steinberger called Hill's effort "one of the outstanding children's books of recent times."

"My purpose," Hill explained to *SATA* about his books in general, "is to illuminate the inner lives of my characters; to try to elicit understanding in my readers; to use my art in such a way that they are able to contemplate these matters without themselves being damaged; and, of course, to show the power of the imagination not only to surmount crises, but also to reassert the decencies and our common humanity. We authors are fortunate in Australia that our children's book publishers support us in these endeavors. The only real test is whether or not we succeed with our material."

■ Works Cited

Knoth, Maeve Visser, review of *The Burnt Stick, Horn Book,* November-December, 1995, p. 743.
Menaldi-Scanlan, Nancy, review of *The Burnt Stick, School Library Journal,* October, 1995, pp. 133-34.
Steinberger, Kevin, review of *The Burnt Stick, Magpies,* March, 1995, p. 27.

■ For More Information See

PERIODICALS

Australian Book Review, February, 1995, p. 58.
Bulletin of the Center for Children's Books, July/August, 1995, pp. 15-16.
Kirkus Reviews, June 15, 1995.
Publishers Weekly, July 10, 1995, p. 58.
School Librarian, August, 1995, p. 108.

HILLERT, Margaret 1920-

■ Personal

Born January 22, 1920, in Saginaw, MI; daughter of Edward Carl (a tool and die maker) and A. Ilva (Sproul) Hillert. *Education:* Bay City Junior College, A.A., 1941; University of Michigan, R.N., 1944; Wayne University (now Wayne State University), A.B., 1948. *Hobbies and other interests:* Cats, walking, gardening, tennis.

■ Addresses

Home—Birmingham, MI. *Office*—Children's Department, Royal Oak Public Library, 222 East Eleven Mile Road, Royal Oak, MI 48067.

■ Career

Author, poet, and reteller. Primary school teacher in public schools in Royal Oak, MI, 1949-82. Affiliated with the Royal Oak Public Library. Lecturer at writers' conferences, library seminars, and book fairs. *Member:* International League of Children's Poets, Society of Children's Book Writers and Illustrators, Emily Dickinson Society, Poetry Society of Michigan, Detroit Women Writers.

■ Awards, Honors

David W. Longo Prize through the *Lyric,* 1990; Chicago Children's Reading Round Table Annual Award for outstanding contributions to the field of children's literature, 1991; Michigan Bookwoman of the Year, Women's National Book Association, 1993; numerous awards for her poetry from the Poetry Society of Michigan; award from the Friends of the Royal Oak Public Library for volunteerism.

■ Writings

POETRY FOR CHILDREN

Farther Than Far, illustrated by Betty Fraser, Follett, 1969.
I Like to Live in the City, Golden Press, 1970.
Who Comes to Your House?, Golden Press, 1973.
The Sleepytime Book, Golden Press, 1975.
Come Play with Me, illustrated by Kinuko Craft, Follett, 1975.
What Is It?, illustrated by Kinuko Craft, Follett, 1978.
I'm Special ... So Are You!, Hallmark Books, 1979.
Fun Days, illustrated by Joe Rogers, Follett, 1982.
The Cow That Got Her Wish, illustrated by Krystyna Stasiak, Follett, 1982.
Rabbits and Rainbows, Standard Publishing, 1985.
Dandelions and Daydreams, illustrated by Judy Hand, Standard Publishing, 1988.
Lightning Bugs and Lullabies, illustrated by Judy Hand, Standard Publishing, 1988.
God's Big Book: Verse for the Earliest Reader, illustrated by Linda Hohag, Standard Publishing, 1988.
Sing a Song of Christmas, Standard Publishing, 1989.

MARGARET HILLERT

The Sky Is Not So Far Away: Night Poems for Children, illustrated by Thomas Werner, Wordsong/Boyds Mills Press, 1996.

EASY READERS

The Three Bears (retelling), illustrated by Irma Wilde, Follett, 1963.
The Three Little Pigs (retelling), Follett, 1963.
The Funny Baby (retelling), Follett, 1963.
The Birthday Car, illustrated by Kelly Oechsli, Follett, 1966.
The Magic Beans (retelling), illustrated by Mel Pekarsky, Follett, 1966.
The Little Runaway, illustrated by Irv Anderson, Follett, 1966.
The Yellow Boat, illustrated by Ed Young, Follett, 1966.
The Snow Baby, illustrated by Liz Dauber, Follett, 1966.
Circus Fun, illustrated by Elaine Raphael, Follett, 1966.
Cinderella at the Ball (retelling), illustrated by Janet LaSalle, Follett, 1970.
A House for Little Red, illustrated by Kelly Oechsli, Follett 1970.
Little Puff, illustrated by Sid Jordan, Follett, 1973.
Play Ball, illustrated by Dick Martin, Follett, 1978.
The Cookie House (retelling), illustrated by Kinuko Craft, Follett, 1978.
The Golden Goose (retelling), illustrated by Monica Santa, Follett, 1978.
The Baby Bunny, illustrated by Robert Masheris, Follett, 1980.
What Am I? (riddles), illustrated by Sharon Elzaurdia, Follett, 1980.
Run to the Rainbow, illustrated by Barbara Corey, Follett, 1980.
Away Go the Boats, illustrated by Robert Masheris, Follett, 1980.
Not I, Not I (retelling), illustrated by Diana Magnuson, Follett, 1980.

The Little Cookie (retelling), illustrated by Ronald Charles, Follett, 1980.

Four Good Friends (retelling), illustrated by Krystyna Stasiak, Follett, 1980.

The Little Cowboy and the Big Cowboy, illustrated by Dan Siculan, Follett, 1981.

Who Goes to School?, illustrated by Nan Brooks, Follett, 1981.

City Fun, illustrated by Barbara Corey, Follett, 1981.

The Witch Who Went for a Walk, illustrated by Krystyna Stasiak, Follett, 1981.

Take a Walk, Johnny, illustrated by Yoshi Miyake, Follett, 1981.

The Purple Pussycat, illustrated by Krystyna Stasiak, Follett, 1981.

Away Go the Boats, illustrated by Robert Masheria, Follett, 1981.

The Magic Nutcracker (retelling), illustrated by Patricia Iverson, Follett, 1982.

Pinocchio (retelling), illustrated by Laurie Hamilton, Follett, 1982.

Let's Have a Play, illustrated by Sharon Eizaurdia, Follett, 1982.

Up, Up, and Away, illustrated by Robert Masheris, Follett, 1982.

I Like Things, illustrated by Lois Axeman, Follett, 1982.

Why We Have Thanksgiving, illustrated by Dan Siculan, Follett, 1982.

The Ball Book, illustrated by Nan Brooks, Follett, 1982.

Tom Thumb (retelling), illustrated by Dennis Hockerman, Follett, 1982.

The Boy and the Goats (retelling), illustrated by Yoshi Miyake, Follett, 1982.

Little Red Riding Hood (retelling), illustrated by Gwen Connelly, Follett, 1982.

The Funny Ride, illustrated by Jeozef Sumichrast, Follett, 1982.

Guess, Guess: Bible Riddles for the Earliest Readers (riddles), illustrated by Ruth O'Connell, Standard Publishing, 1988.

The Birth of Jesus: The Nativity Story for the Earliest Readers (nonfiction), illustrated by Helen Endres, Standard Publishing, 1988.

Jesus Grows Up (nonfiction), Standard Publishing, 1988.

"DEAR DRAGON" SERIES

Happy Birthday, Dear Dragon, illustrated by Carl Kock, Follett, 1977.

I Love You, Dear Dragon, illustrated by Kock, Follett, 1980.

Happy Easter, Dear Dragon, illustrated by Kock, Follett, 1980.

Let's Go, Dear Dragon, illustrated by Kock, Follett, 1980.

Merry Christmas, Dear Dragon, illustrated by Kock, Follett, 1980.

It's Halloween, Dear Dragon, illustrated by Kock, Follett, 1980.

Go to Sleep, Dear Dragon, illustrated by David Helton, Modern Curriculum Press, 1985.

Help for Dear Dragon, illustrated by Helton, Modern Curriculum Press, 1985.

Come to School, Dear Dragon, illustrated by Helton, Modern Curriculum Press, 1985.

It's Circus Time, Dear Dragon, illustrated by Helton, Modern Curriculum Press, 1985.

I Need You, Dear Dragon, illustrated by Helton, Modern Curriculum Press, 1985.

A Friend for Dear Dragon, illustrated by Helton, Modern Curriculum Press, 1985.

OTHER

Also author of *The Three Goats* (retelling for children beyond the easy-reading stage), Ernest Benn, 1973; *Let's Take a Break* and *Doing Things,* action verse collections on duplicating masters for Continental Press; *Action Verse in the Primary Classroom* for T.S. Denison; and *Seasons, Holidays, Anytime,* poems for action verse and choral speaking for Partner Press. Contributor of hundreds of poems for children and adults to numerous periodicals, including the *Horn Book Magazine, Jack and Jill, Humpty Dumpty, My Weekly Reader, Cricket, Christian Science Monitor, Saturday Evening Post, Lyric,* and *Western Humanities Review.* Work represented in anthologies, textbooks, and books on cassettes; individual poems made into transparencies and used in posters and on television programs. Hillert's books have been translated into Danish, German, Portuguese, and Swedish.

■ Sidelights

The author of seventy-six books for children, Hillert is best known as the creator of stories and poems for new readers ranging in age from five to seven years old. Popular with both young children and their teachers, she writes realistic and fantasy stories as well as combinations of the two; in addition, she is the reteller of familiar folk and fairy tales such as "Cinderella" and "The Three Bears" and children's stories such as *Pinocchio.* She has also written several volumes of poetry for children as well as a variety of individual poems for adults. In her easy readers, Hillert uses a controlled vocabulary, mostly one-syllable words and sentences light on nouns and adjectives, and designs her books to entertain children with interesting subjects and stories while helping them to develop their reading skills. In his award presentation speech to the Reading Round Table of Chicago in 1991, Tom McGowen noted, "Margaret Hillert's books aren't merely helping kids catch onto another form for entertaining, they're helping kids do something positive about their futures."

A widely published poet, Hillert has been writing poetry and stories since the third grade, although she did not start submitting her work for publication until 1961. "Nobody ever really encouraged me to try to get my stuff published," she told Barbara Woolf in the *Detroit Free Press.* "But from the time I first saw my name in print, you just couldn't keep me from submitting things." When Hillert graduated from high school, she received a scholarship to study nursing at the University of Michigan. However, teaching was her primary ambition, and she stayed a nurse just long enough to cover the cost of education courses at Wayne (now Wayne

The Sky Is Not So Far Away

Night Poems for Children

By Margaret Hillert • Illustrated by Thomas Werner

Hillert seeks to recreate the wonder of childhood dreams and nighttime adventures in this collection of poetry for children.

State) University; in 1948, she received her teacher certification. For the next thirty-four years, Hillert taught first grade at Whittier School in Royal Oak, Michigan.

As a teacher, Hillert came to the realization that the literature then available for students just starting to read was beyond their comprehension; in response, she began to write her easy readers and poetry for children. Her first collection of poetry, *Farther Than Far,* was published in 1969; one of the poems from that volume, "A Saturday Wind," has been widely reprinted and was used by the Canadian Broadcasting Corporation on their long-running children's program "Mr. Dress-Up." Hillert told Woolf: "People have said to me that it must be easy to write children's poems because I work with kids every day, but I really don't take much of my inspiration from my classroom work. Most of what is in *Farther Than Far* came from my own experiences as a child." Commenting on *Farther Than Far,* May Sarton wrote, "I became a child again, recognizing everything. This is a rare gift ... to evoke so much without

'cuteness' or condescension." Hillert's recent collection *The Sky Is Not So Far Away* includes poems for children that center on nighttime themes. In her *School Library Journal* review, Melissa Hudak notes that with this book Hillert "proves herself to be an accomplished poet as well" as a writer of easy readers, and that she writes with "hidden depth that often emerges only with a third or fourth reading"; a reviewer in *Publishers Weekly* comments that her poetry here "is sweet without being entirely corny."

Hillert is perhaps best known for her "Dear Dragon" series of easy-to-read fantasies about a small boy and his fire-breathing companion. These works, which feature childhood experiences such as enjoying holidays and going to school and the circus, are characterized by Hillert's use of short sentences and repetition of certain words, all of which are reprinted at the back of each book.

■ Works Cited

Sarton, May, comments on *Farther Than Far,* in "Boyds Mills Press Presents Margaret Hillert," promotional piece published by Boyds Mills Press, 1996.

Hudak, Melissa, review of *The Sky Is Not So Far Away, School Library Journal,* September, 1996.

McGowen, Tom, in a transcript of his presentation speech, Children's Round Table Reading Award, Chicago, 1991.

Review of *The Sky Is Not So Far Away, Publishers Weekly,* August 19, 1996.

Woolf, Barbara, "The Royal Oak Teacher Who Writes Poems and Stories Your Children May Be Reading," *Detroit Free Press,* May 6, 1973.

■ For More Information See

BOOKS

Hopkins, Lee Bennett, *Pass the Poetry, Please,* Citation Press, 1972.

Janeczko, Paul, *The Place My Words Are Looking For,* Bradbury, 1990.

LeMaster, J. R., *Poets of the Midwest,* Young Publications, 1966.

PERIODICALS

Bulletin of the Center for Children's Books, September, 1980, p. 12.

Detroit News, September 9, 1996.

School Library Journal, September, 1978, p. 116; School Library Journal, October, 1980, p. 161; December, 1980, p. 70; March, 1985, p. 152.

* * *

HOGARTH, Grace (Weston) Allen 1905-1995
(Grace Allen; Amelia Gay; Allen Weston, a joint pseudonym)

■ Personal

Born November 5, 1905, in Newton, MA: died November 12, 1995; daughter of John Weston (a lawyer) and Caroline (Hills) Allen; married William David Hogarth, August 22, 1936 (died, 1965); married Philip Livermore Sayles, May 22, 1971 (divorced, 1977); children: (first marriage) David Allen, Caroline Mary Barron. *Education:* Attended University of California, Berkeley, 1924-25; Vassar College, A.B., 1927; graduate study at Massachusetts School of Art, 1927-28, and Yale University, 1928-29. *Religion:* Church of England.

■ Career

Oxford University Press, 1929-38, staff artist in New York City, 1929-36, then editor of children's books in London, England, 1936-38; editor of children's books, Chatto & Windus, London, 1938-39, then Houghton Mifflin Co., Boston, MA, 1940-43; British scout for Houghton Mifflin, London, 1943-47, and other U.S. publishers, 1947-56; Constable & Co. Ltd., London, editor of children's books, 1956-63, managing director of Constable Young Books, 1963-68, chairperson, 1966-68; Longman, London, managing director of Longman Young Books, 1968, director, 1968-73; William Collins, London, general editor of Classics for Today and Lifetime Library, beginning 1971. Editor-in-chief, *My Weekly Reader* Family Book Service's Lifetime Library, 1968-71. Member of board of governors, North London and Camden Schools for Girls, 1963-71.

■ Writings

FOR CHILDREN

(And illustrator) *A Bible A B C,* Stokes (Philadelphia), 1940.

(With Joan Colebrook) *Australia: The Island Continent,* illustrated by Howard W. Willard, Houghton, 1943.

(As Amelia Gay) *Lucy's League,* illustrated by Nora S. Unwin, Hodder & Stoughton, 1950, reprinted under name Grace Allen Hogarth, Harcourt, 1951.

(As Amelia Gay) *John's Journey,* illustrated by Nora S. Unwin, Hodder & Stoughton, 1952, reprinted under name Grace Allen Hogarth, Harcourt, 1952.

The Funny Guy, illustrated by Fritz Wegner, Harcourt, 1955.

As a May Morning, Harcourt, 1958.

A Sister for Helen, illustrated by Pat Marriott, Deutsch, 1976.

ADULT NOVELS

(As Grace Allen) *This to Be Love,* J. Cape, 1949.

The End of Summer, J. Cape, 1951.

Children of This World, J. Cape, 1953.

(With Andre Norton, as Allen Weston) *Murders for Sale,* Hammond, 1954, published under name Grace Allen Hogarth as *Sneeze on Sunday,* Tor, 1992.

OTHER

(Editor with daughter, Caroline Hogarth) *American Cooking for English Kitchens,* Hamish Hamilton, 1957.

(Editor with Lee Kingman and Harriet Quimby) *Illustrators of Children's Books, 1967-1976,* Horn Book, 1978.

Contributor to periodicals, including *Horn Book.*

■ Sidelights

An author of many popular books for children and a noted editor of children's titles at major publishing houses, Grace Allen Hogarth has made significant contributions to the genre of children's literature. "Perhaps because she started her career as an art student her interest in book illustration has always been as keen as her insistence on quality in writing," notes Ann Bartholomew in *Twentieth-Century Children's Writers.* Indeed, through Hogarth's active involvement in children's book publishing in both the United States, where she was born, and England, her adopted country, she has allowed children in both countries to share some of the best juvenile literature written during the middle decades of the twentieth century.

Born in Newton, Massachusetts, in 1905, Hogarth began her involvement in children's writing via a rather indirect route—through training in illustration. After graduating from Vassar College and attending two years of art school, she got a job at the American branch of England's prestigious Oxford University Press. There Hogarth worked as a staff artist, "illustrating and editing some of the books on the children's list and ... designing jacket, laying out ads, etc.," as she noted in *Twentieth-Century Children's Literature.* "Although I am not an artist of much ability, I found this experience and training of the greatest help to me when I became a publisher of books for children." Transferred from New York City to London, England, in 1936, Hogarth was promoted to editor of children's books, a position she held at several other noted British publishing houses through the next several decades. From 1943-56, while she was busy raising her two children, she remained involved in the world of children's books by working as a publisher's representative for both U.S. and British firms. Hogarth returned to publishing full-time after 1956, and remained in the field until 1973.

Helen meets her new little sister Katie in Grace Allen Hogarth's *A Sister for Helen,* illustrated by Pat Marriott.

Hogarth's first book for children, *A Bible A B C,* was published in 1940. With its three-color illustrations based on well-known characters and events from the Bible, the book was praised by *Library Journal* contributor Siddie Joe Johnson as an "ideal picture book for the child who has just started Sunday School." *Lucy's League,* published in 1950, was the first of Hogarth's novels for older readers and reflected its author's desire that children from both England and the United States gain a fuller understanding of each other. In this tale London-born Lucy Edwards and her family are planning a trip to visit her Granny Gay in the States; in imitation of the postwar League of Nations, Lucy founds her own "international" league to save money for her overseas holiday. In a sequel, *John's Journey,* the Edwards family's trip to the United States is recounted from the point of view of Lucy's brother. Traveling aboard a steamship bound for Cape Cod, Lucy and John befriend Roger, an American boy who, they learn, has a sister who has been missing for over six years. The mystery of the girl's whereabouts carries the story, with its backdrop of Granny Gay's quaint Cape Cod cottage and the many "oddities" of American life.

The Funny Guy is among the most popular of Hogarth's books for young readers. Taking place in Boston in the early years of the twentieth century, the story features a shy twelve-year-old girl named Helen. With her mother hospitalized and her father devoting most of his time to helping his wife recover from her illness, only-child Helen becomes withdrawn, "odd" in the opinion of her schoolmates. Because of her erratic behavior, she is dubbed the "funny guy" and taunted by everyone except a handful of close friends. Helen finds refuge in reading, writing for *St. Nicholas* magazine, and in setting herself the challenge of earning enough money to buy a bicycle, thereby demonstrating "a kind of grit that ultimately wins her the right to be herself, and not a shadow of others," according to one *Kirkus Reviews* critic. Hogarth's 1976 story *A Sister for Helen* takes place during the same period and features a young protagonist again facing personal trials—and, indeed, life-threatening situations—that change her perceptions of life and the relationships around her. And in *As a May Morning,* written for older readers, seventeen-year-old Jenny MacArthur experiences heartbreak when she falls in love with a U.S. exchange student staying with her family in London for the summer. Like all of Hogarth's stories, *As a May Morning* is a sensitive depiction of intricate and ever-changing human relationships, as well as the individual's progress toward self-awareness and acceptance.

"I owe a great deal of success in life to Vassar College," Hogarth once noted, "not because I was a good student, but because Vassar gave me confidence. I wrote an article for the *Vassar Alumnae/i Quarterly,* 'Confession of a Liberated Woman,' which expresses my thoughts on this subject. In a letter to *Vassar Quarterly* I was attacked as 'neither a liberated woman nor a feminist' because I had 'come to accept as justified male condescension and discrimination against women.' I still feel this criticism to be untrue. Normal women who want home, family, and career, which I did, must have the cooperation and support of their husbands and children."

In addition to her books for young people, Hogarth was the author of several adult novels, as well as *Australia: The Island Continent,* a heavily illustrated work of nonfiction published in 1943; she also co-edited *American Cooking for English Kitchens* with her daughter, Caroline Hogarth.

■ Works Cited

Bartholomew, Ann, "Grace (Weston) Hogarth," *Twentieth-Century Children's Writers,* 4th edition, St. James Press, 1995, pp. 463-64.
Review of *The Funny Guy, Kirkus Reviews,* December 15, 1954, p. 809.
Johnson, Siddie Joe, review of *A Bible A B C, Library Journal,* August, 1941, p. 108.

■ For More Information See

PERIODICALS

Horn Book, March-April, 1951, p. 102; April, 1955, p. 112; June, 1958, p. 208.
Junior Bookshelf, April, 1977.
Library Journal, April 15, 1958, p. 1291.
New York Times Book Review, March 4, 1951, p. 26.*

*   *   *

HOLLANDER, Paul
See SILVERBERG, Robert

*   *   *

HOLLINGSWORTH, Mary 1947-
(Mary Shrode; Professor Scribbler, a pseudonym)

■ Personal

Born October 18, 1947, in Dallas, TX; daughter of Clyde E. (a minister) and Thelma G. (a homemaker; maiden name, Hargrave) Shrode. *Education:* Abilene Christian University, B.S.Ed., 1970. *Politics:* Independent. *Hobbies and other interests:* Singing, travel, collecting Hummel figurines and miniature and rare books.

■ Addresses

Home—1507 Shirley Way, Bedford, TX 76022-6737.
Office—Shady Oaks Studio, 1507 Shirley Way, Bedford, TX, 76022-6737.

■ Career

Sweet Publishing, Fort Worth, TX, managing editor, 1984-95; Shady Oaks Studio, Bedford, TX, owner, author, editor, and consultant, 1988—; owner of A Capella Junction, a mail order distributor of *a capella*

MARY HOLLINGSWORTH

music, 1991—. Special music ministry leader, Richland Hills Church of Christ, 1985—. President, Richland Hills Singers, 1985-94; member of Infinity, an *a capella* jazz ensemble, 1985—. *Member:* Christian Booksellers Association, Society of Children's Book Writers and Illustrators, Christian Education Association (member of board of directors, 1993-96).

■ Awards, Honors

Matrix Award, Women in Advertising Association, for *Just Imagine! with Barney;* included on C. S. Lewis All-Time Top Ten Favorite List, 1993, for *Polka Dots, Stripes, Humps, 'n' Hatracks;* Gold Award, Evangelical Christian Publishers Association, 1995, for *My Little Bible.* Several of her books have appeared on Christian best-seller lists.

■ Writings

JUVENILES

International Children's Story Bible, Word Inc. (Dallas, TX), 1991.
(Reteller) *My Little Bible,* Wordkids (Dallas), 1991.
The Captain, the Countess, and Cobby the Swabby: A Book about Honor, illustrated by Daniel J. Hochstatter, Chariot Family Publishing (Elgin, IL), 1992.

Parrots, Pirates, and Walking the Plank: A Book about Obeying, illustrated by Daniel J. Hochstatter, Chariot Family Publishing, 1992.

A Girl's Diary of Prayers, illustrated by Lois Rosio Sprague, Thomas Nelson (Nashville), 1992.

A Boy's Book of Prayers, illustrated by Lois Rosio Sprague, Thomas Nelson, 1992.

(Under name Mary Shrode) *Just Imagine! with Barney,* illustrated by Mary Grace Eubank, Lyons Group, 1992.

Journey to Jesus: A Four-in-One Story, illustrated by Mary Grace Eubank, Baker Book House (Grand Rapids, MI), 1993.

The Kids-Life Bible Storybook, illustrated by Rick Incrocci, Chariot Family Publishing, 1994.

The Children's Topical Bible, Honor Books (Rapid City, SD), 1994, with activity package, 1994.

Bumper and Noah, Chariot Family Publishing, 1994.

Songs and Rhymes for Wiggle Worms, Questar Publishers (Sisters, OR), 1995.

Who Is Jesus?, Questar Publishers, 1995.

What Does Jesus Say?, Questar Publishers, 1995.

The Story of Jesus, Questar Publishers, 1995.

Bumper the Dinosaur, Chariot Family Publishing, 1996.

Into My Heart: A Treasury of Songs and Rhymes, Questar Publishers, 1996.

The Preschooler's Picture-Reading Bible, Baker Book House, in press.

The Time Trax Bible, Baker Book House, in press.

"CHILDREN OF THE KING" SERIES

The King's Alphabet: A Bible Book about Letters, Worthy Publications (Fort Worth, TX), 1988.

The King's Numbers: A Bible Book about Counting, Worthy Publications, 1988.

The King's Workers: A Bible Book about Serving, Word Inc., 1990.

The King's Manners: A Bible Book about Courtesy, Word Inc., 1990.

The King's Animals: A Bible Book about God's Creatures, Word Inc., 1991.

The King's Children: A Bible Book about God's People, Word Inc., 1991.

"GOD'S HAPPY FOREST" SERIES; ILLUSTRATED BY MARY GRACE EUBANK

Polka Dots, Stripes, Humps, 'n' Hatracks: How God Created Happy Forest, Brownlow (Fort Worth, TX), 1990.

Twizzler, the Unlikely Hero: Bigger Is Not Always Better, Brownlow, 1990.

Christmas in Happy Forest: Love Is the Greatest Gift, Brownlow, 1990.

"MY VERY FIRST BOOK" SERIES; ILLUSTRATED BY RICK INCROCCI; ALL PUBLISHED BY THOMAS NELSON

My Very First Book of Bible Heroes, 1993.

My Very First Book of Bible Lessons, 1993.

My Very First Book of Bible Words, 1993.

My Very First Book of Prayers, 1993.

My Very First Book on God, 1994.

My Very First Book of God's Animals—and Other Creatures, 1994.

My Very First Book of Bible Questions, 1994.

My Very First Book of Bible Fun Facts, 1994.

UNDER PSEUDONYM PROFESSOR SCRIBBLER; ILLUSTRATED BY DAN PEELER

Charlie and the Shabby Tabby: Learning How to Be a Real Friend, Brownlow, 1989.

Charlie and the Missing Music: Learning about God's Concern for the Lost, Brownlow, 1989.

Charlie and the Jinglemouse: Learning about God's Forgiveness, Brownlow, 1989.

Charlie and the Gold Mine: Learning What's Really Valuable in Life, Brownlow, 1989.

OTHER

Help! I Need a Bulletin Board, Quality Publications (Abilene, TX), 1975.

For Mom with Love, Brownlow, 1987.

A Few Hallelujas for Your Ho-Hums: A Lighthearted Look at Life, Brownlow, 1988.

Just between Friends, Brownlow, 1988.

It's a One-derful Life! A Single's Celebration, Brownlow, 1989.

Rainbows, C. R. Gibson (Norwalk, CT), 1989.

Apple Blossoms: A Tribute to Teachers, C. R. Gibson, 1990.

(With Charlotte A. Greeson and Michael Washburn) *The Grief Adjustment Guide: A Pathway through Pain,* Questar Publishers, 1990.

(With Charlotte A. Greeson and Michael Washburn) *The Divorce Recovery Guide,* Questar Publishers, 1991.

(Compiler) *Together Forever: Reflections on the Joys of Marriage,* Word Inc., 1993.

(Compiler) *On Raising Children: Lessons on Love and Limits,* Word Inc., 1993.

(With Fred and Anna Kendall) *Speaking of Love,* Thomas Nelson, 1995.

Reborn! (play), produced in Fort Worth, TX, 1995.

Also author of numerous stories, plays, poetry, and songs; also author of videos based on some of her books. Coeditor, *The International Children's Bible;* editorial director, *The Everyday Study Bible: New Century Version,* Word, 1996; editor of other books. Executive editor, *TEACH Newsletter,* 1985-95. Contributor of articles to periodicals.

Some of Hollingsworth's work has been translated into foreign languages.

■ Work in Progress

The Selfish Giant, a retelling of Oscar Wilde's classic with illustrations by Bill Bell; *Solomon's Song,* a tale of the endangered wolf, illustrations by Lori Salisbury; *A Candle in the Darkness,* an adult book with Dr. M. Norvel Young; *Four-Part Harmony,* a four-in-one storybook; *Working Your Way through Grief,* a personal workbook for people in pain; *The Good Book: The Right-Order Bible for Kids,* for Grapevine Press.

■ Sidelights

Mary Hollingsworth told *SATA:* "As a preschooler I was coaxed into taking a nap by my mom, who took turns with me making up stories and telling them to each other. I'm sure Mom had no idea what long-range impact that little creative ritual would have on me. No doubt, my storytelling career began with my mom, my teddy bear, and my nap blankie.

"Today writing is not only my living but also my life. I can't survive without it, financially or emotionally. I cannot *not* write any more than happy children cannot *not* play. My writing is the essence of me. If you want to know my heart and mind, read my writing.

"I write in various areas and genres—adult nonfiction, gift books, children's nonfiction, children's fiction, plays, songs, articles, scripts, cover copy for books, study guides, and whatever else comes my way. The writing market changes often, and I must be flexible enough to go with the flow, or the flow will simply go without me. Besides, I enjoy the variety.

"Writer's block, to me, is the result of insufficient training. I don't believe in writer's block; it's a luxury that I cannot afford. I write on demand, whether or not I'm in the mood, and whether or not it was my inspiration or someone else's. It's the only way to make it as a freelancer, in my opinion.

"Many people think *Just Imagine! with Barney* is my most important book. And while it was fun to see that one do so well, it is definitely not my most important work. The most significant book I've ever worked on, or ever hope to work on, was the first translation of the Bible ever done for children—*The International Children's Bible.* The task was both humbling and exhilarating. While that book certainly does not carry my name, the experience of working on God's Word changed my career goal and writing style forever. It made me painfully aware that the reader's being able to understand the message far outweighs the importance of my being able to show off my vocabulary and writing flair. It simplified my style, my message, and my life.

"The greatest thrill for me as a writer is to hear children giggling at something funny I wrote, or to have a mother tell me she cried all the way through *For Mom with Love.* One little four-year-old boy came running up to me and said, 'Hi, Professor Scribbler! I can say your book.' Thinking he had made a mistake, I said, 'You mean you can *read* my book?' 'No,' he said, 'I can *say* your book.' And he proceeded to recite from memory the entire text of *The King's Numbers.* I was astounded and so humbled by that incident. What an incredible responsibility I have as a children's author. They trust me; they learn from me; they believe anything I write. It's a fearful and wonderful thing to write for children.

"My right brain loves the freedom to be out of control, but my left brain likes my carefully orchestrated rut. I'm normally at my desk by nine o'clock and work consis-

tently until about five or six. It's a habit developed through the years of working for major corporations and other people. It fits me; it works; I like it. I won't deny a few midnight inspirations and three a.m. creative storms, but those are not the norm for me. My rut is carpeted, draped, and air-conditioned. It's me.

"A glorious parade of writers, poets, composers, playwrights, and others have influenced my work so far. Among them are my all-time favorites: Dr. Seuss, Beatrix Potter, Dr. V. Gilbert Beers, C. S. Lewis, and Calvin Miller. Illustrators that delight me the most are Mary Grace Eubank, Peter Spier, the Nick Butterworth and Mick Inkpen team, the Disney animators, and many others. I love the ones whose little kids inside them are obviously alive and well; they're the best.

"Recently I received a German version of *My Little Bible* from the German publisher. What fun to see my work go international and to think that I might have some small influence even on children around the globe.

"Three other unforgettable experiences stand out for me. First, some of my children's picture books have been developed into animated videos. Second, one of my works is a play, and I got to be at the premiere performance. And third, some of my lyrics have been put to music. The astonishment of seeing and hearing your words moving and speaking, coming to life, dancing across a television screen, and floating on the wind as music, is overwhelming ... at least for me. Nothing can compare to that thrill.

"Every person alive has a legitimate story to tell, and most of us believe our stories deserve book status. Unfortunately, most aspiring writers are unwilling to devote the time, money, and effort to really learn the trade, to do their homework, to become the best in the industry in order to compete with the professionals. Most of the published authors and illustrators I know didn't just 'luck into it.' They are educated, trained, and experienced people, who continually study and upgrade their skills and abilities. They know they have to earn their place in the industry, and they don't expect a handout from publishers and other professionals. Writing and illustrating are careers, not just hobbies. If they are not your career, then you shouldn't expect to make a living at it. If you want to make them your living, then they must become your life.

"If I can make one life a little brighter: if one sentence I write strikes a note of hope, if one poem or song I write lives after I'm gone to encourage other people or make a child laugh, then I will consider myself a successful writer. In truth, I write for God and for me. If other people happen to listen in and are blessed, that's good. If no one ever sees a word I write, I am no less a writer in the eyes of God or when I look in the mirror. Writing is life; mine will stop simultaneously."

HOSTETLER, Marian 1932-

■ Personal

Born February 9, 1932, in Ohio; daughter of M. Harry (a grocer; in insurance) and Esther (a homemaker) Hostetler. *Education:* Goshen College, B.A., 1954; Goshen Biblical Seminary, graduate study, 1957-58; attended Alliance Francaise, Paris, 1960; Indiana University, M.S. (education), 1973. *Religion:* Christian (Mennonite). *Hobbies and other interests:* Writing, reading, painting, music, archeology.

■ Addresses

Home—57717 Seventh St., Elkhart, IN 46517.

■ Career

Mennonite Board of Missions, Elkhart, IN, editorial assistant, 1958-60, teacher in Algeria, 1961-70, writer/editor in Ivory Coast, 1986; Concord Community Schools, Elkhart, elementary teacher, 1970-88; Eastern Mennonite Missions, Salunga, PA, teacher of English as a foreign language in Somalia and Djibouti, 1988-93; currently semi-retired and working part-time for Elkhart Public Library.

MARIAN HOSTETLER

■ Writings

FOR CHILDREN

African Adventure, Herald Press, 1976.
Journey to Jerusalem, Herald Press, 1978.
Fear in Algeria, Herald Press, 1979.
Secret in the City, Herald Press, 1980.
Mystery at the Mall, Herald Press, 1985.
We Knew Paul, Herald Press, 1992.
We Knew Jesus, Herald Press, 1994.

OTHER

Foundation Series Curriculum, Grade 3, Quarter 2, Herald Press, 1977.
(Translator) Pierre Widmer, *Some People Are Throwing You into Confusion,* Herald Press, 1984.
They Loved Their Enemies: True Stories of African Christians, Herald Press, 1988.

Several of Hostetler's works have been translated into Finnish, French, German, Portuguese, and Spanish.

■ Work in Progress

What Is Islam? Who Are the Muslims?, completed but without a publisher; *The Poisoned Potion,* a mystery set in Philippi during New Testament times, completed but unpublished so far.

■ Sidelights

Marian Hostetler told *SATA:* "My first four books of fiction for children are based on my own experiences in Chad (*African Adventure*), the Holy Land (*Journey to Jerusalem*), Algeria (*Fear in Algeria*), and as a church service volunteer in the U.S. (*Secret in the City*). Each had a background theme such as famine and hunger, the political Arab/Israeli situation, Christianity in an Islamic country, the relation of deed and words in Christian service.

"My fifth book, *Mystery at the Mall,* was, I guess, based on my love of reading mysteries. It takes place in that mini-city, The Mall, with the mall manager's daughter playing detective when some robberies occur.

"The sixth, *They Loved Their Enemies,* is nonfiction—true stories about African Christians, from early days to the present, who used Jesus's way of peace when confronted with persecution and death. It has been translated into French and German, but even better, has been published in English in Nairobi, Kenya, for use in Sudan, which has had civil war for many years, as well as being published in English in Nigeria for use in Liberia, also involved in civil war and its aftermath. This book is not specifically for children.

"My last two published books, *We Knew Jesus* and *We Knew Paul,* are Biblical fiction, each chapter supposedly written or told by a young person who knew Jesus or Paul (i.e., Zaccheus's daughter, who was also up in the tree). I wrote them because of my interest in the Bible and in Biblical times, and the desire to make the people of the Bible more real to children."

■ For More Information See

PERIODICALS

Bookstore Journal, January, 1993.
Christian Library Journal, January, 1996.
Church and Synagogue Libraries, November/December, 1994.
Librarian's World, 3rd quarter, 1992-93; summer, 1995.
School Library Journal, January, 1977, p. 93; September, 1978, p. 139; April, 1980, p. 11.

*   *   *

HUNT, Irene 1907-

■ Personal

Born May 18, 1907, in Pontiac, IL; daughter of Franklin Pierce and Sarah (Land) Hunt. *Education:* University of Illinois, A.B., 1939; University of Minnesota, M.A., 1946; graduate work at the University of Colorado, Boulder.

■ Addresses

Home—2307 Brookshire, West Champaign, IL 61821.

■ Career

Oak Park Public Schools, Oak Park, IL, teacher of French and English, 1930-45; University of South Dakota, Vermillion, instructor in psychology, 1946-50; Cicero Public Schools, Cicero, IL, teacher, 1950-65, consultant and director of language arts, 1965-69; writer, 1964—.

■ Awards, Honors

Charles W. Follett Award, 1964, American Notable Book Award, 1965, Newbery Honor Book citation, 1965, Dorothy Canfield Fisher Award, 1965, Clara Ingram Judson Memorial Award, 1965, Lewis Carroll Shelf Award, 1966, and American Library Association Notable Book citation, all for *Across Five Aprils;* Newbery Medal, 1967, and International Board on Books for Young People Honor List citation, 1970, both for *Up a Road Slowly;* Friends of Literature Award and Charles W. Follett Award, both 1971, both for *No Promises in the Wind;* Omar's Book Award, for *The Lottery Rose;* Certificate in Recognition of Contribution to Children's Literature, Twelfth Annual Children's Literature Festival, Central Missouri State University, 1980; Parents' Choice Award, 1985, for *The Everlasting Hills.*

■ Writings

Across Five Aprils, Follett, 1964, Bodley Head (London), 1965.
Up a Road Slowly, Follett, 1966, Macdonald (London), 1967.

IRENE HUNT

Trail of Apple Blossoms, illustrated by Don Bolognese, Follett, 1968, Blackie (London), 1970.
No Promises in the Wind, Follett, 1970.
The Lottery Rose, Scribner, 1976.
William, Scribner, 1978.
Claws of a Young Century, Scribner, 1980.
The Everlasting Hills, Scribner, 1985.

Also contributor to *Horn Book,* August, 1967, and *The Writer's Handbook,* edited by A. S. Burack, 1973. Several of Hunt's manuscripts are housed in the Kerlan Collection of the University of Minnesota at Minneapolis.

■ Adaptations

No Promises in the Wind has been optioned for a motion picture.

■ Sidelights

"With her first book, *Across Five Aprils,*" writes Clyde Robert Bulla in *Twentieth-Century Children's Writers,* "Irene Hunt established herself as one of America's finest historical novelists." In her works Hunt explores places and time periods ranging from 1860s Illinois to the Depression-era Rocky Mountains. Despite what Zena Sutherland of the *Bulletin of the Center for Children's Books* calls her "historically authenticated" details, however, Hunt's strength lies in creating realistic characters learning to cope with their problems and maturing in the process. "Brilliant characterization, a telling sense of story, an uncanny ability to balance fact and fiction, and compassionate, graceful writing mark

Hunt's small but distinguished body of work," maintains commentator Sheryl Lee Saunders in *Children's Books and Their Creators*. Hunt's devotion to quality literature for children brought her a Newbery honor citation in 1965 for *Across Five Aprils,* and her second book, *Up a Road Slowly,* won the Medal itself in 1967. "She has proven that she can write good books for children that please adults as well," notes Philip A. Sadler in the *Dictionary of Literary Biography,* "and she has established an international audience."

Hunt was born in Pontiac, Illinois—a small town about halfway between Springfield and Chicago—in 1907. When she was still quite young, however, her parents, Franklin and Sarah Hunt, moved to Newton, in the southeastern corner of the state. The family was living there in 1914 when her father died. Hunt and her mother relocated to her grandparents' farm nearby. She formed a close relationship with her grandfather, who had grown up during the Civil War and had a plentiful stock of stories about his childhood experiences. Hunt

IRENE HUNT

ACROSS FIVE APRILS

NEWBERY MEDAL HONOR BOOK

"...An intriguing and beautifully written book, a prize to those who take the time to read it, whatever their ages."
—THE NEW YORK TIMES

BERKLEY · 0-425-10241-6 · [$4.99 CANADA] · $3.99 U.S.

Told from the viewpoint of a boy growing to adulthood, Hunt's acclaimed tale of a border-state family divided by the Civil War was inspired by stories from her grandfather.

later drew on her grandfather's memories as the inspiration for *Across Five Aprils.* She based *Up a Road Slowly* on her own experiences.

Hunt began her career as a schoolteacher. For fifteen years, from 1930 until 1945, she worked as a teacher of French and English in the school system of Oak Park, Illinois, a suburb of Chicago. She earned her bachelor's degree from the University of Illinois at Urbana in 1939, and went on to obtain a master's degree from the University of Minnesota at Minneapolis in 1946. Hunt taught psychology at the University of South Dakota in Vermillion for the next four years before returning to Illinois. From 1950 until her retirement in 1969 she taught in the school system in Cicero, Illinois, another Chicago suburb. In her position as director of language arts Hunt found that good historical fiction for younger readers, which she felt was an effective teaching tool, was in short supply. *Across Five Aprils,* Sadler reveals, was "written to fit the needs of her students."

Across Five Aprils differs from other stories about the Civil War, such as Stephen Crane's *The Red Badge of Courage,* because the action of the war takes place, for the most part, elsewhere. The focus of the story is nine-year-old Jethro Creighton and how he grows and matures while the war rages on. "Jethro experiences the war through his relationships with his parents," writes Sadler, "his sisters, Jenny and Mary; his brothers, John and Bill; and his schoolmaster, Shadrach Yale." He has to learn to accept the fact that his brothers enlist to fight for different sides, John for the Union and Bill for the Confederacy. "The family respects their rights to act on their beliefs," Sadler states, "but because Bill's sympathies are with the Confederacy, the family is labeled 'Copperheads' and slated for retribution." "Once the pampered baby of the family," Patricia L. Bradley reveals in *Twentieth-Century Young Adult Writers,* "Jethro advances to adult status amid the disintegration of the family unit in which he had once felt security." In addition, he has to take up most of the responsibilities for the farm when his father suffers a heart attack. "At the end of the war," Sadler concludes, "Jethro, who has come to a knowledgeable understanding of it through letters and conversations, is taken east to school by Shadrach and Jenny, who are now married."

Hunt depicts the destruction and remaking of the Creighton family as a model of the destruction of the United States during the Civil War and the Reconstruction period. One major character, Jethro's cousin Ed, deserts from the Union Army and writes in desperation to President Lincoln for a pardon. Lincoln responds by offering to forgive all the deserters in Ed's party. "Hunt's research of historical details is impeccable," declares Bradley, "and her use of her grandfather's memories of his childhood during the war gives the reader a sense of great intimacy with the lives of the characters." Hunt has, according to a reviewer for *Booklist,* "in an uncommonly fine narrative, created living characters and vividly reconstructed a crucial period of history." "It is withal an intriguing and beautifully written book," states *New York Times Book*

Review contributor John K. Bettersworth—"a prize to those who take the time to read it, whatever their ages."

Up a Road Slowly, Hunt's second book, chronicles ten years in the life of Julie Trelling. Julie's mother dies when she is only seven years old. Her father and her beloved older sister, unable to care for her, send Julie to live with her Aunt Cordelia, a country schoolteacher. "Willful and adventurous," Bradley declares, "Julie clashes frequently with her aunt, a strict and duty-bound woman who nonetheless exerts a loving and powerful influence over Julie." Despite her early problems, Julie matures into a gracious young lady. "Miss Hunt," claims Constantine Georgiou in *Children and Their Literature,* "relates with warmth and sympathetic insight the story of a young girl's growth to maturity."

Critics praised Hunt's depiction of her characters and her grasp of language and difficult themes in *Up a Road Slowly.* "Treating the story with a detached realism tempered with love," Sadler asserts, "Hunt introduces themes of jealousy, first love, parent-child and sibling relationships, foster-family relationships, and snobbishness and handles them in fresh new ways." Ruth Hill Viguers, writing in *Horn Book,* suggests that, while the characters in *Up a Road Slowly* "are no more unusual and varied than are most people's families and friends," Hunt "sees them so much more clearly ... and gives them such vivid life that the reader is quickly and intensely interested in them." "She breaks new ground," concludes Sadler, "shattering old taboos in children's literature, to produce a book devoid of the artificiality and superficiality of many of the teenage novels of the time." "The author is adept at distinguishing the genuine from the spurious," writes a reviewer for *Virginia Kirkus' Service.* "Julie *is* a genuine character, and girls who go up the road with her will share in her growing up."

Like *Across Five Aprils, Up a Road Slowly* draws on Hunt's family history. It reflects her own experience growing up in relative isolation with only one parent after the death of the other. "Just as Hunt had been lonely, bewildered, and frightened upon the loss of her father," Sadler states, "another little girl ... might, in her loneliness, wander into the woods quoting verses from Edna St. Vincent Millay or Shakespeare." Hunt, asserts *New York Times Book Review* contributor Dorothy M. Broderick, "brings off a difficult tour de force and turns personal reminiscence into art." Hunt herself acknowledged this debt in her Newbery acceptance speech, published in *Horn Book.* "Often children are troubled and in a state of guilt," Hunt wrote. "One can say to them, 'You are not unique. There is in all of us only a thin veneer of civilization that separates us from the primitive.'"

Trail of Apple Blossoms, Hunt's third book, drew for its inspiration on the American folk hero John Chapman, better known as Johnny Appleseed. The book "is not a biography, but a historical novel," Bulla reveals, "picturing Johnny Appleseed as he may have been—a heroic man with a reverence for life whose beneficent influence

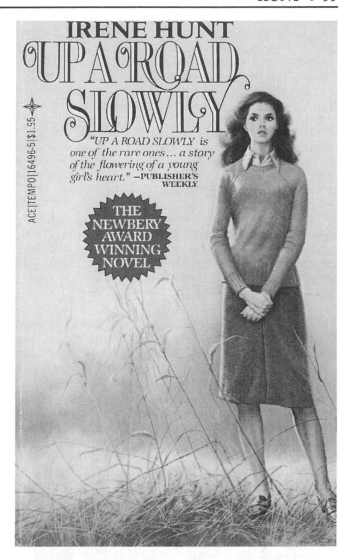

Hunt's Newbery Medal-winning coming-of-age novel chronicles ten critical years in the life of Julie Trelling following the tragic death of her mother.

touched pioneer America." *Trail of Apple Blossoms* focuses not on Chapman's traditional planting and sowing of apple seeds, but on his reputation as a man of peace and a lover of life. The narrator of the story is Hoke Bryant, who is traveling with his parents and his two-year-old sister Rachel from their old home in Boston to a new place in the Ohio Valley. During the trip, Rachel becomes ill and refuses to eat. The Bryants encounter Chapman, who uses his skills to coax Rachel into eating. He becomes a close friend of the Bryant family and his gentle philosophy inspires the adult Hoke to take up a career as a minister. "Irene Hunt," declares Dorothy M. Broderick in the *New York Times Book Review,* "has written one of the best accounts of the gentle man who would harm neither man nor beast." *School Library Journal* contributor Helen Armstrong claims that in *Trail of Apple Blossoms* Hunt "has endowed her subject with a spiritual quality which shines through the story."

In *No Promises in the Wind,* Hunt moves on to the twentieth century and the era of the Great Depression.

The Grodowski brothers, Josh and his little brother Joey, flee their home and their negligent father. In the company of Howie, a friend, the two hop a freight train for the west. However, Howie slips beneath the wheels of a freight car and is killed. Josh and Joey travel on, finding both trials and comfort in their travels. "They are befriended by a kindly truck driver who treats them as his own sons," Sadler writes. "When Josh recovers from a serious illness, the boys leave their benefactor and continue on their wanderings. Joining a carnival group, they again find others who will share with them their meager substance as well as their love.... Even the hungry hoboes offer assistance to the boys." Eventually the boys return home and are reconciled with their repentant father. "With all the problems that exist today," Ruth Hill Viguers writes in *Horn Book,* "such an honest picture of one of our country's most tragic periods may give readers a wider perspective. It is a deeply moving story."

"The writer who takes on a subject like child abuse," writes author Betsy Byars in the *New York Times Book Review,* "faces a problem—whether to show the deed in all its headline horror or to soften it for young readers." *The Lottery Rose* is Hunt's story of Georgie Burgess, neglected by his alcoholic mother and abused by her boyfriend. "In a lottery held by the new owners of a local grocery story, Georgie wins a rose bush," Byars notes. "Beautiful flowers ... are the only meaningful things in his life, and he lavishes his concern on finding a place to plant his rose bush." After a particularly brutal beating Georgie is placed in a Catholic boarding school, where he encounters Mollie Harper, who is in mourning for her husband and son. "In the passage of time," Sadler explains, "Georgie emerges from his withdrawn state." He makes friends with Mrs. Harper's surviving son Robin and, when Robin is lost in an accident, gains her acceptance. "Though the book may not be as strong a novel as her earlier ones," Sadler concludes, "Hunt does provide a touching treatment of a theme out of the ordinary at the time of the book's creation—the abuse of a small child—in a manner suitable for young readers."

William looks at interracial relationships on an intergenerational level. A young, pregnant white teenager named Sarah moves in next door to William's family. William's Mama, the head of the household, helps nurse Sarah through a hurricane strike and the birth of her child. When Mama dies of cancer, states Nancy P. Bailey in *School Library Journal,* "Sarah takes over as head of the family, refusing to let William and his sisters be placed in a foster home." "William recognizes that the situation and the home he has grown up in will never be the same again," Sadler concludes, "but he realizes that he must assume responsibility for the family." "The love and concern for human beings other than oneself are basic elements underlying the development of strong family relationships," explains *Horn Book* reviewer Mary M. Burns. "Through the skill with which the author delineates the characters, their ultimate triumph over multiple adversities is made believable, and each one emerges as a distinct personality."

Hunt looks at feminist issues in *Claws of a Young Century,* the story of a young suffragette working for women's rights in the early years of the century. "On New Year's Eve, 1899, seventeen-year-old Ellen Archer has hopes of bringing change and progress into her life and into the lives of other women," writes *Horn Book* contributor Ann A. Flowers. She leaves her unenlightened father to live with her college-educated brother Alex, falls in love with his journalist friend Philip Wrenn, and becomes pregnant. Ellen and Philip marry, but separate and divorce so that Philip can work overseas as a foreign correspondent and Ellen can continue her campaign for women's rights. "Ellen goes to jail for her beliefs," explains Cyrisse Jaffee in *School Library Journal,* "and the brutal treatment she receives there proves fatal." "When Philip returns after sixteen years abroad to find Ellen dying," Sadler concludes, "they realize their love and that pride has kept them apart. He promises to continue her work for the ratification of the suffrage amendment."

The Everlasting Hills, published in 1985, is set in the Rocky Mountains during the 1930s. The protagonist is Jeremy Tydings, who has a learning disability. Alienated from his unfeeling father, Jeremy finds solace in his relationship with his sister Bethany. When he realizes that Bethany is sacrificing her own life in order to care for him, he runs away. Jeremy finds shelter with an old hermit named Ishmael. "In the time he spends with Ishmael, Jeremy matures and grows in self-esteem," writes Barbara Chatton in *School Library Journal.* "After Ishmael dies, Jeremy returns to the cabin and embarks upon a project the two had dreamed of together and a difficult reconciliation with his father." "Their relationship ... [is] delicately portrayed," Bulla states, "and reveal[s] some of Hunt's finest qualities."

Critics continue to celebrate Hunt's literary accomplishments. Bradley states that Hunt "demonstrates her virtuosity as a storyteller by never duplicating her use of characters, setting, and plot within the genre of historical fiction. In addition, all of Hunt's novels consistently demonstrate other important elements such as poetic yet simple language and a delicate appreciation of the natural world." "Irene Hunt has a strong faith in the enduring qualities of courage, love, and mercy," Sadler concludes. "It is to reiterate this faith that she writes her books."

■ Works Cited

Review of *Across Five Aprils, Booklist and Subscription Books Bulletin,* July 1, 1964, p. 1002.

Armstrong, Helen, review of *Trail of Apple Blossoms, School Library Journal,* May, 1968, p. 79.

Bailey, Nancy P., review of *William, School Library Journal,* April, 1977, p. 77.

Bettersworth, John K., review of *Across Five Aprils, New York Times Book Review,* May 10, 1964, pp. 8, 10.

Bradley, Patricia L., "Irene Hunt," *Twentieth-Century Young Adult Writers,* St. James Press, 1994, pp. 312-14.

Broderick, Dorothy M., review of *Up a Road Slowly, New York Times Book Review,* November 6, 1966, pp. 8, 12.

Broderick, Dorothy M., review of *Trail of Apple Blossoms,* New York Times Book Review, April 14, 1968, p. 20.

Bulla, Clyde Robert, "Irene Hunt," *Twentieth-Century Children's Writers,* 3rd edition, St. James Press, 1989, pp. 481-82.

Burns, Mary M., review of *William, Horn Book,* October, 1977, pp. 540-41.

Byars, Betsy, review of *The Lottery Rose, New York Times Book Review,* May 16, 1976, pp. 16, 18.

Chatton, Barbara, review of *The Everlasting Hills, School Library Journal,* September, 1985, p. 134.

Flowers, Ann A., review of *Claws of a Young Century, Horn Book,* October, 1980, pp. 525-26.

Georgiou, Constantine, *Children and Their Literature,* Prentice-Hall, 1969, p. 379.

Hunt, Irene, "Books and the Learning Process," *Horn Book,* August, 1967, pp. 424-29.

Jaffee, Cyrisse, review of *Claws of a Young Century, School Library Journal,* August, 1980, p. 77.

Sadler, Philip A., "Irene Hunt," *Dictionary of Literary Biography, Volume 52: American Writers for Children since 1960: Fiction,* Gale, 1986, pp. 202-208.

Saunders, Sheryl Lee, "Irene Hunt," *Children's Books and Their Creators,* edited by Anita Silvey, Houghton Mifflin, 1995, p. 331.

Sutherland, Zena, review of *Across Five Aprils, Bulletin of the Center for Children's Books,* July-August, 1964, p. 171.

Review of *Up a Road Slowly, Virginia Kirkus' Service,* November 15, 1966, p. 1188.

Viguers, Ruth Hill, review of *Up a Road Slowly, Horn Book,* February, 1967, p. 73.

■ **For More Information See**

BOOKS

Children's Literature Review, Volume 1, Gale, 1976.

Hopkins, Lee Bennett, *More Books by More People,* Citation Press, 1974.

Larrick, Nancy, *A Parent's Guide to Children's Reading,* 3rd edition, Doubleday, 1969.

PERIODICALS

Booklist, August, 1985, p. 1665.

Commonweal, May 24, 1968.

Horn Book, June, 1970.

New Yorker, December 14, 1968.

New York Times Book Review, November 6, 1966; March 19, 1967; April 14, 1968; April 5, 1970; May 16, 1976.

Publishers Weekly, March 13, 1967; March 22, 1976, p. 46.

School Library Journal, April, 1976, p. 74; August, 1993, pp. 50-51; September, 1994, p. 140.

Writer, March, 1970.

Young Readers' Review, June, 1968.

J

JACKSON, Dave 1944-

■ Personal

Born July 16, 1944, in Glendale, CA; son of Louis (an aircraft metalworker) and Helen (a homemaker) Jackson; married Neta Thiessen (a writer), October 15, 1966; children: Julian, Rachel Berg, Samantha Sang (a Cambodian foster daughter). *Education:* Judson College, B.A., 1969. *Politics:* Independent. *Religion:* Christian. *Hobbies and other interests:* Bow hunting, fishing, vegetable gardening, camping, mountain bike riding, watching *Mystery* and *Masterpiece Theater* on PBS.

■ Addresses

Home and office—917 Ashland Ave., Evanston, IL 60202.

■ Career

David C. Cook Publishing Co., Elgin, IL, editor, 1980-85; freelance writer, 1985—. Member of pastoral staff at Reba Place Church, 1973-82. *Member:* Children's Reading Round Table (Chicago, IL).

■ Awards, Honors

Silver Angel Award, Excellence in Media, 1994, for *Listen for the Whippoorwill,* and 1995, for *Attack in the Rye Grass;* Gold Medallion Award, Evangelical Christian Publishers Association, 1994, for *Breaking Down Walls: A Model for Reconciliation in an Age of Racial Strife;* Best Children's Book of the Year, Christian Booksellers Association, 1995, for the "Trailblazer" series; Best Children's Book, Christian Booksellers New Zealand, 1995, for the "Trailblazer" series; C. S. Lewis Award for Best Series, 1995, for the "Trailblazer" series.

■ Writings

FOR CHILDREN

(With wife, Neta Jackson) *Hero Tales: A Family Treasury of True Stories from the Lives of Christian Heroes,* Bethany House (Minneapolis, MN), 1996.

"TRAILBLAZER" SERIES; WITH WIFE NETA JACKSON; ILLUSTRATED BY SON, JULIAN JACKSON; PUBLISHED BY BETHANY HOUSE

The Queen's Smuggler, 1991.
Kidnapped by River Rats, 1991.
Spy for the Night Raiders, 1992.
The Hidden Jewel, 1992.
Escape from the Slave Traders, 1992.
The Chimney Sweep's Ransom, 1992.
The Bandit of Ashley Downs, 1993.
Imprisoned in the Golden City, 1993.
Shanghaied to China, 1993.
Listen for the Whippoorwill, 1993.
Attack in the Rye Grass, 1994.
Trial by Poison, 1994.
Flight of the Fugitives, 1994.
The Betrayer's Fortune, 1994.
Abandoned on the Wild Frontier, 1995.
Danger on the Flying Trapeze, 1995.
The Thieves of Tyburn Square, 1995.
The Runaway's Revenge, 1995.
Quest for the Lost Prince, 1996.
The Warrior's Challenge, 1996.
Traitor in the Tower, 1997.
The Drummer Boy's Battle, 1997.

Several titles in the "Trailblazer" series have been translated into various languages, including German, Norwegian, Korean, Spanish, and Swedish.

"SECRET ADVENTURE" SERIES; WITH NETA JACKSON; ILLUSTRATED BY JULIAN JACKSON; PUBLISHED BY BROADMAN AND HOLMAN (NASHVILLE, TN)

Spin: Truth, Tubas, and George Washington, 1994.
Snap: How to Act Like a Responsible Almost Adult, 1994.

Smash: How to Survive Junior High by Really Trying, 1994.

Snag: I'm Dreaming of a Right Christmas, 1994.

"STORYBOOKS FOR CARING PARENTS" SERIES, ILLUSTRATED BY SUSAN LEXA; PUBLISHED BY CHARIOT BOOKS (ELGIN, IL)

Scared, But Not Too Scared to Think, 1985.
Bored, But Not Too Bored (to Pretend), 1985.
Tired, But Not Too Tired (to Finish), 1985.
Angry, But Not Too Angry (to Talk), 1985.
Shy, But Not Too Shy, 1986.
Stubborn, But Not Too Stubborn, 1986.
Disappointed, But Not Too Disappointed, 1986.
Unfair, But Not Too Unfair, 1986.

The "Storybooks for Caring Parents" series has been translated into Chinese.

FOR ADULTS

Coming Together, Bethany House, 1978.
Dial 911: Peaceful Christians and Urban Violence, Herald Press, 1981.
(With Patricia Brandt) *Just Me and the Kids: A Course for Single Parents,* D. C. Cook (Elgin, IL), 1985.
(With Matthew and Lea Dacy) *Teen Pregnancy,* D. C. Cook, 1989.

Dave and Neta Jackson.

Lost River Conspiracy, Good Books (Intercourse, PA), 1995.

FOR ADULTS; WITH NETA JACKSON

Living Together in a World Falling Apart, Creation House (Carol Stream, IL), 1974.
(Editor) *Storehouse of Family-Time Ideas: Fall and Winter,* D. C. Cook, 1987.
(Editor) *Storehouse of Family-Time Ideas: Spring and Summer,* D. C. Cook, 1987.
(Also with Ed Hurst) *Overcoming Homosexuality,* D. C. Cook, 1987.
Glimpses of Glory: Thirty Years of Community: The Story of Reba Place Fellowship, Brethren Press (Elgin, IL), 1987.
(Also with Brother Andrew) *A Time for Heroes,* Vine Books (Ann Arbor, MI), 1988.
(Also with Kenneth E. Schemmer) *Between Life and Death: The Life-Support Dilemma,* Victor Books (Wheaton, IL), 1988.
(Also with Grace A. Wenger) *Witness: Empowering the Church through Worship, Community, and Mission,* Herald Press (Scottdale, PA), 1989.
On Fire for Christ: Stories of Anabaptist Martyrs, Herald Press, 1989.
(Editors with Beth Landis) *The Gift of Presence: Stories that Celebrate Nurses Serving in the Name of Christ,* Herald Press, 1991.
(Also with Gordon R. McLean) *Cities of Lonesome Fear,* Moody Press (Chicago, IL), 1991.
(Also with Kenneth E. Schemmer) *Tinkering with People* ("What You Need to Know about the Medical Ethics Crisis" Series), Scripture Press, 1992.
(Also with Howard Jones) *Heritage & Hope: The Legacy and Future of the Black Family in America,* Victor Books, 1992.
(Also with Steve Wilke) *When We Can't Talk Anymore: Stories about Couples Who Learned to Communicate Again* ("Recovering Hope in Your Marriage" Series), Living Books (Wheaton, IL), 1992.
(With Wilke) *When It's Hard to Trust,* Tyndale House, 1992.
(Also with John D. Bradley) *Switching Tracks: Advancing Through Five Crucial Phases of Your Career,* Fleming H. Revell (Grand Rapids, MI), 1994.
(Also with Raleigh Washington and Glen Kehrein) *Breaking Down Walls: A Model for Reconciliation in an Age of Racial Strife,* Moody Press, 1994.
(Also with Steve Wilke) *When Alcohol Abuses Our Marriage,* New Leaf Press, 1995.
(With Wilke) *When the Odds Are Against Us,* New Leaf Press, 1995.
(With Wilke) *When We Fight All the Time,* New Leaf Press, 1995.

Living Together in a World Falling Apart has been translated into Swedish and Finnish.

■ Work in Progress

Research on circuit-riding preachers in the early 1800s; a second volume of *Hero Tales.*

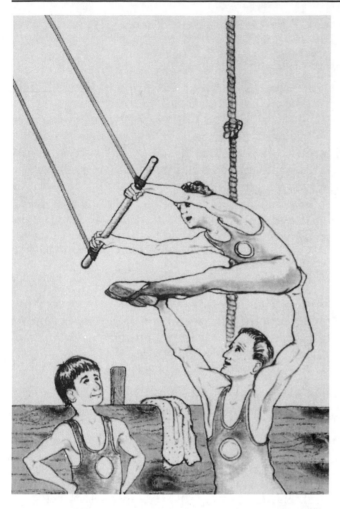

Casey Watkins has two weeks to learn to "fly on the trapeze" before the circus arrives in Chicago for the World's Fair. (From *Danger on the Flying Trapeze,* by Dave and Neta Jackson. Illustrated by Julian Jackson.)

■ Sidelights

An author of juvenile fiction and adult self-help books, Dave Jackson has received widespread commendation for his fictional biographies about young men and women whose lives are influenced by historical Christian figures. Jackson is perhaps best known for the "Trailblazer" series of books he initiated with his wife and coauthor Neta Jackson in 1991. The "Trailblazer" works are fictionalized biographies of men and women whose pioneering efforts left a significant mark on history and Christianity.

In addition to coauthoring the "Trailblazer" series, Jackson and his wife teamed to create a collection of "Secret Adventure" books featuring lively action designed to teach children Christian virtues and underscore positive values. The same thematic emphasis permeates Jackson's *Lost River Conspiracy,* a story about a young Mennonite man who becomes involved in a fierce Indian war. While traveling home to Lost River, Oregon, Abraham Miller meets a young pioneer named Mary and her father. When Miller hears that a war has broken out near Mary's home, he decides to try to help diffuse the situation between the Modoc tribe and the United States Army. Miller, acting as a go-between for the Army's Peace Commission and the Modoc warriors, tries to resolve the conflict. After his peace-keeping efforts fail and war erupts, Miller chooses to remain with the Indian tribe and attempt to right the many injustices they suffered at the hands of the United States government. Writing in *Voice of Youth Advocates,* Lisa Prolman commended Jackson's ability to create a character who "shows how a person can stand for his or her beliefs even when those beliefs run counter to majority opinion." Although admitting the book's opening was "slow-going," Prolman also said that she found the book "compelling" after a few chapters and appreciated the afterword about the history of the Modoc uprising in 1872. In *Booklist,* a critic found Jackson's recreation of Captain Jack and Scarface Charley, two famous Modoc warriors, "very much to life." Furthermore, the critic praised Jackson's "sure sense" of northern Nevada and the lava beds into which the defeated Indians retreat.

■ Works Cited

Review of *Lost River Conspiracy, Booklist,* November 1, 1995, p. 455.
Prolman, Lisa, review of *Lost River Conspiracy, Voice of Youth Advocates,* April, 1996, p. 26.

■ For More Information See

PERIODICALS

Booklist, April 1, 1995, p. 1391; September 1, 1995, p. 56; January 1, 1996, p. 834; March 15, 1996, p. 1264.
Bookstore Journal, October, 1994, p. 99.
Christianity Today, November 9, 1992, p. 76.
Los Angeles Times Book Review, September 7, 1986.
School Library Journal, December, 1995, p. 104.

* * *

JACKSON, Mike 1946-
(Robert Arley)

■ Personal

Born October 1, 1946. *Education:* Trent Polytechnic, Nottingham, B.Sc. (with honors), 1970; Wolverhampton Polytechnic, Certificate in Education, 1979. *Hobbies and other interests:* Sailing.

■ Addresses

Office—Severn Pictures, Dovecote Barn, The White House, Suckley, Worcester WR6 5DF, England.

■ Career

Associated Television (ATV) Network Ltd., Birmingham, England, scriptwriter, 1972-78; City of Birmingham Polytechnic, media studies course director, 1980-

MIKE JACKSON

84; Central TV, Birmingham, producer and director of children's Independent Television (ITV), 1984-89; Severn Pictures Ltd., Worcestershire, England, managing director, 1989—. Freelance TV and theatre producer and director; producer and director (under name Robert Arley) of ITV entertainment series *Gaz Top Non Stop,* 1995; media studies lecturer. *Member:* Producers Association for Cinematography and Television, Royal Yacht Association.

■ Awards, Honors

Best Theatre Director, *Birmingham Post and Mail,* 1977-78; First Prize, *The European,* 1994, for short story "The Video Vicar."

■ Writings

AS ROBERT ARLEY

Along the Beach, Creative Publishing, 1994.
Clothes from Many Lands, Raintree Steck-Vaughn, 1995.
Homes around the World, Raintree Steck-Vaughn, 1995.

Also author of short story, "The Video Vicar."

PLAYS

The Man Who Knew, produced at King's Head Theatre, London, 1974.
Carbon Monoxide, produced by Birmingham Pub Theatre Company tour, 1975.
Cut!, produced at Everyman Theatre, Cheltenham, England, 1994.

Also author of *Spaghetti Junction,* produced in Birmingham, 1991.

OTHER

Author of episodes of the comedy-drama television series *The Kids from 47A,* ATV, 1974.

■ Work in Progress

The Fun Factory, a comic novel about the TV industry; *Dead Lucky!,* a movie screenplay, optioned by Ken Topolski Productions in Los Angeles.

■ Sidelights

"A student of CVs will have spotted the nearly twenty-year gap between performed plays," Mike Jackson pointed out to *SATA.* "What happened?

"I had an early enthusiasm for writing, inspired by comic fringe theatre plays, which got me a job as a promotions scriptwriter with ATV. Here I had lots of fun and some frustration, which eventually caused me to leave to become a lecturer in media.

"But the small screen drew me back, and I got to be responsible for the presentation and promotion of all children's programming on the ITV Channel in the U.K. This was a fantastic job ... dealing with everything from bullish programme controllers to directing puppets for live segments to a daily audience of over four million.

"And I had some say in the output that reached those kids ... until a series turned up that I honestly felt was unsuitable for children. I argued against it, and kind of won, then kind of lost ... and subsequently wrote a black comedy play about the TV industry, *Cut!*

"I also made a behind-the-scenes programme for Columbia Pictures and ITV about 'The Real Ghostbusters' in Los Angeles, and was encouraged—by Dan Aykroyd, no less—to write a film screenplay. Five scripts later, I've got options on American stories, which, for a non-native, I feel is pretty good.

"Now, while working as a producer/director in factual TV, I'm trying to write the definitive comic novel about the TV industry."

*   *   *

JACKSON, Neta 1944-

■ Personal

Born October 26, 1944, in Winchester, KY; daughter of Isaac (a school administrator) and Margaret (a teacher) Thiessen; married Dave Jackson, October 15, 1966; children: Julian, Rachel Berg, Samantha Sang (a Cambodian foster daughter). *Education:* Wheaton College, B.A., 1966. *Politics:* Independent. *Religion:* Christian. *Hobbies and other interests:* Horseback riding, flower gardening, camping, mountain bike riding, watching *Mystery* and *Masterpiece Theater* on PBS, genealogy, creating photo albums.

■ Addresses

Home and office—917 Ashland Ave., Evanston, IL 60202.

■ Career

David C. Cook Publishing Co., Elgin, IL, editor, 1980-85; freelance writer, 1985—. *Member:* Children's Reading Round Table (Chicago, IL).

■ Awards, Honors

Silver Angel Award, Excellence in Media, 1994, for *Listen for the Whippoorwill,* and 1995, for *Attack in the Rye Grass;* Gold Medallion Award, Evangelical Christian Publishers Association, 1994, for *Breaking Down Walls: A Model for Reconciliation in an Age of Racial Strife;* Christian Booksellers Association, Best Children's Book of the Year, 1995, for the "Trailblazer" series; Best Children's Book, Christian Booksellers New Zealand, 1995, for the "Trailblazer" series; C. S. Lewis Award for Best Series, 1995, for the "Trailblazer" series.

■ Writings

FOR CHILDREN

Loving One Another—Beginner's Stories on Being a Good Friend, Questar Publishers (Sisters, OR), 1994.

(With husband, Dave Jackson) *Hero Tales: A Family Treasury of True Stories from the Lives of Christian Heroes,* Bethany House (Minneapolis, MN), 1996.

"TRAILBLAZER" SERIES; WITH HUSBAND, DAVE JACKSON; ILLUSTRATED BY SON, JULIAN JACKSON; PUBLISHED BY BETHANY HOUSE

The Queen's Smuggler, 1991.
Kidnapped by River Rats, 1991.
Spy for the Night Raiders, 1992.
The Hidden Jewel, 1992.
Escape from the Slave Traders, 1992.
The Chimney Sweep's Ransom, 1992.
The Bandit of Ashley Downs, 1993.
Imprisoned in the Golden City, 1993.
Shanghaied to China, 1993.
Listen for the Whippoorwill, 1993.
Attack in the Rye Grass, 1994.
Trial by Poison, 1994.
Flight of the Fugitives, 1994.
The Betrayer's Fortune, 1994.
Abandoned on the Wild Frontier, 1995.
Danger on the Flying Trapeze, 1995.
The Thieves of Tyburn Square, 1995.
The Runaway's Revenge, 1995.
Quest for the Lost Prince, 1996.
The Warrior's Challenge, 1996.
Traitor in the Tower, 1997.
The Drummer Boy's Battle, 1997.

Twelve-year-old Rosebud Jackson seeks freedom from slavery on Harriet Tubman's Underground Railroad. (Cover illustration by Julian Jackson.)

Several titles in the "Trailblazer" series have been translated into various languages, including German, Norwegian, Korean, Spanish, and Swedish.

"SECRET ADVENTURE" SERIES; WITH DAVE JACKSON; ILLUSTRATED BY JULIAN JACKSON; PUBLISHED BY BROADMAN & HOLMAN (NASHVILLE, TN)

Spin: Truth, Tubas, and George Washington, 1994.
Snap: How to Act Like a Responsible Almost Adult, 1994.
Smash: How to Survive Junior High by Really Trying, 1994.
Snag: I'm Dreaming of a Right Christmas, 1994.

"PET PARABLES" SERIES; PUBLISHED BY MULTNOMAH PRESS

The Parrot Who Talked Too Much, 1991.
The Hamster Who Got Himself Stuck, 1991.
The Cat Who Smelled Like Cabbage, 1991.
The Dog Who Loved to Race, 1991.

FOR ADULTS

A New Way to Live, Herald Press, 1983.
Building Christian Relationships, Bethany House, 1984.

Who's Afraid of a Virgin, Wolf?, Meriwether Publishers (Colorado Springs, CO), 1991.

From Sod Shanty to State Senate (a biography of C.R. Thiessen), Castle Rock Publishers (Evanston, IL), 1992.

FOR ADULTS; WITH DAVE JACKSON

Living Together in a World Falling Apart, Creation House (Carol Stream, IL), 1974.

(Editor) *Storehouse of Family-Time Ideas: Fall and Winter*, D. C. Cook (Elgin, IL), 1987.

(Editor) *Storehouse of Family-Time Ideas: Spring and Summer*, D. C. Cook, 1987.

(Also with Ed Hurst) *Overcoming Homosexuality*, D. C. Cook, 1987.

Glimpses of Glory: Thirty Years of Community: The Story of Reba Place Fellowship, Brethren Press (Elgin, IL), 1987.

(Also with Brother Andrew) *A Time for Heroes*, Vine Books (Ann Arbor, MI), 1988.

(Also with Kenneth E. Schemmer) *Between Life and Death: The Life-Support Dilemma*, Victor Books (Wheaton, IL), 1988.

(Also with Grace A. Wenger) *Witness: Empowering the Church through Worship, Community, and Mission*, Herald Press (Scottdale, PA), 1989.

On Fire for Christ: Stories of Anabaptist Martyrs, Retold from Martyrs Mirror, Herald Press, 1989.

(Editor with Beth Landis) *The Gift of Presence: Stories that Celebrate Nurses Serving in the Name of Christ*, Herald Press, 1991.

(Also with Gordon R. McLean) *Cities of Lonesome Fear*, Moody Press (Chicago), 1991.

(Also with Kenneth E. Schemmer) *Tinkering with People* ("What You Need to Know about the Medical Ethics Crisis" Series), Scripture Press, 1992.

(Also with Howard Jones) *Heritage & Hope: The Legacy and Future of the Black Family in America*, Victor Books, 1992.

(Also with Steve Wilke) *When We Can't Talk Anymore: Stories about Couples Who Learned to Communicate Again* ("Recovering Hope in Your Marriage" Series), Living Books (Wheaton, IL), 1992.

(With Wilke) *When It's Hard to Trust*, Tyndale House, 1992.

(Also with John D. Bradley) *Switching Tracks: Advancing Through Five Crucial Phases of Your Career*, Fleming H. Revell (Grand Rapids, MI), 1994.

(Also with Raleigh Washington and Glen Kehrein) *Breaking Down Walls: A Model for Reconciliation in an Age of Racial Strife*, Moody Press, 1994.

(Also with Steve Wilke) *When Alcohol Abuses Our Marriage*, New Leaf Press, 1995.

(With Wilke) *When the Odds Are Against Us*, New Leaf Press, 1995.

(With Wilke) *When We Fight All the Time*, New Leaf Press, 1995.

Living Together in a World Falling Apart has been translated into Swedish and Finnish.

■ Work in Progress

Research on circuit-riding preachers in the early 1800s.

■ Sidelights

One-half of a husband-wife writing duo, Neta Jackson is the coauthor of several series of children's books, including one focusing on the lives of important Christian figures in history. Interestingly, Jackson told *Bookstore Journal* that while growing up, she never aspired to be a writer, but instead an artist. "I loved to draw and was horse-crazy as a kid. . . . But in junior high, I started writing stories about horses instead of just drawing them. Eventually, my interest in writing stories overtook my interest in art."

Along with her husband Dave, Jackson began the "Trailblazer" series in 1991, a fictionalized biography series about men and women who had a significant impact on history and Christianity, such as Harriet Tubman, Martin Luther, and Menno Simons. In *The Betrayer's Fortune,* for instance, fifteen-year-old Adriaen begins to question his Anabaptist faith when his mother is imprisoned for her beliefs. Set in the early 1500s, the story shows how a young man struggles with his faith in a God who allows suffering among His followers. Writing in *Booklist*, Shelly Townsend-Hudson praises the "compelling" plot which follows the growth of "an initially unsympathetic boy into a courageous young man."

Jackson tries to teach readers about history by creating fictional characters whose lives are influenced by real men and women from the past. *Danger on the Flying Trapeze* features a fourteen-year-old boy who convinces his mother to join a traveling circus after his father dies. While preforming at the Chicago World's Fair, Casey loses his courage on the trapeze bar after a bad fall. However, he happens to meet the evangelist D. L. Moody who encourages him to try the stunt again. Casey succeeds and decides to continue following the teachings of Moody. While in a *Booklist* review Townsend-Hudson complains that the references to Moody are slight, not allowing the reader to "gain a real sense of the man," she does go on to say that Jackson's biographical sketch of Moody "will interest some readers." In *School Library Journal*, Renee Steinberg contends that "the message is heavy-handed and the characters are flat," but she is enthusiastic about the dramatic events in the book, saying "there is a lot of action."

Jackson told *SATA* that the "burning issue" she and her husband share is "the need to confront racism in ourselves and our culture, and to work for racial reconciliation in every area of our lives—but especially the church."

■ Works Cited

Jackson, Neta, comments in *Bookstore Journal*, October, 1994, p. 99.

Steinberg, Renee, review of *Danger on the Flying Trapeze, School Library Journal,* December, 1995, p. 104.

Townsend-Hudson, Shelly, review of *The Betrayer's Fortune, Booklist,* April, 1, 1995, p. 1391.

Townsend-Hudson, Shelly, review of *Danger on the Flying Trapeze, Booklist,* September 1, 1995, p. 54.

■ For More Information See

PERIODICALS

Booklist, September 1, 1995, p. 56; January 1, 1996, p. 834; March 15, 1996, p. 1264.
Christianity Today, November 9, 1992, p. 76.

* * *

JANSEN, Jared
See CEBULASH, Mel

* * *

JOHNSON, Lois Walfrid 1936-

■ Personal

Born November 23, 1936, in Starbuck, MN; daughter of Alvar Bernhard (a clergyman) and Lydia (a business manager and bookkeeper; maiden name, Christiansen)

LOIS WALFRID JOHNSON

Walfrid; married Roy A. Johnson (an elementary school teacher and delinquency prevention counselor), June 26, 1959; children: Gail, Jeffrey, Kevin. *Education:* Gustavus Adolphus College, B. A. (magna cum laude), 1958; University of Oklahoma, graduate study, 1968-71. *Politics:* Independent. *Religion:* Christian. *Hobbies and other interests:* Spending time with family and friends, hiking, biking, swimming, cross-country skiing, reading, listening to music, playing the piano, traveling, photography.

■ Addresses

Office—c/o Bethany House, 11300 Hampshire Ave. S., Minneapolis, MN 55438.

■ Career

English teacher, Wayzata, MN, 1958-59; author and speaker, 1969—. *Writer's Digest School,* editorial associate, 1974-77. Teacher of writing for children and adults at schools, libraries, and universities. Presenter at writing workshops and conferences, 1971—. *Member:* Society of Children's Book Writers and Illustrators, Children's Reading Round Table of Chicago, Council for Wisconsin Writers.

■ Awards, Honors

Distinguished Alumni Citation, Gustavus Adolphus College, 1983, for body of work; Gold Medallion, Evangelical Christian Publishers Association, and C. S. Lewis Medal for Best Series Published in 1988, both 1989, both for "Let's-Talk-about-It Stories for Kids" series, including *You're Worth More than You Think!, Secrets of the Best Choice, Thanks for Being My Friend, You Are Wonderfully Made!;* Book Award of Merit for Distinguished Service to History, State Historical Society of Wisconsin, 1991, "Adventures of the Northwoods" series; Silver Angel Award, Excellence in Media, 1991, for *The Disappearing Stranger,* 1992, for *Trouble at Wild River,* 1994, for *The Runaway Clown,* 1995, for *Disaster on Windy Hill,* and 1996, for *Escape into the Night;* Arthur Tofte Juvenile Book Award, Council for Wisconsin Writers, 1992, for *Trouble at Wild River;* Award of Merit, Excellence in Media, 1993, for *Grandpa's Stolen Treasure;* C. S. Lewis Honor Book (Silver Medal), 1995, for *Escape into the Night.*

■ Writings

FOR CHILDREN; PUBLISHED BY AUGSBURG

Just a Minute, Lord, 1973.
Aaron's Christmas Donkey (picture book), 1974.
Hello, God! (picture book), 1975.
You're My Best Friend, Lord, 1975.

"LET'S-TALK-ABOUT-IT STORIES FOR KIDS" SERIES; PUBLISHED BY NAVPRESS

Secrets of the Best Choice, 1988.
You're Worth More Than You Think!, 1988.
Thanks for Being My Friend, 1988.
You Are Wonderfully Made!, 1988.

"ADVENTURES OF THE NORTHWOODS" SERIES;
    PUBLISHED BY BETHANY HOUSE

The Disappearing Stranger, 1990.
The Hidden Message, 1990.
The Creeping Shadows, 1990.
The Vanishing Footprints, 1991.
Trouble at Wild River, 1991.
The Mysterious Hideaway, 1992.
Grandpa's Stolen Treasure, 1992.
The Runaway Clown, 1993.
Mystery of the Missing Map, 1994.
Disaster on Windy Hill, 1994.

"RIVERBOAT ADVENTURES" SERIES; PUBLISHED BY
    BETHANY HOUSE

Escape into the Night, 1995.
Race for Freedom, 1996.
Midnight Rescue, 1996.
The Swindler's Treasure, 1997.

FOR ADULTS; PUBLISHED BY AUGSBURG

Gift in My Arms: Thoughts for New Mothers, 1977.
Either Way, I Win, 1979.
Songs for Silent Moments, 1980.
Falling Apart or Coming Together, 1984.

OTHER

Also author of over 225 shorter pieces, including articles, poetry, and song lyrics. Some of Johnson's work has been published in the United Kingdom, Australia, New Zealand, and other English-speaking countries throughout the world, translated into twelve languages for publication in other countries, and printed in braille for the blind.

■ Work in Progress

Additional novels for the "Riverboat Adventures" series; revised edition of *Either Way, I Win.*

■ Sidelights

A former high school English teacher, Lois Walfrid Johnson is the creator of several popular pre-teen books, including the "Riverboat Adventures" series. This series revolves around the experiences of twelve-year-old Libby Norstad who, after living with a rich aunt in Chicago, joins her riverboat captain father. In the first book, *Escape into the Night,* Libby meets Caleb, her father's thirteen-year-old cabin boy. A conductor on the Underground Railroad, Caleb is involved in helping slaves escape from the South, which forces Libby to examine her own thoughts about slavery. Soon, Libby finds herself in the midst of a dangerous struggle to help three runaway slaves find freedom. Applauding the "fast-paced plot," *Booklist* reviewer Lois Schultz praised Johnson's ability to weave history "with well-developed characters, believable dialogue, and crisp description." In a *School Library Journal* review, Joyce Adams Burner lauded the depth of Johnson's characters, "especially Libby, whose transformation from a spoiled brat into a self-sacrificing heroine rings true."

Lois Walfrid Johnson told *SATA:* "Often people ask me, 'How did the "Adventures of the Northwoods" series begin?' Some time ago, my husband and I moved from Minneapolis to northwest Wisconsin. I began hearing stories from people who had been friends and neighbors for three and four generations. I valued these stories and the way of life they represented. I felt that these memories, and the values, love, and courage they represented, were too good to be lost.

"Then one warm May evening when the air was sweet with lilac and plum blossoms, I took a walk near our home. I came to a field where trees had grown up inside the cellar of an old house. As I looked at the broken foundation of what had once been a log home, I asked myself, *What if a farm family lived here? What if there was a girl named Kate who moved from Minneapolis to northwest Wisconsin? What if she had a step-brother named Anders who teased her all the time? And someone like Erik who could become a special friend?* That was the beginning. I kept thinking about Kate, Anders, Erik, and the Windy Hill folks until I felt as though that family were mine.

"Because I want readers to have fun with my novels, I often include a mystery. I try to write about universal problems true to any time of history. Sometimes the experiences of my characters reflect my own life. Before our marriage, my husband, Roy, was a widower, just like Papa Nordstrom. When Roy and I were married, Roy's daughter, Gail, became our flower girl. In time, two additional children, Jeffrey and Kevin, were born and grew tall like Anders and Erik. While Kate is my viewpoint character, I wanted strong male characters because of my experience in having sons.

"I set the series in 1906-7 for two reasons. Those were transition years in northwest Wisconsin. It was still possible to see the old way of doing things—horse power, hand pumps, clearing of the land. Yet the new was coming in—electricity, rural telephones, even automobiles. Also, Big Gust, a much loved 360-pound, seven-foot, six-inch Swedish immigrant, was the village marshall in Grantsburg, Wisconsin during those years.

"Whenever I could, I used historic characters—people who actually lived in the time and place about which I wrote. I wove the lives of these people into what my fictional characters were doing. A note at the front of each novel tells which characters really lived.

"Kate had Irish and Swedish parents, and soon discovered that she, Harry Blue, and Rev. Pickle were the only non-Swedes in the Trade Lake area. Being Swedish was true to the settlement of that part of northwest Wisconsin, but I also wrote out of what I knew from my own background.

"Within the novels are 'secrets' that reflect both my family and that of my husband, Roy. We are still close to the immigrant heritage that made America strong. As a young woman, Roy's mother came from Norway. In a wave of homesickness she had her picture taken and sent back to her family. The result was the family picture described in *The Disappearing Stranger* and other novels. Roy's father also immigrated from Norway, and the two met in Milwaukee.

"Carl Nordstrom is named after two more immigrants—my Swedish grandfather, Carl Johnson, and my Swedish grandmother, Mathilda Nordstrom. While a young woman, Grandma worked on a farm outside Walnut Grove, Minnesota, and often watched wagon trains pass through to settle in the West.

"When Grandpa and Grandma Johnson were married, they bought a farm on the banks of Plum Creek. My father grew up there, and many of my stories about runaway horses come out of his experience in riding and breaking broncos. Years later, during summer vacations, my sisters and I often played in Plum Creek. From where we waded, the water flowed under a bridge into the land once owned by the family of Laura Ingalls Wilder.

"The Danish side of my family is also represented in the Northwoods novels. When my Grandpa Christiansen came to America, he worked for about a year to save enough money to bring my grandmother and their three-year-old daughter, Lydia, across the Atlantic. While passing through Ellis Island, Grandma and Lydia had pieces of paper pinned on their coats, as described in *Grandpa's Stolen Treasure.*

"Although they are called Swedish, that novel described my Danish grandparents as they looked when I was a child. From that point on, the story was fiction, or so I thought. A few months after the book was published, I learned that when Grandma came to Rochester, Minnesota, as an immigrant, there was a mix-up at the depot. Grandpa 'lost' her and Lydia for an entire day! As you might guess, three-year-old Lydia grew up to be my mother.

"Some of the country school experiences in the Northwoods novels also came out of my own childhood. I attended my first four grades in a two-room country school on the shores of Goose Lake, near Scandia, Minnesota. Miss Sundquist gives spelling words exactly as my teacher, Miss Guslander, did. There were drafts through the knotholes in the floor at Goose Lake, too, as well as box socials, a woodshed, and a large wood stove. Even as a child, I knew it was special to attend a school with woods and water for a playground.

"In addition to being a wonderful encourager, my husband, Roy, helps me in the development of ideas. After writing a number of Northwoods novels, I told him, 'I'm having so much fun doing this. I'll miss my characters when it's time to stop. What could we do next?'

"That morning Roy went out for coffee. Taking a napkin, he wrote down some thoughts. When he told me his idea for the 'Riverboat Adventures' series, I said, 'That's it!'

"We felt that by having my main characters live on the steamboat *Christina,* they could travel as needed to make a story work. For three years, while I was still writing 'Northwoods' novels, Roy and I traveled up and down the Mississippi River, researching for ideas and historical accuracy. Soon the year 1857 became especially interesting to me. I could reflect the golden era of steamboats, for rivers were the highways of that time. I could show the pioneers using those steamboats to reach their new homes along the waterways of the Midwest. But I could also bring to life the social and political upheaval of the times by telling the story of the Underground Railroad.

"Again I use a girl as my viewpoint character—Libby, who comes from Chicago to join her father, a steamboat captain. Again I use strong boy characters—Caleb, who has worked with the Underground Railroad since the age of nine, and Jordan, a fugitive slave who escapes from his cruel master. With every novel I try to create strong reader interest by having fast moving plots and cliff hangers at the end of each chapter. I also seek to reflect important truths of our American heritage, giving perspective on the freedoms sought in the Declaration of Independence.

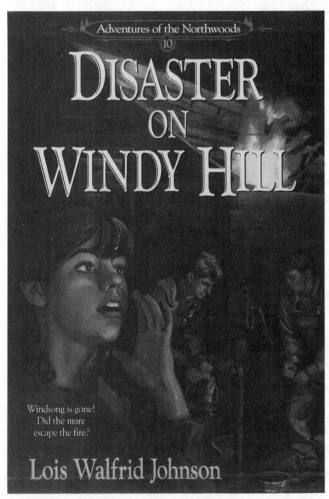

Kate is mystified when her scruffy, newly acquired horse is sought after by crooks in this "Adventures of the Northwoods" tale.

THE RIVERBOAT ADVENTURES

ESCAPE INTO THE NIGHT

LOIS WALFRID JOHNSON

Life on a steamboat in 1857 becomes tense in Johnson's story about two young people who help a fugitive slave escape captors. (Cover illustration by Andrea Jorgenson.)

"To research these books, my husband and I visited Underground Railroad sites in a number of states. We grew to love and value the runaway slaves about whom we learned. We grieved about their hardship and suffering. We also respected their courage and daring, as well as the integrity and honor of the people who helped them.

"When readers write to say, 'I want to know what happens to Jordan's family,' I feel deeply moved. I, too, want to discover what happens to his family!

"By now Libby, Caleb, and Jordan have become part of our lives. When Roy and I talk, we sometimes say, 'Could Libby do that?' Often we think of something that would be perfect for such a leap-before-she-looks person. Other times we decide, 'No, that would fit Caleb or Jordan better.' Like my readers, we often wonder, *What will these characters do next?*"

■ Works Cited

Burner, Joyce Adams, review of *Escape into the Night,* *School Library Journal,* October, 1995, p. 134.
Schultz, Lois, review of *Escape into the Night, Booklist,* November 15, 1995, p. 559.

■ For More Information See

PERIODICALS

Children's Book Watch, September, 1991, p. 3.
Library Journal, October 15, 1974, p. 2721.
Voice of Youth Advocates, June, 1984, p. 120; February, 1985, p. 51.

*   *   *

JORGENSON, Ivar
See SILVERBERG, Robert

K

KELLER, Beverly L(ou)
(B. L. Harwick)

■ Personal

Born in San Francisco, CA; daughter of Wearne E. and Ruth (Burke) Harwick; married William Jon Keller, June 18, 1949 (died, 1964); children: Lisa, Kristen, Michele. *Education:* University of California, Berkeley, B.A., 1950.

■ Career

Author, newspaper columnist, and feature writer. *Member:* Society for the Prevention of Cruelty to Animals (director and officer for Yolo County, 1976-78; 1991-93).

■ Awards, Honors

Fiona's Bee was selected a Best Book of 1975 by *School Library Journal.*

■ Writings

FOR CHILDREN

Fiona's Bee, Coward, 1975.
The Beetle Bush, Coward, 1976.
Don't Throw Another One, Dover!, Coward, 1976.
(Under name B. L. Harwick) *The Frog Prints,* Raintree Editions, 1976.
The Genuine Ingenious Thrift Shop Genie, Clarissa Mae Bean and Me, Coward, 1977.
Pimm's Place, Coward, 1978.
The Sea Watch, Four Winds Press, 1980.
Fiona's Flea, Coward, 1981.
The Bee Sneeze, Coward, 1982.
My Awful Cousin Norbert, Lothrop, 1982.
No Beasts! No Children!, Lothrop, 1983.
A Small, Elderly Dragon, Lothrop, 1984.
When Mother Got the Flu, Lothrop, 1984.
A Garden of Love to Share, Parker Brothers, 1984.
Rosebud, with Fangs, Lothrop, 1985.
Desdemona: Twelve Going on Desperate, Lothrop, 1986.

Beverly L. Keller, writer and animal rights activist, with the rescued dogs who share her home.

Only Fiona, HarperCollins, 1988.
Fowl Play, Desdemona, Lothrop, 1989.
Desdemona Moves On, Bradbury, 1992.
Camp Trouble, Scholastic, 1993.
The Night the Babysitter Didn't Come, 1994.
The Amazon Papers, Browndeer, 1996.

OTHER

The Baghdad Defections (adult suspense novel), Bobbs-Merrill, 1973.
Consumer Skills, Quercus, 1986.
A Car Means Out, Quercus, 1987.
Cliffhanger, Quercus, 1987.
Beam Me Up, He Said, Quercus, 1987.

Also contributor to textbooks, including *Hide and Seek,* Scott Foresman, 1985. Contributor to anthologies, including *The Best from Fantasy and Science Fiction,* edited by Edward Ferman, Doubleday, 1974; and *The Random House Book of Humor for Children,* Random House, 1988. Contributor to periodicals, including *Atlantic, Fantasy and Science Fiction, Cosmopolitan,* and *American Voice. Fiona's Bee* has been produced as an audio recording by Listening Library in 1976, re-released, 1991. Some of Keller's books have been published in Japanese and Spanish.

■ Work in Progress

A series for children.

■ Sidelights

Beverly L. Keller is the author of two popular series of children's books, one about a dog-loving girl named Fiona and another starring a pre-teen protagonist named Desdemona. The story of ten-year-old Fiona Foster begins in *Fiona's Bee* when she purchases a dog dish in hopes of befriending a dog and its owner. However, Fiona doesn't expect a bee to land on her hand and interfere with her friend-making plan. Instead of panicking, the brave girl reasons that if she slowly walks to an area packed with flowers, the insect will fly off in search of sweet nectar. The scheme works, but with an unexpected bonus—along the way to the park she meets many new friends impressed by her pet bee. A critic in *Kirkus Reviews* lauded Keller's "sharp, empathic humor," while in *Horn Book,* Ann A. Flowers described the story as "simple and kindly."

In *Only Fiona,* Keller's third book in the series, Fiona and her family have moved to a new town and once again she finds herself in the uncomfortable situation of making new friends. By the end of the story, Fiona does gain new playmates, but not without causing a few problems. Intensely interested in the welfare of animals, she interrupts neighborhood events, including two outdoor weddings, first to save a beetle, and then to help a bumblebee. Although she contended that Fiona's naivety and a "determined cuteness" detract from the story, Zena Sutherland added in *Bulletin of the Center for Children's Books,* "the writing style is brisk and the dialog and characters convincing." Calling Fiona a "real, three-dimensional person," a *Kirkus Reviews* critic stated that children should be entertained by Fiona's antics and applauded "Keller's sharply portrayed characters."

In 1983, Keller introduced young readers to the world of Desdemona Blank in *No Beasts! No Children!* After her parents separate, Desdemona and her five-year-old twin brother and sister go and live with her psychologist father in the only place in the city that allows both kids and pets. When the rich landlord tries to evict the Blank family because of all the commotion they and their animals make, he is surprised to discover that his son Sherman spends much of his free time with Desdemona. In the end, the landlord allows the family to stay and even realizes that he should give more time and attention to his own son. Zena Sutherland of the *Bulletin of the Center for Children's Books* wrote that the

"characters are exaggerated but colorful and funny, as is the dialogue," but found the "intensity of the ceaseless action" a bit tiresome. In *School Library Journal,* Elaine E. Knight praised the swift, humorous action, saying "the misadventures of this menagerie are irresistible."

Desdemona's spirited adventures continue in *Desdemona: Twelve Going on Desperate,* Keller's 1986 sequel to *No Beasts! No Children!* In this fast-paced story, Desdemona and her family must fight her landlord's plan to level the family's house and build luxury condos on the site. Making matters worse, the landlord, who hopes to be elected mayor, is also the father of Sherman, Desdemona's best friend. Mixups always seem to happen to Desdemona—she mistakes a bottle of varnish for shampoo and serves dog food instead of truffles at a party she caters for Sherman's father. Yet throughout the book, Desdemona keeps her head up and eventually helps her family keep their home. Ilene Cooper of *Booklist* described Keller's characters as "strong and funny" and Betsy Hearne of the *Bulletin of the Center for Children's Books* praised Keller's "gift to connect absurd characters, themes, and situations with a logical certainty that

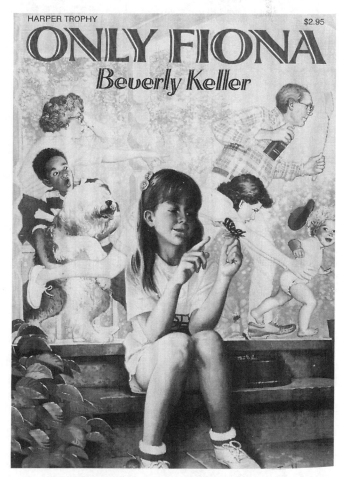

Keller's comical tale relates the plight of ten-year-old Fiona Foster, whose attempts to make friends in a new town are often undermined by her simultaneous efforts to impress upon others the importance of being humane to animals and insects. (Cover illustration by Tom Newsom.)

builds into farce." In a *School Library Journal* review, Linda Wicher called Desdemona's life "zany and appealing," while noting that Keller manages to include some "food for thought about slumlords, image-conscious politicians, and true friends."

Fowl Play and *Desdemona Moves On* continue the series about the Blank family. In *Fowl Play,* Desdemona decides to help her vegetarian friend's crusade against the eating of turkeys for Thanksgiving. Always finding herself in messy situations, Desdemona discovers that the printer confused her "save-a-turkey" flyers with ones advertising adult entertainers after she and Sherman already inserted them in the program for the school play. Although *Booklist* reviewer Ilene Cooper criticized some of Keller's minor persons as "stock characters who are little more than cartoons," she went on to applaud the "funny moments as well as several sobering ones that work well." Ranking Keller's Desdemona with Lois Lowry's Anastasia and Constance Greene's Al, *School Library Journal* contributor Sally T. Margolis lauded Keller's even handed approach to teaching children about animal rights without sounding like a "tract."

Once again, in *Desdemona Moves On,* the Blank family is facing eviction, this time just before Christmas. However, Desdemona's father finally manages to secure a new house which even has a swimming pool. After they move in, they are surprised to find the Chinese Olympic swim team practicing every day in their back yard. While she cautioned in *School Library Journal* that "some situations seem contrived," Mary Lou Budd claimed "the plot flows smoothly" and suggested this book for reluctant readers.

In 1996, Keller ventured into the world of young adult literature with her fast-paced book *The Amazon Papers.* When she's not working on cars or reading a book of philosophy, fifteen-year-old protagonist Iris Hoving—a straight-A student whose disappointed mother would rather her daughter be a popular cheerleader—is desperately seeking the attention of a handsome high school dropout and pizza delivery boy, Foster Prizer. When her mother goes on vacation, Iris arranges to meet Foster at a pool hall, but the evening becomes a disaster when Iris suffers a broken foot and vandals strip her mother's car. "Iris' narrative voice is dryly rueful and oddly suitable for a bright, unconventional young woman exasperatedly trying to figure out how she 'fits,'" noted Janice M. Del Negro of the *Bulletin of the Center for Children's Books.* In a *School Library Journal* review, Susan R. Farber called Iris "a wonderful, fully fleshed-out character," and praised the "true to life" ending in which Iris realizes she needs the help of an adult to get everything back in order.

Keller told *SATA:* "As a child, I didn't live anywhere, but travelled with my parents. Wherever we stayed, my father let it slip that he was really Lawrence Tibbett, the great Metropolitan opera star, secretly married to my mother, who was really Gertrude Ederle, the first woman to swim the English Channel. My mother weighed ninety pounds and was terrified of any body of water larger than a bathtub, but fortunately, nobody pressed her to do a few strokes.

"I knew what it was like to be treated like a star. We had flowers and fruit baskets and prime tables. Now and then the band leader would beg my father to honor the guests with an aria. Now and then my father obliged.

"So we changed schools often. By the time I was in high school, I'd attended thirteen schools, and in the process missed learning English grammar entirely. One compensates.

"I married in my junior year at UC Berkeley, and as soon as I was graduated, began writing a newspaper column at forty cents a column inch. As soon as I sold one piece to the *Atlantic* and another to *Women's Home Companion,* I decided that I would never work again for forty cents a column inch.

"By this time we had two daughters, and we lived for the next few years in Baghdad and Beirut. I got caught in a

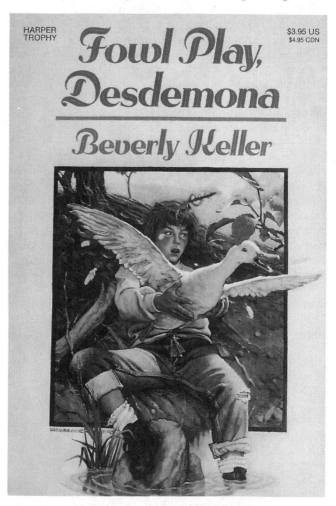

Keller's popular protagonist Desdemona Blank turns to her friend Sherman for help when she finds herself in charge of making posters for the school play, unaware that an opportunistic Sherman has ideas of his own for the poster campaign. (Cover illustration by Mike Wimmer.)

camel migration in Iraq, and we arrived in Beirut in time for the Suez Canal crisis. At its height, we drove through the Middle East and Europe, sleeping in abandoned villas on the Aegean, arriving in Rome at the outbreak of the Hungarian Revolution.

"We lived in a penthouse which had belonged to Count Ciano, Mussolini's son-in-law. It wound around the building—vast terraces, a marble foyer, bar, and sitting room, an enormous den full of assegais, spears, shields, guns ... and there were rooms I never cared to enter.

"Afterward we traveled third class by rail through Europe with two small children, which explains why I have looked my age for many years."

"I started doing precinct work when I was seven, passing out political flyers, and continued doing political volunteer work for years, serving as county co-chair for several presidential campaigns.

"If you have ever seen the Booth cartoon, 'Write about Dogs,' you may have some inkling of my working conditions. My dogs, which are large and many, doze and shed on bills, correspondence, and work in progress. I also knock myself out for cats in trouble, shelter spiders, and feed ants. I can't say my friends understand, but they're fond of me."

■ Works Cited

Review of *Only Fiona, Kirkus Reviews,* April 15, 1988, p. 619.

Budd, Mary Lou, review of *Desdemona Moves On, School Library Journal,* December, 1992, p. 112.

Cooper, Ilene, review of *Desdemona: Twelve Going on Desperate, Booklist,* October 1, 1986, p. 273.

Cooper, Ilene, review of *Fowl Play, Desdemona, Booklist,* April 1, 1989, p. 1385.

Del Negro, Janice M., review of *The Amazon Papers, Bulletin of the Center for Children's Books,* November, 1996, p. 101.

Farber, Susan R., review of *The Amazon Papers, School Library Journal,* October, 1996, pp. 147-48.

Review of *Fiona's Bee, Kirkus Reviews,* October 1, 1975, p. 1128.

Flowers, Ann A., review of *Fiona's Bee, Horn Book,* April, 1976, p. 151.

Hearne, Betsy, review of *Desdemona: Twelve Going on Desperate, Bulletin of the Center for Children's Books,* December, 1986, p. 70.

Knight, Elaine E., review of *No Beasts! No Children!, School Library Journal,* May, 1983, p. 72.

Margolis, Sally T., review of *Fowl Play, Desdemona, School Library Journal,* May, 1989, p. 110.

Sutherland, Zena, review of *No Beasts! No Children!, Bulletin of the Center for Children's Books,* March, 1983, p. 153.

Sutherland, Zena, review of *Only Fiona, Bulletin of the Center for Children's Books,* January, 1988, p. 93.

Wicher, Linda, review of *Desdemona: Twelve Going on Desperate, School Library Journal,* November, 1986, p. 90.

■ For More Information See

PERIODICALS

Booklist, December 15, 1975, p. 582; July 15, 1976, p. 1602; October 15, 1982, p. 317; September 1, 1983, p. 87; May 1, 1984, p. 1248; October 15, 1986, p. 359.

Bulletin of the Center for Children's Books, April, 1976, p. 126; October, 1976, p. 26; May, 1977, p. 144; May, 1978, p. 143; June, 1981, p. 196; June, 1982, p. 190; June, 1984, p. 188; July, 1984, p. 207; March, 1989, p. 173.

Horn Book, August, 1984, p. 466.

Kirkus Reviews, June 15, 1973, p. 659; June 1, 1976, p. 633; December 1, 1976, p. 1263; January 1, 1978, p. 3; February 15, 1979, p. 195; March 1, 1981, p. 283; August 1, 1981, p. 939; February 1, 1983, p. 121; February 15, 1989, p. 294.

Library Journal, August, 1973, p. 2342.

New York Times Book Review, August 19, 1973, p. 13.

Publishers Weekly, June 25, 1973, p. 69; June 4, 1982, p. 67.

School Library Journal, December, 1975, pp. 31, 62; December, 1976, p. 64; March, 1977, p. 133; March, 1978, p. 130; February, 1979, p. 43; May, 1981, p. 82; November, 1981, p. 106; February, 1982, p. 37; August, 1982, p. 98; December, 1982, p. 77; May, 1983, p. 32; May, 1984, p. 81; October, 1984, p. 148; October, 1985, p. 174; April, 1988, p. 101.

Voice of Youth Advocates, August, 1984, p. 147; December, 1996, p. 271.

*   *   *

KELLY, Kate 1958-

■ Personal

Born January 11, 1958, in Baraboo, WI; daughter of John Michael (a journalist) and Berneice (a journalist; maiden name, Schlemmer) Kelly; married Carleton Cato Ealy (in corporate development), March 22, 1986; children: Kendra Leigh. *Education:* Attended School for Irish Studies, Dublin, Ireland, 1978-79; Yale University, B.A., 1980. *Politics:* "Moderate/unaffiliated." *Religion:* Episcopalian. *Hobbies and other interests:* Cooking, gardening, dogs, natural history, archaeology, volunteering for local school and church activities.

■ Addresses

Home—129 Beechwood Ave., Trumbull, CT 06611. *Office*—632 Broadway, New York, NY 10012.

■ Career

William Morrow, New York City, editor, 1980-82; Facts On File, New York City, senior editor and executive editor, 1983-89; Simon & Schuster, New York City, executive editor, 1989-91; Irving Place, Inc., New York City, co-founder and principal, 1991—. *Member:* Yale Club of New York City.

■ Writings

FOR CHILDREN; "HOMEWORK REFERENCE" SERIES

(With Anne Zeman) *Everything You Need to Know about American History Homework: A Desk Reference for Students and Parents,* Scholastic, 1994.

(With Zeman) *Everything You Need to Know about Math Homework: A Desk Reference for Students and Parents,* Scholastic, 1994.

(With Zeman) *Everything You Need to Know about Science Homework: A Desk Reference for Students and Parents,* Scholastic, 1994.

(With Zeman) *Everything You Need to Know about World History Homework,* Scholastic, 1995.

(With Zeman) *Everything You Need to Know about English Homework,* Scholastic, 1995.

(With Zeman) *Everything You Need to Know about Geography,* Scholastic, 1997.

FOR ADULTS

What Color Is Your Toothbrush?, Pocket Books, 1985.
(Editor) *BBQ and All the Fixin's,* Macmillan, 1994.
Kindergarten Basics, Black Dog & Leventhal, 1995.
(Editor) *100 Easy Old-Fashioned Flowers,* Holt, 1995.
(Editor) *Encyclopedia Mysteriosa,* Prentice Hall, 1995.
(Editor) *New Native American Cooking,* Random House, 1996.

■ Work in Progress

The French Roast Cafe Breakfast and Brunch Book; Virginia Country Homes; The Three Maidens, about Native American food, lore, and recipes; *Thanksgiving,* "a historical cookbook of America's first holiday;" *Adirondack High Camp,* "examining the grand traditions of camping, from lean-tos to luxury hotels, in New York's Adirondack Mountains."

■ Sidelights

Kate Kelly told *SATA:* "The publishing industry has provided me with a flexible and fulfilling professional home for the past sixteen years, first as an editor, rising though the ranks at such houses as William Morrow, Facts On File, and Simon & Schuster, then (since 1991) as a book packager and author of nearly a dozen books. My career has also allowed me to introduce in the most sincere way a love of books and reading to my daughter."

*   *   *

KNOX, Calvin M.
  See SILVERBERG, Robert

KUNTZ, J(ohn) L. 1947-

■ Personal

Surname has an umlaut over the "u"; born August 23, 1947, in Banner Elk, NC; son of William C. (a truck driver) and Norma L. (a teacher) Whitehead-Kuntz; children: Christine Villabona Kuntz. *Education:* University of Maryland, B.S. (cum laude), 1979; Washington College, M.A., 1982; The Johns Hopkins University, M.L.A., 1985, C.A.S., 1989; additional graduate work at Anne Arundel College and University of Nevada-Reno, 1991-94; English Ph.D. candidate, Bath College, U.K. *Religion:* Southern Baptist. *Hobbies and other interests:* Mountain biking, cross-country skiing, mountaineering and rock climbing, hiking, studying Southern mythology and folklore.

■ Addresses

Home—560 Glen Ct., Glen Burnie, MD 21061-4734; and 4224 Belvoir Dr., East Ridge, Chattanooga, TN 37412.

■ Career

U.S. Air Force-U.S. Army, 1966—, served as Army Special Forces Intelligence and Demolition Sergeant and senior mountaineering instructor, currently AGR Battalion Operations Sergeant-Major, SGM, E-9, and

J. L. KUNTZ

works as operations and training specialist for the 29th Light Infantry Division, Towson, MD. Taught literature, writing, and psychology at Queen Anne's County High School, 1979-80.

■ Writings

Tennessee Tiger (children's novel), illustrated by Tina Wells Davenport, Winston-Derek, 1996.

Has also published a short story entitled "In the Shed," Tropos Press, 1986.

■ Work in Progress

Ocoee, a completed children's novel; *The Ravenel,* a children's novel in progress.

■ Sidelights

J. L. Kuntz told *SATA:* "I feel that I am ready to make the transition from the military to a civilian career. This comes at a rather ironic moment, as Congress is 'downsizing' the military force. I have always wanted to teach on the college level, and I feel that I have a lot of personal experiences that would be beneficial to young people. I plan on completing my Ph.D. as soon as possible. I now have my third children's novel in the final-draft stage, as I began doing the research work on the novel three years ago in Charleston, S.C. I am fortunate that I have been in military training over the past thirty years. It has brought me into close contact with peoples of different cultures, from wide areas of location. I have been an instructor and advisor in Estonia, Alaska, Italy, Norway, and all over the United States in Military Training affairs. It has caused my life to be exciting and meaningful. I view the college classroom as an arena to continue the teaching experience."

*   *   *

KURTZ, Jane 1952-

■ Personal

Born April 17, 1952, in Portland, OR; daughter of Harold (a Presbyterian minister) and Pauline Kurtz; married Leonard Goering, 1979; children: David, Jonathan, Rebekah. *Education:* Monmouth College, B.A., 1973; University of North Dakota, M.A., 1995.

■ Addresses

Home—1210 Lincoln Dr., Grand Forks, ND 58201. *Office*—English Dept., University of North Dakota, Grand Forks, ND 58202-7209. *Electronic Mail*—jkurtz@badlands.nodak.edu. *Agent*—Pesha Rubinstein Literary Agency, 1392 Rugby Rd., Teaneck, NJ 07666.

JANE KURTZ

■ Career

Carbondale New School, Carbondale, IL, teacher/director, 1975-81; Trinidad Catholic High School, Trinidad, CO, teacher, 1984-89; University of North Dakota, Grand Forks, lecturer, 1995—. *Member:* Society of Children's Book Writers and Illustrators.

■ Writings

FICTION

I'm Calling Molly, illustrated by Irene Trivas, Albert Whitman, 1990.
Fire on the Mountain, illustrated by Earl B. Lewis, Simon & Schuster, 1994.
Pulling the Lion's Tail, illustrated by Floyd Cooper, Simon & Schuster, 1995.
Miro in the Kingdom of the Sun, illustrated by David Frampton, Houghton, 1996.
(With Christopher Kurtz) *Only a Pigeon,* illustrated by Earl B. Lewis, Simon & Schuster, 1997.
Trouble, illustrated by Durga Bernhard, Harcourt, 1997.
The Storyteller's Beads, Harcourt, in press.
My Father's Wild Home, illustrated by Michael Bryant, Harcourt, in press.

NONFICTION

Ethiopia: The Roof of Africa, Dillon/Macmillan, 1991.
The American Southwest Resource Book: The People, Eakin Press, 1996.

OTHER

Contributor to *School Library Journal*. Reviewer for "Book Connection," a weekly children's book review column in Knight-Ridder newspapers.

■ Work in Progress

All the Wisdom in the World, Harcourt; *Etta Baker: Music Maker,* Harcourt; a historical novel set in South Dakota.

■ Sidelights

"When I was two years old," Jane Kurtz told *SATA,* "living in Portland, Oregon, my parents decided to move to Ethiopia to work for the Presbyterian church there. I often trace my career as a writer back to that decision. All of my early childhood memories are of Maji, a small village in southwestern Ethiopia, where my sisters and I explored, made up and acted out stories, and listened to stories told by my father and by other people around us. Though the whole town had only two or three motorized vehicles, no television, no radio stations, no computer games, no movies, I never felt a lack of entertainment. Life was full of sensations, interesting people, and adventures."

Drawing from these experiences, Kurtz's books are typically either about or set in Ethiopia, as is the case with *Ethiopia: The Roof of Africa,* a nonfiction work for middle schoolers about life in Ethiopia. Similarly, her fictional stories, such as *Fire on the Mountain, Pulling the Lion's Tale,* and *Trouble,* are the retelling of popular tales Kurtz heard as a youngster in Ethiopia and include characters based on some of her childhood friends.

Her first work, *I'm Calling Molly,* is a story about friendship featuring four-year-old protagonist Christopher and his friend Molly. After learning how to call Molly over the phone, Christopher invites her over for a play date. She turns him down, however, because she is already playing with another friend. Hurt and disappointed, Christopher plays by himself. After Molly's friend leaves, she calls Christopher to play and the two resolve their differences. Complimenting Kurtz's presentation of an occurrence common among children, reviewer Marge Loch-Wouters noted in *School Library Journal* that "Kurtz and [illustrator Irene] Trivas catch the essence of children's spats and casual rejections without making the situations uncomfortable or cruel."

Turning to nonfiction, Kurtz published *Ethiopia: The Roof of Africa* in 1991, describing in this work many aspects of present-day Ethiopian life, including food, markets, festivals, and legends, famine, emigration, and war. Reviewer Loretta Kreider Andrews, writing for *School Library Journal,* maintained that "Kurtz conveys a lively sense of reality through concrete descriptions of . . . Ethiopian life." Information for this work was taken from the author's personal knowledge of the country in addition to formal research. Kurtz told *SATA* that it "was an important and healing thing to do research on the geography and history of the country

where I grew up, things I never studied because I was being prepared to come back to the U.S. schools."

A few years after writing *Ethiopia: The Roof of Africa,* Kurtz began devoting her attention to the retelling of folk tales, some of which are from Ethiopia, and others variants from other cultures. "I began to do my own versions of stories I had heard as a child in Ethiopia, putting characters into them who were like the playmates I grew up with," Kurtz explained to *SATA. Fire on the Mountain,* a picture book based on a well-known Ethiopian tale, focuses on Alemayu, an orphaned boy searching for his sister, who works as a cook for a wealthy and boastful man. After finding his sister, Alemayu takes a job as a cowherd, working for the same man. Challenged by his employer to spend a cold night alone in the mountains wearing only light clothing, Alemayu wins the bet by imagining himself warmed by a distant fire. His sore-losing boss, however, refuses to admit he lost and won't pay up. Left to their own wits, the siblings devise a clever plan that causes the man to keep his end of the bargain. Janice Del Negro, writing for *Booklist,* admired how Kurtz retells the tale "in a strong narrative voice: her language is simple and spare yet evocative." *School Library Journal* contributor Jos N. Holman noted that "this is a well-written retelling that's sure to be enjoyed whether read individually or aloud."

Pulling the Lion's Tale is based on the Ethiopian folktale *The Lion's Whiskers,* a story about a mother who had lost the love of her son. Kurtz retells the tale by focusing on a stepmother and stepdaughter relationship. In Kurtz's version, Almaz tries to win her stepmother's love by pulling some hair from the tale of a lion. "Kurtz's language has a tender lyricism further empha-

Almaz's grandfather teaches her to value patience in Kurtz's *Pulling the Lion's Tail*. (Cover illustration by Floyd Cooper.)

sized by [Floyd] Cooper's oil paintings," wrote Loretta Kreider Andrews in *School Library Journal.*

In *Miro in the Kingdom of the Sun*—a familiar folktale in many cultures—Kurtz focuses on the Ecuadoran Inca variant. She tells of a heroic girl who saves the life of an ailing prince (along with her bird friends) by bringing him water containing magical healing powers from a faraway lake. Those who attempted to collect the water before had failed, including her brothers, who were imprisoned for presenting ordinary water as the real thing. A reviewer for *Publishers Weekly* praised the way Kurtz "deftly weaves in details of pre-Conquest Inca life, giving readers a glimpse of a vanished culture as well as a good story." Similarly, a commentator for *Kirkus Reviews* appreciated the way Kurtz "combines formal language and a contemporary style to make the story at once accessible and otherworldly."

Kurtz returned to the United States twice during her childhood years. Of her experiences during these lengthy visits she told *SATA:* "Ethiopia was home and I generally felt like a stranger among my peers in the United States, who hardly knew what questions to ask and—if they did manage a question—were likely to blurt out something like 'Did you see Tarzan?'" After moving back to the United States to attend college, Kurtz decided to play down her years in Ethiopia and focus on American life. "Nearly twenty years later, my feelings of homesickness and longing led to the realization that I could connect with my childhood—through the books and stories I was writing," Kurtz revealed. "My books have given me a way to connect with my own memories, with Ethiopian friends here in the United States and in Ethiopia, and with school children. For the first time, I can comfortably go into a classroom and talk about growing up in a beautiful country far away from where I now live."

■ Works Cited

Andrews, Loretta Kreider, review of *Ethiopia: The Roof of Africa, School Library Journal,* May, 1992, p. 123.

Andrews, Loretta Kreider, review of *Pulling the Lion's Tale, School Library Journal,* December, 1995, p. 83.

Del Negro, Janice, review of *Fire on the Mountain, Booklist,* October 15, 1994, p. 432.

Holman, Jos N., review of *Fire on the Mountain, School Library Journal,* December, 1994, p. 99.

Loch-Wouters, Marge, review of *I'm Calling Molly, School Library Journal,* March, 1990, p. 198.

Review of *Miro in the Kingdom of the Sun, Kirkus Reviews,* January 15, 1996, p. 137.

Review of *Miro in the Kingdom of the Sun, Publishers Weekly,* April 8, 1996, p. 67.

■ For More Information See

PERIODICALS

Booklist, September 1, 1995, p. 87.
Five Owls, November, 1995, p. 35.
Horn Book, November-December, 1994, p. 739.
New Advocate, summer, 1995, pp. 213-14.

L

LEHMAN, Bob

■ Personal

Born in Wilkinsburg, PA; son of Roy F. (a printer and mechanic) and Ellen E. (a homemaker) Lehman; married Elaine Pawelek (a writer and teacher), August 28, 1976; children: Scott, Craig, Debra, Susan, Lynn, Deborah. *Education:* Northrop University, graduate of Aircraft Maintenance Engineering program; Brevard Community College, A.A.; studied at Florida Technological University. *Politics:* Independent. *Religion:* "Deeply spiritual! but not a member of a church." *Hobbies and other interests:* Rebuilding antique, classic aircraft, warbirds, and round engines.

■ Addresses

Office—943 Sudden Valley, Bellingham, WA 98226-4825.

■ Career

Cape Canaveral, FL, rocket engineer, 1956-77; worked as an airframe and powerplant mechanic in Maryland, Virginia, and Oregon, 1977-1994; freelance writer, 1994—. *Military service:* U.S. Air Force, jet fighter specialist and flight chief, 1950-54; served in Philippine Islands for two years during Korean conflict. *Member:* Society of Automotive Engineers, American Motorcycle Association, Good Sam Recreational Vehicle Club.

■ Writings

(With wife, Elaine Lehman) *Petey the Peacock Breaks a Leg,* Winston-Derek (Nashville, TN), 1995.

■ Work in Progress

Petey the Peacock Is a Daddy.

A baby peacock gets into trouble when he strays away from his mother in this illustrated adventure.

■ Sidelights

"I'm a doer," Bob Lehman told *SATA.* "I have to be busy with my hands. After twenty-one years as a rocket engineer at Cape Canaveral, Florida, I changed careers and locations to help straighten out my delinquent son.

120

Because of him, my wife, Elaine, and I are very concerned about the nation's out-of-control youth. Every children's book we write will be aimed at helping to reach young children before they get into the drugs, drop-out, teen pregnancy, and crime lifestyle.

"I rebuild antique and classic aircraft, warbirds, and round engines. This type of work brings me great pleasure. I also have been involved, along with Elaine, with improving any house we live in. This certainly keeps my hands busy. But, as if that were not enough, I'm now learning to play the piano."*

* * *

LEHMAN, Elaine

■ Personal

Daughter of Stanley J. (a school supervisor) and Constance (an assistant school superintendent) Pawelek; married Bob Lehman (a writer and rocket engineer and mechanic), August 28, 1976; children: Scott, Craig, Debra, Susan, Lynn, Deborah. *Education:* Towson State University, B.S., 1958. *Politics:* Independent. *Religion:* "Deeply spiritual, but not a member of a church."

■ Addresses

Office—943 Sudden Valley, Bellingham, WA 98226-4825.

■ Career

Writer. Worked as a public school teacher in Baltimore, MD, 1957-60.

■ Writings

(And illustrator; with husband, Bob Lehman) *Petey the Peacock Breaks a Leg,* Winston-Derek (Nashville, TN), 1995.

■ Work in Progress

Petey the Peacock Is a Daddy.

■ Sidelights

"I am deeply involved with personal growth and spiritual development," Elaine Lehman told *SATA*. "I spent the last thirty-five years learning everything I could about human behavior—and changed my own in the process. It's a passion I expect will go on for the rest of my life.

"Peacock relationships and behaviors are amazing. Both *Petey the Peacock Breaks a Leg* and *Petey the Peacock Is a Daddy* contain information about peacocks that has never before been published. Petey was a real peacock on our ranch in the Willamette Valley of Oregon. *Petey the Peacock Breaks a Leg* is a true story and contains healthy values for both inner city and suburban youth

and their parents. *Petey the Peacock Is a Daddy* is a fictional story about our real little peacock. Without deviating from true peacock behavior, this story shows Petey taking charge of his own naughty chick.

"My husband, Bob, and I are co-authors, and I do the illustrating. We are opposites, and we work together comfortably and compatibly. After exploring other careers, we embarked on this one—and it's a labor of love! We each have an office in our home, and balance our writing with travel and reading."

"Bob and I love to improve any house we live in, and I actively seek creative ideas which my talented husband carries out. As another hobby, I write a family newsletter at least once a month. With six adult children spread all across the nation, their spouses, and our four grandchildren, I do a LOT of communicating!"

* * *

LIGHTBURN, Ron 1954-

■ Personal

Born June 24, 1954, in Cobourg, Ontario, Canada; son of Thomas George (a court reporter) and Mary Veronica (an antique dealer; maiden name Scarisbrick) Lightburn; married Sandra Rosemarie Meyer (an author), June 9, 1975. *Education:* Attended Alberta College of

RON LIGHTBURN

Art, 1973-75. *Hobbies and other interests:* Film studies, travel.

■ Addresses

Home—803-1034 Johnson St., Victoria, British Columbia, Canada V8V 3N7.

■ Career

Illustrator, 1975—; lecturer throughout Canada, 1992—. *Member:* Canadian Children's Book Centre, Canadian Society of Children's Authors, Illustrators, and Performers (CANSCAIP), International Board on Books for Young People (IBBY), Society of Children's Book Writers and Illustrators (SCBWI), Children's Writers and Illustrators of British Columbia, Society of Illustrators.

■ Awards, Honors

Waiting for the Whales received the Governor General's Literary Award for Children's Illustration, the Amelia Frances Howard-Gibbon Illustrators Award, and the Elizabeth Mrazik Cleaver Canadian Picture Book Award, all in 1992. *How Smudge Came* received Mr. Christie's Book Award and the Sheila A. Egoff Children's Literature Prize, both in 1996.

■ Illustrator

Sheryl McFarlane, *Waiting for the Whales,* Orca Book Publishers (Victoria, British Columbia, Canada), 1991, Philomel, 1993.
Patti Farmer, *I Can't Sleep!,* Orca Book Publishers, 1992.
Sheryl McFarlane, *Eagle Dreams,* Orca Book Publishers, 1994, Philomel, 1995.
Nan Gregory, *How Smudge Came,* Red Deer College Press, 1995.
Sandra Lightburn, *Driftwood Cove,* Doubleday, 1997.

Contributor of illustrations to *Mother Goose—A Canadian Sampler,* Groundwood Books, 1994. Illustrated over two dozen book covers for a number of Canadian and American publishers, including Doubleday, Kids Can Press, HarperCollins, and Scholastic. Works selected for a number of reference books, including *The Very Best of Children's Book Illustration, The Best of Colored Pencil,* and *The Best of Colored Pencil Two.*

■ Sidelights

Ron Lightburn is an illustrator noted for his joyful and luminous colored-pencil picture book drawings. Although Lightburn has been illustrating for more than two decades, he didn't start working on picture books until 1991, when Orca Book Publishers commissioned him to create pictures for Sheryl McFarlane's *Waiting for the Whales.*

Waiting for the Whales, the winner of Canada's prestigious Governor General's Literary Award for Children's

Lightburn's colored-pencil drawings for Sheryl McFarlane's *Waiting for the Whales* earned him the Amelia Frances Howard-Gibbon Award for illustration.

Illustration, is the story of an old man who lives alone in a cottage by the sea. He occupies his time by gathering firewood and collecting clams during the winter, planting a huge garden in the spring, and waiting for the whales to swim by his beach in summer. When his daughter and granddaughter move in with him, he is happy to share his love of nature with them. Eventually the old man dies, leaving his family to care for his garden. Applauding Lightburn's illustrations, *School Library Journal* contributor Kathleen Odean wrote, "The lovely colored-pencil drawings ... beautifully capture the sense of waiting and stillness." A *Publishers Weekly* reviewer added: "His use of light and shade ... proves remarkable."

Lightburn illustrated *I Can't Sleep!,* by Patti Farmer, in 1992, and another book by Sheryl McFarlane, *Eagle Dreams,* in 1994. *Eagle Dreams* is the story of a young boy who finds an injured eagle while flying his kite and wants to help it, but his farmer father feels the boy is too busy to take care of it. Against his father's wishes, the boy cares for the large bird and has a veterinarian set its broken wing. The bird eventually recovers and leaves the farm with a powerful exit. "Lightburn's dramatically changing perspectives entice readers to note the many subtle details while reflecting on the mood of each," commented Ronald Jobe for *School Library Journal.* In order to make these pictures come to life, Lightburn told *SATA* that he "accompanied veterinarians on their rounds to farms and found a dairy farm family to portray the characters in the book."

In 1995 Lightburn illustrated Nan Gregory's *How Smudge Came,* the story of Cindy—who lives in a group home that doesn't allow dogs—and her newly found puppy Smudge. Next came *Driftwood Cove* (written by his wife, Sandra), which is about a friendship that develops between campers from the city and squatters who live on the beach. In addition to picture book illustrations, Lightburn has created over two dozen book covers for a number of publishers and has also contributed drawings to *Mother Goose—A Canadian Sampler.*

Lightburn told *SATA,* "As a child growing up in West Vancouver, British Columbia, Canada, I enjoyed making coloured pencil drawings and reading books, such as the Rupert Bear annuals by British author Alfred Bestall. Since that time, I have had a continuing interest in making pictures that tell a story. Two years of studies at the Alberta College of Art gave me the opportunity to experiment with a variety of artistic mediums and introduced me to the world of art history. Settling in Victoria in 1975, I soon established a career as an illustrator with commissions for a variety of North American publications. In 1982 coloured pencils became my medium of choice. Recently I have been using oil paints for some of my illustration projects.

"My most important influence is the world around me. I'm always looking for the best way to tell the story I am working on and to ensure that the words and pictures are in perfect harmony."

■ Works Cited

Jobe, Ronald, review of *Eagle Dreams, School Library Journal,* June, 1995, pp. 91-92.
Odean, Kathleen, review of *Waiting for the Whales, School Library Journal,* June, 1993, p. 83.
Review of *Waiting for the Whales, Publishers Weekly,* March 15, 1993, p. 86.

■ For More Information See

PERIODICALS

Booklist, May 15, 1993, p. 1696; May 1, 1995, p. 1580; March 15, 1996, p. 1262.

*   *   *

LIGHTBURN, Sandra 1955-

■ Personal

Born May 5, 1955, in Calgary, Alberta, Canada; daughter of Conrad Adam (a welding instructor) and Ethel Regina (a homemaker; maiden name, Schappert) Meyer; married Ron Lightburn (an illustrator), June 9, 1975. *Hobbies and other interests:* "Reading while enjoying Earl Grey tea and florentines."

■ Addresses

Home—803-1034 Johnson St., Victoria, British Columbia, Canada V8V 3N7.

SANDRA LIGHTBURN

■ Career

Writer.

■ Writings

Driftwood Cove, illustrated by Ron Lightburn, Doubleday, 1997.

■ Sidelights

Sandra Lightburn told *SATA,* "I am a child in an adult's body. Opening a new package of crayons still thrills me. Reading and re-reading my collection of children's books refreshes me.

"My love of children's literature led me to write a story of my own, *Driftwood Cove,* which is about a friendship that develops between campers from the city and squatters who live on a beach. I have lived on the West Coast for the past twenty-one years and drew upon my knowledge of my coastal environment for the story's setting.

"Ron Lightburn, my husband and award-winning illustrator, readily agreed to illustrate *Driftwood Cove.* As we discussed the images that were in my mind when I wrote the story, I was able to participate in the process of turning my words into pictures. This is an experience rarely shared by authors and illustrators."

*   *   *

LUTTRELL, Ida (Alleene) 1934-

■ Personal

Surname is accented on first syllable; born April 18, 1934, in Laredo, TX; daughter of Pelton Bruce (a rancher) and Helen (a teacher and rancher; maiden name, Sewell) Harbison; married William S. Luttrell (in real estate and insurance), January 20, 1959; children: Robert, Anne, Billy, Richard. *Education:* University of Texas, B.A., 1955; also attended University of Houston, 1960, and Houston Baptist University, 1969-71. *Religion:* Protestant. *Hobbies and other interests:* "One of my favorite activities is helping in the school library and reading to the primary grades. I also enjoy birding, gardening, plays, family get-togethers, and sharing my husband's interest in old and contemporary art glass. I also like to do needlework occasionally, including designing and stitching quilts."

■ Addresses

Home—12211 Beauregard, Houston, TX 77024.

■ Career

University of Texas, Main University (now University of Texas at Austin), Austin, TX, laboratory technician at Biochemical Institute, 1954-55; Texas Children's Hospital, Houston, TX, bacteriologist, 1955-63; Luttrell Insurance Agency, Houston, part-time secretary, 1963—. Writer. *Member:* Society of Children's Book Writers and Illustrators, Authors Unlimited of Houston.

■ Awards, Honors

Le Prix Bernard Versele (Belgium), Ligue des Familles, 1991, for *One Day at School; Three Good Blankets* and *Milo's Toothache* were selected to Bank Street College's Children's Book of the Year list.

■ Writings

Not Like That, *Armadillo,* illustrated by Janet Stevens, Harcourt, 1982.
One Day at School, illustrated by Jared D. Lee, Harcourt, 1984.
Lonesome Lester, illustrated by Megan Lloyd, Harper, 1984.
Tillie and Mert, illustrated by Doug Cushman, Harper, 1985.
Mattie and the Chicken Thief, illustrated by Thacher Hurd, Dodd, 1988.
Ottie Slockett, illustrated by Ute Krause, Dial, 1990.
Three Good Blankets, illustrated by Michael McDermott, Atheneum, 1990.
The Bear Next Door, illustrated by Sarah Stapler, HarperCollins, 1991.

Be Nice to Marilyn, illustrated by Lonnie Sue Johnson, Atheneum, 1992.
Milo's Toothache, illustrated by Enzo Giannini, Dial, 1992.
Mattie's Little Possum Pet, illustrated by Betsy Lewin, Atheneum, 1993.
The Star Counters, illustrated by Korinna Pretro, Tambourine Books, 1994.

Contributor to several books, including *Collectible Glass,* edited by A. Christian Revi, Everybody's Press, 1980, and *Three Ingredient Cookbook,* edited by Phyllis Prokop, 1981. Contributor of articles to periodicals such as *Antique Trader, Collectible Glass,* and *Spinning Wheel.*

■ Sidelights

Growing up on a ranch as a child, Ida Luttrell learned to enjoy the companionship of animals, and she continues to express that love for small creatures in her books for children. In her first picture book, *Not Like* That, *Armadillo,* Luttrell tells cheerful short stories about a silly Armadillo who relies on his friends to teach him life's small intricacies, for instance explaining to Armadillo why he must first purchase a glass of lemonade before he can buy a refill. While Rabbit and Turtle often disappoint Armadillo's good intentions, such as when Armadillo rubs bananas all over his body because he hears they are good for his skin, the two friends also help Armadillo make his wish come true when he throws a lucky penny into a swimming hole instead of a wishing well. A reviewer in *Publishers Weekly* calls *Not Like* That *Armadillo* an easy-to-read book "enticing to beginners," and Denise M. Wilms in *Booklist* notes that even though the use of animals in children's books "isn't fresh, the stories are humorous."

Luttrell's experiences as a child on the wide open, sparsely populated ranches of Texas surface in her 1984 book about a lonely prairie dog named Lester. In *Lonesome Lester,* Luttrell teaches children that there is all kinds of company. Living on the outskirts of a prairie, Lester wishes someone, anyone would come and see him. After being visited by an army of ants who eat everything in sight, a kindly aunt who tries to preserve everything in wax, and a lost little rabbit who refuses to stop crying for his mother, Lester realizes that some guests are better than others and perhaps being alone is not all so bad. Commenting in *School Library Journal,* Kay McPherson applauds "the droll incongruous humor of Lester" and adds that "his predicaments will appeal both to those who can read the easy-to-read text and to younger children." Although there are four stories, Karen Stang Hanley notes in *Booklist* that children will find no problem reading them all in one storytime and compliments the maps of Lester's town drawn on the bookflaps, saying they are "a nice extension of the story for older viewers."

When she thinks a thief is after her chickens, Mattie decides to take action in Luttrell's 1988 picture book, *Mattie and the Chicken Thief.* Using everything from

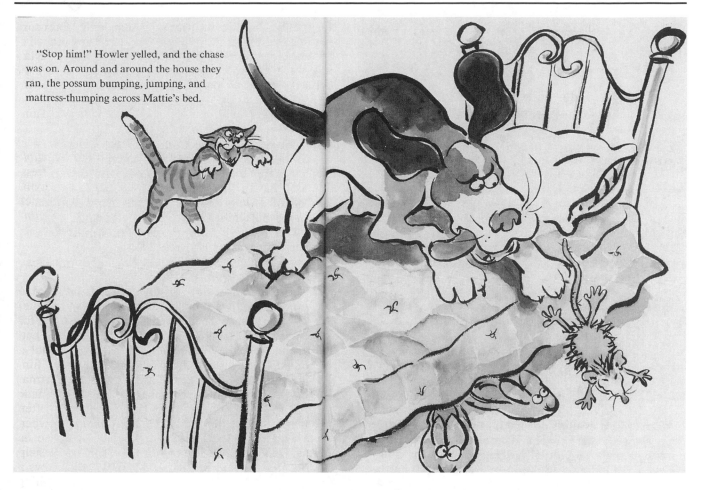

"Stop him!" Howler yelled, and the chase was on. Around and around the house they ran, the possum bumping, jumping, and mattress-thumping across Mattie's bed.

Mattie's new pet, a baby possum, creates havoc for her dog and cat in Ida Luttrell's comical *Mattie's Little Possum Pet*, illustrated by Betsy Lewin.

pots and pans to old bedsprings, Mattie builds an intricate trap to catch the chicken thief, not realizing that it is her own cat and dog, Prowler and Howler, who have frightened away the chickens. When Prowler and Howler see Mattie's trap, they decide that they should go out into the woods and try to drive the hens back into their house. On the way, however, the animals set off the oddly-built trap, surprising everyone with the terrible racket. Describing *Mattie and the Chicken Thief* as "a rollicking picture book," Bessie Egan, writing in *School Library Journal*, claims "children will enjoy the humorous antics of Maggie and her friends in this visually attractive picture book." In *Horn Book*, reviewer Ethel R. Twichell calls the story "less than exciting," but adds that the explosion of Mattie's contraption "will provide moments of round-eyed enjoyment." A critic in *Kirkus Reviews* praises Luttrell's "economic style that makes comic use of concrete description" and notes that the story "should be a satisfying addition to picture book hours."

Mattie, Prowler, and Howler all appear again in *Mattie's Little Possum Pet*. This time, Mattie finds a possum lying belly-up and, not realizing the critter is just playing dead, brings the poor creature to her farm. Soon, chaos erupts, and Prowler and Howler are blamed when the possum spills the milk, breaks the eggs, and jumps on the bed. Finally, the crafty cat and dog devise a plan to expose the possum for the troublemaker he is. "Kids will love the fury," says Hazel Rochman in *Booklist*, "as well as the gleeful reversal." A critic in *Publishers Weekly* finds the text "lively" and thinks Luttrell and illustrator Betsy Lewin created "an animated, expressively illustrated work." "A story-hour favorite," claims a critic in Kirkus Reviews who describes *Mattie's Little Possum Pet* as "folksy in language, spirited in delivery, a winning read-aloud or alone."

A greedy king is the central character in Luttrell's *The Star Counters*. His royal highness thinks he owns every star in the night sky and tries to count each one, making sure no stars are missing. The king soon finds the task tiresome and tries to find someone else to look after his stars, first hiring a turtle, who can't count past ten; then a fox, who won't count things prettier than himself; and finally a quiet, reliable cow. Never trusting anyone, the king watches over the cow, making sure she doesn't steal a single star. All goes well until he sees the cow drinking out of a small pond and accuses her of stealing the reflected stars. As the king looks up at the sky for his missing celestial wonders, he sees shooting stars, chases after them, and is never seen again. In *Booklist*, Kay Weisman calls *The Star Counters* a "comic look at obsession gone too far."

A greedy king assumes ownership of all the stars in the sky and seeks the help of a quiet, reliable cow to keep track of them in Luttrell's whimsical tale *The Star Counters,* illustrated by Korinna Pretro.

Ida Luttrell once commented to *SATA:* "I grew up on a small ranch in south Texas, in a family where children were plentiful and money was scarce. We could not buy books, but I can still remember the thrill of checking out my first book from the county library—*Angus and the Ducks* by Marjorie Flack, the even greater thrill when I could finally read it, and the longing to have A. A. Milne's *Winnie the Pooh* for my very own. Because ranch life was so isolated, books were a great diversion for us, as well as taming baby rabbits, mice, quail, owls, or ground squirrels for pets, and the joy we found in the profusion of wild flowers that bloomed in the fields and pastures.

"Both parents stressed the importance of an education, and there was never any doubt that we would all go to college. So I went to the University of Texas and became a bacteriologist. During the time I worked at Texas Children's Hospital I met my husband, and we now have four children. Through my children I once again became interested in children's books. I have very happy memories of reading to my children when they were small, and the closeness that sharing pleasures brings.

"Because books and reading have been so important to me, it distresses me to hear of the cutbacks in funding for public libraries. Citizens whose only source of reading material is the public library are being robbed of the enrichment books provide. With test scores declining, we need more exposure to books, and I feel the cutbacks could be made in other areas."

■ Works Cited

Egan, Bessie, review of *Mattie and the Chicken Thief,* School Library Journal, February, 1989, p. 72.

Hanley, Karen Stang, review of *Lonesome Lester, Booklist,* May 1, 1984, p. 1251.

Review of *Mattie and the Chicken Thief, Kirkus Reviews,* September 15, 1988, p. 1406.

Review of *Mattie's Little Possum Pet, Kirkus Reviews,* September 15, 1993, p. 1205.

Review of *Mattie's Little Possum Pet, Publishers Weekly,* July 19, 1993, p. 253.

McPherson, Kay, review of *Lonesome Lester, School Library Journal,* May, 1984, p. 67.

Review of *Not Like That Armadillo, Publishers Weekly,* November 12, 1982, p. 67.

Rochman, Hazel, review of *Mattie's Little Possum Pet, Booklist,* August, 1993, p. 2071.

Twichell, Ethel R., review of *Mattie and the Chicken Thief, Horn Book,* November-December, 1988, p. 774.

Weisman, Kay, review of *The Star Counters, Booklist,* May 15, 1994, p. 1683.

Wilms, Denise M., review of *Not Like That, Armadillo, Booklist,* September 15, 1982, p. 122.

■ For More Information See

BOOKS

Goettsche, Jacque, and Phyllis Prokop, *A Kind of Splendor,* Broadman (Nashville, TN), 1980.

PERIODICALS

Booklist, October 15, 1985, p. 342; December 1, 1988, p. 652; April 1, 1990, p. 1561; April 1, 1991, p. 1578; November 1, 1992, p. 521.

Bulletin of the Center for Children's Books, November, 1984, p. 50; January, 1986, p. 90.

Children's Book Review Service, spring, 1984, p. 1251; July, 1994, p. 148.

Horn Book, November, 1990, p. 730.

Kirkus Reviews, November 15, 1985, p. 1265; June 1, 1990, p. 806; March 15, 1991, p. 404; October 15, 1992, p. 1312.

New York Times Book Review, August 14, 1994, p. 22.

Publishers Weekly, December 13, 1985, p. 53; October 12, 1988, p. 72; April 13, 1992, p. 59; August 31, 1992, p. 78.

School Library Journal, December, 1982, p. 78; October, 1984, p. 149; December, 1985, p. 109; June, 1990, p. 104; January, 1991, p. 77; June, 1991, p. 85; November, 1992, p. 73; January, 1993, p. 81; September, 1993, p. 210.

M

MacCARTER, Don 1944-

■ Personal

Born July 9, 1944, in Great Falls, MT; son of Douglas and Dorothy MacCarter; married Jane Susan MacCarter (a writer); children: Mindy, Kent. *Education:* University of Montana, B.S., 1967; Humboldt State University, M.S., 1971. *Politics:* Independent.

■ Addresses

Home—2884 Plaza Blanca, Santa Fe, NM 87505. *Office*—141 East DeVargas St., Santa Fe, NM 87501.

■ Career

New Mexico Department of Game and Fish, Santa Fe, NM, assistant chief of public affairs, 1983—, and official photographer.

■ Awards, Honors

Western Regional Environmental Education Council, Project WILD, Project Learning Tree.

PHOTOGRAPHER

Jennifer Owings Dewey, *Wildlife Rescue: The Work of Dr. Kathleen Ramsay*, Boyds Mills Press, 1994.

Jane MacCarter, *The New Mexico Wildlife Viewing Guide*, Falcon Press, 1994.

Photographs regularly featured in *New Mexico Wildlife*, the magazine of the New Mexico Department of Game and Fish.

MANN, Kenny 1946-

■ Personal

Born May 1, 1946, in Nairobi, Kenya. *Children:* Sophie. *Education:* University of East Africa, Nairobi, B.Sc.,

KENNY MANN

1968; Bristol University, Bristol, England, diploma in film and theatre arts, 1969; Bank Street College of Education, M.Sc., 1992. *Hobbies and other interests:* Music ("all kinds"), dance ("modern"), theatre ("experimental").

■ Addresses

Office—29 Henry St., Sag Harbor, NY 11963.

■ Career

Author, editor, and educator. Bank Street Publications, New York City, editor and writer, 1990-92; Simon & Schuster/Dillon Press, Parsippany, NJ, author and picture researcher, 1993—; Marshall-Cavendish Benchmark Books, White Plains, NY, author, 1995—; Institute of Children's Literature, Redding, CT, member of faculty, 1996—. Faculty member of Southampton College and Friends World College. Freelance educational consultant. Also worked as a documentary filmmaker and radio show producer and host in Hamburg, Germany, and as a tour and public relations manager for Polydor Records in Germany. *Member:* African Studies Association, Association for Supervision and Curriculum Development, Authors Guild, Earthwatch.

■ Awards, Honors

Excellence in Educational Journalism Award, National Educational Press Association, 1994.

■ Writings

"AFRICAN KINGDOMS OF THE PAST" SERIES; PUBLISHED BY SIMON AND SCHUSTER/DILLON PRESS

The Western Sudan: Ghana, Mali, Songhay, 1996.
The Guinea Coast: Oyo, Benin, Ashanti, 1996.
Monomotapa, Great Zimbabwe, Zululand, Lesotho: Southern Africa, 1996.
Kongo Ndongo: West Central Africa, 1996.
Zenj, Buganda: East Africa, 1996.
Egypt, Kush, Aksum: Northeast Africa, 1996.

OTHER

I Am Not Afraid! Based on a Masai Tale, illustrated by Richard Leonard, Bantam/Doubleday/Dell, 1993.
Yellow Dog Dreaming (fiction), illustrated by Gabrielle T. Raacke, Wise Acre Publications, 1995.
The Ancient Hebrews, Marshall-Cavendish/Benchmark Books (White Plains, NY), 1997.

Coauthor of play, *Viva la Vida,* about artist Frida Kahlo; creator of documentary film *Megillah* that depicts the escape of Mann's parents from Europe during the Holocaust. Contributor of numerous articles to periodicals, including *Newsday, Southwest Art, Sesame Street Parents,* and *Creative Classroom.*

■ Sidelights

Kenny Mann told *SATA:* "I have been a writer since I was six years old—it is the only real skill that I have! I was editor of my elementary and high school publications and a contributor to my college magazine. In Kenya, where I grew up, I was also a keen participant in amateur theatre, both in acting and in production.

"I started my writing career at sixteen as a cub reporter for the *East African Standard,* Kenya's national newspaper. I spent two years in England, where I published articles in various magazines, followed by twelve years in Hamburg, Germany, where I worked on a series of documentary films on animal behavior and ecology and published hundreds of articles on everything from pop music and popular culture to environmental issues and science. I also worked in radio, producing and hosting a live show for teenagers. For four years, I accompanied rock groups around the country as tour and PR manager for Polydor Records. In 1982, I moved to the U.S.A. where I continued to publish extensively in many magazines and newspapers. In 1992, I earned my M.Sc. in education from Bank Street College—the best thing I ever did, for it opened the doors to the educational world for me. I realized, at the age of forty-six, that I have always been a writer, teacher, and educator, and that is now my entire focus. I write books and curriculum, hold staff development workshops, and teach

Based on an old Masai folktale, this exciting adventure of two brothers illuminates the difference between fear and respect. (From *"I Am Not Afraid!",* written by Kenny Mann and illustrated by Richard Leonard and Alfredo Alcala.)

writing to the fourth through twelfth grades and college freshmen.

"My career seems to have been very varied, but in fact, it has all led to one point—teaching and education. Through my books, I am able to reach a wide audience and, through my workshops, I meet my students face-to-face.

"I have developed three mottos that seem to cover my career and life philosophy: 1) *Nothing is ever lost*—nothing I ever did or learned has been wasted; sooner or later, it gets used; 2) *Always ask*—never be afraid to ask questions; 3) *C.Y.A.*—no explanation needed.

"I am a person of varied interests and have finally found a niche in which those interests can be explored and even bring me an income. What could be better! My focus for the future will be to develop as a teacher of teachers of social studies, especially African history. As a teacher mainly of teachers, I want to expand knowledge of global issues, such as the plight of indigenous peoples, and to explore the great themes common to the study of history. I shall continue to combine writing and teaching until I drop dead—hopefully in front of a room full of enthusiastic students. And P.S.—despite my name, I am a woman!"

*   *   *

MANN, Pamela 1946-

■ Personal

Born August 5, 1946, in Barnsley, Yorkshire, England; daughter of Arthur and Jessie (Bird) Robinson; married Brian Mann (a gardener), September 16, 1967; children: Richard, Helen. *Education:* Open University, B.A., 1987. *Religion:* Anglican. *Hobbies and other interests:* "Touring Scotland by motorcaravan, country walking with my dog."

■ Addresses

Home—149 Galway Crescent, Retford, Nottinghamshire, England, DN22 7YR.

■ Career

Nottinghamshire County Council Leisure Services/Libraries, senior library assistant, 1983—; writer. *Member:* Library Association, Society of Authors (Great Britain), National Trust (Great Britain).

■ Writings

The Frog Princess?, illustrated by Jill Newton, All Books for Children (London), 1995, Gareth Stevens (Milwaukee, WI), 1995.

Author's work has been translated into nine languages, including Spanish and Chinese.

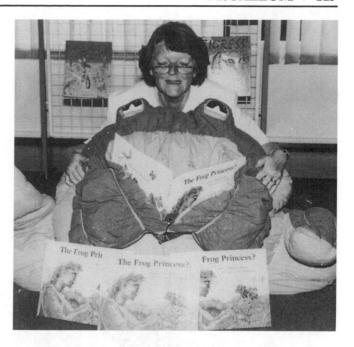

PAMELA MANN

■ Work in Progress

The Rabbit Detector, a picture book.

■ Sidelights

"I have always adored books," explains Pamela Mann to *Something about the Author*, "so my job in a library is ideal, not like work at all. During school holidays, we have events for children, using themes from books. I love to read picture books to the children as a basis for craft activities.

"In 1993 the Library Association of Great Britain had a National Library Week, which was the inspiration for the story *The Frog Princess?* . . .

"Writing is a hobby for me, but it is really good when I see someone borrow my book from the library. Brilliant!"

*   *   *

MARA, Jeanette
See CEBULASH, Mel

*   *   *

McCALLUM, Stephen 1960-

■ Personal

Born August 18, 1960, in Victoria, British Columbia, Canada; son of James Bruce (a naval officer) and Margaret Elizabeth (a nurse; maiden name, Vann) McCallum; married June Lauren Beatty (a museum curator), September 25, 1993. *Education:* Camosun College (Victoria, British Columbia), diploma in fine

STEPHEN McCALLUM

arts, 1981. *Politics:* Left. *Religion:* None. *Hobbies and other interests:* Playing guitar and singing in a folk-rock band; playing ice hockey and tennis; hiking.

■ Addresses

Home and office—2412 Central Ave., Victoria, BC V8S 2S6, Canada.

■ Career

Children's book illustrator. National Film Board of Canada, Vancouver, animator, 1984-92; Hanna Barbera, Taipei, Taiwan, animation supervisor, 1993; Sanctuary Woods, Victoria, BC, animator for computer software, 1994—. *Member:* Vancouver Island Illustrators Society.

■ Awards, Honors

Reader's Choice Award, Canadian Children's Book Center, 1993, for *Belle's Journey.* Best short fiction film, International Environmental Film Festival, Brazil, 1992, and award of excellence, PIMA Conference, Victoria, BC, both for film *From Flores.*

■ Illustrator

Jacolyn Caton, *The Potter,* Coteau Books, 1992.
Marilynn Reynolds, *Belle's Journey,* Orca Books, 1993.

Marilynn Reynolds, *A Dog for a Friend,* Orca Books, 1994.
Marilynn Reynolds, *The New Land,* Orca Books, 1997.

■ Sidelights

Stephen McCallum told *SATA:* "Illustrating for children's books is a wonderfully meditative way to spend time. I enjoy visualising a story and immersing myself in the process of discovering what the characters and events look like on paper. I have now completed four books for children. If the royalties continue to improve I might be able to pursue this full-time one day. For now, though, I support myself in other ways but always with some connection to the arts."

* * *

McKINNEY, Nadine 1938-

■ Personal

Born January 1, 1938, in Lincoln County, WV; daughter of Bruce (a carpenter) and Elvetta (Bias) Spurlock; married Cecil Edward McKinney (an auto mechanic), May 28, 1956; children: Teresa Barton, Cecil Edward, Jr. *Education:* University of Charleston, B.A., 1973. *Politics:* Democrat. *Religion:* Baptist.

NADINE McKINNEY

■ Addresses

Home—P.O. Box 248, Peytona, WV 25154.

■ Career

Boone County Board of Education, Madison, WV, elementary teacher, 1970-85; writer, beginning 1989. *Member:* West Virginia Writers.

■ Writings

Eyes in the Attic, May Davenport (Los Altos Hills, CA), 1995.

"Bread and Butter," a short story, was included in an anthology published by Mountain State Press, 1985; poems have been published in newspapers.

■ Work in Progress

A Year of Tears and *The Last Rose,* both young adult novels; *The Shanty Man, The Dead Man's Finger,* and *Look! It's Alive,* middle grade readers.

■ Sidelights

"I've always loved pencils and paper," author Nadine McKinney told *SATA.* "But these simple items that we take for granted today were not easy to come by in the 'forties. There were sixteen of us kids living in the head of a hollow and we truly were 'as poor as church mice.' But there was one occasion, I remember in particular, when I felt quite rich. It was the last day of school, when I was in the first grade. Most of the students were in a hurry to toss their used pencils into the waste basket. Loving pencils the way I did, I went for the toss-aways. The teacher saw my interest and asked the students to give them to me.

"I loved every pencil, no matter how chewed or how small, and felt rich to have such treasures. Needless to say, I put those pencils to use that summer, drawing and writing poems and stories on meat-wrapping paper. My many brothers and sisters boosted me on with their enthusiasm over my creations.

"My most treasured writings are drawn from those childhood memories I wish to share with others. I've completed a series of three books based on the kids of the hollow. They are: *Look! It's Alive; The Dead Man's Finger;* and *The Shanty Man.* This brief introduction used for the series tells it like it was: 'Where one survived on whatever was there, and varmints ruled the night; where neighbors were few and far between, and the creek traveled the same path as the road; and where vehicles or Santa couldn't get to you ... that was the hollow. And those that endured the hardships; the laughs; the cries; the scares; the sickness; and made every day unique ... those were the kids of the hollow.'"*

METCALF, Doris H(unter)

■ Personal

Married to Weston Metcalf; children: Rockell, Kendric, Sevante. *Education:* Stillman College, B.S., 1962; Ohio State University, M.A., 1971; University of North Alabama, Ed.S., 1978; University of Alabama, A.A. certification, 1982. *Religion:* Baptist.

■ Addresses

Home—2201 Edwards Ave., Muscle Shoals, AL 35661. *Office*—Hibbett School, 1601 Appleby Blvd., Florence, AL 35630. *Electronic mail*—dmet1942@aol.com.

■ Career

Marengo High School, Dixon Mills, AL, chemistry and science teacher, 1962-67; Burrell-Slater High School, Florence, AL, science teacher, 1968-70; Forest Hills School, Florence, science teacher, 1971-77, gifted education, 1978-95; Hibbett School, Florence, teacher of gifted, 1996—. Has presented lectures at seminars and conferences. *Member:* National Educational Association, National Council of Negro Women, Alabama Education Association, Florence Education Association, Delta Sigma Theta Sorority.

DORIS H. METCALF

■ Writings

Earth Mysteries: A Learning Center, Engine-uity Publishing, 1981.

Thinking Upside Down: A Resource Book of Creative Thinking Activities, GCT Publishing, 1983.

Computers: An Independent Learning Project, Interact Publishing, 1984.

Rocks and Minerals, TOPS Learning Systems, 1989.

Portraits in Black: A Resource Activity Book about the Achievements of African-Americans, Good Apple, 1990.

African-Americans: Their Impact on U.S. History, Good Apple, 1992.

Portraits of Contemporary African-Americans, Good Apple, 1993.

Portraits of Exceptional African-American Scientists, illustrated by Marilynn G. Barr, Good Apple, 1994.

Portraits of African-American Achievers, Good Apple, 1995.

Portraits of African-American Women, Good Apple, 1996.

Portraits of Outstanding Explorers, Good Apple, 1996.

Fifty Fun Things for Kids to Do with Catalogs, Good Apple, 1996.

Contributor to periodicals, including *Challenge, Oasis,* and *GCT Magazine.* Also contributor of articles to newspapers.

■ Sidelights

Doris H. Metcalf told *SATA:* "About fifteen years ago, I began writing curriculum units of study for my gifted students. Gifted education was relatively new then, and there was not much material available for use in my classes. I sent some materials that I had developed to a publishing company. They bought it for a flat fee, which was disappointing as I review it, but I did get my 'feet in the door.' Sometimes one has to go backward in order to move forward.

"That first published piece was a real inspiration to me. I then believed that I could write. This gave me the encouragement to continue to write. Now, almost twelve books later, I know that my first published piece simply gave me the determination to get a better royalty base fee.

"My objectives for writing have changed now. With the coming of age of the multi-cultural curriculum, there is a commitment for schools to explore and recognize the contributions of minorities. My aim is to provide easily accessible information for the study of African-American contribution. I do this by writing historical information followed by interesting, motivating activities that require little or no teacher preparation time.

"In a few more years, when I am retired, my writing will probably take another direction. I want so much to write a book about my autistic son in the hope that it might serve as a source of information for other parents of autistic children. I also have a southern folklore book that I hope to get published in the near future. In the meantime, I will keep doing 'small things' until something 'big' comes along."

* * *

MILLER, Robert H. 1944-

■ Personal

Born March 22, 1994, in San Antonio, TX; son of Margauret (a high school teacher) and stepson of Eugene (a reverend) Boyd. *Education:* Attended Linfield College, 1962-65; University of District of Columbia, B.S., 1973, M.S., 1975; Temple University, Ph.D. candidate, 1995—. *Politics:* Independent. *Religion:* "Nondenominational."

■ Addresses

Home—503 South Sixth St., Camden, NJ 08103. *Agent*—Robin Rue, Diamant Agency, 310 Madison Ave., Suite 1105, New York, NY 10017.

■ Career

Writer.

■ Writings

Reflections of a Black Cowboy, illustrated by Richard Leonard, Book 1: *Cowboys,* Book 2: *Buffalo Soldier,* Book 3: *Pioneers,* Book 4: *Mountain Men,* Silver Burdett, 1991.

ROBERT H. MILLER

A Pony for Jeremiah, Silver Burdett, 1996.

"STORIES OF THE FORGOTTEN WEST" SERIES

The Story of "Stagecoach" Marcy Fields, illustrated by Cheryl Hanna, Silver Burdett, 1994.
Buffalo Soldiers: The Story of Emanuel Stance, illustrated by Michael Bryant, Silver Burdett, 1995.
The Story of Jean Baptiste Du Sable, illustrated by Richard Leonard, Silver Burdett, 1995.
The Story of Nat Love, illustrated by Michael Bryant, Silver Burdett, 1995.

■ Work in Progress

A Knight to Remember: The Legend of Morien, the story of a fourteen-year-old African knight during the time of King Arthur.

■ Sidelights

Robert H. Miller is the author of historical children's books that focus on the lives of determined African Americans. Most of these courageous men and women, who sought to escape slavery or improve their lives after being freed, helped tame the Wild West.

In his four-volume work *Reflections of a Black Cowboy,* Miller tells the tales of many almost-forgotten African Americans through the narrator, an old black cowboy whose only companion is his dog. Most of the heroes and heroines in the set survived their adventures in the Western frontier through sheer determination. "All of my characters are strong African American men and women," Miller told *SATA.* "When young readers pick up *Reflections of a Black Cowboy,* they are taken back into history to relive the adventures of African American cowboys, pioneers, explorers, and mountain men, who helped shape and make the face of America."

In the "Stories of the Forgotten West" series, Miller again focuses on almost-forgotten African American figures, but this time he writes about individual achievers rather than groups. For example, *The Story of "Stagecoach" Mary Fields* highlights the adventures of Mary Fields—a freed slave who was the first African American woman to deliver the U.S. mail via stagecoach. In a review for *Booklist,* Kay Weisman complimented Miller on his presentation of a "strong, independent woman who never allowed others to take advantage of her." In *The Story of Nat Love,* Miller relates the colorful adventures of Nat Love, a former slave turned cowboy headed West. "Young readers will delight in Nat's exciting adventures," remarked Lauren Peterson for *Booklist.* Noting Miller's contribution to history in a review for *School Library Journal,* John Sigwald wrote that "this book will help to fill a glaring void in Wild West folklore."

About writing for children, Miller told *SATA,* "I write about African American cowboys and pioneers because I want young African American boys to understand that even during a time of slavery in this country, black people were not all picking cotton or singing hymns on

Miller's lively tale of Mary Fields, ex-slave and bandit-wrestling mail-carrier, brings a fresh African American perspective to Wild West folklore. (From *The Story of Stagecoach Mary Fields,* illustrated by Cheryl Hanna.)

some plantation. They were cowboys in every sense of the word, pioneers, builders of churches, schoolteachers, and ranchers. They went West to escape slavery and the plantation system and build a solid future for themselves, and their families. Obstacles, however, never eluded them even out West, but with strength and determination they committed themselves to securing a stable future."

■ Works Cited

Peterson, Lauren, review of *The Story of Nat Love, Booklist,* January 1, 1995, p. 824.
Sigwald, John, review of *The Story of Nat Love, School Library Journal,* January, 1995, p. 104.
Weisman, Kay, review of *The Story of Stagecoach Mary Fields, Booklist,* April 15, 1995, p. 1503.

■ For More Information See

PERIODICALS

Kirkus Reviews, January 1, 1992, p. 55.
School Library Journal, September, 1991, p. 290.

*   *   *

MISHICA, Clare 1960-

■ Personal

Born March 4, 1960, in Calumet, MI; daughter of Ronald and Rosemary (Rost) Crouch; married Gary Mishica (an industrial arts teacher), July 17, 1982; children: Stephanie and Amanda (twins), Christina, Joel. *Education:* Western Michigan University, B.A.

Clare Mishica with her family.

(summa cum laude), 1981; completed course from the Institute for Children's Literature, Redding, CT. *Religion:* Catholic. *Hobbies and other interests:* Reading, sewing, cross-country skiing, looking for agates along the shoreline of Lake Superior.

■ **Addresses**

Home—R.R. 1, Box 187-A, Calumet, MI 49913.

■ **Career**

Author and educator. Teacher in White River, SD, 1982-83, and Point Lay, AK, 1983-85; Suomi College, Teaching and Learning Center, Hancock, MI, 1993—. *Member:* Upper Peninsula Writer's Association.

■ **Writings**

Billions of Bugs, illustrated by Roberta K. Loman, Standard Publishing Company (Cincinnati, OH), 1993.
The Penguin's Big Win, illustrated by Terri Steiger, Standard Publishing, 1994.
Charlie the Champ, illustrated by Kathleen Estes, Standard Publishing, 1994.
Max's Answer, illustrated by Patrick Girouard, Standard Publishing, 1994.
A Friend for Fraidy Cat, Standard Publishing, 1994.

Contributor of short stories, essays, and crafts articles to periodicals, including *Canadian Messenger, Catholic Digest, Daily Meditation, Family Digest, Highlights for Children, Humpty Dumpty, Nature Friend, On the Line, Our Family, Pockets, R-A-D-A-R, Sunshine, Sunday Digest, Turtle Magazine* and *Vista,* as well as contributor of puzzles to "Puzzlemania" series of books published by *Highlights.*

■ **Work in Progress**

Short stories for children; a Bible encyclopedia for Standard Publishing.

■ **Sidelights**

"I began writing stories for children while living and teaching with my husband in a small Eskimo village, Point Lay," author Clare Mishica told *SATA.* "I write because I love to imagine and create. It's one kind of job that never, *ever* seems dull. I find it exciting and challenging to invent characters, motivations, and situations. I also like to try to write stories to fit specific formats, particularly Beginning Readers, as I taught reading at one time. I usually work in the morning when my house is quiet and the kids are in school. My children and fourteen nieces and nephews give me ample ideas for stories and I also often remember significant events that affected me as a child. I've always loved reading and would be hard pressed to name a favorite—I love to read a variety of authors and still love reading some children's books today. To aspiring writers, my advice would be to persevere. When you least expect it, your first sale will happen."

*   *   *

MOBLEY, Joe A. 1945-

■ **Personal**

Born February 11, 1945; son of John W. and Shirley R. Mobley; married Kathleen B. Wyche (an editor), December 30, 1995. *Education:* North Carolina State University, B.A., 1971, M.A., 1976. *Hobbies and other interests:* Fly fishing, jogging, gardening.

■ **Addresses**

Home—1222 Dixie Tr., Raleigh, NC 27607. *Office*—109 East Jones St., Raleigh, NC 27601-2807.

■ **Career**

North Carolina Division of Archives and History, Raleigh, archivist, 1974-76, researcher, 1976-82, editor, 1983-96. *Military service:* United States Marine Corps, 1963-67; became sergeant. *Member:* Association of Documentary Editors, Historical Society of North Carolina, Association of Historians in North Carolina (president, 1980), North Carolina Literary and Historical Association.

■ **Writings**

James City: A Black Community in North Carolina, 1863-1900, North Carolina Division of Archives & History (Raleigh), 1981.
The USS North Carolina: Symbol of a Vanished Age, North Carolina Division of Archives & History, 1985.

Pamlico County: A Brief History, North Carolina Division of Archives & History, 1991.

Ship Ashore! The U.S. Lifesavers of Coastal North Carolina, North Carolina Division of Archives & History, 1994.

(Editor) *The Papers of Zebulon Baird Vance,* North Carolina Division of Archives & History, Volume 2: *1863,* 1995, Volume 3, 1997.

Contributor to books, including *The Craft of Public History: An Annotated Select Bibliography,* edited by David M. Trask, Robert W. Pomeroy III, and others, Greenwood Press (Westport, CT), 1983; *Dictionary of North Carolina Biography,* University of North Carolina Press (Chapel Hill), Volume 3, 1988; and *American National Biography,* Oxford University Press (New York), in press. Also a contributor to periodicals, including *North Carolina Historical Review, Carolina Comments, Tar Heel Junior Historian,* and *Alabama Historical Quarterly.*

■ Work in Progress

Tarheel Commanders in Grey: The Confederate Generals of North Carolina; A Children's Book of Pirates.

■ Sidelights

Joe A. Mobley told *SATA:* "I believe that the study of history on the local levels—community, county, and

JOE A. MOBLEY

state—provides much insight into large historical events and personalities—especially for young readers. One of my favorite quotations is by the well-known American historian Ray Allen Billington: 'Good local history is not really local history at all; instead it views the universality of the human experience through the tiny lens of a single community.'"*

* * *

MODESITT, L(eland) E(xton), Jr. 1943-

■ Personal

Born October 19, 1943, in Denver, CO; son of Leland Exton (an attorney) and Nancy Lila (Evans) Modesitt; married Christina Alma Gribben (an educator), October 22, 1977 (divorced 1991); married Carol Ann Hill (a singer and professor of voice; maiden name, Janes), January 4, 1992; children: (first marriage) Leland Exton III, Susan Carnall, Catherine Grant, Nancy Mayo, Elizabeth Leanore, Kristen Linnea; (step-children) Lara Beth Hill, Kevin Lawrence Hill. *Education:* Williams College, B.A., 1965; graduate study at University of Denver, 1970-71. *Politics:* Republican. *Religion:* Episcopalian.

■ Addresses

Home—255 South Sunny View Rd., Cedar City, UT 84720.

■ Career

C. A. Norgren Co. (industrial pneumatics company), Littleton, CO, market research analyst, 1969-70; Koelbel & Co. (real estate and construction firm), Denver, CO, sales associate, 1971-72; legislative assistant to U.S. Representative Bill Armstrong, 1973-79; administrative assistant and staff director for U.S. Representative Ken Kramer, 1979-81; U.S. Environmental Protection Agency, Washington, DC, director of Office of Legislation and Congressional Affairs, 1981-83, special assistant, Office of External Affairs, 1984-85; Multinational Business Services, Inc., Washington, DC, regulatory/communications consultant, 1985-89; independent regulatory and communications consultant, 1989—; writer. Lecturer in science fiction writing at Georgetown University, 1980-81; lecturer in English and writing, Plymouth State College (New Hampshire), 1990-93. *Military service:* U.S. Navy, 1965-69; became lieutenant.

■ Writings

SCIENCE FICTION

The Fires of Paratime, Timescape (New York City), 1982.

Hammer of Darkness, Avon, 1985.

The Ecologic Envoy, Tor Books, 1986.

The Ecolitan Operation, Tor Books, 1989.

The Ecologic Secession, Tor Books, 1990.

(With Bruce Scott Levinson) *The Green Progression,* Tor Books, 1992.

L. E. MODESITT, JR.

Timedivers' Dawn, Tor Books, 1992.
The Timegod, Tor Books, 1993.
Of Tangible Ghosts, Tor Books, 1994.
The Parafaith War, Tor Books, 1996.
Adiamante, Tor Books, 1996.
The Ecolitan Enigma, Tor Books, 1997.
The Soprano Sorceress, Tor Books, 1997.

Contributor to science fiction magazines, including *Analog Science Fiction/Science Fact, Galaxy,* and *Isaac Asimov's Science Fiction Magazine.*

SCIENCE-FICTION; "FOREVER HERO" TRILOGY

Dawn for a Distant Earth, Tor Books, 1987.
The Silent Warrior, Tor Books, 1987.
In Endless Twilight, Tor Books, 1988.

FANTASY; "RECLUCE" SERIES

The Magic of Recluce, Tor Books, 1991.
The Towers of the Sunset, Tor Books, 1992.
The Magic Engineer, Tor Books, 1994.
The Order War, Tor Books, 1995.
The Death of Chaos, Tor Books, 1995.
Fall of Angels, Tor Books, 1996.
The Chaos Balance, Tor Books, in press.

The Magic of Recluce, The Towers of the Sunset, and *The Magic Engineer* have also appeared in British editions published by Orbit. Some of the books in the "Recluce" series are scheduled to be published in German.

■ Work in Progress

The Ghost of the Revelator; The Spellsong War.

■ Sidelights

The environmentally focused science fiction and fantasy novels of L. E. Modesitt, Jr. have been praised for their finely crafted plots rich in technological detail. In both his "Forever Hero" trilogy and the six-part series about the island kingdom of Recluce, as well as his other novels, Modesitt has woven diverse ecological theories and technologies into the storyline. From ghosts re-enacting their untimely deaths to the adventures of the scattered survivors of a post-nuclear holocaust earth, Modesitt's novels boast intriguing characters and imaginative plots in tales that both entertain and enlighten readers.

Categorized under the science fiction subgenre referred to as "hard" science fiction, works such as Modesitt's "Forever Hero" trilogy and 1996's *The Parafaith War* and *Adiamante* stress intricately devised plots. In the "Forever Hero" novels, which include 1987's *Dawn for a Distant Earth* and *The Silent Warrior,* as well as 1988's *In Endless Twilight,* the earth has been destroyed by nuclear war. Modesitt's epic revolves around the adventures of MacGregor Corson Gerswin, a strong, resourceful, and seemingly indestructible loner who manages to survive on what little the earth's surface still produces. He and others like him join together as trainees for the army of a powerful intergalactic empire that has added the weakened Earth to its collection of colonial outposts.

In *Dawn for a Distant Earth,* which opens the trilogy, the surface of the earth has degenerated into poisoned oceans and barren deserts, its unwholesome atmosphere broken by violent climatic outbursts that include hail and tornadoes. Survivors of the nuclear holocaust are divided between the suspicious "shambletowners," whose small, tattered communities dot the landscape, and "devilkids" who, like Gerswin, live in isolation, stealing what they cannot glean from the land. Now a lieutenant with the Imperial Army and stationed back on planet Earth, Gerswin dedicates himself to terraforming his home planet—reworking the atmospheric conditions to allow Earth to support life again—while also attempting to stop the Empire from using the earth as a dump-site for sub-standard life-forms from other worlds.

In *Endless Twilight* recounts Gerswin's attempts to break the grip of the powerful Empire and continue to restore the ecology of planet Earth. The protagonist draws upon his knowledge of genetic engineering to help the people of several worlds dominated by the ruthless intergalactic superpower to create sufficient food and shelter for themselves. Meanwhile, through his creative genius he finds a way to undermine the greedy Empire's network for robbing each of these worlds of their riches. While a broad technological knowledge provides the series with an intricate plotline, some critics contended that Gerswin, the Forever Hero, is too invulnerable. Comparing *In Endless Twilight* to the popular "Star Wars" books, Tom Pearson notes in *Voice of Youth Advocates* that "Gerswin would be more interesting and believable if, like Luke Skywalker, he had a sense of humor or some interesting friends, or a superhuman villain like Darth Vader to oppose him."

Modesitt's *The Parafaith War* finds Trystin Desoll, an officer in the Eco-Tech army, involved in a long-standing racially based interstellar battle with opposing Revenant forces. He is also fighting the prejudice of his own people because, due to his fair complexion and blue eyes, he looks more Revenant than Eco-Tech. A man of great intelligence and perception, Desoll is eventually ordered to infiltrate the Revenant stronghold of Wystuh and assassinate that group's leader; instead, he devises a way to end the war peacefully, using the Revenants' fanatical religious beliefs as the means.

Washington, D.C., where Modesitt once served as director of legislation for the Environmental Protection Agency (EPA), represents one wellspring of ideas for his science fiction novels. While works like the "Forever Hero" trilogy have loose ties to his EPA experiences, 1992's *The Green Progression* is a direct outgrowth of his career as an environmental consultant. Coauthored with consultant Bruce Scott Levinson, *The Green Progression* is a science fiction thriller concerning a Soviet effort to sap the power of the U.S. industrial base by trapping it within a web of regulatory bureaucracy. Jack McDarvid and Jonnie Black, consultants to an international chemical company known as JAFFE, become savvy to the Russian plot after their boss is murdered on the job. The two consultants soon discover that environmental restrictions against pesticides and other industrial technologies have been pushed into law with the backing of Soviet agents who use U.S. environmental lobbyists as puppets in a covert Cold War battle plan.

Other forays into the world of ecological science fiction taken by Modesitt include 1986's *The Ecologic Envoy,* 1989's *The Ecolitan Operation,* 1990's *The Ecologic Secession,* and *Of Tangible Ghosts,* published in 1994. Taking place in an alternate world where ghosts and psychic phenomenon exist, *Of Tangible Ghosts* sets forth an alternative history of our own planet. Northeast Columbia (which represents the United States and Canada) is a Dutch-based culture (the British never won colonial control of North America) that features a quiet, dedicated workforce with a love of hot chocolate. It is one of two competing superpowers; the other is the power-hungry Austro-Hungarian Empire. The great psychic energy of the spirit world is the only thing preventing these powerful governments from going to war over world domination; ghosts' habits of haunting the sites of their untimely deaths and replaying the means of their murder has made the thought of creating battlefields—sites of mass death—untenable. Doktor Johan Eschbach, a teacher of environmental economics

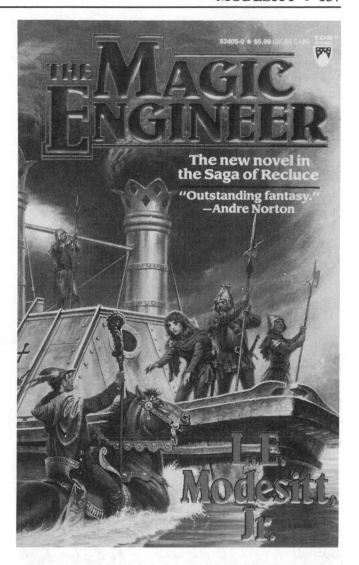

One of Modesitt's absorbing fantasies about the otherworldly island of Recluce. (Cover illustration by Darrell K. Sweet.)

who formerly worked as an agent for the Columbian government, is drawn into the struggle for world domination after a colleague is murdered and he encounters her ghost, who demands justice. As he seeks his friend's murderer, Eschbach discovers that a computer-driven technology able to harness the power of ghosts and channel it to serve human interests has been developed; this frightening technology is being fought over by Northeast Columbia and the sinister Austro-Hungarian Empire. Modesitt "excels in using subtle details to enhance the credibility of an imaginary parallel world," notes a *Library Journal* reviewer. And Jennifer D. Kubenka adds her praise for the novel in *Voice of Youth Advocates:* "an engaging and all-too-human protagonist, a finely realized world, and misused technology that is vaguely familiar yet exotic and different makes for a reading experience that will linger in the reader's mind and sense long after the last page has been turned."

Fantasy has also proved to be a fertile ground for Modesitt's storytelling abilities. In his six-part "Recluce" series, which includes the novels *The Magic*

Engineer and *The Death of Chaos,* he recounts the history of an otherworldly island called Recluce, wherein a balance exists between the forces of Order and those of Chaos: if chaotic activity increases, then order must also increase to balance it. The wellspring of this world's "magic" increases as such balances are struck; White Wizards promote Chaos, while Black Wizards work to promote Order, and both fight the natural balance of nature. In *The Magic of Recluce,* which introduces readers to the series, a woodworker's apprentice named Lerris is forced to leave his home in a test that moves him from childhood to maturity after he criticizes the island's laws. Temporarily exiled from Recluce, Lerris is helped in coming to terms with Order-dominated island culture by a gray wizard. He also encounters Antonin, the master of the laws of Chaos, who uses his power to disrupt and destroy law, thereby increasing his own supply of chaotic magic. Lerris eventually grows up and begins to both understand and appreciate the impor-tance of laws in preserving the stability of his island home.

Published five years after *The Magic of Recluce, Fall of Angels* is the prequel to the saga of the battle between Order and Chaos. A spaceship full of female "Angels" who are involved in a battle against "demons" enters an alien universe and lands on a planet where all but the highest elevations are hot enough to kill them. To make matters worse, some of the planet's inhabitants already wield the magic of Chaos, against which the order of these Amazonian warriors and one male engineer must prevail. Other "Recluce" novels recount various other segments of the saga. *The Towers of the Sunset* describes the island's founding, as Creslin, son of a powerful female military leader and himself a Black Storm Wizard able to control the heavens, flees from an arranged marriage in order to find himself. Pursued by his distraught and slightly annoyed fiance, Megaera, with whom he shares an empathic bond (when he feels pain, she does as well, and vice versa), as well as by the White Wizards of Chaos who feel threatened by his growing power, Creslin finds refuge upon a desolate island and vows to start a new life. "The concept of a necessary maintenance between Order and Chaos is an interesting departure from most SF and fantasy ideas," writes Diane Yates in a *Voice of Youth Advocates* review of the second "Recluce" novel.

As in *The Magic of Recluce,* 1994's *The Magic Engineer* also centers around a young man. But this time, rather than a bored youth, the young man is Dorrin, the ambitious son of a Black Wizard. Fascinated by the forbidden art of metallurgy—an orderly process that unfortunately generates chaos through its byproducts, air and water pollution—he is exiled to the land of Chaos where he continues to dream of building machinery. Eventually Recluce becomes threatened by White Wizards and Dorrin must choose between following his dream of practicing Chaotic arts or defending his Order-driven island home. The battle between controlled technological advancement and chaos continues in *The Order War* as yet another smith, Justen, engages in direct battle with the armies of Chaos, who have taken over much of the world in the wake of the steam engine's development. "Modesitt is as clever as his blacksmith heroes," notes Tom Easton in a review of *The Order War* for *Analog,* "finding ways to discuss today's environmental concerns and technological hubris in ways that can reach a public that prefers wish-fulfillment fantasy to more hard-nosed SF."

Modesitt told *SATA:* "One of my motivations in writing fantasy was to create 'real' places with 'real' people, economics, and politics, not pale copies of might-have-been medieval societies that once existed on earth. Some of the 'Recluce' books have technology, and that technology impacts and is impacted by order/chaos magic. Both technology and magic have an impact on their users, and often a high price to pay. One reason for that is my observation that talented individuals, whatever their field, usually pay a high price for their talent,

OF TANGIBLE

GHOSTS

L.E.MODESITT, JR.

"Possibly Modesitt's best book, it's certainly highly recommended."
—*Booklist*

In this popular science fiction mystery, Modesitt cleverly sets forth an alternative history of our own planet in an otherworldly universe of restless ghosts and psychic phenomena. (Cover illustration by Nicholas Jainschigg.)

In this sequel to the popular *Magic of Recluce*, the new challenge before wizard-hero Lerris pits Order against Chaos, as well as Good against Evil. (Cover illustration by Darrell K. Sweet.)

and I felt that would be true of talented magicians as well."

"Writers write," Modesitt once explained. "They have to, or they would not be writers. I am a writer who worked at it long enough to become an author. Virtually all of my early and formal training in writing was devoted to poetry—where I had a choice! I did not write my first science fiction story for publication until I was twenty-nine, and my first novel was published just before my thirty-ninth birthday."

Modesitt commented that the motivation for his fiction comes from several sources. "Although the various aspects of power and how it changes people and how government systems work and how they don't are themes underlying what I write, I try to concentrate on people—on heroes in the true sense of the word. A man who has no fear is not a hero. He's a damned fool. A hero is a man or woman who is shivering with fear and who conquers that fear to do what is right. I also believe

that a writer simultaneously has to entertain, educate, and inspire. If he or she fails in any of these goals, the book will somehow fall flat."

■ Works Cited

Easton, Tom, review of *The Order War, Analog Science Fiction/Science Fact,* June, 1995, pp. 167-68.

Kubenka, Jennifer D., review of *Of Tangible Ghosts, Voice of Youth Advocates,* April, 1995, pp. 37-38.

Review of *Of Tangible Ghosts, Library Journal,* September 15, 1994.

Pearson, Tom, review of *In Endless Twilight, Voice of Youth Advocates,* December 1988, p. 247.

Yates, Diane, review of *The Towers of the Sunset, Voice of Youth Advocates,* February 1991, pp. 354-55.

■ For More Information See

PERIODICALS

Analog Science Fiction/Science Fact, August 1994, pp. 161-62.

Booklist, May 1, 1991, p. 1698; March 1, 1994, p. 1185; October 1, 1994, p. 245; January 1995, p. 803; September 1, 1995, p. 48.

Environmental Forum, October 1982; April 1983.

Kirkus Reviews, December 1, 1995, p. 1673.

Library Journal, March 14, 1994, p. 104; December 1994, pp. 138-39; September 15, 1995, p. 97.

Los Angeles Times Book Review, December 19, 1982.

Publishers Weekly, November 22, 1991, p. 38; January 2, 1995, p. 63; August 28, 1995, p. 106.

Voice of Youth Advocates, August/September, 1987, p. 132; August, 1995, p. 174; February, 1996, p. 385.

Washington Times, February 3, 1988.

*   *   *

MORRIS, Deborah 1956-

■ Personal

Born August 23, 1956, in Opa-Locka, FL; daughter of Ray (a treasure-hunter and engineer) and Delphine (a homemaker; maiden name, Benton) Snyder; married Terrel L. Morris (an engineer), April 20, 1974; children: Elisabeth Anne, Rachel Dawn, Steven Lee, Sean Michael. *Religion:* Christian (non-denominational). *Hobbies and other interests:* Reading, camping, boating, taking in stray animals.

■ Addresses

Home and office—P.O. Box 461572, Garland, TX 75046-1572. *Electronic mail*—deb@realkids.com; (website) www.realkids.com. *Agent*—(literature) Karen Solem, Writer's House, West 26th St., New York, NY; (film) Scott Henderson, Favored Artists, South Robertson Blvd., Los Angeles, CA.

DEBORAH MORRIS

■ Career

Merritt Island, FL, commercial fisher, 1974-75; "The 1896 Mine," Yarnell, AZ, gold miner, 1980-81; Avon Products, Garland, TX, assistant district manager, 1982-88; children's book author and magazine freelancer, 1985—; Building and Fire Code Board, Garland, 1988-89; Tejas Writer's Roundtable, Dallas, TX, co-founder and host, 1991—; speaker, 1992—; Springcreek Community Church, Garland, youth leader, 1994-96; National Stop Youth Violence in America, Inc., advisory board member, 1995—; Writer's Roundtable Conferences, director and speaker, 1996—. *Member:* Society of Children's Book Writers and Illustrators, Texas Freelance Writers' Association; Tejas Writer's Roundtable.

■ Writings

REAL KIDS, REAL ADVENTURES SERIES

Book 1: *Firestorm!, Plane Crash on Christmas Day, Lost in Hidden Treasure Mine,* Broadman & Holman, 1994.
Book 2: *Adrift in the Atlantic, Blizzard in Wildcat Hills, Blinded at Big Hole,* Broadman & Holman, 1994.
Book 3: *Runaway Balloon, Rescue in the Trinity River, Apartment Inferno!* Broadman & Holman, 1995.
Book 4: *Shark Attack! Rescue at Nordic Valley, Emergency at Chitek Lake,* Broadman & Holman, 1995.

Book 5: *Over the Edge, Kidnapped!, Swept Underground,* Broadman & Holman, 1995.
Book 6: *Tornado!, Hero on the Blanco River, Attacked by Wild Dogs,* Broadman & Holman, 1995.

OTHER

Trapped in a Cave! A True Story, Broadman & Holman, 1993.

Has published over ninety articles in *Reader's Digest, Family Circle, Good Housekeeping,* and other publications.

■ Work in Progress

"Real Kids, Real Adventures" books 7 and 8; *When Bad Kids Happen to Good Families,* a nonfiction book co-authored with adolescent psychologist Dr. Barbara Rila.

■ Sidelights

Deborah Morris told *SATA:* "I'm often asked what 'inspired' me to start writing real-life dramas, but the fact is it was an accident—literally! Early in my writing career, my family was on vacation in Florida when a tractor-trailer ran us off the highway and sent us spinning end over end down into a ravine. It should have killed us, but we all walked away from it. I wrote the story for *Guideposts* magazine, and that's how I discovered dramatic storytelling was a lot of fun. Soon I was writing dramas for *Reader's Digest, Good Housekeeping* and other magazines. The idea of the 'Real Kids, Real Adventures' series emerged gradually as I realized during interviews involving both kids and adults that I consistently found the kids' stories much more interesting than the adults'!

"For instance, in the story *Runaway Balloon!* an eleven-year-old boy is trapped alone in a hot air balloon after the pilot gets dumped out during a botched landing. The boy's only chance for survival is to learn to fly the balloon before the fuel runs out. So what does he do? In the middle of following the pilot's frantic instructions over the radio, he takes time out to scoop up snow from the floor of the gondola, make some snowballs, and 'bomb' cows he spots in a pasture far below. True story. When writing for adults, a detail like that would be routinely omitted as unimportant, but to kids things like that *are* important. I find the kid version a lot more fun to write.

"Probably what I like best about writing the 'Real Kids, Real Adventures' series, though, is that it shatters the notion that today's youth are all jaded and less caring than previous generations. Despite the negative press they get, kids today are still very idealistic. When they see someone in trouble, they don't stop to consider the risks or to weigh whose life is more important; they leave that kind of rationalizing to adults. Kids just do what they think is *right*—and almost without exception they see helping someone in trouble as *the right thing to do.* They're natural-born heroes. They just don't all get the opportunity to prove it."

MOST, Bernard 1937-

■ Personal

Born September 2, 1937, in New York, NY; son of Max (a painter) and Bertha Most; married Amy Beth Most, February 12, 1967; children: Glenn Evan, Eric David. *Education:* Pratt Institute, B.F.A. (with honors), 1959. *Politics:* Independent.

■ Addresses

Home—Scarsdale, NY. *Office*—c/o Harcourt Brace, 525 B St., San Diego, CA 92101.

■ Career

McCann-Erickson, Inc. (advertising agency), New York City, art director, 1959-65; Benton & Bowles, Inc. (advertising agency), New York City, associate creative director, 1965-78; MCA Advertising, Inc., New York City, senior vice president and creative director, 1978-86; Bernie & Walter, Inc. (consulting company), partner, 1986-89; writer and illustrator, 1989—.

■ Awards, Honors

Awards from Art Directors Club, Type Directors Club, and American Institute of Graphic Arts; Clio Award; Andy Award; *If the Dinosaurs Came Back, There's an Ant in Anthony, My Very Own Octopus,* and *Boo!* were each selected as a Children's Choice Book by the International Reading Association and Children's Book Council; *There's an Ant in Anthony* was chosen as an ALA Notable Book; *Dinosaur Cousins?* received the Washington Irving Award.

■ Writings

SELF-ILLUSTRATED CHILDREN'S BOOKS

If the Dinosaurs Came Back, Harcourt, 1978.
There's an Ant in Anthony, Morrow, 1980.
Turn Over, Prentice-Hall, 1980.
My Very Own Octopus, Harcourt, 1980.
Boo!, Prentice-Hall, 1980.
There's an Ape behind the Drape, Morrow, 1981.
Whatever Happened to the Dinosaurs?, Harcourt, 1984.
Dinosaur Cousins?, Harcourt, 1987.
The Littlest Dinosaurs, 1989.
Four & Twenty Dinosaurs, HarperCollins, 1990.
The Cow That Went Oink, Harcourt, 1990.
A Dinosaur Named after Me, Harcourt, 1990.
Pets in Trumpets: And Other Word-Play Riddles, Harcourt, 1991.
Happy Holidaysaurus, Harcourt, 1992.
Zoodles, Harcourt, 1992.
Where to Look for a Dinosaur, Harcourt, 1993.
Can You Find It?, Harcourt, 1993.
How Big Were the Dinosaurs?, Harcourt, 1994.
Hippopotamus Hunt, Harcourt, 1994.
Catbirds & Dogfish, Harcourt, 1995.
Dinosaur Questions, Harcourt, 1995.
Cock-a-Doodle-Moo!, Harcourt, 1996.

BERNARD MOST

OTHER

Contributor of illustrations to national magazines. *If the Dinosaurs Came Back* has been translated into Chinese, Japanese, French, and Spanish; *The Cow That Went Oink* has been translated into Spanish.

■ Sidelights

Author and illustrator Bernard Most is noted for his colorfully illustrated books featuring dinosaurs and animals that entertain and teach readers, both young and old alike. Most's popular word game books challenge readers to look for words inside other words. "My books are 'concept books,'" Most once told *SATA.* "They get children to participate in the ideas of the books beyond the actual reading of them."

A former advertising executive whose "enthusiasm for dinosaurs seems boundless," as noted by Stephanie Zvirin in *Booklist,* Most's dinosaur books feature dinosaurs of all sizes and species, from the most widely recognized to the most obscure. In addition, each book is filled with thought-provoking facts and comparisons to everyday objects in an effort to help readers remember dinosaur names and traits. For example, in *The Littlest Dinosaurs,* published in 1989, Most focuses on dinosaurs small enough to be house pets and emphasizes their actual size and weight by comparing them to familiar objects. To help children (and adults) read the names more easily, the book includes a pronunciation guide. Writing for the *New York Times Book Review,* Karen Leggett noted that "*The Littlest Dinosaurs* offers a fine opportunity to expand a child's interest in dinosaurs beyond the big toothy fighters." A reviewer for *Publishers Weekly,* however, noted that Most's approach to everyday objects "distances readers from a real understanding of how these little ones lived." *How Big Were the Dinosaurs?,* published in 1994, also employs the technique of comparing dinosaurs to everyday objects. Here, however, Most concentrates mainly on those creatures found at the larger end of the dinosaur spectrum.

In his next dinosaur book, *Happy Holidaysaurus,* Most pairs twenty-seven dinosaurs with the same number of holidays. The pairs are typically made according to each beast's personal characteristics, habitat, or name. Every match contains a two- to three-line explanation of the holiday and a factoid about the dinosaur. A *Publishers Weekly* reviewer commented that the book could "serve as a mnemonic device to help readers remember dinosaur traits and names." *Booklist* contributor Denia Hester appreciated the "pleasant blend of fact and whimsy," and "the cheerful illustrations ... done with bright, bold markers."

Where to Look for a Dinosaur, published in 1993, maps out where twenty-five dinosaurs once existed around the world and shows readers what it would be like for a dinosaur if it existed there today. One example included in the book is the Alamosaurus. If it were alive today, it would live near the Alamo in San Antonio, Texas. "Kids just might remember more than they mean to," expressed a reviewer for *Publishers Weekly.* However, Stephanie Zvirin, in her review for *Booklist,* pointed out that "the book's maps, though filled with carefully placed miniature dinosaurs, don't identify the countries mentioned."

Most's talent for dinosaur books is matched by his collections of word games, particularly those involving a search for words within words. Among the books he has written and illustrated using word play is *Can You Find It?,* which features fifteen word-plays centered around the word "it." One-sentence clues, large illustrations of everyday activities, and boldfacing the word "it" help young readers to solve the puzzles more easily: for example, "When playing baseball, one can find 'it' in one's mitt." Janice Del Negro, writing for *Booklist,* found the book "culturally inclusive, lighthearted, and fun." Lisa S. Murphy commented in *School Library Journal* that "youngsters ... will enjoy turning the pages to discover the author's creative solutions."

Another popular word-game book by Most is his 1994 *Hippopotamus Hunt,* which features five young hunters and a friendly hippo traveling through a colorful jungle

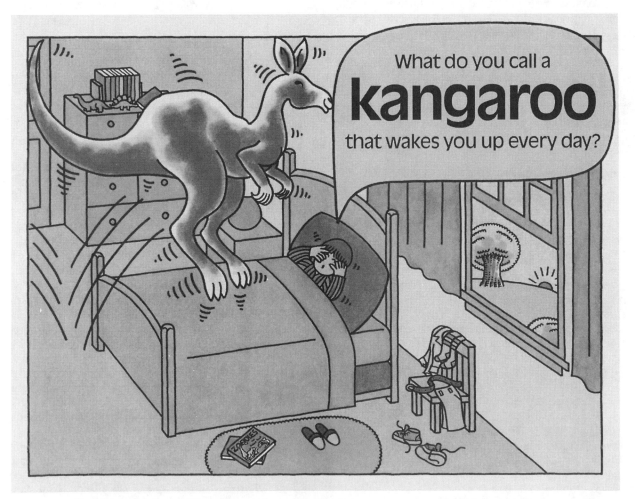

Hilarious word-play and fantastic animals entertain children in Most's self-illustrated *Zoodles*.

Children on a word hunt in the jungle find much to ponder over in the lengthy name of their traveling companion. (From *Hippopotamus Hunt,* written and illustrated by Most.)

hunting for words found in the word hippopotamus. The words are derived from a variety of objects the group encounters along the way. After a successful adventure, the hunters—and reader—leave the jungle with fifty-three words in their crate, including south, hut, hats, shoot, and pots.

Most's word-play riddle books include *Zoodles* and *Pets in Trumpets: And Other Word-Play Riddles*. *Zoodles* contains fifteen riddles in which the answers cross one animal with another, such as: "what do you call a stubborn emu? An emule!" Highlighting the answer is an illustration of the two animals interacting with each other. A writer for *Kirkus Reviews* complimented Most on his "boldly drawn, cartoon-like illustrations," which the critic found "lively and amusing."

Books by Most that feature animals include *Catbirds & Dogfish* and *The Cow That Went Oink*. Animals who are named after other animals fill the pages of *Catbirds & Dogfish*. In addition to including animal facts, the book contains pictures of the animals, for example the spider monkey, and pictures of make-believe animals—imaginative interpretations of the animals' names. In *The Cow That Went Oink,* Most draws on his wit to create the story of a cow who "oinks" and a pig who "moos." In spite of the other barnyard animals who laugh at them, the two animals work together to become fluent in

each other's language. "Older readers will appreciate the humor, and will absorb such subtle messages as the importance of helping others," declared a reviewer for *Publishers Weekly.*

Interested in art since he was about four years old, Most enjoys sharing his talent with others. He also likes to encourage people, children and adults alike. Most once told *SATA* that "desire and believing in yourself is more important than 'natural' talent. You must love what you do and work very hard to make your own 'luck' happen."

■ Works Cited

Review of *The Cow That Went Oink, Publishers Weekly,* August 10, 1990, p. 442.

Del Negro, Janice, review of *Can You Find It?, Booklist,* November 15, 1993, pp. 628-29.

Hester, Denia, review of *Holidaysaurus, Booklist,* March 15, 1992, p. 1385.

Review of *Holidaysaurus, Publishers Weekly,* February 10, 1992, p. 82.

Leggett, Karen, review of *The Littlest Dinosaurs, New York Times Book Review,* June 24, 1990, p. 29.

Review of *The Littlest Dinosaurs, Publishers Weekly,* July 28, 1989, p. 218.

Most, Bernard, *Pets in Trumpets: And Other Word-Play Riddles,* Harcourt, 1991.
Most, Bernard, *Can You Find It?,* Harcourt, 1993.
Murphy, Lisa S., review of *Can You Find It?, School Library Journal,* April, 1994, p. 121.
Review of *Where to Look for a Dinosaur, Publishers Weekly,* February 22, 1993, p. 95.
Review of *Zoodles, Kirkus Reviews,* October 15, 1992, p. 1314.
Zvirin, Stephanie, review of *Where to Look for a Dinosaur, Booklist,* February 15, 1993, p. 1064.
Zvirin, Stephanie, review of *Dinosaur Questions, Booklist,* October 1, 1995, p. 324.

■ For More Information See

PERIODICALS

Booklist, February 15, 1987, p. 902; April 1, 1995, p. 1421.
Kirkus Reviews, October 15, 1994, p. 1413.
Publishers Weekly, April 18, 1994, p. 60; October 24, 1994, pp. 60-61.
School Library Journal, May, 1987, p. 90; May, 1990, p. 100; March, 1992, p. 232; June, 1993, p. 99; April, 1994, p. 110; November, 1994, p. 86.

*   *   *

MYERS, Arthur 1917-

■ Personal

Born October 24, 1917, in Buffalo, NY; son of Edward A. (a Western Union executive) and Isabel (Baker) Myers. *Education:* Hobart College, B.A., 1939.

■ Addresses

Home—60 Grove St., #6202, Wellesley, MA 02181.

■ Career

Rochester Times-Union, Rochester, NY, various editorial posts, 1948-53; *Washington Post,* Washington, DC, assistant city editor, 1955-57; *Berkshire Eagle,* Pittsfield, MA, reporter and feature writer, 1957-64; *Bergen Record,* Hackensack, NJ, columnist, 1970-71; *Berkshire Sampler,* Pittsfield, MA, executive editor, 1971-77; freelance writer. *Military service:* U.S. Army; served during World War II. *Member:* American Society of Journalists and Authors, PEN, Mensa.

■ Awards, Honors

Three Associated Press awards for reporting.

■ Writings

(With Jeffrey O'Connell) *Safety Last,* Random House, 1966.
Careers for the Seventies: Journalism, Crowell-Collier, 1971.

ARTHUR MYERS

Analysis: The Short Story, Foothills (Pittsfield, MA), 1975.
Analysis: The Personal Profile Magazine Article, Foothills, 1976.
The Ghost Hunters, illustrated by Peter Coes, Messner, 1979.
Kids Do Amazing Things, illustrated by Anthony Rao, Random House, 1980.
Sea Creatures Do Amazing Things, illustrated by Jean D. Zallinger, Random House, 1981.
(With Irma Myers) *Why You Feel Down and What You Can Do about It,* Scribner, 1982.
The Ghostly Register: Haunted Dwellings, Active Spirits—a Journey to America's Strangest Landmarks, Contemporary Books (Chicago), 1986, also published as *Ghostly Register: A Guide to Haunted America,* Marboro Books, 1990.
Ghosts of the Rich and Famous, Contemporary Books, 1988.
The Ghostly Gazetteer: America's Most Fascinating Haunted Landmarks, Contemporary Books, 1990, also published as *Ghostly American Places,* Random House, 1995.
The Cheyenne, F. Watts, 1992.
The Pawnee, F. Watts, 1993.
The First Movies, McGraw-Hill/Macmillan, 1993.
The First Football Games, McGraw-Hill/Macmillan, 1993.
The Ghosthunter's Guide: To Haunted Landmarks, Parks, Churches, and Other Public Places, Contemporary Books, 1993.
The First Baseball Games, McGraw-Hill/Macmillan, 1993.

Drugs and Peer Pressure, Rosen, 1995.
World's Most Terrifying "True" Ghost Stories, Sterling, 1995.
Drugs and Emotion, Rosen, 1996.

Contributor of over 150 stories and articles to magazines, including *American Girl, Boys' Life, Collier's, Coronet, Cricket, Ladies' Home Journal, Saturday Review, Sports Illustrated,* and *Women's Day.* Also author of articles and stories for remedial reading material published by Educational Development Laboratories, Random House, and Houghton Mifflin.

■ Work in Progress

Film scripts; nonfiction books; various journalistic and teaching commitments.

■ Sidelights

Journalist and author Arthur Myers has devoted his life to writing. "When I was a small boy in Buffalo, New York, my father, who loved to read, used to read to me," he once recalled to *SATA.* "One great day, when I was about six, I discovered that I could read myself. I even remember the book I picked up that I found I could read. It was *Doctor Dolittle,* and that was in 1923, about the time, I believe, of its first publication.

"When I was in the fourth grade, we began to write compositions. Since I had had so much exposure to the written word, I was able to write very good pieces. With some other good composition writers, I was sent throughout the school reciting my compositions. I thought this was just dandy, and resolved, at age nine, to become a writer."

Myers has kept to his resolve; he has been a writer throughout his adult life. "I started as a newspaperman," he told *SATA,* "because I figured that was a good way to write and still have enough money coming in to eat regularly." After working as a journalist in northeastern U.S. cities from Washington, D.C., to Rochester, New York, he began writing short stories and articles for magazines. He also began writing books; at last count, Myers had "published about twenty books, and written several others, particularly novels, that haven't been published." He has also served as a magazine editor and has passed along his enthusiasm and skills by serving as a writing instructor in various colleges.

"I got into writing for young people by accident several years ago," Myers explained about the latest shift in his career track. "I have been listed in several reference books on writers, and in one I apparently listed education as one of my interests. This derived from the fact that for a time I was the education reporter of a newspaper. One day an editor called me up, said she had seen my name, and asked me if I would like to write articles and stories that would be used in remedial reading classes. These articles and stories had to be very interesting, she said, to hold the interest of people who were having problems with reading.

"As a result, I began writing many stories and articles for this company and other companies that put out this sort of material. One day, I decided that with this experience I would try writing straight children's and young adult books, and since then I've published a dozen of these." Among the many books to his credit are several works of young adult nonfiction, including *The Cheyenne, The Pawnee, The First Baseball Games,* and a guidebook for teens called *Drugs and Peer Pressure.*

"My favorite books are several I have written on the occult," noted Myers, acknowledging his personal interest in the unknown. Myers's books on this subject include *The Ghostly Register, The Ghostly Gazetteer, World's Most Terrifying "True" Ghost Stories,* and *The Ghosthunter's Guide,* the latter praised by Ann E. Cohen in *Library Journal* as "a truly fascinating, memorable romp and unique vacation experience." "They are serious investigations of hauntings, cases of possession, and other such phenomena," Myers adds. "I have written many newspaper and magazine articles on unusual subjects: a clairvoyant healer, people who can heal through their hands or simply through thought, and so on. I've written articles on spiritual groups such as the Sufis, the followers of Muktananda, dowsers, and others. These are people who are seeking higher consciousness through meditation and other practices.

"I suspect that the world is moving toward a greater awareness of what life and death and the universe is all about, that we're moving into an Aquarian Age that will be much more enlightened than the Piscean Age that we've supposedly been in for the past 2,000 years," he added. "I suspect that the children being born into the world today will be creators of this better, more spiritual age. That's why I like to write for young people. Which goes to show, you can be a senior citizen and still be an idealist."

■ Works Cited

Cohen, Ann E., review of *The Ghosthunter's Guide, Library Journal,* May 15, 1993, p. 87.

■ For More Information See

PERIODICALS

Booklist, September 15, 1993, p. 137; February 15, 1994, p. 1078; April 15, 1994, p. 1554.
School Library Journal, March, 1987, p. 181; October, 1995, p. 164.
Voice of Youth Advocates, August, 1992, p. 187.

N

ROBERT NEWCOME

NEWCOME, Robert 1955-

■ Personal

Born September 25, 1955, in Aldershot, England; son of John (in business) and Jane (Scobie) Newcome; married Zita Paterson (an artist), December 10, 1983; children: Henry, Claudia. *Education:* Marlborough College, 1973;

degree (with honors) from Exeter University, 1983. *Politics:* Conservative. *Religion:* Church of England.

■ Addresses

Home—31 Ray Park Ave., Maidenhead, Berkshire SL6 8DZ, England.

■ Career

John Lewis Partnership, London, England, department manager, then management trainer, 1983-96; ITMS, Wokingham, England, consultant, 1996—. *Military service:* British Army, 1974-80; began as officer cadet, became lieutenant. *Member:* Central Register of Advanced Hypnotherapists.

■ Awards, Honors

Northern Ireland General Service Medal.

■ Writings

Herbert the Harmonious Hippo, illustrated by wife, Zita Newcome, Medici Society, 1989.
Little Lion, illustrated by Zita Newcome, Random Century (London), 1993.

Also author of two other children's books about hippos illustrated by Zita Newcome and published by the Medici Society.

■ Work in Progress

Assisting Zita Newcome with text for children's books.

■ Sidelights

"My main career is in management training," Robert Newcome told *SATA.* "This varies in content, but usually involves running residential training courses for middle managers on subjects ranging from leadership to making presentations. Linked to this I am a practicing hypnotherapist and see clients for problems such as smoking, self-confidence, phobias, and any generally persistent problems.

"However, I have always been interested in writing, which I see very much as a hobby. I have written a novel—as yet unpublished—and a number of articles for an in-house business magazine. When my wife, Zita, was looking for someone to write a children's story that she could illustrate she naturally turned to her husband! Initially I wrote three stories about hippos for her, then *Little Lion*. On her more recent works I have helped her with text, rhyming, etc."

*   *   *

NI DHUIBHNE, Eilis 1954-
(Elizabeth O'Hara)

■ Personal

Born February 22, 1954, in Ireland; daughter of Edward (a carpenter) and Margaret (a homemaker; maiden name, O'Hara) Deeney; married Bo Almquist (a professor), 1982; children: Ragnar, Olaf. *Education:* University College Dublin, Ireland, B.A., 1974, M.Phil., 1976, Ph.D., 1982. *Hobbies and other interests:* Reading.

■ Addresses

Home—Dublin, Ireland.

■ Career

University College Dublin, Dublin, Ireland, folklore collector, 1978-80; assistant keeper, National Library, 1980-95; folklore lecturer, People's College, 1986-92; writer of books for children, 1990—. Has lectured widely on folklore, literature, and related topics. *Member:* Irish Writers' Union (secretary, 1992-93; chairperson, 1994-95).

■ Awards, Honors

Listowel Poetry Award, 1985; Art Council Bursary, 1986; Bisto Merit Award, 1994; Bisto Book of the Year, 1995; Readers' Association of Ireland Overall Winner, 1995.

■ Writings

FOR CHILDREN

The Uncommon Cormorant, illustrated by Carol Betera, Poolbeg Press, 1990.
Hugo and the Sunshine Girl, illustrated by Carol Betera, Poolbeg Press, 1991, Dufour, 1991.

FOR CHILDREN; UNDER PSEUDONYM ELIZABETH O'HARA

The Hiring Fair, Poolbeg Press, 1992, Dufour, 1993.
Blaeberry Sunday, Poolbeg Press, 1994.

FOR ADULTS

The Bray House, Attic Press, 1990.

EILIS NI DHUIBHNE

Eating Women Is Not Recommended, Attic Press, 1991.
Singles, Basement Press (Dublin), 1994.
(Editor and author of introduction) *Voices on the Wind: Women Poets of the Celtic Twilight,* New Island Books, 1995.

Also author of many short stories and a play.

■ Work in Progress

Penny Farthing Sally; The Burn; Summer Pudding; a long article on Irish women storytellers.

■ Sidelights

"I have wanted to write and have enjoyed writing since I was eight years old," Irish author Eilis Ni Dhuibhne, who also writes for children under the pseudonym Elizabeth O'Hara, told *SATA.* "I realized it was fun and that I seemed to have a knack for it. (I was not a very self-confident or talkative child, and that may have been a motivating factor.) I loved reading as a child and still do. I suppose I write because I want to, and also because I believe literature (including visual literature—films, etc.) is one of the most important of human creations. I have never been able to live without books."

■ For More Information See

PERIODICALS

Bulletin of the Center for Children's Books, September, 1994, p. 22.
School Library Journal, September, 1994, p. 220.*

NORMENT, Lisa 1966-

■ Personal

Born August 9, 1966, in Everett, WA; daughter of William L. and Eleanor (a consultant; maiden name, Graham) Norment; married Michail A. Reid, May 27, 1995. *Education:* Syracuse University, B.A.

■ Addresses

Office—c/o E. Norment, 1600 South Eads St., Arlington, VA 22202.

■ Career

Teacher of language arts in New York City. *Member:* Society of Children's Book Writers and Illustrators.

■ Writings

Once Upon a Time in Junior High (juvenile fiction), Scholastic, 1994.

■ Work in Progress

The Black House; Down the Street, a picture book; research on African-American female adolescent educational progress in independent schools.

■ Sidelights

Lisa Norment told *SATA:* "I am deeply concerned about the lack of positive children's literature written for and about African-American young people. There is especially a lack of contemporary literature where black kids are portrayed as well-adjusted, functional young people. My goal is to write about 'real' kids and take away the focus from the stereotypical ones. I adore young people, especially their energy and spirit. It is important that writers of children's literature capture this in their novels."

* * *

NORTH, Andrew
See NORTON, Andre

* * *

NORTON, Alice Mary
See NORTON, Andre

* * *

NORTON, Andre 1912-
(Andrew North; Allen Weston, a joint pseudonym)

■ Personal

Given name Alice Mary Norton; name legally changed, 1934; born February 17, 1912, in Cleveland, OH; daughter of Adalbert Freely and Bertha (Stemm) Norton. *Education:* Attended Western Reserve University (now Case Western Reserve University), 1930-32. *Politics:* Republican. *Religion:* Presbyterian. *Hobbies and other interests:* Collecting fantasy and cat figurines and paper dolls, needlework.

■ Addresses

Home—High Hallack, 4911 Calf Killer Highway, Monterey, TN 38574. *Agent*—Russell Galen, 381 Park Ave. S., Suite 1020, New York, NY 10016.

■ Career

Cleveland Public Library, Cleveland, OH, children's librarian, 1930-41, 1942-51; Mystery House (book store and lending library), Mount Ranier, MD, owner and manager, 1941; special librarian for a citizenship project in Washington, DC, and at the Library of Congress, 1941; novelist, 1947—; editor, Gnome Press, 1950-58. *Member:* Science Fiction Writers of America, Swordsmen and Sorcerers Association.

■ Awards, Honors

Award from Dutch government, 1946, for *The Sword Is Drawn;* Ohioana Juvenile Award honor book, 1950, for *Sword in Sheath;* Boys' Clubs of America Medal, 1951, for *Bullard of the Space Patrol;* Hugo Award nominations, World Science Fiction Convention, for novel *Star Hunter,* 1962, for novel *Witch World,* 1964, and for story "Wizard's World," 1968; Headliner Award, Theta

LISA NORMENT

ANDRE NORTON

Sigma Phi, 1963; Invisible Little Man Award, Westercon XVI, 1963, for sustained excellence in science fiction; Boys' Clubs of America Certificate of Merit, 1965, for *Night of Masks;* Phoenix Award, 1976, for overall achievement in science fiction; Gandalf Master of Fantasy Award, World Science Fiction Convention, 1977, for lifetime achievement; Andre Norton Award, Women Writers of Science Fiction, 1978; Balrog Fantasy Award, 1979; Ohioana Award, 1980, for body of work; named to Ohio Women's Hall of Fame, 1981; Fritz Leiber Award, 1983, for work in the field of fantasy; Nebula Grand Master Award, Science Fiction Writers of America, 1984, for lifetime achievement; Jules Verne Award, 1984, for work in the field of science fiction; Second Stage Lensman Award, 1987, for lifetime achievement; Science Fiction Book Club Reader's Award, First Place, 1991, for *The Elvenbane.* Several of Norton's books have been named Junior Literary Guild and Science Fiction Book Club selections.

■ Writings

SCIENCE FICTION

Star Man's Son, 2250 A.D., Harcourt, 1952, published as *Daybreak, 2250 A.D.* (bound with *Beyond Earth's Gates* by C. M. Kuttner), Ace Books, 1954.

Star Rangers ("Central Control" series), Harcourt, 1953, published as *The Last Planet,* Ace Books, 1955.

The Stars Are Ours! ("Astra" series), World Publishing, 1954.

Star Guard ("Central Control" series), Harcourt, 1955.

The Crossroads of Time ("Time Travel" series), Ace Books, 1956.

Star Born ("Astra" series), World Publishing, 1957.

Sea Siege, Harcourt, 1957.

Star Gate, Harcourt, 1958.

Secret of the Lost Race, Ace Books, 1959 (published in England as *Wolfshead,* Hale, 1977).

The Beast Master ("Beast Master" series), Harcourt, 1959.

The Sioux Spaceman, Ace Books, 1960.

Storm over Warlock ("Planet Warlock" series), World Publishing, 1960.

Star Hunter, Ace Books, 1961.

Catseye, Harcourt, 1961.

Lord of Thunder ("Beast Master" series), Harcourt, 1962.

Eye of the Monster, Ace Books, 1962.

Judgment on Janus ("Janus" series), Harcourt, 1963.

Ordeal in Otherwhere ("Planet Warlock" series), Harcourt, 1964.

Night of Masks, Harcourt, 1964.

Quest Crosstime ("Time Travel" series), Viking, 1965 (published in England as *Crosstime Agent,* Gollancz, 1975).

The X Factor, Harcourt, 1965.

Victory on Janus ("Janus" series), Harcourt, 1966.

Operation Time Search, Harcourt, 1967.

Dark Piper, Harcourt, 1968.

The Zero Stone ("Zero Stone" series), Viking, 1968.

Uncharted Stars ("Zero Stone" series), Viking, 1969.

Ice Crown, Viking, 1970.

Android at Arms, Harcourt, 1971.

Breed to Come, Viking, 1972.

Here Abide Monsters, Atheneum, 1973.

Forerunner Foray, Viking, 1973.

Iron Cage, Viking, 1974.

The Many Worlds of Andre Norton (short stories), edited by Roger Elwood, Chilton, 1974, published as *The Book of Andre Norton,* DAW Books, 1975.

Outside, Walker & Co., 1975.

(With Michael Gilbert) *The Day of the Ness,* Walker & Co., 1975.

Knave of Dreams, Viking, 1975.

No Night without Stars, Atheneum, 1975.

Perilous Dreams (short stories), DAW Books, 1976.

Voor Loper, Ace Books, 1980.

Forerunner ("Forerunner" series), Tor Books, 1981.

Moon Called, Simon & Schuster, 1982.

Voodoo Planet [and] *Star Hunter,* Ace Books, 1983.

Forerunner: The Second Venture ("Forerunner" series), Tor Books, 1985.

Brother to Shadows, Morrow, 1993.

"SOLAR QUEEN" SCIENCE FICTION SERIES

(Under pseudonym Andrew North) *Sargasso of Space,* Gnome Press, 1955, published under name Andre Norton, Gollancz, 1970.

(Under pseudonym Andrew North) *Plague Ship,* Gnome Press, 1956, published under name Andre Norton, Gollancz, 1971.

(Under pseudonym Andrew North) *Voodoo Planet,* Ace Books, 1959.

Postmarked the Stars, Harcourt, 1969.

(With P. M. Griffin) *Redline the Stars,* Tor Books, 1993.

"TIME WAR" SCIENCE FICTION SERIES

The Time Traders, World Publishing, 1958.
Galactic Derelict, World Publishing, 1958.
The Defiant Agents, World Publishing, 1962.
Key out of Time, World Publishing, 1963.
(With P. M. Griffin) *Firehand,* Tor Books, 1994.

"MOON MAGIC" SCIENCE FICTION SERIES

Moon of Three Rings, Viking, 1966.
Exiles of the Stars, Viking, 1971.
Flight in Yiktor, Tor Books, 1986.
Dare to Go A-Hunting, Tor Books, 1990.

"STAR KA'AT" SCIENCE FICTION SERIES; WITH DOROTHY MADLEE

Star Ka'at, Walker & Co., 1976.
Star Ka'at World, Walker & Co., 1978.
Star Ka'ats and the Plant People, Walker & Co., 1979.
Star Ka'ats and the Winged Warriors, Walker & Co., 1981.

EDITOR; SCIENCE FICTION

Malcolm Jameson, *Bullard of the Space Patrol,* World Publishing, 1951.
Space Service, World Publishing, 1953.
Space Pioneers, World Publishing, 1954.
Space Police, World Publishing, 1956.
(With Ernestine Donaldy) *Gates to Tomorrow: An Introduction to Science Fiction,* Atheneum, 1973.
Grand Masters' Choice, Tor Books, 1991.

FANTASY

Rogue Reynard (juvenile), Houghton, 1947.
Huon of the Horn (juvenile), Harcourt, 1951.
Steel Magic, World Publishing, 1965, published as *Gray Magic,* Scholastic, 1967.
Octagon Magic, World Publishing, 1967.
Fur Magic, World Publishing, 1968.
Dread Companion, Harcourt, 1970.
High Sorcery (short stories), Ace Books, 1970.
Dragon Magic, Crowell, 1972.
Garan the Eternal (short stories), Fantasy Publishing, 1973.
Lavender-Green Magic, Crowell, 1974.
Merlin's Mirror, DAW Books, 1975.
Wraiths of Time, Atheneum, 1976.
Red Hart Magic, Crowell, 1976.
Yurth Burden, DAW Books, 1978.
Quag Keep, Atheneum, 1978.
Wheel of Stars, Simon & Schuster, 1983.
Were-Wrath, Cheap Street, 1984.
The Magic Books, Signet, 1988.
Moon Mirror, Tor Books, 1989.
Wizards' Worlds, Tor Books, 1990.
(With Susan M. Shwartz) *Imperial Lady,* Tor Books, 1990.
(With Marion Zimmer Bradley and Julian May) *Black Trillium,* Doubleday, 1990.
(With Mercedes Lackey) *The Elvenbane,* Tor Books, 1991.
Mark of the Cat, Ace Books, 1992.

Golden Trillium, Bantam Books, 1993.
(With Susan M. Shwartz) *Empire of the Eagle,* Tor Books, 1993.
The Hands of Lyr, Morrow, 1994.
(With Mercedes Lackey) *Elvenblood,* Tor, 1995.
The Mirror of Destiny, Morrow, 1995.
(With Marion Zimmer Bradley and Mercedes Lackey) *Tiger Burning Bright,* Morrow, 1995.
The Monster's Legacy (juvenile), illustrated by Jody A. Lee, Atheneum, 1996.

"WITCH WORLD" FANTASY SERIES

Witch World, Ace Books, 1964.
Web of the Witch World, Ace Books, 1964.
Three against the Witch World, Ace Books, 1965.
Year of the Unicorn, Ace Books, 1965.
Warlock of the Witch World, Ace Books, 1967.
Sorceress of the Witch World, Ace Books, 1968.
Spell of the Witch World (short stories), DAW Books, 1972.
The Crystal Gryphon (first volume in "Gryphon" trilogy), Atheneum, 1972.
The Jargoon Pard, Atheneum, 1974.
Trey of Swords (short stories), Ace Books, 1977.
Zarthor's Bane, Ace Books, 1978.
Lore of the Witch World (short stories), DAW Books, 1980.
Gryphon in Glory (second volume in "Gryphon" trilogy), Atheneum, 1981.
Horn Crown, DAW Books, 1981.
'Ware Hawk, Atheneum, 1983.
(With A. C. Crispin) *Gryphon's Eyrie* (third volume in "Gryphon" trilogy), Tor Books, 1984.
The Gate of the Cat, Ace Books, 1987.
(Editor) *Tales of the Witch World,* Tor Books, 1987.
Four from the Witch World, Tor Books, 1989.
(With P. M. Griffin) *Storms of Victory* (first volume in "The Turning"), Tor Books, 1991.
(With P. M. Griffin and Mary H. Schaub) *Flight of Vengeance* (second volume in "The Turning"), Tor Books, 1992.
(With A. C. Crispin) *Songsmith,* Tor Books, 1992.
(With Patricia Matthews and Sasha Miller) *On Wings of Magic* (third volume in "The Turning"), Tor Books, 1994.
(With Lyn McConchie) *The Key of Klepian,* Warner, 1995.
(With Mary H. Schaub) *The Magestone,* Warner, 1996.
The Warding of Witch World, Warner, 1996.

EDITOR; FANTASY

(With Robert Adams) *Magic in Ithkar,* Tor Books, 1985.
(With Robert Adams) *Magic in Ithkar II,* Tor Books, 1985.
(With Robert Adams) *Magic in Ithkar III,* Tor Books, 1986.
(With Robert Adams) *Magic in Ithkar IV,* Tor Books, 1987.
(With Martin H. Greenberg) *Catfantastic,* DAW Books, 1989.
(With Martin H. Greenberg) *Catfantastic II,* DAW Books, 1992.

(With Martin H. Greenberg) *Catfantastic III,* DAW Books, 1994.

(With Martin H. Greenberg) *Catfantastic IV,* DAW Books, 1996.

HISTORICAL NOVELS

The Prince Commands, Appleton, 1934.

Ralestone Luck, Appleton, 1938.

Follow the Drum, Penn, 1942.

The Sword Is Drawn, (first volume of "Swords" trilogy), Houghton, 1944.

Scarface, Harcourt, 1948.

Sword in Sheath (second volume of "Swords" trilogy), Harcourt, 1949 (published in England as *Island of the Lost,* Staples Press, 1954).

At Sword's Points (third volume of "Swords" trilogy), Harcourt, 1954.

Yankee Privateer, World Publishing, 1955.

Stand to Horse, Harcourt, 1956.

Shadow Hawk, Harcourt, 1960.

Ride Proud, Rebel!, World Publishing, 1961.

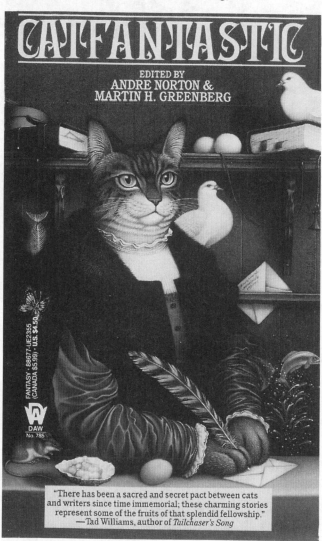

"There has been a sacred and secret pact between cats and writers since time immemorial; these charming stories represent some of the fruits of that splendid fellowship."
—Tad Williams, author of *Tailchaser's Song*

Featuring cats of varied times and dimensions, this 1989 collection of fifteen original tales includes an introduction and story by master fantasy writer Norton. (Cover illustration by Braldt Bralds.)

Rebel Spurs, World Publishing, 1962.

OTHER

(With Grace Hogarth, under joint pseudonym Allen Weston) *Murder for Sale* (mystery), Hammond, 1954, reprinted under names Andre Norton and Grace Hogarth as *Sneeze on Sunday,* Tor Books, 1992.

(With mother, Bertha Stemm Norton) *Bertie and May* (biography), World Publishing, 1969.

(Editor) *Small Shadows Creep: Ghost Children,* Dutton, 1974.

The White Jade Fox (gothic novel), Dutton, 1975.

(Editor) *Baleful Beasts and Eerie Creatures,* Rand McNally, 1976.

Velvet Shadows (gothic novel), Fawcett, 1977.

The Opal-Eyed Fan (gothic novel), Dutton, 1977.

Snow Shadow (mystery), Fawcett, 1979.

(With Phyllis Miller) *Seven Spells to Sunday* (juvenile), McElderry, 1979.

Iron Butterflies (gothic novel) Fawcett, 1980.

Ten Mile Treasure (juvenile mystery), Pocket Books, 1981.

(With Enid Cushing) *Caroline,* Pinnacle, 1982.

(With Phyllis Miller) *House of Shadows* (mystery), Atheneum, 1984.

Stand and Deliver, Tor Books, 1984.

(With Phyllis Miller) *Ride the Green Dragon* (mystery), Atheneum, 1985.

(With Robert Bloch) *The Jekyll Legacy* (horror), Tor Books, 1991.

Contributor to numerous periodicals and anthologies. Many of Norton's early novels have been reprinted by Del Rey, Ace Books, Fawcett, and other publishers. Her works have been translated into eighteen languages.

■ Adaptations

The Beast Master was made into a film by MGM/UA in 1982; a recording was made of *Witch World,* and numerous licenses have been granted by Norton for *Witch World* items, such as maps, stationery, and acrylic sculptures.

■ Work in Progress

Scent of Magic, a fantasy novel for Avon; *Elvenborn* and *Elvenbred,* both with Mercedes Lackey, both for Tor Books.

■ Sidelights

Andre Norton was one of the first women to break into science fiction writing, a largely male domain until her time. So male-dominated was the genre, in fact, that Norton legally changed her given name from Mary Alice to Andre in 1934, thus lending her title-pages the 'proper' gender appearance. Initially a writer of juvenile historical novels and adventures, Norton began writing science fiction in the 1950s and turned to fantasy by the mid-1960s. Because of her early associations with juvenile literature in a time before publishers had pinpointed young adults as a separate audience, Norton's later works have suffered some critical neglect, lumped as they are into the juvenile fiction grab-bag. Norton, however, writes for all ages and is, as a reviewer for *Library Journal* noted, "one of the first women sf/fantasy writers with the selling clout to match the Asimovs and the Heinleins." The author of over 150 books, Norton has a readership spanning generations and several of her books have sold over a million copies. Her first science fiction book, *Star Man's Son, 2250 A.D.,* like many of her other novels, remains in print decades after its initial publication. "A skilled teller of stories" is how Francis J. Molson described Norton in *Dictionary of Literary Biography*. She is one of a handful of writers who have won both a Nebula Grand Master Award from the Science Fiction Writers of America, and a Gandalf Award—a special Hugo—from science fiction fans. In a review of her 1994 science fiction novel *Firehand,* published six decades after her first novel, a reviewer for *Voice of Youth Advocates* commented that "this author has staying power."

Born in Ohio in 1912, Norton was almost two decades younger than her sister and was thus brought up as if she were an only child. Books were highly valued in the Norton household, as was an appreciation for history. Norton's parents both had deep roots in the country's history: on her mother's side were some of the first settlers in Ohio, and ancestors on her father's side came to America in 1634. Norton early on developed a love for both books and history. Some of her early reading included the Oz books and novels by H. G. Wells and Jules Verne. Science fiction stories found in the pulp magazines of the time also formed staples of her reading diet. Writing also began early for Norton, who wrote fiction and book reviews for her school paper. During high school Norton wrote her first novel, *Ralestone Luck,* published almost a decade later after several re-writings.

Writing, however, was put on hold upon graduation from high school. Norton attended Western Reserve University in hopes of qualifying as a history teacher. But with the onset of the Great Depression, Norton had to leave school and find work, becoming a librarian in the Cleveland Public Library system. She held this position for the next two decades, excepting a one-year leave in 1941 when she opened a book shop of her own in Maryland. Meanwhile, she also began taking night classes at Western Reserve, especially in creative writing. Her interest in science fiction continued, but that genre was only a short story market at the time, and Norton did not care for short-story writing. Instead, she tackled juvenile historical fiction. Because she was then working as a children's librarian, this was a logical choice. Her first published novel was *The Prince Commands,* sold when Norton was twenty-two. Her output was not great at first: only four books in the next decade. The fourth, however, was a turning point for Norton. *The Sword Is Drawn* began what turned out to be a trilogy about the Dutch resistance in World War II, a series of books that would win her an award from the Dutch government for its authenticity. Many of Nor-

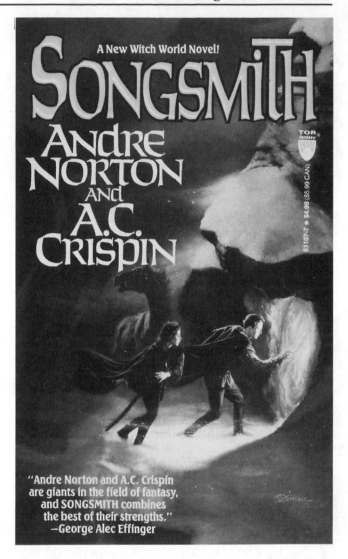

Eydrth must find a way to rescue her father from evil without recourse to magic in this 1992 romantic fantasy from the popular "Witch World" series. (Cover illustration by Doriau.)

ton's early books featured juvenile male protagonists and were pure escapist reading, though based on thorough research.

Norton's career as a librarian ended when she was diagnosed with agoraphobia, a condition that made her more or less of an invalid for decades, though more recent treatment has allowed her some mobility. Ironically, it was that condition that spawned a new career for Norton, one that has made her a very public figure. From 1950 to 1958 she worked as a reader at Martin Greenberg's Gnome Press, and also helped to edit science fiction anthologies for World Publishing. The science fiction market had been transformed in the intervening decades. No longer was it only to be found between the covers of pulp magazines; by the 1950s mainstream publishers were offering book contracts for such works. Thus, with publishing contacts and credits in place, Norton sold her first science fiction novel, *Star Man's Son, 2250 A.D.,* to Harcourt Brace in 1952. Brought out initially as a juvenile work, the book sold well enough for Ace Paperbacks to reissue the book as an adult novel two years later, and it has sold over a million copies over the years. The popularity of this and other early science fiction titles enabled Norton to write full time. In *Star Man's Son, 2250 A.D.,* which introduces many of the themes and elements found in other Norton works, the descendants of the survivors of a nuclear war on a distant planet try to create a new life for themselves. A young mutant, Fors, spurned by his tribe, is tested by a dual mission: to keep warring tribes from making the same mistakes as the Old Ones, and to find himself and his own destiny. He is aided in this endeavor by a telepathic cat and a young black leader from another tribe.

Here, in short, is the Norton formula, developed and refined over the next forty-five years: a youthful protagonist, an outsider, coming to grips with his or her own identity while battling for a just cause. As Molson noted, "one theme, above all others, is pervasive in Norton's science fiction and fantasy: the centrality of the passage or initiation." Or, in terms of young adult writing, the classic coming-of-age story, which explains Norton's continuing popularity with young readers. Also present in this first science fiction novel is Norton's preoccupation with animals—especially telepathic ones—which act as guides to humans. Her books are full of such sentient creatures: dolphins, horses, and birds, but most of all cats, for which she has a personal fondness. The black youth also introduces the element of ethnicity Norton so often and so early displayed in her work, later installments of which would include Native Americans and Asians as well as African Americans. Additionally, as with the nuclear holocaust in *Star Man's Son, 2250 A.D.,* there is a strong bias in many Norton books against the evils wrought by unrestrained science and technology. Sandra Miesel, in her introduction to a 1978 edition of Norton's *Sargasso of Space,* explained the Norton formula: "The typical Norton hero is a misfit seeking his rightful place. He is usually poor, young, powerless, and frequently a victim, orphan, cripple or outcast. His character-building struggle against his enemies is commonly plotted as chase-capture-escape-confrontation. The hero grows in wisdom, knowledge, and virtue under stress.... Finally, the victorious hero saves others besides himself." What is important for Norton is that her protagonists deal not only with physical tests, but also with ethical ones.

Many of Norton's science fiction novels are inter-linked, constructed in the same universe with the same villains and protagonists recurring throughout. The "Forerunners" series posits a mysterious race of beings who lived on Terra—Norton's stand-in for planet Earth—several thousand years ago. These star-travelling precursors have left behind tantalizing clues about themselves in the form of artifacts scattered about various planets. Themes such as the danger of trading cartels—the Free Traders—and organized crime—the Thieves' Guild—are repeated in the "Solar Queen" series of novels, as is Norton's distrust for large bureaucratic institutions. Throughout all her books, Norton also displays a skill that sets her apart from the crowd of science fiction or

fantasy writers: her ability "to construct a fantastic never-never land of new color, new sound, new motion," as Jane Manthorne described it in a *Horn Book* review of *The X Factor.*

In 1993, Norton returned to one of her most popular science fiction series, "Solar Queen," with *Redline the Stars.* Rather than following the adventures of the male protagonist, Dane Thorson, Norton was now able to use a female lead, Rael Cofort, something that was unthinkable in the early days of science fiction. Co-authored by P. M. Griffin, *Redline the Stars* is a compilation of "agreeable, well-crafted adventures," according to *Kirkus Reviews.* In *Brother to Shadows,* Norton also peripherally revisits her Forerunners "in classic Norton style," according to Roland Green in *Booklist.* Here are all the familiar Norton elements: the exiled young warrior searching for Forerunner remains in the Solar Queen's universe, and the use of what Green termed "grungy realistic detail" to give the book a feel of authenticity. A

Jofre, who has been expelled from the Brotherhood, travels through time and space with his reptilian companion in this gripping science fiction mystery centering on honor, courage, and duty. (Cover illustration by Daniel Horne.)

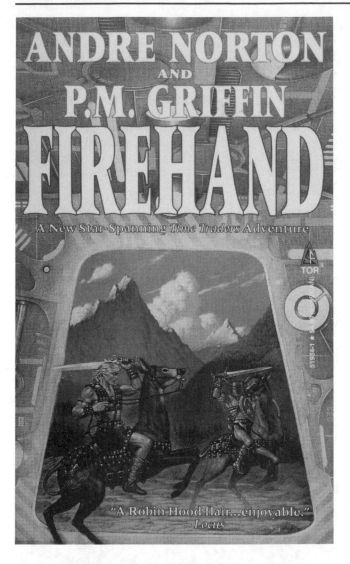

Petty criminal turned hero Ross Murdoch must try to live up to his new image when the feudal people of Dominion seek his leadership in a war against aliens in this classic "Time Trader" series tale. (Cover illustration by Walter Velez.)

reviewer for *Voice of Youth Advocates* commented that this 1993 addition to the writer's science fiction works has "lots of action, a vivid presentation of alien cultures, and an unbreakable code of honor," which combine to produce a "page-turner that is vintage Norton." A later addition to Norton's science fiction catalogue of works is the 1994 *Firehand,* co-authored with Griffin, which pays a return visit to the "Time Traders" series of books. Dealing with the coming-of-age adventures of a time-travelling mercenary, the book could simply be a potboiler, but as *Voice of Youth Advocates* noted, "It is an emphasis on characterization and a completely realized alien civilization that really hooks the readers."

Many of Norton's favorite themes are also employed in her fantasy novels, books which account for much of her production since the mid-1960s. Some of the best known of these fantasy novels are in the "Witch World" series, which debuted in 1964. Although Norton has said that she never intended to write series books, the use of the same characters and worlds in various books created strong interrelationships between the books. With the first of these, *Witch World,* a group of telepathic witches do battle with invaders from a parallel universe. These Kolder invaders are mechanized, industrialized villains, the repository for much of what Norton finds wrong with the "civilized" world. "In the name of progress more than one crime is committed nowadays," one of her characters says in *Octagon Magic.* Talismans and magic counteract such mechanized evils in Norton's fantasy books; female witches in touch with the natural rhythm of the world, connected to the land, battle uncontrolled science and malevolent progress.

At the height of her productivity, Norton was able to turn out three books per year. However, arthritis and age have combined to slow her down. Much of Norton's recent work has been co-authored, as she has teamed up with Dorothy Madlee, Phyllis Miller, Mercedes Lackey, Susan Shwartz, and Marion Zimmer Bradley, among others. With Lackey, Norton produced the popular and award-winning *Elvenbane,* in which a decadent society of elves controls a human slave population. A half-breed human/elf child—the typical Norton outsider—uses magic to lead a revolt of other such half-breeds against their elven overlords. *Publishers Weekly* commented that this tale, with its "excellent evocations of dragon lore and society," would "rank as one of the season's liveliest and most appealing fantasy epics." Roland Green noted in *Booklist* that the book was a "well-told tale in all respects," while *Kirkus Reviews* dubbed it "an entertaining adventure." Norton and Lackey repeated their teamwork with the 1995 *Elvenblood,* another yarn about the evil elven empire and youthful battlers against its tyranny. The book's two spunky female protagonists would, decided Mary Anne Hoebeke in *Voice of Youth Advocates,* "provide two good role models for young women."

Working with A. C. Crispin, Norton wrote two additions to Witch World: *Gryphon's Eyrie* and *Songsmith.* The latter book, the story of the young songsmith Eydryth, might "expand the audience for fantasy," according to *School Library Journal* contributor Barbara Hawkins, with its "fast-paced and single-threaded plot." Employing a mixture of Celtic mythology and English folklore, Norton's fantasy novels also involve cooperation between males and females in their plot resolution. In *Flight of Vengeance,* co-authored with Griffin and Schaub, "a man and woman must overcome obstacles to fight evil and find each other," according to Green in *Booklist.* Writing solo in the 1993 *Golden Trillium*—a companion book to *Black Trillium*—Norton continued the story of the land of Ruwenda which is threatened by a legacy of the Vanished Ones, an ancient race of people. Young Kadiya, a female warrior, is the only one who can save the land, and she does so by discovering the Vanished Ones in a parallel world. Calling Norton "the grande dame of sf and fantasy," a reviewer for *Library Journal* went on to comment that *Golden Trillium* "bears witness to [Norton's] mastery of no-frills storytelling." *Publishers Weekly* concluded that Norton's portrayal of aboriginal life, "with its dedication to nature, and ... the emotional growth of a strong yet uncertain and lonely woman are finely wrought."

While the "Witch World" series and other Norton fantasy novels were written with an adult audience in mind, many young adult readers are also attracted to the books. However, *The Monster's Legacy,* written in 1996, was specifically targeted at a young adult audience and serves up many of the usual Norton elements and themes: a quest by a young woman, a dreadful monster who provides the test, and a magic talisman that gives gentle Sarita, the protagonist, the power to see into the future. "Mix in fast-paced adventure, a sense of constant danger, and a mystery about long-gone dragons and their legacy—and you have a satisfying tale," noted Sally Estes in a *Booklist* review of the book. In addition to her myriad science fiction and fantasy novels, Norton has also proved an able editor of anthologies. One of her most popular fantasy series is *Catfantastic,* co-edited with Martin H. Greenberg—a natural for Norton with her love of cats.

Throughout her long and varied career in writing, Norton has maintained an allegiance to the theme of self-discovery, no matter in what genre she was writing.

How can Sarita, a needlework apprentice in charge of the Earl's infant son, escape and survive when the castle is attacked? (From *The Monster's Legacy,* written by Norton and illustrated Jody A. Lee.)

Yet she has managed to develop that and other themes without becoming didactic. "The primary concern of fiction is to tell an entertaining story," Norton told Paul Walker in a *Luna Monthly* interview. Norton went on to relate that she was not "one of the 'new wave' writers, but rather a very staid teller of old-fashioned stories with firm plots and morals ... [with] a hero or heroine who stands up to difficulties as best as he or she can and does not 'cop out' when the going gets rough." In his introduction to *The Many Worlds of Andre Norton,* Norton's former editor at Ace, Donald Wollheim, nicely summed up Norton's achievement. "Andre Norton is at home telling wonder stories," Wollheim wrote. "She is telling us that people are marvelously complex and marvelously fascinating.... She is weaving an endless tapestry of a cosmos no man will fully understand, but among whose threads we are meant to wander forever to our personal fulfillment."

■ Works Cited

Review of *Brother to Shadows, Voice of Youth Advocates,* February, 1995, p. 350.

Review of *The Elvenbane, Kirkus Reviews,* September 1, 1991, p. 1123.

Review of *The Elvenbane, Publishers Weekly,* September 20, 1991, p. 124.

Estes, Sally, review of *The Monster's Legacy, Booklist,* April 1, 1996.

Review of *Firehand, Voice of Youth Advocates,* December, 1994, p. 288.

Review of *Golden Trillium, Publishers Weekly,* May 15, 1993, p. 70.

Review of *Golden Trillium, Library Journal,* June 15, 1993, p. 104.

Green, Roland, review of *The Elvenbane, Booklist,* October 15, 1991, p. 416.

Green, Roland, review of *Flight of Vengeance, Booklist,* December 15, 1992, p. 718.

Green, Roland, review of *Brother to Shadows, Booklist,* October 15, 1993, p. 422.

Review of *Hands of Lyr, Library Journal,* February 15, 1994.

Hawkins, Barbara, review of *Songsmith, School Library Journal,* December, 1992, p. 148.

Hoebeke, Mary Anne, review of *Elvenblood, Voice of Youth Advocates,* February, 1996, p. 386.

Manthorne, Jane, review of *The X Factor, Horn Book,* December, 1965, p. 636-7.

Miesel, Sandra, introduction to *Sargasso of Space* by Andre Norton, Gregg Press, 1978.

Molson, Francis J., "Andre Norton," *Dictionary of Literary Biography, Volume 52: American Writers for Children since 1960: Fiction,* Gale, 1986, pp. 267-78.

Norton, Andre, *Octagon Magic,* World Publishing, 1967.

Review of *Redline the Stars, Kirkus Reviews,* February 1, 1993, p. 104.

Walker, Paul, "An Interview of Andre Norton," *Luna Monthly,* September, 1972.

Wollheim, Donald, introduction to *The Many Worlds of Andre Norton,* Chilton, 1974.

■ For More Information See

BOOKS

Contemporary Literary Criticism, Volume 12, Gale, 1980.
Dictionary of Literary Biography, Volume 8, Gale, 1981.
The Encyclopedia of Science Fiction, Granada, 1979.
Schlobin, Roger C., *Andre Norton,* Gregg Press, 1979.
Schlobin, Roger C., *Andre Norton: A Primary and Secondary Bibliography,* G. K. Hall, 1980.
Twentieth-Century Young Adult Writers, edited by Laura Standley Berger, St. James Press, 1994.

PERIODICALS

Children's Literature in Education, No. 4, 1996.
Horn Book, April, 1966, p. 216; December, 1967, p. 760; June, 1984, p. 331.
Kliatt, Fall, 1985, p. 24; September, 1987, p. 28; January, 1989, p. 23; April, 1991, p. 21; July, 1994, p. 16; September, 1995, p. 24.

New York Times Book Review, August 31, 1952, p. 12; December 14, 1958, p. 18; December 3, 1967, p. 103; September 20, 1970, p. 47; February 24, 1974, p. 8; January 25, 1976, p. 12.
School Library Journal, August, 1985, p. 88; November, 1985, p. 89; May, 1986, p. 117; February, 1993, p. 126; September, 1993, p. 261.
Voice of Youth Advocates, August, 1985, p. 193; October, 1985, p. 268; April, 1986, p. 41; August, 1986, p. 164; February, 1988, p. 290; June, 1989, p. 117; August, 1989, p. 164; February, 1990, p. 373; June, 1990, p. 118; October, 1990, p. 258; December, 1990, p. 304; August, 1991, p. 182; April, 1992, p. 45; August, 1992, p. 178; December, 1992, p. 294; April, 1993, p. 10; June, 1993, p. 103; October, 1993, p. 232; December, 1993, p. 281; April, 1994, p. 39; August, 1994, p. 158.

—Sketch by J. Sydney Jones

O–P

OFFENBACHER, Ami 1958-

■ Personal

Born August 29, 1958, in Rockford, IL; daughter of Delbert LeRoy and Billie Laurence (Reed) Franklin; married Steven Offenbacher (a research scientist), February 21, 1987; children: Elsa Marie, Cody Michael. *Education:* Attended LaSalle Extension University, 1979; attends University of North Carolina, 1995—. *Politics:* "Flexible—usually Democrat." *Religion:* Lutheran. *Hobbies and other interests:* Music, reading, ballet, soccer, walking, pets, gardening.

■ Career

Emory University Clinic, Atlanta, GA, Medicare account supervisor, 1980-86; homemaker, 1988—. Holy Trinity Lutheran Church, choir member, 1991—. *Member:* Natural Resources Defense Council, National Wildlife Federation, National Audubon Society, Friends of the Lakota Indian Children.

■ Writings

The Dragonfly, Winston-Derek, 1996.

■ Work in Progress

"The Trilogy—A Love Story," three novels in the historical romance genre; *In a Child's Mind,* a collection of poetry about children for adults; "The Adventures of Amanda Chesterfield," a series; "Cindy, Mindy & Lindy," a series of picture/story books.

■ Sidelights

Ami Offenbacher told *SATA:* "My earliest memories of writing are those of corresponding with my maternal grandmother. It seemed to me that she lived thousands of miles away, although in actuality it was only about four hundred. Still, finances being what they were, our visits were brief and only once a year.

AMI OFFENBACHER

"Our relationship was enriched through our letter writing, I a child of five and she, well, of grandmotherly age anyway. I would write long, drawn out letters relating the complicated life of a five year old and she would reply in turn with tales of canning okra, picking cotton, or finding a lost hunting dog. I never could figure out how a hunting dog could get lost, although I, of course, was only five.

"We corresponded regularly into my early twenties. By that time I had accumulated quite a few pen pals, due to our numerous moves, and several of them suggested that my letters often sounded like stories. Putting real events onto paper and perhaps exaggerating them slightly

157

helped me to get through the difficult teenage years, and unknowingly at that time, I began developing the skills I would need to become a writer.

"I was staggered by my grandmother's passing and was left feeling unsatisfied by writing only to pen pals. I decided to put my writing to the test and enrolled in the LaSalle Extension University course for fiction writing. After two years I was awarded their diploma in fiction writing and began writing in earnest for the first time.

"*The Dragonfly* is my first published children's book. I have several others in progress and have completed the first in a series entitled 'Cindy, Mindy & Lindy'—which will cover the antics of three little squirrels having real life adventures.

"I am currently working on an adult historical romance/adventure novel that will eventually evolve into a trilogy of love stories involving the same characters. Another series of children's books is also in the making and I plan to call them 'The Adventures of Amanda Chesterfield.'"

*   *   *

O'HARA, Elizabeth
See NI DHUIBHNE, Eilis

*   *   *

OSBORNE, David
See SILVERBERG, Robert

*   *   *

PARKS, Deborah A. 1948-

■ Personal

Born February 26, 1948, in Great Barrington, MA; daughter of John J. (a builder and executive) and Haroldine Catherine (a psychiatric nurse; maiden name, Gold) Keeler. *Education:* State University of New York at Stony Brook (now Stony Brook University), B.A., 1970; attended City College of the City University of New York, 1970-72, New York University, 1971-72, Columbia University Teachers College, 1973, and State University of New York College at New Paltz, 1973. *Hobbies and other interests:* Mountaineering, rock climbing.

■ Addresses

Home—1167 Rte. 52, Ste. 220, Fishkill, NY 12524. *Electronic mail:* MtDeb@aol.com (America Online).

■ Career

Freelance researcher/writer, 1971-72; market researcher/writer for BBDO Advertising Agency, 1972-73; secondary school teacher at Somers High School, West-chester Board of Co-Operative Education, 1973-76; freelance editor, writer, and educational consultant, 1976-77; Prentice-Hall, Inc., Englewood Cliffs, NJ, associate editor, 1977-79; Scholastic Inc., New York City, staff writer/editor, 1979-81; Harcourt Brace Jovanovich, Inc., New York City, senior supervisory editor, 1981-85; president/owner of Editorial Directions, 1985-91; editorial consultant and author/editor/reporter for publishing clients and news magazines, Fishkill, NY, 1991—. Member of Dutchess County Association for Retarded Citizens; volunteer with inner-city youth projects. *Member:* National Council of the Social Studies, Sierra Club, Appalachian Mt. Club, Yosemite Association, The Access Fund, Himalayan Explorers Club, South American Explorers Club.

■ Writings

Climb Away: A Mountaineer's Dream (adventure), Silver Burdett, 1996.

Author and developer of numerous U.S. and world history books. Contributor to *African Americans in U.S. West, Hispanic America to 1776,* and *Native Americans: the Struggle for the Plains,* all Globe Fearon, 1993-94.

DEBORAH A. PARKS

■ Work in Progress

A manuscript on a group of young Latino runners; a manuscript on a climbing-based children's adventure.

■ Sidelights

Deborah A. Parks told *SATA:* "Traveling around the world has never uprooted my heart from New York's Hudson Valley. I heard the folklore of the region while working in gardens alongside my mother and grandmother. When old enough to join with the family's women over late-night cups of tea, I knew enough of the stories to retell them myself. 'A coven,' one of my boyfriends called us as he heard us laughing each evening. But this story-coven, as it were, inspired my first writings. Unpublished to this day, the stories taught me to read my writing aloud—to make sure they caught the cadence of everyday speech.

"As ever-present as the stories were the Catskill Mountains. I traveled mentally to these mountains many times before ever leaving home. So perhaps it was natural that when I first set out to travel far from family and friends it would be into the mountains. The mountain journeys were never intended to form a book. (As a freelance writer, I wrote many non-mountain stories instead.) But the women of my family taught me to be a storyteller. So when an editor asked me to write a book on the mountains I had climbed it turned out to be a collection of chronological stories—read aloud by phone, chapter by chapter, to the women in my family and in my life. The result was my first trade title, *Climb Away: A Mountaineer's Dream,* stories retold by me for children of all ages."

* * *

PEARSON, Susan 1946-

■ Personal

Born December 21, 1946, in Boston, MA; daughter of Allen M. (a Swedish masseur) and Chloris (a secretary; maiden name, Horsman) Pearson. *Education:* St. Olaf College, Northfield, MN, B.A., 1968.

■ Addresses

Home—Minneapolis, MN.

■ Career

Author and editor. Volunteers in Service to America (VISTA), Columbia, SC, volunteer worker, 1968-69; Quaker Oats Co., Minneapolis, MN, sales representative, 1969-71; Viking Press, New York City, assistant, 1971-72; Dial Press, New York City, editor, 1972-78; Carolrhoda Books, Minneapolis, MN, editor in chief, 1978-84; freelance editor and writer, 1985—.

■ Awards, Honors

Izzie was named one of the *New York Times'* Outstanding Books of the Year and one of Child Study Association's Children's Books of the Year, 1975; *Saturday I Ran Away* was selected one of the International Reading Association's Children's Choices, 1982.

■ Writings

Izzie, illustrated by Robert Andrew Parker, Dial, 1975.

Monnie Hates Lydia, illustrated by Diane Paterson, Dial, 1975.

That's Enough for One Day, J.P.!, illustrated by Kay Chorao, Dial, 1977.

Everybody Knows That!, illustrated by Diane Paterson, Dial, 1978.

Monday I Was an Alligator, illustrated by Sal Murdocca, Lippincott, 1979.

Molly Moves Out, illustrated by Steven Kellogg, Dial, 1979.

Karin's Christmas Walk, illustrated by Trinka H. Noble, Dial, 1980.

Saturday I Ran Away, illustrated by Susan Jeschke, Lippincott, 1981.

Happy Birthday, Grampie, illustrated by Ronald Himler, Dial, 1987.

Baby and the Bear, illustrated by Nancy Carlson, Viking, 1987.

The Day Porkchop Climbed the Christmas Tree, illustrated by Rick Brown, Prentice Hall, 1987.

When Baby Went to Bed, illustrated by Nancy Carlson, Viking, 1987.

My Favorite Time of Year, illustrated by John Wallner, Harper & Row, 1988.

Porkchop's Halloween, illustrated by Rick Brown, Simon & Schuster, 1988.

(Reteller) *Jack and the Beanstalk,* illustrated by James Warhola, Simon & Schuster, 1989.

The Bogeyman Caper, illustrated by Gioia Fiammenghi, Simon & Schuster, 1990.

The Campfire Ghosts, illustrated by Gioia Fiammenghi, Simon & Schuster, 1990.

Eagle-Eye Ernie Comes to Town, illustrated by Gioia Fiammenghi, Simon & Schuster, 1990.

The Tap Dance Mystery, illustrated by Gioia Fiammenghi, Simon & Schuster, 1990.

Well, I Never, illustrated by James Warhola, Simon & Schuster, 1990.

The Green Magician Puzzle, illustrated by Gioia Fiammenghi, Simon & Schuster, 1991.

The 123 Zoo Mystery, illustrated by Gioia Fiammenghi, Simon & Schuster, 1991.

The Spooky Sleepover, illustrated by Gioia Fiammenghi, Simon & Schuster, 1991.

The Spy Code Caper, illustrated by Gioia Fiammenghi, Simon & Schuster, 1991.

Lenore's Big Break, illustrated by Nancy Carlson, Viking, 1992.

■ Adaptations

Everybody Knows That! was filmed and released as a video, directed by Chris Pelzer, Phoenix Films and Video, 1984.

■ Sidelights

Susan Pearson, who has written over twenty books for beginning readers, had "an idyllic childhood," as she once told *SATA*. An only child, she grew up in Massachusetts, Virginia, and Minnesota. "Few restrictions were placed on me. I was never expected to play with dolls or to fit into a particular mold, and was encouraged in all my interests," she recalled.

Pearson began writing as early as the second grade, when one of her teachers insisted that she create a booklet for each subject they studied. "I decided I wanted my *own* booklet," she related. "The first thing I ever wrote was entitled, 'My Booklet.' It consisted of

drawings, very short stories, and some poems." When Pearson was a teenager, her family moved to Minnesota, where she began to approach writing more seriously. "I think adolescence has something to do with that," she noted. "Many female writers I know started writing in earnest during their adolescence, when they were too embarrassed to tell people what they were really feeling."

Pearson attended St. Olaf College in Northfield, Minnesota, where she majored in English. Lacking just a few credits for graduation, she convinced her advisors to let her write and illustrate a children's book as an independent study project. When she completed the book, which was illustrated with silkscreens, her professor was so impressed that he sent it out to several publishers. Though this early effort was never published, Pearson admitted to *SATA* that its positive reception helped her believe that she could make writing her career. Her senior year "instilled in me a real feeling of confidence, a feeling that, 'Gee, maybe I really could....'"

Martha finds the perfect gift for her blind grandfather in Susan Pearson's picture book *Happy Birthday, Grampie*, illustrated by Ronald Himler.

After college, Pearson worked at a variety of office jobs. Each time she saved about one thousand dollars, however, she would quit her job and concentrate on writing. She learned a great deal about the publishing industry while working as an editor at Dial Press in New York City, and it was during her tenure there that her first book, *Izzie,* was published in 1975. Three years later Pearson became editor-in-chief of Carolrhoda Books in Minneapolis, where she remained until she decided to write full-time in 1984.

Pearson received critical praise for her book *Happy Birthday, Grampie,* published in 1987. Every Sunday after church, young Martha accompanies her family to the nursing home to visit her beloved grandfather. She remembers Grampie when he was strong enough to push her on the swings, but now he is frail and blind and has reverted to speaking only his native Swedish. This Sunday happens to be his eighty-ninth birthday, so Martha makes a special card with raised letters that spell out "I love you, Grampie" in an attempt to reconnect with him. Suspense builds as Grampie studies the card with his fingertips, until finally he laughs and says, "Martha, I love you, too." A writer for *Kirkus Reviews* called Pearson's book "a lovely, realistic evocation of the American family at its best," while *Horn Book* contributor Hanna B. Zeiger noted that "this story of a strong Swedish-American family is a welcome addition to book collections."

In 1990 and 1991, Pearson published a series of books featuring child detective Ernestine Jones, nicknamed Eagle-Eye Ernie. In *Eagle-Eye Ernie Comes to Town,* Ernie has just moved to Minnesota from Virginia and started classes at a new school. Some of the kids make fun of her clothes and the way she talks, and they blame her when food mysteriously disappears from their lunches. Ernie discovers that William, one of the nicest boys in her class, has been taking the food because an older bully has been stealing his lunch. She helps William get revenge on the bully and earns her classmates' respect in the process. Lisa Smith, in a review for *School Library Journal,* predicted that "children will relate to both the situations and the characters, who are realistic and well drawn."

In *Lenore's Big Break,* published in 1992, Pearson uses the plight of an unpopular adult to show children that there are positive aspects to being different. Nerdy Lenore is the object of much ridicule at her office job, but the only thing important to her is her secret dream of training birds. Every night she returns to her small apartment with bread, insects, worms, and small fish to feed the variety of birds who live with her. Among her many amazing feats, Lenore trains pelicans to tap dance, puffins to walk a tightrope, and flamingoes to perform a ballet. Before long, she appears with her performing feathered friends on television, gets her big break into show business, and becomes famous, leaving the snide remarks of her former co-workers far behind. A reviewer for *Publishers Weekly* noted that "Pearson's snappy text skillfully holds the reader's attention as Lenore's double life unfolds." Ilene Cooper, writing in

Scapegoat Ernestine Jones finds the lunch-bag thief in Pearson's entertaining school mystery. (From *Eagle-Eye Ernie Comes to Town,* illustrated by Gioia Fiammenghi.)

Booklist, added that "there is a real message here for children who may need encouragement to follow a different drummer."

Describing her writing process, Pearson told *SATA:* "I usually write in the morning. I have a separate room, and everything is there. It's a very cheerful room and I enjoy the sunlight and the company of my cats." She had the following advice for hopeful young writers: "To be a writer, you have to 'write.' You must believe that you can do it. If you want it badly enough, you can do it. But there is no point in wanting it for the glamour because writing isn't glamorous, it's a lot of hard work, and if you don't love words there's not much point in getting involved."

■ Works Cited

Cooper, Ilene, review of *Lenore's Big Break, Booklist,* January 15, 1992, p. 949.

Review of *Happy Birthday, Grampie, Kirkus Reviews,* March 15, 1987, p. 475.

Review of *Lenore's Big Break, Publishers Weekly,* December 13, 1991, p. 55.

Smith, Lisa, review of *Eagle-Eye Ernie Comes to Town, School Library Journal,* April, 1991, p. 101.

Zeiger, Hanna B., review of *Happy Birthday, Grampie, Horn Book,* May-June, 1987, pp. 333-34.

■ For More Information See

BOOKS

Authors of Books for Young People, Scarecrow, 1990.

PERIODICALS

Booklist, January 15, 1989, p. 874; February 1, 1989, p. 936; June 15, 1989, p. 1826; November 15, 1990, p. 667; April, 1991, p. 101.

Kirkus Reviews, January 1, 1988, p. 59; August 15, 1990, p. 1178.

Publishers Weekly, February 27, 1987, p. 161; January 15, 1988, p. 94; May 19, 1989, p. 82.

School Library Journal, April, 1987, p. 88; March, 1989, p. 168; February, 1991, p. 73; December, 1991, p. 99; February, 1992, p. 76; March, 1992, p. 223; June, 1992, p. 100.

Wilson Library Bulletin, April, 1987, pp. 54-55.*

* * *

PINE, Nicholas 1951-
(Andrew Coleman, Nicholas Adams)

■ Personal

Born December 11, 1951, in Harlan, KY. *Education:* St. Petersburg Junior College, A.A., 1971; University of West Florida, M.A., 1976. *Hobbies and other interests:* Fishing, gardening.

■ Addresses

Office—P.O. Box 551, Center Conway, NH 03813. *Agent*—The Vines Agency, 409 East 6th Street #4, New York, NY 10009.

■ Career

Writer.

■ Writings

UNDER PSEUDONYM NICHOLAS ADAMS; YOUNG ADULT HORROR

Horror High, HarperCollins, 1991.
Mr. Popularity, HarperCollins, 1991.
Resolved: You're Dead, HarperCollins, 1991.
Heartbreaker, HarperCollins, 1991.
Hard Rock, HarperCollins, 1991.
The New Kid on the Block, HarperCollins, 1991.

YOUNG ADULT HORROR; "TERROR ACADEMY" SERIES; ALL PUBLISHED BY BERKLEY BOOKS

Lights Out, 1993.
Stalker, 1993.
Sixteen Candles, 1993.
Spring Break, 1993.
The New Kid, 1993.
Student Body, 1993.
Breaking Up, 1994.
The In-Crowd, 1994.
Night School, 1994.

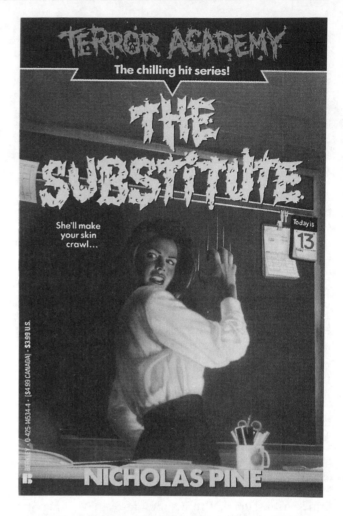

In this installment of Nicholas Pine's popular "Terror Academy" series, Iris discovers her new teacher has magical powers that she will share—for a price.

Summer School, 1994.
Science Project, 1994.
The Prom, 1994.
The Substitute, 1995.
School Spirit, 1995.
Boy Crazy, 1995.

UNDER PSEUDONYM ANDREW COLEMAN; YOUNG ADULT SUSPENSE

Mirror Image ("Nightshade" series), HarperCollins, 1996.
Attitude Problem ("Nightshade" series), HarperCollins, 1996.

Also author of six books in the "Escape from Lost Island" series, under the pseudonym Clay Coleman, and twenty-six westerns.

■ Work in Progress

Currently researching a historical mystery.

■ Sidelights

Nicholas Pine told *SATA:* "My 'hero' authors are John D. MacDonald (creator of Travis McGee), Robert E. Howard (creator of Conan the Barbarian), F. Scott Fitzgerald, William Faulkner, and Willa Cather. People who have been instrumental in my career: Damaris Rowland (editor), Chris Fortunato (editor of *Horror High*), Gary Goldstein (editor of the "Terror Academy" series), and Nicholas Guest (actor) who helped me very early in my career."

"Though I have written for adult audiences, I prefer to write for young adults," Pine continued. "Most of my fan mail comes from children in elementary and middle school. I enjoy hearing from kids, because I think they are the best audience in the world. Young people are often given the bad rap of 'Johnny can't read.' I disagree. There is a large section of the young audience who read all the time. This audience has always been there, and it will always be there. Reading stirs the imagination, letting the reader fill in a lot of the details with a formed picture in the mind. Reading provides pleasure and satisfaction that cannot be found in television and movies. I hope and pray that reading will never disappear.

"When I am interviewed for newspaper and magazine articles, the interviewer will often ask: 'Have you ever thought about writing something serious?' Well, when I write for the young adult audience, I am extremely serious. To engage and entertain a young reader is very gratifying. I write because it's a great way to make a living. I wrote my first story when I was eight years old, a contribution to the camp newspaper. I also have a theatrical background which gave me a sense of drama, a sense of timing, and an appreciation of words.

"I love words. Communication is everything. In today's educational venues, there is much talk of how to teach children. Teach them language skills and they can adapt. To be able to interpret information is an invaluable asset to anyone entering the modern work force. Without language, you might as well be blind, hearing-impaired, and mute.

"Words rule. Believe in them. Learn them. Love them."*

*   *   *

POPP, K. Wendy

■ Personal

Daughter of Kermit William Popp and Rosemary E. Jeppi; married William R. Simmons (an architect), October 1, 1983; children: Zoe Raine. *Education:* Pratt Institute, B.F.A. (with honors), 1981; studied at Maryland Institute of Art.

■ Addresses

Home—19 Hall Ave., Larchmont, NY 10538. *Office*—Illustration Department, Parsons School of Design, 66 Fifth Avenue, New York, NY.

■ Career

Artist and illustrator. Instructor of drawing and concepts in illustration at foundation and junior levels, Parsons School of Design, New York City, 1991—. Lecturer and juror for funding institutions for the arts. *Exhibitions:* Work has been shown in exhibitions throughout the U.S. and Japan and in juried annual exhibitions including the Society of Illustrators Museum of American Illustration; The Art Directors Club; The Society for Publication Designers; The Master Eagle Gallery; Parson's Gallery of New York; Perrot Memorial Library; Old Greenwich, Connecticut; The Oresman Gallery; and The Mamaraneck Artist Guild Gallery in Larchmont.

■ Awards, Honors

Time/Life grants, 1979, 1980; Hallmark Grant of Kansas City, 1994.

■ Illustrator

Marc Harshman, *Moving Days,* Cobblehill, 1994.
John Warren Stewig, *Princess Florecita and the Iron Shoes: A Spanish Fairy Tale,* Knopf, 1995.

K. WENDY POPP

Popp has over three hundred illustrations in print, including covers for the works of such authors as Robert Cormier, Paula Fox, Margaret Craven, Bette Greene, Henry James, and Sinclair Lewis. Interior illustrations for numerous volumes published by Reader's Digest, Time Life Books, and The Franklin Library.

■ Work in Progress

A children's picture book on the topic of racism; Marybeth Lorbiecki, *Sister Anne's Hands,* for Dial Books.

■ For More Information See

PERIODICALS

Booklist, September 1, 1994; October 1, 1995.
School Library Journal, October, 1994; January, 1996, p. 107.

*   *   *

POURNELLE, Jerry (Eugene) 1933-
(Wade Curtis)

■ Personal

Born August 7, 1933, in Shreveport, LA; son of P. Eugene (a radio station owner) and R. Ruth (Lewis) Pournelle; married Roberta Jane Isdell (a reading specialist), July 18, 1959; children: Alexander, Francis Russell, Phillip, Richard Stefan. *Education:* Attended University of Iowa, 1953-54; University of Washington, B.S., 1955, M.S., 1957, Ph.D. (psychology), 1960, Ph.D. (political science), 1964. *Politics:* Republican. *Religion:* "Anglo-Catholic." *Hobbies and other interests:* Sailing, backpacking, computers, war gaming.

■ Addresses

Home—12190 1/2 Ventura Blvd., Box 372, Studio City, CA 91604. *Agent*—Eleanor Wood, Spectrum Agency, 111 Eighth Ave., Suite 1501, New York, NY 10011.

■ Career

University of Washington Medical School, Seattle, research assistant, 1954-57; Boeing Corp., Seattle, aviation psychologist and systems engineer, 1957-64; Aerospace Corp., San Bernadino, CA, manager of special studies, 1964-65; systems scientist, North American Aviation, 1964-65; research specialist and proposal manager, American Rockwell Corp., 1965-66; Pepperdine University, Los Angeles, professor of history and political science, 1966-69; executive assistant to mayor of Los Angeles and director of research, Los Angeles, 1969-70; freelance writer, lecturer, and consultant, 1970—. Member of Republican Board of Governors, San Bernadino Co., 1960-64; chairman of board, Seattle Civic Playhouse, 1962-63; member of board of directors, Ocean Living Institute. Adviser to numerous futurist and space-oriented organizations. *Military service:* U.S. Army, 1950-52. *Member:* Science Fiction Writers of America (president, 1973-74), Mystery Writers of America, American Institute of Aeronautics and Astronautics, Operations Research Society of America (fellow), American Association for the Advancement of Science (fellow), American Academy of Arts and Sciences (fellow), American Rocket Society, Institute for Strategic Studies, American Security Council, University Professors for Academic Order (director, 1971), Society for Creative Anachronism, Military and Hospitaler Order of St. Lazarus of Jerusalem (officer).

■ Awards, Honors

Bronze Medal from American Security Council, 1967; Republic of Estonia Award of Honor, 1968; John W. Campbell Award for Best New Writer of 1972, World Science Fiction Convention, 1973; Evans-Freehafer Award, 1977; Nebula Award nomination (with Larry Niven), Science Fiction Writers of America, 1977, for *Inferno;* Hugo nomination (with Larry Niven), World Science Fiction Convention, 1978, for *Lucifer's Hammer;* American Book Award nomination, science fiction hardcover, 1980, for *Janissaries.*

■ Writings

SCIENCE FICTION

A Spaceship for the King, DAW, 1972, revised and expanded as *King David's Spaceship,* Pocket Books, 1980.
Escape from the Planet of the Apes (novelization of screenplay), Award (New York City), 1974.
(With Larry Niven) *The Mote in God's Eye,* Simon & Schuster, 1974.
Birth of Fire, Laser (Toronto), 1976, Pocket Books, 1978.
(With Niven) *Inferno,* Pocket Books, 1976.
West of Honor, Laser, 1976, Pocket Books, 1978.
The Mercenary, Pocket Books, 1977.
(With Larry Niven) *Lucifer's Hammer,* Playboy Press (Chicago), 1977.
High Justice (short stories), Pocket Books, 1977.
Exiles of Glory, Ace Books, 1978, revised, Baen, 1993.
Janissaries, Ace Books, 1979.
(With Larry Niven and John Eric Holmes) *Mordred,* Ace Books, 1980.
(With Larry Niven and Richard S. McEnroe) *Warrior's Blood,* Ace Books, 1981.
(With Niven and McEnroe) *Warrior's World,* Ace Books, 1981.
(With Niven) *Oath of Fealty,* Phantasia Press (Huntington Woods, MI), 1981.
(With Roland Green) *Janissaries II: Clan and Crown,* Ace Books, 1982.
(With Larry Niven and John Silbersack) *Roger's Rangers,* Ace Books, 1983.
(With Niven) *Footfall,* Ballantine (New York City), 1985.
(With Roland Green) *Janissaries III: Storms of Victory,* Ace Books, 1987.
(With Larry Niven and Steven Barnes) *The Legacy of Heorot,* Simon & Schuster, 1987.
Prince of Mercenaries, Baen, 1989.

(With Larry Niven, Dean Ing, and S. M. Stirling) *Man-Kzin Wars II*, Baen, 1989.

Falkenberg's Legion (includes *West of Honor* and *The Mercenary*), Baen, 1990, published as *Future History*, Orbit (London), 1991.

(With Larry Niven, Poul Anderson, and S. M. Stirling) *Man-Kzin Wars III* (short stories), Baen, 1990.

(With S. M. Stirling) *Go Tell the Spartans*, Baen, 1991.

(With Stirling) *The Children's Hour*, Baen, 1991.

(With Larry Niven and Michael Flynn) *Fallen Angels*, Easton (Norwalk, CT), 1991.

(With Larry Niven, S. M. Stirling, and Thomas T. Thomas) *Man-Kzin Wars IV* (short stories), Baen, 1992.

(With S. M. Stirling) *Prince of Sparta*, Baen, 1993.

Exiles to Glory, Baen, 1993.

(With Larry Niven) *The Gripping Hand* (sequel to *The Mote in God's Eye*), Pocket Books, 1993, published as *The Moat around Murcheson's Eye*, HarperCollins (London), 1993.

(With Ben Bova, Frederik Pohl, and Charles Sheffield) *Future Quartet* (novellas), Morrow, 1994.

Invasion, Baen, 1994.

(With Larry Niven and Steven Barnes) *Beowulf's Children* (sequel to *The Legacy of Heorot*), Tor Books, 1995, published as *The Dragons of Heorot*, Gollancz (London), 1995.

(With Charles Sheffield) *Higher Education*, Tor Books, 1996.

EDITOR

20/20 Vision, Avon, 1974.

(And contributor) *Black Holes and Other Marvels*, Orbit, 1978, Fawcett, 1979.

(And contributor) *The Endless Frontier*, Ace Books, 1979.

(With John F. Carr) *The Survival of Freedom*, Fawcett, 1981.

(With Carr) *The Endless Frontier 2*, Ace Books, 1981.

(With Carr) *Nebula Award Stories 16*, Holt, 1982.

(With Carr, and contributor) *There Will Be War*, Tor Books, 1983.

(With Carr, and contributor) *There Will Be War: Men of War*, Tor Books, 1984.

(With Carr) *There Will Be War 2: Blood and Iron*, Tor Books, 1984.

(With Carr) *Silicon Brains*, Ballantine, 1985.

(With Carr) *Science Fiction Yearbook 1984*, Baen, 1985.

(With Carr) *There Will Be War 3: Day of the Tyrant*, Tor Books, 1985.

(With Jim Baen and John F. Carr) *Far Frontiers*, Baen, 4 volumes, 1985-86.

(With John F. Carr) *Imperial Stars: The Stars at War*, Baen, 1986.

(With Carr) *There Will Be War 4: Warrior*, Tor Books, 1986.

(With Carr) *Imperial Stars 2: Republic and Empire*, Baen, 1987.

(With Carr) *There Will Be War 5: Guns of Darkness*, Tor Books, 1987.

(With John F. Carr and Roland Green) *War World 1: The Burning Eye*, Baen, 1988.

(With John F. Carr) *There Will Be War 6: Call to Battle*, Tor Books, 1988.

(With Carr) *Imperial Stars 3: The Crash of Empire*, Baen, 1989.

(With Carr) *There Will Be War 6: Armageddon!*, Tor Books, 1989.

War World 2: Death's Head Rebellion, Baen, 1990.

(With Carr) *There Will Be War 7: After Armageddon*, Tor Books, 1990.

(With Carr) *There Will Be War 8: Men of War*, Tor Books, 1990.

(With Carr) *War World 3: Sauron Dominion*, Baen, 1990.

(With Carr) *Endless Frontier: Cities in Space*, Baen, 1991.

CoDominium: Revolt on War World, Baen, 1992.

(With John F. Carr) *Endless Frontier 2: Life among the Asteroids*, Baen, 1992.

War World 5: Blood Feuds, Baen, 1993.

War World 6: Blood Vengeance, Baen, 1994.

NONFICTION

(With Stefan T. Possony) *The Strategy of Technology: Winning the Decisive War*, Dunellen (New York City), 1970.

That Buck Rogers Stuff, edited by Gavin Claypool, Extequer (Pasadena, CA), 1977.

(With R. Gagliardi) *The Mathematics of the Energy Crisis*, Intergalactic Publishing (Westmont, NJ), 1978.

A Step Farther Out (essays), W. H. Allen (London), 1980, Ace Books, 1983.

(With Dean Ing) *Mutual Assured Survival: A Space-Age Solution to Nuclear Annihilation*, Baen, 1984.

The User's Guide to Small Computers, Baen, 1985.

Adventures in Microland, Baen, 1985.

(With Michael A. Banks) *Pournelle's PC Communications Bible: The Ultimate Guide to Productivity with a Modem*, Microsoft Press (Redmond, WA), 1992.

Also author of *Human Temperature Tolerance in Astronautic Environments*, 1959; *Stability and National Security*, 1968; *Congress Debates Viet Nam*, 1971; and *The Right to Read*, 1971. Contributor to *The Craft of Science Fiction*, edited by Reginald Bretnor, Harper, 1976. Contributor of nonfiction articles to *Analog*, *Galaxy*, *Info World*, and *American Legion*. Author of column "Notes from Chaos Manor," *Byte;* science columnist, *Galaxy Science Fiction Magazine;* computer columnist, *Popular Computing*.

OTHER

(Under pseudonym Wade Curtis) *Red Heroin* (novel), Berkley Publishing, 1969, reprinted under name Jerry Pournelle, Ace Books, 1985.

(Under pseudonym Wade Curtis) *Red Dragon* (novel), Berkley Publishing, 1971, reprinted under name Jerry Pournelle, Ace Books, 1985.

■ **Sidelights**

With his background in the field of technology, author Jerry Pournelle writes in what is known as the "hard" science fiction genre. Advances in technology are directly related to the progress of the human race in Pournelle's fast-paced adventure novels, while complicated social issues are dealt with as they relate to technological advances. "Pournelle develops his plots logically," notes Don D'Ammassa in *St. James Guide to Science Fiction Writers,* "with a good sense of timing and judicious use of suspense and other devices. Most of his fiction is essentially action-oriented, with clear-cut issues and sympathetic characters."

Born August 7, 1933, in Shreveport, Louisiana, Pournelle graduated from high school and went on to earn degrees in history and engineering from the University of Washington, before continuing his education by obtaining advanced degrees in psychology and political science. During the late 1950s he got a job in the space industry, spending two years as chief of the Experimental Stress Program at Boeing's Seattle-based Human Factor Laboratories. After government budget cuts reduced the demand for space research in the 1960s, he decided to become a science fiction writer. "It wasn't really a big jump," Pournelle tells Jeffrey M. Elliot in *Science Fiction Voices Number Three: Interviews with Science Fiction Writers,* "especially since I had done considerable research on alternative futures and technologies."

Pournelle's first novel was 1972's *A Spaceship for the King,* later republished as *King David's Spaceship.* Highlighting its author's belief in the importance of scientific advancement, the novel recounts the efforts of a planet's Imperial Navy to regain its technological aptitude so that it can join a rejuvenated galactic empire. Also characteristic of many of Pournelle's later novels, *King David's Spaceship* takes place in the future—in "future history," as Pournelle terms it. Comparing the novel to the "old-fashioned science fiction" of the 1930s and 1940s, *Washington Post Book World* contributors Alexei and Cory Panshin believe that "this novel is a romp, a technological fairy tale, but it can't be taken seriously for a moment. Even to partake of its exuberance, you must close your eyes, promise not to think, and turn the clock back."

"My work reflects my own view of the world, particularly my view of science and technology," the author explained to Elliot. "As I see it, not all technology is good, but it's certainly not all bad. It affords you a host of choices." This theme characterizes much of Pournelle's fiction: scientific advances create options for mankind, but the outcomes that result from human choices about the best use of those advances may be good or bad. In *Higher Education,* for example, the increasing fear of lawsuits and a corrupted educational system have ultimately created an illiterate work force, but technological advances have also created opportunities for some young people in the area of asteroid mining. While the working conditions for miners-in-training like *Higher Education* protagonist Rick Luban are at least as unpleasant as army boot camp, the payoffs prove to be great in this young adult novel by Pournelle and coauthor Charles Sheffield. Space travel provides

Cadmann, the lone warrior on a Utopian civilization in space, faces his Grendel like the ancient Beowulf in this 1987 adventure by coauthors Jerry Pournelle, Larry Niven, and Steven Barnes. (Cover illustration by Richard Pracher.)

Pournelle with another means of creating options, and it figures strongly in such novels as 1976's *West of Honor,* 1977's *The Mercenary,* and *Exiles of Glory,* first published in 1978.

Although he has been successful as a solo novelist—his 1979 adventure novel *Janissaries* was nominated for an American Book Award—and has served as editor or coeditor of numerous collections of short stories, Pournelle's fiction writing in collaboration with Larry Niven, among others, has brought him the greatest recognition of his long career. As Niven remarks to Charles Platt in *Dream Makers Volume II: The Uncommon Men and Women Who Write Science Fiction,* "I would say that we're the most successful collaboration in science-fiction history." The two men first joined forces on *The Mote in God's Eye,* a 1974 novel that takes place in Pournelle's future history. Later novels, such as *Lucifer's Hammer, Oath of Fealty,* and a sequel to *Mote* entitled *The Gripping Hand,* established the duo as bestselling authors even among non-science fiction buffs. Describing what happens after a comet strikes the earth, *Lucifer's Hammer* "is one of the most ambitious disaster novels to date," writes Richard Freeman in the *New York Times Book Review,* describing one of the pair's more popular collaborative efforts. "For all its portentous length, the narrative pace seldom flags, and the stick-figure characters are sufficiently animated."

Another collaboration between Pournelle and Niven, *Oath of Fealty* relates the efforts of an independent, self-contained city called Todos Santos to prevent outsiders from destroying it. While some critics have faulted *Oath of Fealty* for being somewhat one-dimensional, *Science Fiction and Fantasy Book Review* contributor Lawrence I. Charters believes that the novel differs from most escapist science fiction: "Most SF dealing with explosive political or social issues is placed in the far future," he explains, noting that "*Oath* does not provide this soothing distance; try as you might, the world about you and the world you are reading about seem uncomfortably close.... *Oath of Fealty* is, without question, a book worth reading, and arguing about."

Pournelle and Niven's 1985 novel, *Footfall,* is the account of an alien invasion of earth by the elephant-like Fithp, which land in Kansas amid a hail of deadly meteorites. Achieving the initial surrender of the earthlings, the simple-minded Fithp eventually come under nuclear attack from the combined forces of Earth's superpowers. Praising the coauthors for presenting a detailed portrait of an alien culture and history, *Chicago Tribune Book World* contributors James Park Sloan and Eugene Sloan call Pournelle "the master of plot and adventure, while Niven ... provides the leavening of hard science." The critics also praise the authors for giving a unique perspective to humankind by depicting them from an alien point of view. While some critics have objected to the length of the novel, *Science Fiction Review* writer Richard E. Geis terms *Footfall* "gut tensing, emotional bedrock stuff," "impossible to put down," and praises it as "probably the finest novel of alien invasion ever written."

The Gripping Hand, which Pournelle and Niven wrote as a sequel to their popular *The Mote in God's Eye,* was published in 1993. In the original novel, a group of earth-born explorers encounter an alien race known as "Moties." Because these quickly regenerating and amazingly adaptive aliens have evolved in a highly specialized manner—with biological characteristics grouped around several subspecies that include artists, warriors, and engineers—the humans quarantine the Moties within their own planetary system. Now, twenty-five years later, the aliens are about to escape their confines and their superiority, not to mention their animosity, will undoubtedly pose a threat to Earth. "Some of the intriguing subtexts, such as the prevailing xenophobia, are disturbing," comments Sybil Steinberg in *Publishers Weekly,* "while others, including warnings about overpopulation, enlighten."

In 1987 Pournelle and Niven joined fellow author Steven Barnes in writing *The Legacy of Heorot,* a reworking of the classic Beowulf legend; the novel was followed eight years later by *Beowulf's Children.* Set on a planet called Avalon, which appears to have a simple ecology and present little danger, the novel depicts the attempts of a group of Earth-born scientists to colonize the planet. All goes well until a group of deadly amphibious predators appear and surround their island home. Dubbed "grendels" by the colonists, these beings are unlike the clumsy monsters of many science fiction stories. They come equipped with complex body mechanisms that allow for rapid attack and escape. After security chief Cadmann Weyland defeats the monsters, the colonists realize that their own presence on the planet is upsetting the ecological balance of this peaceful world and sparking the creation of yet another race of killer creatures. In the novel's sequel, which takes place twenty-five years later, members of the next generation—sons and daughters of the original colonists—attempt to move to the mainland, only to encounter a race of man-eating insects and a grendel that has evolved into an air-breathing creature even more threatening than its predecessors. While questioning the wisdom of dressing the classic Old English epic up in science fiction clothing, *Los Angeles Times Book Review* contributor Mary Dryden believes that *The Legacy of*

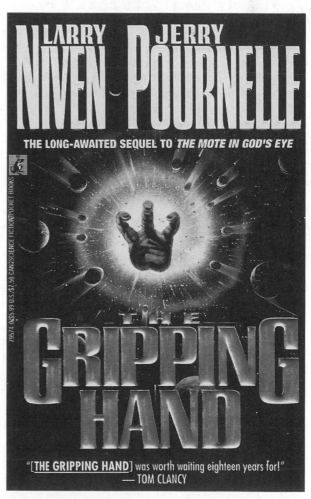

Pournelle teams again with Larry Niven to tell of a group of highly evolved and amazingly adaptive aliens who have escaped a twenty-five year confinement at the hands of earth-born explorers. (Cover illustration by Lee MacLeod.)

Heorot "undertakes that presumptuous exercise not only without disappointment but with substantial success."

When asked why his collaboration with Niven has been so successful, Pournelle explains to Elliot that Niven brings an exceptional imagination to the table. "He comes up with some great ideas, but he's not always capable of executing them in the context of a realistic story .... On the other hand, I'm not as good at coming up with these fantastic attention-getters. Larry's much better at that than I am. I tend to do the nuts-and-bolts work, making sure that all the loose ends are well thought out. The end result," concluded Pournelle, "is that we usually come up with a product that neither of us could have created separately."

Whether writing in tandem with Niven or alone, Pournelle feels that his work should entertain his readers. "I see myself as the modern-day counterpart of the chap in the Bronze Age who used to wander around from camp fire to camp fire with a lyre in his hand," he tells Elliot. "He would see this group of guys sitting around a camp fire, and he'd say, 'Boys, if you'll fill up my cup with some of that wine, and cut me off a chunk of that roast boar, I'll tell you a story about a virgin and a bull that you just won't believe.' Well, that's what I do for a living. I sing songs for my supper and, fortunately, I get a pretty good supper out of it. Hopefully, they're pretty good songs, too." "And given any luck at all," Pournelle once told *SATA*, "I'll live to write a column from the moon."

■ Works Cited

Charters, Lawrence I., review of *Oath of Fealty, Science Fiction and Fantasy Book Review,* April, 1982, p. 7.

D'Ammassa, Don, "Jerry Pournelle," *St. James Guide to Science Fiction Writers,* edited by Jay P. Pederson, St. James Press, 1995, pp. 745-47.

Dryden, Mary, review of *The Legacy of Heorot, Los Angeles Times Book Review,* August 2, 1987, p. 11.

Elliot, Jeffrey M., *Science Fiction Voices Number Three: Interviews with Science Fiction Writers,* Borgo Press, 1980.

Freeman, Richard, review of *Lucifer's Hammer, New York Times Book Review,* November 13, 1977, p. 26.

Geis, Richard E., review of *Footfall, Science Fiction Review,* May 1985, p. 45.

Panshin, Alexei, and Cory Panshin, review of *King David's Spaceship, Washington Post Book World,* April 26, 1981.

Platt, Charles, *Dream Makers Volume II: The Uncommon Men and Women Who Write Science Fiction,* Berkley Publishing, 1983.

Sloan, James Park, and Eugene Sloan, review of *Footfall, Chicago Tribune Book World,* July 28, 1985, p. 10.

Steinberg, Sybil, review of *The Gripping Hand, Publishers Weekly,* December 28, 1992, p. 62.

■ For More Information See

PERIODICALS

Analog, December 1979, p. 167; February 1986, p. 177; January 1996, pp. 273-74.

Booklist, June 1, 1987, p. 1466; July 1987, p. 1655; October 15, 1995, p. 389.

Chicago Tribune Book World, March 22, 1981.

Detroit News, April 19, 1981.

Library Journal, April 15, 1979, p. 979; January 15, 1981, p. 168; November 15, 1988, p. 30.

Los Angeles Times Book Review, November 8, 1981; February 24, 1985.

Magazine of Fantasy and Science Fiction, August, 1985.

New York Times, February 26, 1985.

New York Times Book Review, January 31, 1993, p. 25.

Publishers Weekly, October 16, 1995, p. 46.

School Library Journal, January 1982, p. 92; December 1985, p. 113; January 1988, p. 97.

Science Fiction Review, February 1976.

Tribune Books (Chicago), July 12, 1987.

Voice of Youth Advocates, April 1982, p. 40; October 1983, p. 216; August 1985, p. 192; December 1991, pp. 324-25; August, 1993, p. 169.

Washington Post Book World, December 27, 1981; July 28, 1985.*

*   *   *

PROFESSOR SCRIBBLER
See HOLLINGSWORTH, Mary

R

RANDALL, Robert
See SILVERBERG, Robert

*   *   *

REINSMA, Carol 1949-

■ Personal

Born September 27, 1949, in Worthington, MN; daughter of John W. (a farmer) and Gertrude (a homemaker; maiden name, Fransen) Vander Kooi; married Jerry Reinsma, June 28, 1975; children: John, Kathryn. *Education:* Dordt College, B.A., 1972; attended State University of New York at Stony Brook, 1973-74 and Pikes Peak Community College, 1982.

■ Addresses

Home and office—1690 Big Horn Tr., Colorado Springs, CO 80919.

■ Career

West Sayville Christian, West Sayville, NY, first grade teacher, 1972-79; part-time preschool teacher, 1979-89; writer and substitute teacher, 1989—. Volunteer for Job Assistance Program, Ecumenical Social Ministries. *Member:* Society of Children's Book Writers and Illustrators.

■ Writings

Friends Forever, illustrated by Nathan Cori, Standard Publishing, 1993.
A Place in the Palace, illustrated by Nathan Cori, Standard Publishing, 1993.
The Secret of the Ring in the Offering, illustrated by Jennifer Schneider, Standard Publishing, 1993.
The Picnic Caper, illustrated by Nathan Cori, Standard Publishing, 1994.
The Shimmering Stone, illustrated by Nathan Cori, Standard Publishing, 1994.

(With Bonnie Bruno) *The Young Reader's Bible,* Standard Publishing, 1994.
Wanna Trade?, CRC Publications, 1995.
With a Cherry on Top (devotional), CRC Publications, 1997.

■ Work in Progress

Research for a biography of Fanny Crosby.

■ Sidelights

Carol Reinsma told *SATA:* "My mother's closet was narrow and deep; the further back I went the more

CAROL REINSMA

mysterious the clothes became—there was something with fur and something with sequins. Who wore these clothes? Someone of long ago or someone who used the closet late at night? My imagination explored the mystery and feeling brave, I stepped through the rows— through the fabrics that touched my skin with little shivers.

"I loved inventing mysteries. Discovering a sealed-off room in the almost one hundred-year-old farm house and wall drawings in the shed fueled my imagination.

"But it was the real mysteries of life and death that frightened me. My sister died of cancer, then a brother died in an accident. The sadness bound me as it wrapped tightly around me. Then a miracle happened. God came to me in a way I couldn't explain—he came to comfort and let me know he was real. From my Bible with a black leather cover and red-edged pages, I read the Psalms—they spoke of sadness, joy, and promises of God. Somehow it all mysteriously fit into my life. But how? Finally I started a journal and wrote about it. Bits and pieces came together and I was hooked on writing. So at the age of twelve, I wrote that I would always write and someday I'd write stories for people like me who were trying to sort through the mystery of God, hurts, and joys.

"I became a teacher, but I still wanted to write, and write from my child's heart.

"First I tried books—no one was interested. To reach my goals, I needed to study writing. I attended workshops, critique groups, read about writing, and read and re-read my favorite authors. Finally I sold a short story—then some more before writing books again.

"My first books, the 'Proverb Pals,' resulted from seeking the wisdom of Solomon in Proverbs. I liked the small but wise animals he talked about—the ant, the coney, the locust, and the lizard. So from my experience in teaching first graders, I wrote beginning readers about these characters. Each of the books features one animal and has a hidden secret about God.

"Next, I worked on *The Young Reader's Bible.* That was great, too, because the Bible not only gives us clues about an awesome and mysterious God, it has great stories that teach us about his ways.

"After that I wrote *Wanna Trade,* which is a book that explores Bible stories and the ways young people can compare their actions to what the Bible teaches.

"I hope I can write for a long time because there are so many more things I want to explore. There are mysteries of life, soul, and childhood that go back deep into many rows past furs and sequins."

RICE, Eve (Hart) 1951-

■ Personal

Born February 2, 1951, in New York, NY; daughter of Henry Hart (a real estate broker) and Grace (a teacher; maiden name, Hecker) Rice; married Timothy Mattison (a physician), 1978. *Education:* Yale University, B.A. 1972, graduate study, 1972-73; New School for Social Research, graduate study, 1973-74. *Hobbies and other interests:* Walking, bicycling, exploring New York City, hiking in the country, collecting wild flowers, history, calligraphy, etching, collecting children's books, swimming.

■ Career

Freelance writer and illustrator of children's books, New York City, 1973—.

■ Awards, Honors

Children's Book Showcase designation, 1977, for *What Sadie Sang.*

■ Writings

FOR CHILDREN; SELF-ILLUSTRATED

Oh, Lewis!, Macmillan, 1974.
New Blue Shoes, Macmillan, 1975.
Mr. Brimble's Hobby, and Other Stories, Greenwillow, 1975.
Ebbie, Greenwillow, 1975.
What Sadie Sang, Greenwillow, 1976.
Papa's Lemonade and Other Stories, Greenwillow, 1976.
Sam Who Never Forgets, Greenwillow, 1977.
The Remarkable Return of Winston Potter Crisply, Greenwillow, 1978.
(Adapter) *Once in a Wood: Ten Tales from Aesop,* Greenwillow, 1979.
Goodnight, Goodnight, Greenwillow, 1980.
Benny Bakes a Cake, Greenwillow, 1981.

FOR CHILDREN

City Night (poem), illustrated by Peter Sis, Greenwillow, 1987.
Aren't You Coming Too?, illustrated by Nancy Winslow Parker, Greenwillow, 1988.
Peter's Pockets, illustrated by Nancy Winslow Parker, Greenwillow, 1989.
At Grammy's House, illustrated by Nancy Winslow Parker, Greenwillow, 1990.
Swim, illustrated by Marisabina Russo, Greenwillow, 1996.

ILLUSTRATOR

Helen Puner, *I Am Big; You Are Little,* Young Scott (Reading, MA), 1973.
Carla Stevens, *Stories from a Snowy Meadow,* Seabury Press (New York), 1976.

■ Adaptations

New Blue Shoes was adapted for filmstrip, Insight Productions, 1976.

■ Sidelights

"Few authors are as successful as Eve Rice in capturing the essence of the ritual events that make the most potent childhood memories," proclaimed *School Library Journal* reviewer Jeanne Marie Clancy. An author and illustrator, Rice creates tales that reflect a strong sensitivity to the myriad feelings, insecurities, joys, and emotions of childhood. In her many works, such as *City Night, Aren't You Coming Too?,* and the highly praised 1990 picture book *At Grammy's House,* the world of childhood is warmly and lovingly evoked through both text and drawings.

"If my fourth grade teacher is out there somewhere listening, I am sure that she is quite surprised to find that this particular ex-pupil is a writer," Rice once admitted to *SATA,* "since in those early days I was none too fond of the written word—a source of some distress to my well-read parents. Getting me to read a book was about as easy as pulling teeth." Instead, the future writer/illustrator's idea of fun was to "put on a pair of sturdy rubber boots and wade downstream in search of salamanders, bullfrogs, and turtles." Overcast or rainy days would find her indoors, curled up and busily drawing with "a cache of crayons and paints and a seemingly inexhaustible supply of paper." Although she never suspected that she would one day be a writer, Rice always knew that art would be in her future.

An inventive mother solves the problem of pocket-less Peter, who needs a place to carry the treasures he finds outside. (From *Peter's Pockets,* written by Rice and illustrated by Nancy Winslow Parker.)

Rice was busy drawing by the time she reached the age of three, aided by her mother, a former art teacher, who kept her daughter well supplied with paper and pencils. "The earliest pictures were of New York City, where I was born, but we moved out to the 'country' at about the time that I picked up my first paintbrush." While attending middle school in Armonk, New York, Rice decided upon her career: "I wanted to illustrate children's books. And with that goal in mind, I trooped off to Yale University where I soon found myself involved with all the nuances of a major in English history, and even flirted, briefly, with the idea of becoming a professional historian before returning to the fold."

In college Rice "discovered the great joys of reading" and began to consider combining her artistic talents with creative writing. "In spite of my earlier reluctance to pick up a book, I have always adored words and language and storytelling," she explained, commenting that the love of spoken language is a "good preparation for a writer since [writing] is ultimately a discipline of the ear as much as the intellect." Indeed, writing came easily to her; "now, to ask me to choose between the two, would be to ask the impossible."

Rice has written books for children of all ages, from toddler to teenager. "But I find myself drawn again and again to the creation of picture books for the very youngest child," she said. "There is something wonderful and special about that period when everything is new, when language has just been learned and walking means a first independence. And the striking moments and great stories for that age are to be found everywhere in the wonders of daily life which has yet to become banal or routine: a walk to the end of the block, buying a new pair of shoes, a simple 'good-night' from a neighbor, baking a birthday cake. Even in such quiet moments as these, the attentive writer can find real tales of comedy and tragedy—and with luck, be able to translate them into words and pictures that will touch a three-year-old." Her first book, *Oh, Lewis!,* was published in 1974, followed the next year by *New Blue Shoes.* "Rebecca, the heroine of *New Blue Shoes,* was originally an extension of Ellie, the little sister in *Oh, Lewis!,* although she quickly developed a personality of her own. The story has a lot to do with my own childhood. I was very particular about the kind of shoes, or anything else, that I would wear and, not surprisingly, my mother's patience often wore thin on those shopping expeditions."

Mr. Brimble's Hobby and Other Stories is a collection of tales about members of the fun-loving Brimble family. "A number of stories influenced the contents of the individual chapters," noted Rice. "[When] I first visited the collection of musical instruments at the Metropolitan Museum of Art in New York ... I was tremendously impressed by the shapes, colors, and variety of the instruments, as well as by the craftsmanship employed in their creation and their beauty as objects of art. 'Mr. Brimble's Hobby,' the story of an ardent collector of musical instruments, grew from that experience."

Rice got the idea for her 1976 book *What Sadie Sang* while on a visit to Cambridge, Massachusetts. "It was a warm, sunny day in October," she recalled. "A woman came down the street pushing a small child in a stroller and the little girl started making a strange, screechy noise. I was sure the child would start crying any minute—but she didn't cry and only continued making the sound. I realized then that the child was smiling and that the noise was probably her way of saying how nice a day she thought it was.

"The incident stuck in my mind and I sensed that it was the beginning of a story. While playing with the idea, I remembered a number of walks a year earlier when I had helped a friend push a Sadie-like child in a stroller around Brooklyn Heights. And then, too, I thought I could recall how nice it was to be pushed around the neighborhood with Mama doing the legwork. When I began writing, the phrases took on a sort of rhythm with sounds that seemed to complement each other and make the words nice to say." Featuring a simple story line, *What Sadie Sang* comes to life through its illustrations. "I began to fill in Sadie's world based on my earliest city memories and details from my many Greenwich Village walks—ornamented doorways, fancy iron railings, windowsills with orange cats, friendly people sitting on the stoops, and other urban bits and pieces."

Rice has always loved to draw animals. "I often drew the members of our resident household menagerie," she recalled of her childhood; "any one of the three dogs, a cat, snakes, polliwogs, frogs, turtles, beetles, etc. But I also enjoyed drawing the exotic animals I found only in books or at the zoo. Domestic or wild, they all seemed to come in fascinating shapes and sizes, to make curious noises, and to have very particular and interesting ways of moving."

The Central Park Zoo was a frequent haunt for Rice while she lived in New York City. "It seemed to be such a magical place—with so much color and noise and movement.... It is quite a marvelous thing to be able to stand in front of a rhinoceros and stare him straight in the eye. I loved the patterns made by the spots that ran down the giraffe's long neck, the equally impressive stripes of the zebra, the sinister glint in the crocodile's eye, the knowing look of the orangutan, and the frightening roar of the lion."

Not surprisingly, Rice's experience at the zoo later inspired some of her works. *Sam Who Never Forgets* features a zookeeper as its main character, and the zoo that he takes care of is certainly not an ordinary zoo. "Sam runs an ideal zoo where all the animals are happy and well cared for by their indefatigable friend and

Benny's dog eats the child's birthday cake but Dad saves the day in Eve Rice's self-illustrated *Benny Bakes a Cake.*

EVE RICE
City Night
pictures by PETER SIS

Rice's pulsating verse presents the sights and sounds of the city at night to her picture-book audience.

keeper," said Rice. A trip to the zoo also figures prominently in 1988's *Aren't You Coming Too?*, as young Amy watches her neighbors pass by her window on their way to work, to school, or to play; "Are you coming too?" is the question she imagines each passerby asking as they see her alone in her house with nowhere to go. Finally, who should appear but Grandpa, who takes her on a trip to the zoo. A *Booklist* reviewer praised Rice for her "sure touch with early childhood sensibilities," especially her sensitivity to a young child's fear of being left out or left behind.

A strong trust in family ties and other childhood emotions are captured and reflected in such books as *Peter's Pockets* and *Benny Bakes a Cake.* In the first book, published in 1989, Peter is proud of his new trousers until a trip with his Uncle Nick becomes problematic: all the treasures that he finds must be stored in his uncle's pockets because Peter's pants have none. Fortunately, his mother is attuned to the needs of young boys and girls and makes Peter's fine new pants even better, sewing on, as she tells her son, "a pocket for

each good thing you've found." "As Eve Rice has proven in other highly successful books for young children . . . ," wrote *Horn Book* contributor Ellen Fader in her review of *Peter's Pockets,* "she has that unique and rare talent that enables her to create small dramas that are acutely sensitive to what is most important to a young child." In *Benny Bakes a Cake,* Benny's chance to help bake and ice his own fourth birthday cake turns into a disaster when the finished cake, left uncovered on the kitchen counter, proves too much of a temptation for the hungry family dog. Benny is devastated by the disappearance of his birthday cake, until his mother and father find a way to solve the problem and a happy birthday celebration is had by all. *At Grammy's House* is the classic portrayal of the time-honored visit to Grandma's country home for a weekend, complete with pieces of homemade chocolate cake and a turn at the butter churn, while the scents of the farm mix with fresh, clean air and the inviting aroma of Sunday dinner cooking in an old cast-iron stove.

Two children enjoy their weekly dinner at Grandmother's farm, where there is always plenty to discover and do. (From *At Grammy's House*, written by Rice and illustrated by Nancy Winslow Parker.)

Goodnight, Goodnight, published in 1980, was inspired by Rice's view of the city from her studio window. "My studio had a big window that overlooked a wonderful jumble of rooftops, watertowers, clock towers, penthouse gardens, etc.," she told *SATA*. Every evening she would watch hundreds of neighborhood lights go on; late at night, while she sat at work at her drawing table, she would watch as most eventually went out. "It occurred to me that each time a light was switched off, someone was saying 'Goodnight.' And in some peculiar fashion, that thought translated itself into a very simple, rhythmic manuscript about a town going to sleep, and as it does, the familiar 'Goodnight' is called by its numerous inhabitants. It is a funny sort of story because the main character is the town itself—and in counterpoint, one poor, small, lost (and ultimately found) kitten." In illustrating the story, Rice felt that it was important to stress the high contrast between light and shadow. "Through trial and error, I slowly developed a mixed-media technique that enabled me to get a lithographic quality," she explained. "I started each illustration with

a very detailed pencil drawing, which was then heavily crosshatched in India ink, and then shaded with a layer of lithographic crayon, and reshaded with a layer of black color pencil before being scraped with an X-Acto knife and finally touched up with white paint."

As well as being high in contrast, the illustrations for *Goodnight, Goodnight* gave Rice the chance to incorporate much of the architectural detail that she had observed during her years walking past many of New York City's older buildings. "It was an opportunity to create my own city—by rearranging cornices, doorways, columns, lintels, and keystones of the real New York in any way I pleased and inventing other decorative details to my heart's content."

Indeed, the city landscape is one that Rice has returned to again and again in her books, but perhaps nowhere more successfully than in 1987's *City Night*, which was illustrated by Peter Sis. Featuring a young girl and her family's after-dark exploration of a small neighborhood street fair, *City Night* is a poem that reflects the nighttime rhythms and energies of a benign carnival atmosphere. "City children will respond to this urban love poem," wrote Ilene Cooper of *Booklist,* "while other youngsters may find it a lively introduction to an arresting milieu." A reviewer for *Publishers Weekly* similarly noted that "urban life after dark shines and glows in [*City Night*]," and *School Library Journal* contributor Cathy Woodward praised Rice's work as "an exquisite book for an adult to share with a child, for story hours, or for children to discover on their own."

■ Works Cited

Review of *City Night, Publishers Weekly,* August 28, 1987, p. 76.
Clancy, Jeanne Marie, review of *At Grammy's House, School Library Journal,* May, 1990, p. 91.
Cooper, Ilene, review of *City Night, Booklist,* September 15, 1987, p. 152.
Fader, Ellen, review of *Peter's Pockets, Horn Book,* May-June, 1989, p. 363.
Rice, Eve, *Peter's Pockets,* Greenwillow, 1989.
Wilms, Denise M., review of *Aren't You Coming Too?, Booklist,* May 1, 1988, p. 1529.
Woodward, Cathy, review of *City Night, School Library Journal,* December, 1987, p. 82.

■ For More Information See

PERIODICALS

Booklist, September 15, 1979, p. 128; March 1, 1989, p. 1196.
Bulletin of the Center for Children's Books, September, 1975, p. 98; April, 1976, p. 132; September, 1976, p. 16; January, 1977; May, 1978, p. 148; March, 1980, p. 125; January, 1982, p. 93; June, 1989, p. 263.
Horn Book, February, 1977, p. 44; August, 1978, p. 397; October, 1979; October, 1981, p. 529; November/December, 1987, p. 730; July/August, 1988, p. 484; May/June, 1990, p. 328.
Junior Bookshelf, August, 1982, p. 135.
Publishers Weekly, February 12, 1988, p. 85.
Times Literary Supplement, July 18, 1980, p. 809.

*   *   *

RITTHALER, Shelly 1955-

■ Personal

Born September 26, 1955, in McCook, NE; daughter of Joe Cassinat (a music teacher and businessman) and Alice Kuhn (a teacher); stepfather: John T. Kuhn (a government worker); married Reuben R. Ritthaler (a rancher), October 19, 1976; children: Min Dee Lin. *Education:* Attended University of Wyoming, Black Hills State University, and Sheridan College; Eastern Wyoming College, A.A., 1988. *Hobbies and other interests:* Taking classes, reading, walking, bird watching, animals, collecting wildflowers, watching movies.

■ Addresses

Home—P.O. Box 160, Upton, WY 82730-0160.

■ Career

Works with her husband on their ranch. Has taught creative writing for Eastern Wyoming College; trustee of the University of Wyoming. *Member:* Society of Children's Book Writers and Illustrators, National Writers Club, Mystery Writers of America, Western Women in the Arts, Rocky Mountain Fiction Writers, Wyoming Writers (past president and board member), Bear Lodge Writers, Women Writing the West.

■ Awards, Honors

First place, Manuscripts International Award, for short story; Black Hills Pen Women award, for short story; Award for Meritorious Achievement, Weston County Historical Society, and Award for Excellence, Wyoming State Historical Society, 1989, both for *Weston County—The First 100 Years;* Spur Award for Short Nonfiction, Western Writers of America, 1991, for *The Ginger Jar;* Children's Choice selection, International Reading Association and Children's Book Council, 1995, for *Dinosaurs Alive.*

SHELLY RITTHALER

■ Writings

FOR CHILDREN

Dinosaurs for Lunch, Avon, 1993.
Dinosaurs Wild, Avon, 1994.
Dinosaurs Alive, illustrated by Gioia Fiammenghi, Avon, 1994.
Heart of Hills (young adult novel), Avon, 1996.
With Love, Amanda (young adult novel), Avon, 1997.

OTHER

Weston County—The First 100 Years, Curtis Media, 1989.
The Ginger Jar (essays), Raven Creek Press, 1990.
Through the Cooperation of People—Fifty Years of Service, Tri-County Electric and Raven Creek Press, 1995.

Author of a monthly column called "The Ginger Jar," for *The Black and the White* magazine, 1988-89; contributing writer to *Art of the West* magazine. Contributor to periodicals, including *Wyoming Hub of the Wheel, Borderland, Sheep Industry News, True West,* and *Guideposts Magazine.* Contributor of short stories to *My Weekly* (Scotland) and *Norsk Ukeblad* (Norway), and poems to anthologies, including *Pegasus, If You Would Love Wyoming,* and *Writings from the High Plains.*

■ Work in Progress

Historical fiction based on Wyoming historical events; research into the lives of memorable Wyoming women.

■ Sidelights

Shelly Ritthaler told *SATA:* "I come from a family of readers. My earliest memories are of my grandfather, who had so many books that he had them stacked along the walls of his bedroom like a wainscot. My mother gathered my siblings and me at her knee at night and read aloud to us when we were children. I grew up loving books, but never dreamed or even thought of becoming a writer myself.

"When I was older I married my husband, Reuben, a rancher from northeast Wyoming. We moved to the family ranch to begin our adult lives. Shortly after that, a neighbor needed someone to ride with her to an evening creative writing class in a town about fifty miles away. She asked me to go with her. I refused, telling her I was a reader, not a writer. She asked again and, knowing I loved Mexican food, promised to stop at Taco John's for soft-shell tacos after each class. I couldn't refuse her bribe. Although I was originally only there for the tacos, in the course of the class I found something special. I discovered the power of words and writing, and that I possessed an ability to tap into that power and could put words and thoughts together to make people laugh, cry, and think.

"From there to the present, my writing career has been an exploration of that ability. I have tried writing many different kinds of things, looking to find what genre, medium, and for which audience I like to write best. I am still searching for those answers and have serious doubts if I will ever find them. I'm not sure, at this point, that it really matters—just writing, and writing well, is what is most important. I have to say, however, my most enjoyable projects are the ones for children.

"Today, my life seems to be a constant balancing act between writing, family, our ranching business (which I am active in), and a personal commitment to community service. Reuben and I have a daughter, Min Dee. I love people and am lucky to enjoy a wide circle of friends and acquaintances. I enjoy taking classes, reading, walking, bird watching, animals, collecting wildflowers, and watching movies. I teach numerous writing workshops to audiences of all ages, consider myself to be an amateur historian, and serve the state of Wyoming as a trustee for the University of Wyoming."

*   *   *

ROBINSON, Lloyd
See SILVERBERG, Robert

*   *   *

ROBINSON, Nancy K(onheim) 1942-1994

■ Personal

Born August 12, 1942, in New York, NY; died of cancer, March 15, 1994, in New York, NY; daughter of Norris David (in advertising) and Natalie (Barnett) Konheim; married Peter Beverly Robinson, May 6, 1966 (divorced, 1987); children: Kenneth Beverly, Alice Natalie. *Education:* Vassar College, A.B., 1964.

■ Career

Free-lance writer and researcher.

■ Awards, Honors

U.S. Customs Award, 1978, for a historical article about New York's first coast guard cutter, the *Vigilant;* Four Leaf Clover Award, Scholastic Book Services, 1981, for her contribution to the reading pleasure of seven and eight year olds.

■ Writings

Jungle Laboratory: The Story of Ray Carpenter and the Howling Monkeys (nonfiction), illustrated by Bill Tinker, Hastings House, 1973.
Firefighters! (nonfiction), Scholastic, 1979.
Wendy and the Bullies, illustrated by Ingrid Fetz, Hastings House, 1980.
Just Plain Cat, Scholastic, 1981.
Mom, You're Fired, illustrated by Ed Arno, Scholastic, 1981.

NANCY K. ROBINSON

Veronica, the Show-Off, illustrated by Sheila Greenwald, Scholastic, 1982.

Oh Honestly, Angela!, illustrated by Richard Williams, Scholastic, 1985.

Veronica Knows Best, illustrated by Rosanne Kaloustian, Scholastic, 1987.

Angela, Private Citizen, Scholastic, 1989.

Veronica Meets Her Match, Scholastic, 1990.

Angela and the Broken Heart, Scholastic, 1991.

The Ghost of Whispering Rock, illustrated by Ellen Eagle, Holiday House, 1992.

Countess Veronica, Scholastic, 1994.

Wendy on the Warpath, Scholastic, 1994.

Also writer of "Men of Bronze," a documentary that was broadcast by Public Broadcasting System (PBS-TV), February, 1978.

"T*A*C*K" SERIES; WITH MARVIN MILLER; ILLUSTRATED BY ALAN TIEGREEN; PUBLISHED BY SCHOLASTIC

T*A*C*K to the Rescue, 1982.
T*A*C*K Secret Service, 1983.
T*A*C*K Into Danger, 1983.
T*A*C*K Against Time!, 1983.

"TRIPPER AND SAM" SERIES; PUBLISHED BY SCHOLASTIC

The Phantom Film Crew, 1986.
Danger on the Sound Track, 1986.
The Ghost Who Wanted to Be a Star, 1987.

■ Sidelights

Nancy K. Robinson wrote more than twenty books for children before her tragic death caused by cancer in 1994. While her first published books were works of nonfiction, her primary contributions to the genre of children's literature were through her fiction. She wrote stories about a family of characters, Nathaniel, Tina, and Angela Steele, which critics compared with Beverly Cleary's Ramona Quimby books. Robinson was also known for *Just Plain Cat* and the "Veronica" books, which allow readers to sympathize with an otherwise disagreeable character.

Chris, the protagonist of *Just Plain Cat,* begins third grade with a few problems. His photographer father doesn't make enough money to provide Chris with the things their neighbor, Veronica, has. Veronica attends a fancy private school, has a special cat, and two color television sets—and she doesn't hesitate to tell Chris all about them. When Chris finally gets a cat, Tiger, Veronica informs him that the cat is a plain one. In addition to his troubles with Veronica, Chris must deal with his feelings toward his best friend in school, Peter. As the story progresses, Chris realizes that Veronica has her own problems when she reveals that she is having a difficult time at her private school, and he also begins to better appreciate his own school. Tiger the cat almost spoils everything when he gets into Chris's father's precious negatives, but the story ends happily. "Appealing, often funny, with a feel for a third-grader's experiences," commented a *Kirkus Reviews* critic.

While Veronica may be, according to Denise M. Wilms of *Booklist,* "an incidental, obnoxious character" in *Just Plain Cat,* her character is probed more deeply in *Veronica, the Show-Off.* Readers learn why she is unhappy and why she behaves the way she does. Veronica's parents are divorced; she lives with her mother and rarely sees her father. Veronica is upset that the girls at her private school are slow to befriend her. She tries to impress them by bragging, and even tells lies. To make matters worse, she throws a fit in the library because her favorite books are not in, and writes nasty notes to the girl who has them checked them out. When she finally finds some friends, Veronica makes some sincere attempts to change her ways. According to Zena Sutherland of the *Bulletin of the Center for Children's Books,* Robinson's characterization of Veronica in *Veronica, the Show Off* "evokes sympathetic understanding" from readers. "Readers' hearts will go out to Veronica the show-off, and that's quite an achievement," explained a *Kirkus Reviews* critic.

Veronica Knows Best continues the title heroine's story. Still determined to improve her behavior, Veronica helps a friend prepare for a tryout for a play instead of

In Robinson's humorous 1985 tale of sixth-grader Tina and her exasperating little sister Angela, the whole family learns what is truly important. (From *Oh Honestly, Angela!*, illustrated by Richard Williams.)

pursuing a part for herself. Veronica's plans are ruined when her protege demonstrates little talent; her plans to visit with her father in California, despite some surprises, turn out better. "Veronica is a lively and likable heroine despite some unattractive personality traits," wrote Ilene Cooper of *Booklist*. Although suggesting weaknesses in plot and characterization in the story, Zena Sutherland of the *Bulletin of the Center for Children's Books* described *Veronica Knows Best* as "pleasantly light, often amusing, [and] nicely written."

Veronica gets a new neighbor in *Veronica Meets Her Match*. Although she befriends Crystal herself, Veronica resents how quickly Crystal becomes popular at school. "Readers will identify with Veronica's anxiety to be liked and will recognize her maturity when she accepts her new friend's success," observed Carolyn Noah in a review of Robinson's book in *School Library Journal*. A final addition to the "Veronica" books, *Countess Veronica*, finds Robinson's popular heroine attempting to play matchmaker to her divorced parents. Believing one of her mother's acquaintances to be royalty, Veronica invites him to their home for dinner; at the same time, she loses her friend the librarian when the woman moves to Santa Barbara—where, coincidentally, Veronica's unmarried father also resides. When Veronica subsequently learns that her father has remarried, she is

very upset and refuses to communicate with him; she finally reads one of his letters to find that his new wife is her old librarian! Noting that "readers who are hooked on Veronica will be anxious to see if she has reformed at all" in this latest story, *Booklist* contributor Susan DeRonne described *Countess Veronica* as "age-appropriate soap-opera reading."

Oh Honestly, Angela!, the sequel to *Mom, You're Fired*, develops the characters of the Steele children, thirteen-year-old Nathaniel, Tina, eleven years old, and Angela, who is just five years old. Angela, in the words of Ann A. Flowers of *Horn Book*, "is a real charmer, naive and tenderhearted." A gentle story about the everyday life of these children, *Oh Honestly, Angela!* describes humorous episodes that result when the young people misunderstand adult conversations and behavior. "An old-fashioned story, realistic, funny, and heart-warming," concluded Flowers in her review for *Horn Book*. Ilene Cooper of *Booklist* similarly found *Oh Honestly, Angela!* "warm, eminently likable family fare with a strong theme about generosity and giving."

The story in *Angela, Private Citizen* again shows how Angela, now six, manages to make trouble out of good

This final addition to Robinson's "Veronica" books finds the popular heroine getting embroiled in matchmaking for her divorced parents.

intentions. This time, Angela is concerned about the national debt, so she decides to send the government all her money. Unfortunately, she uses a blank 1040 tax form her parents must sumbit by the tax deadline the following day! Zena Sutherland, in a review in *Bulletin of the Center for Children's Books,* asserted that *Angela, Private Citizen* possesses "the same kind of warmth and humor" as Beverly Cleary's Ramona books.

Angela and the Broken Heart finds Angela in the second grade. When she learns that her brother has a crush on a girl who seems to have no intention of returning his affection, Angela tries to heal his broken heart. Her friend Mandy has an older sister who would be perfect for Nathaniel. When Mandy's sister turns out to be the girl Nathaniel has been in love with all along, the story ends happily. "A warm, funny story, sure to be popular with Angela's fans," concluded a *Kirkus Reviews* critic. *Booklist* contributor Leone McDermott, in her review of *Angela and the Broken Heart,* voiced a widely shared view of Robinson's contributions to children's literature when she asserted that the author "writes with humorous insight into children's feelings and the problems of growing up."

■ Works Cited

Review of *Angela and the Broken Heart, Kirkus Reviews,* April 1, 1991, p. 475.

Cooper, Ilene, review of *Oh Honestly, Angela!, Booklist,* November 1, 1985, p. 413.

Cooper, Ilene, review of *Veronica Knows Best, Booklist,* October 15, 1987, pp. 399-400.

DeRonne, Susan, review of *Countess Veronica, Booklist,* February 1, 1994, p. 1007.

Flowers, Ann A., review of *Oh Honestly, Angela!, Horn Book,* March-April, 1986, p. 203.

Review of *Just Plain Cat, Kirkus Reviews,* February 15, 1983, p. 185.

McDermott, Leone, review of *Angela and the Broken Heart, Booklist,* April 1, 1991, p. 1568.

Noah, Carolyn, review of *Veronica Meets Her Match, School Library Journal,* December, 1990, p. 106.

Sutherland, Zena, review of *Veronica, the Show-Off, Bulletin of the Center for Children's Books,* May, 1983, pp. 176-77.

Sutherland, Zena, review of *Veronica Knows Best, Bulletin of the Center for Children's Books,* February, 1988, p. 123.

Sutherland, Zena, review of *Angela, Private Citizen, Bulletin of the Center for Children's Books,* January, 1990, p. 120.

Review of *Veronica, the Show-Off, Kirkus Reviews,* February 15, 1983, p. 186.

Wilms, Denise M., review of *Veronica, the Show-Off, Booklist,* April 15, 1983, pp. 1097-98.

■ For More Information See

PERIODICALS

Kirkus Reviews, November 15, 1989, p. 1677.
Publishers Weekly, October 30, 1987, p. 72.

School Library Journal, January, 1990, p. 60; October, 1992, p. 121.

■ Obituaries

PERIODICALS

New York Times, March 20, 1994, p. 42.*

*   *   *

ROETS, Lois F. 1937-

■ Personal

Born March 4, 1937, in Breda, IA; daughter of Charles G. (a farmer and hybrid seed-corn developer) and Mary (Goecke) Schelle; married Philip G. Roets (a teacher, writer, and biblical scholar), June 7, 1969; children: Jacqueline, Ron. *Education:* Viterbo College, B.S., 1965; University of Wisconsin-Madison, M.S., 1975; International Institute for Advanced Studies, Ed.D., 1984. *Religion:* Christian. *Hobbies and other interests:* Collecting significant old bibles and commentaries, watching nature.

■ Addresses

Office—P.O. Box 8358, Des Moines, IA 50301.

LOIS F. ROETS

■ Career

Teacher of general education, then administrator and curriculum director of gifted and talented children and adults in schools in Iowa and Wisconsin, beginning 1960; Drake University, Des Moines, IA, adjunct instructor, beginning 1984; Leadership Publishers, Des Moines, IA, founder, 1982. Board member, Odyssey of the Mind, Iowa, 1986-90; member of Sheridan scholarship committee, 1985-88. *Member:* American Educators Research Association, National Association for Gifted Children, Iowa Talented and Gifted Educators Association.

■ Writings

INSTRUCTIONAL PROGRAMS

Leadership: A Skills Training Program, Leadership Publishers, 1981, seventh edition, 1992.
Readers' Theatre (three volumes), Leadership Publishers, 1992-95.
Incomplete Plays, Leadership Publishers, 1982, third edition, 1990, fourth edition, 1995.
Public Speaking: Grades 2-12, Leadership Publishers, 1982, third edition, 1989.
Survey and Public Opinion Research, Leadership Publishers, 1983, second edition, 1988.
Understanding Success and Failure, Leadership Publishers, 1983, second edition, 1988.
Writing Fiction: Grades Three and Above, Leadership Publishers, 1987.
Philosophy and Philosophers, Leadership Publishers, 1987, second edition, 1994.
Student Projects: Ideas and Plans, Leadership Publishers, 1994.

OTHER

How to Survive and Thrive as Educator of the Gifted and Talented in Large and Small School Districts, Leadership Publishers, 1987, second edition, 1990, third edition, 1996.
How to Write and Market Your Own Educational Materials, Leadership Publishers, 1988.
In-Service Manual for Gifted and Talented, Leadership Publishers, 1987, second edition, 1995.
Modifying Standard Curriculum for High-Ability Learners, Leadership Publishers, 1987, fourth edition, 1993, fifth edition, 1997.
Giving Your Child Roots and Wings: How to Survive and Thrive as Parents of Gifted and Talented High-Ability Children, Leadership Publishers, 1996.

Contributor of articles and book reviews to magazines, including *Challenge, Gifted Child Today, Library Journal, Mailbox, Oasis, Small School Administrator Newsletter,* and *School Administrator.*

■ Work in Progress

Plays for two people; articles for parents and general public on dealing with loss and revising school curriculum for contemporary needs.

■ Sidelights

"I write, teach, publish, and share what I know because I am driven from within to do so," author Lois Roets told *SATA.* "That determination is coupled with my life's purpose of leaving this earth a little better than how I found it. Several books were written specifically from this motivation: *Leadership: A Skills Training Program, Philosophy and Philosophers, How to Survive and Thrive as Educator of the Gifted and Talented,* and *Giving Your Child Roots and Wings: How to Survive and Thrive as Parents of Gifted and Talented High-Ability Children.*

"I was born and raised on a farm in western Iowa. I share my parents' sense of roots and my father's need to explore multiple avenues of interest. He developed seed corn by cross-pollination plants he considered good for whatever variable he was seeking. I could calculate percentages before I went to school because all of the testing and records were kept in samples of one hundred. I thought all kids could do that. With this type of childhood—isolated from other children and permitted to be with parents—it was natural that I would pursue multiple interests and enjoy these pursuits.

"Since 1980 I have worked with talented and gifted, high-ability children and adults. This population has drive, ambition, worries, intensities, habits, and needs that are unique—not in their presence but in their capacity and intensity. For that purpose I developed the leadership program, based on a 'Lead yourself; lead others' approach. Leadership permits people to be in charge of their own life and yet be in charge of others or projects—as time, energy, and ambition dictates. It was this same population for which I wrote and taught seminars on philosophy and philosophers. It is philosophy that helps us thread together our lives—past, present, and projected futures. It is philosophers who analyze current trends and help us find our way through life—a path we get to tread but once.

"I do as many seminars, workshops, and speeches as time and ability permit. In addition to the information given, I'm told I 'inspire' people to believe in themselves and to move forward. This is deeply satisfying. Early in my educational career, the principal wrote on the bottom of the daily bulletin, 'Give a man a fish and he eats for a day. Teach a man to fish and he eats for a lifetime.' I don't know the author of that phrase, nor did the principal who quoted it. When I 'inform' as well as 'inspire' I am teaching someone to 'fish.'

"My next project? I don't know—but I'll recognize it when I see it."

*   *   *

ROSS, Kent 1956-

■ Personal

Born in 1956; son of Chapin and Alice Ross; married Linda Panter. *Education:* Abilene Christian University

KENT ROSS

(M.Div.); graduate study at University of Texas at Arlington. *Religion:* Christian.

■ Addresses

Home—225 North 27th, Arkadelphia, AR 71923.

■ Career

Minister at University Church of Christ, Arkadelphia, AR. Also a storyteller and writing workshop leader for schools and libraries.

■ Writings

(With parents, Alice and Chapin Ross), *Whistle Punk* (middle-level historical fiction), Texas Christian University Press, 1994.

(With mother, Alice Ross), *Cemetery Quilt* (picture book), illustrated by Rosanne Kaloustian, Houghton Mifflin, 1995.

(With Alice Ross), *The Copper Lady* (early reader), illustrated by Leslie Bowman, Carolrhoda Books, 1996.

■ Work in Progress

Jezebel's Spooky Spot, a picture book for Dutton about a young black girl living during the Civil War. Also working on an adult "Christian" fantasy novel, plus several picture book manuscripts.

■ Sidelights

Kent Ross's first book, *Whistle Punk,* which he wrote with his parents, Alice and Chapin Ross, is set in East Texas during World War II. Because of the war, Mac Johnson's father is having difficulties with his failing lumber business. To help with the labor, he makes an arrangement with the government to allow German prisoners of war to work for him. Mac, however, is upset by his father's decision because his brother, Donald, was killed fighting the Germans. Many of the townspeople are also against the idea, which causes tensions to rise in the town. Mac decides to form a plot with his friend, Arlen, to get revenge against the Germans. "How Mac's plans develop, what he learns about the German POWs and ... himself provide fast paced reading," according to *Voice of Youth Advocates* contributor Kathleen D. Hutchins. Hutchins also praised the authors for their well-balanced characterizations and historically accurate setting, concluding that the novel is a "fascinating" coming-of-age tale.

In another collaboration, this time with his mother only, Kent wrote the picture book *Cemetery Quilt,* "a bleakly atmospheric story about a rebellious girl reluctant to go to her grandfather's funeral with her mother," as one *Kirkus Reviews* critic described it. When ten-year-old Josie finds the quilt upon which coffins are sewn with the names of family members who have died, she is at first shocked and disturbed by it, but her grandmother explains that the quilt is simply a way of dealing with grief. How this helps Josie deal with Papaw's death is the message of the book, but some critics have found the transition from grief to acceptance abrupt. As Vanessa Elder wrote in a *School Library Journal* review, for example, "Josie's initial thoughts about the funeral and the quilt are so believably negative that it's jarring when she comes around."

The next book Ross wrote with his mother is *The Copper Lady,* part of the "On My Own" historical fiction series published by Carolrhoda Books. Written for children in kindergarten through the third grade, the series features innovative, brave characters living in real historical settings. In *The Copper Lady* a young boy from France intervenes to save "his lady," the Statue of Liberty.

■ Works Cited

Review of *Cemetery Quilt, Kirkus Reviews,* August 15, 1995.

Elder, Vanessa, review of *Cemetery Quilt, School Library Journal,* September, 1995, pp. 185-86.

Hutchins, Kathleen D., review of *Whistle Punk, Voice of Youth Advocates,* August, 1994.

■ For More Information See

PERIODICALS

Booklist, September 15, 1995, p. 176.
Children's Book Review Service, September, 1995, p. 3.
Hungry Mind Review, 1995-96, pp. 54-55.

* * *

RUCKER, Mike 1940-

■ Personal

Born August 9, 1940, in Pinehurst, NC; son of Henry C., Jr. (a teacher and wildlife conservationist) and Phoebe Katherine (a homemaker; maiden name, Price) Rucker; married Harriet Allen Jones (a homemaker), September 20, 1969; children: Derek Peck. *Education:* Virginia Polytechnic Institute, B.S., 1963. *Hobbies and other interests:* Running, automotive history.

■ Addresses

Home—1003 West Centennial Dr., Peoria, IL 61614-2828. *Office*—Caterpillar Inc., 100 North East Adams St., Peoria, IL 61629-9420.

■ Career

Caterpillar Inc., Peoria, IL, service representative and supervisor, 1963—. George H. Rucker Realty Corp., member of board of directors, 1980—; Peoria Area Arts and Sciences Council, 1984—; Lakeview Museum of Arts and Sciences, member of board of directors, 1987—; Peoria City Housing Commission, 1988-96; Southern Financial Bank, member of board of directors, 1991—. *Member:* Society of Automotive Engineers, Illinois Valley Striders Running Club, Rails to Trails,

MIKE RUCKER

The Nature Conservatory, Appalachian Trail Conference, Friends of Bradley University Cullom-Davis Library, 1994—(president, 1996—).

■ Writings

Terry the Tractor, illustrated by Bob Burchett, Aegina Press (Huntington, WV), 1993.
Terry and the Bully, illustrated by Burchett, Aegina Press, 1994.
Terry the Athlete, illustrated by Burchett, Aegina Press, 1995.
Terry and the Super Powerful Fuel, illustrated by Burchett, Aegina Press, 1996.

■ Work in Progress

Terry and the Elephant.

■ Sidelights

Mike Rucker told *SATA:* "I have always liked mechanical things. My career with Caterpillar Inc., my employer since 1963, bears this out. During much of this time, I have been a service representative concerned with the care and operation of earthmoving machines at many locations around the world.

"While residing with my family in Australia during the mid-1970s, I began to make up tales for my young son, Derek, about a small, diligent tractor named Terry. After searching for a publisher for a number of years, I had my first in the *Terry* series released under the University Editions mark of Aegina Press, Huntington, West Virginia.

"That first book, *Terry the Tractor,* explains how a tractor is built on an assembly line and the importance of proper use and care. The second, *Terry and the Bully,* involves working as a team and establishing a work plan. The third, *Terry the Athlete,* emphasizes sportsmanship and always trying one's best. It is built upon my experiences as a competitive runner. The next is *Terry and the Super Powerful Fuel.* It deals with the problem of drug abuse. I have several more planned for the series, including *Terry and the Elephant.*

"While it is clear from the subject matter that I like 'mechanical things,' it is also obvious that I understand the feelings of children. Until I began this series, I never realized how much emotion could be engendered by the storybook experiences of one small sincere, young tractor."

* * *

RYDELL, Katy 1942-

■ Personal

Born March 24, 1942, in Port Washington, NY; daughter of Clarence Oliver (an accountant) and Jessie Guerry (an artist) Tuck; married C. Peter Rydell (a researcher),

KATY RYDELL

October 27, 1962. *Education:* Temple University, B.A. (German), 1964; University of California, Los Angeles, M.A. (folklore and mythology), 1988. *Hobbies and other interests:* "I love hiking, skiing, summers in Maine, vegetable soup, apple cake, my friends, my family, my husband Peter."

■ Addresses

Home—12600 Woodbine St., Los Angeles, CA 90066.

■ Career

Self-employed professional storyteller, 1985—; editor and publisher of *Stories: A Western Storytelling Newsletter,* Los Angeles, CA, 1987—. *Member:* Society of Children's Book Writers and Illustrators, National Storytelling Association.

■ Writings

Wind Says Good Night, illustrated by David Jorgensen, Houghton Mifflin, 1994.

■ Sidelights

Katy Rydell told *SATA:* "I love telling stories, and I read barrels of books, looking for ones I might want to tell out loud. Whenever I write a story, I am always thinking about how to tell it, too."

Rydell's *Wind Says Good Night* is a bedtime story in which a little girl cannot sleep because Mockingbird is singing, but Mockingbird sings because the cricket is playing, and the cricket is playing because the frog is strumming, and the frog strums while the moth dances, and on it goes until the wind carries a cloud over the moon, bringing an end to the moth's dancing and setting off another chain reaction that brings rest to all. "Rydell captures the peaceful rhythms of nighttime in this witty, cumulative bedtime tale," noted *Booklist* reviewer Stephanie Zvirin, who added that *Wind Says Good Night* presents "a comical cast of stubborn characters, none of whom wants to be the first to fall asleep." Roger Sutton of the *Bulletin of the Center for Children's Books* praised Rydell's effort in this work, maintaining that "the writing is expertly cadenced, and by the last page you'll find yourself whispering."

■ Works Cited

Sutton, Roger, review of *Wind Says Good Night, Bulletin of the Center for Children's Books,* May, 1994, p. 301.
Zvirin, Stephanie, review of *Wind Says Good Night, Booklist,* April 1, 1994, p. 1463.

■ For More Information See

PERIODICALS

Kirkus Reviews, March 1, 1994, p. 309.

*   *   *

RYDEN, Hope

■ Personal

Born in St. Paul, MN; daughter of Ernest E. (a minister) and Agnes (Johnson) Ryden. *Education:* Attended Augustana College, Rock Island, IL; University of Iowa, B.A.

■ Addresses

Home—345 East 81st St., #7A, New York, NY 10028. *Agent*—N. S. Bienstock, 850 7th Ave., New York, NY 10019.

■ Career

Freelance documentary film producer, photographer, and writer. Drew Associates (affiliate of Time-Life Broadcast), New York City, film producer, 1960-64; Hope Ryden Productions, New York City, film producer, writer, and director, 1965; American Broadcasting Corp., New York City, feature producer for ABC-TV evening news, 1966-68. Member of board of directors, Defenders of Wildlife, 1977—, Society for Protective Animal Legislation, 1983—, and American Society for Protection of Animals, 1984—.

■ Awards, Honors

"Oppie" Award for best book in Americana category, 1970, and *Library Journal* citation as one of the 100 best sci-tech titles, 1970, for *America's Last Wild Horses;* Screen Writers Guild nomination for best film documentary, 1970, for *Missing in Randolph;* New York Public Library citations for *God's Dog* and *America's Last Wild Horses;* Cine Golden Eagle award for *The Wellsprings;* Emmy Award, Clarion Award, and Society of the Silurians Award, all for *Angel Dust: Teenage Emergency;* Library of Congress Award, Notable Book award, Outstanding Science Book for Children award, Notable Book in Field of Social Studies award, and Children's Choice award, all 1978, for *The Little Deer of the Florida Keys;* Humanitarian of the Year Award, American Horse Protection Association, 1979; Joseph Wood Krutch Award, Humane Society of the United States, 1981; Outstanding Achievement Award, Augustana College Alumni Association, 1981; Outstanding Science Book for Children award, 1983, for *Bobcat;*

HOPE RYDEN

Books Can Develop Empathy award, 1990, for *Wild Animals of Africa ABC.*

■ Writings

NONFICTION; AND PHOTOGRAPHER

America's Last Wild Horses, Dutton, 1970, revised edition, Lyons & Burford, 1990.
The Wild Colt: The Life of a Young Mustang, Coward, 1972.
Mustangs: A Return to the Wild, Viking, 1972.
God's Dog: The North American Coyote, Coward, 1975.
The Wild Pups: The True Story of a Coyote Family, Putnam, 1975.
The Little Deer of the Florida Keys, Putnam, 1978, revised edition, Florida Classics Library, 1986.
Bobcat Year, Viking, 1981.
Bobcat, Putnam, 1983.
America's Bald Eagle, Putnam, 1985.
The Beaver, Putnam, 1986.
Wild Animals of America ABC, Lodestar, 1988.
Wild Animals of Africa ABC, Lodestar, 1989.
Lily Pond: Four Years with a Family of Beavers, Morrow, 1989.
The Raggedy Red Squirrel, Lodestar, 1992.
Your Cat's Wild Cousins, Lodestar, 1992.
Joey: The Story of a Baby Kangaroo, Tambourine, 1994.
Your Dog's Wild Cousins, Lodestar, 1994.
Out of the Wild: The Story of Domesticated Animals, Dutton, 1995.
ABC of Crawlers and Flyers, Clarion, 1996.

DOCUMENTARY FILMS; AND PRODUCER AND DIRECTOR

Susan Starr, produced by Drew Associates/Time-Life Films, 1962.
Jane, produced by Drew Associates/Time-Life Films, 1963.
Mission to Malaya, produced by Drew Associates/ABC-TV Network News, 1964.
Operation Gwamba, produced by Hope Ryden Productions and CBS-TV, 1965.
To Love a Child, broadcast by ABC-TV News, 1969.
Missing in Randolph, broadcast by ABC-TV news, 1970.
Strangers in Their Own Land: The Chicanos, broadcast by ABC-TV News, 1971.
The Wellsprings, broadcast by PBS-TV, 1976.
Beginning Again at Fifty, broadcast by CBS-TV, 1977.
The Forties: A Crossroad, broadcast by CBS-TV, 1977.
Angel Dust: Teenage Emergency, broadcast by CBS-TV, 1978.

OTHER

Backyard Rescue (fiction), illustrated by Ted Rand, Morrow, 1994.

Contributor of articles to periodicals, including *Look, Children's Day, National Geographic, Reader's Digest, National Parks,* and *Conservation Magazine;* contributor of photographs to *National Geographic, Time, New York Times, Reader's Digest, Children's Day,* and other periodicals.

HOPE RYDEN
Backyard Rescue
pictures by TED RAND

When Greta has to move away, she fears losing her best friend Lindsay and their backyard wildlife hospital.

■ Sidelights

Hope Ryden is a photographer, filmmaker, and author best known for her nature books for children and young adults. She is especially noted for her works about North American animals like the coyote, beaver, bobcat, bald eagle, and Florida deer, which are illustrated with her own black-and-white photographs. For some of her books, including *Lily Pond: Four Years with a Family of Beavers* and *God's Dog: The North American Coyote,* Ryden spent years out in the field studying her subjects firsthand.

"I feel very little attention has been paid to North American wildlife," Ryden once commented. "Most people are more concerned with animals on other continents whose fate is beyond our control. Our own animals are exploited by commercial interests or removed if they have little or no commercial value and stand in the way of fuller exploitation of some other facet of nature. Though many people are enlightened regarding the balance of nature, the concept is not practiced in wildlife management. I wish to make this understood."

In a critically acclaimed 1978 story, *The Little Deer of the Florida Keys,* Ryden describes the plight of an endangered species. The rare miniature Key deer, once thought to be extinct, has been making a comeback since the establishment of the National Key Deer Refuge in 1957. Illustrated with both color and black-and-white photographs, the work explores the creatures' environment and behavior. Reviewing *The Little Deer of the Florida Keys,* Sarah Gagne of *Horn Book* stated that Ryden "skillfully creates tension by alternating an account of the deer's natural living habits with the story of its near extinction."

Another award-winning work, *Bobcat,* examines the lives of its solitary title creatures. Ryden includes information about the bobcat's mating habits, care of young, and hunting skills, and discusses natural selection and the evolution of a species. Though Zena Sutherland of the *Bulletin of the Center for Children's Books* felt that the text was "authoritative but diffuse in organization," a *Kirkus Reviews* critic deemed the work an "unusually interesting, intelligent, and smoothly knit introduction" to the life of the bobcat, adding that Ryden's photos "are truly illustrative and visually varied."

To research her 1989 book, *Lily Pond: Four Years with a Family of Beavers,* Ryden spent almost every night for four years observing a group of beavers living in a pond in New York state. During that time, the beaver family grew from four to six members and maintained a 150-foot-long, five-foot-high dam. The author became involved with the animals, bringing them food during a severe winter, helping them reconstruct the dam after vandals damaged it, and hand-feeding the elderly "Lily" before her death. "This is captivating natural history," remarked a *Publishers Weekly* reviewer, and *Booklist* contributor Mary Ellen Sullivan praised the author's "lively and perceptive prose" and "infectious passion" for her subjects.

In a more recent work, *Out of the Wild: The Story of Domesticated Animals,* Ryden traces the domestication of fifteen different animals, including dogs, cats, elephants, and pigs. Arranged chronologically, beginning with the domestication of the dog some 15,000 years ago, *Out of the Wild* looks at the reasons why each animal proved useful to humans and discusses the methods scientists have used to unlock this information. Though some reviewers criticized Ryden for anthropomorphizing, especially in the introduction, most commentators felt she produced an informative, entertaining work. A *Kirkus Reviews* critic remarked that Ryden "speaks persuasively of the combined efforts of human and beast to bring each other out of the wild," and *Booklist* reviewer Mary Harris Veeder called *Out of the Wild* a "good treatment" of complicated issues.

■ Works Cited

Review of *Bobcat, Kirkus Reviews,* March 1, 1983, p. 248.

Gagne, Sarah, review of *The Little Deer of the Florida Keys, Horn Book,* October, 1978, pp. 541-43.

Review of *Lily Pond: Four Years with a Family of Beavers, Publishers Weekly,* August 18, 1989, p. 46.

Review of *Out of the Wild: The Story of Domesticated Animals, Kirkus Reviews,* May 1, 1995.

Sullivan, Mary Ellen, review of *Lily Pond: Four Years with a Family of Beavers, Booklist,* November 15, 1989, p. 628.

Sutherland, Zena, review of *Bobcat, Bulletin of the Center for Children's Books,* September, 1983, p. 16.

Veeder, Mary Harris, review of *Out of the Wild: The Story of Domesticated Animals, Booklist,* June 1, 1995, p. 1768.

■ For More Information See

PERIODICALS

Appraisal: Science Books for Children, winter, 1986, pp. 31-32; summer, 1992, pp. 48-49; winter, 1995, p. 60; winter-spring, 1996, p. 52.

Booklist, September 1, 1981, p. 11; July, 1985, p. 1560; December 1, 1986, p. 581; August, 1994, p. 2047.

Bulletin of the Center for Children's Books, September, 1972, p. 15; April, 1988, p. 166.

Horn Book, November-December, 1989, p. 793; September-October, 1992, p. 601; May-June, 1994, pp. 336-37.

Kirkus Reviews, July 1, 1978, p. 693; August 15, 1989, p. 1230.

New York Times Book Review, April 30, 1978, p. 47.

Publishers Weekly, September 11, 1981, p. 68.

School Library Journal, January, 1976, pp. 40, 60; October, 1989, p. 108; September, 1994, p. 234; January, 1995, p. 110; July, 1995, p. 90.

Voice of Youth Advocates, October, 1985, pp. 279-80.

S

SUZANNE M. SAMSON

SAMSON, Suzanne M. 1959-

■ Personal

Born in Levitown, PA; daughter of Richard and Iola Samson; married David Arnold, March, 1990. *Education:* University of North Carolina at Chapel Hill, B.A., B.S., 1981; San Francisco State teaching credential, 1988.

■ Addresses

Office—Glenshire Elementary, 10990 Dorchester, Truckee, CA 96161.

■ Career

Elementary school teacher in Redwood City and Truckee, CA; children's book writer.

■ Writings

Fairy Dusters and Blazing Stars: Exploring Wildflowers with Children, illustrated by Preston Neel, Roberts Rhinehart, 1994.
Sea Dragons and Rainbow Runners: Exploring Fish with Children, illustrated by Preston Neel, Roberts Rhinehart, 1995.
Tumblebugs and Hairy Bears: Exploring Insects with Children, illustrated by Preston Neel, Roberts Rhinehart, 1996.

■ Work in Progress

Roadrunners and Sandwich Terns: Exploring Birds with Children, illustrated by Preston Neel; *Sun and Shadow; Jelly Babies and Turkey-tails: Exploring Mushrooms with Children; Coachwhips and Waterdogs: Exploring Reptiles and Amphibians with Children.*

■ Sidelights

Suzanne M. Samson told *SATA:* "I am in the process of writing a nature series that will hopefully encourage children to appreciate their environment and motivate them to learn more about it. Children have a natural curiosity about the world around them; my books tap into that playful, creative part of learning. My goal is to make children and adults more observant so they will more fully enjoy the beauty which surrounds them.

"Another goal of mine is to share with children my love of reading. Books open up new worlds for people and stimulate the imagination. My friend and illustrator, Preston Neel, and I are having a wonderful time creating each book in the series."

*   *   *

SATTGAST, L. J.
See SATTGAST, Linda J.

SATTGAST, Linda J. 1953-
(L. J. Sattgast)

■ Personal

Born September 4, 1953, in Fort Worth, TX; daughter of Homer C. (a missionary) and Kathleen (a missionary) Parry; married Charlie Sattgast (a minister), March 5, 1982; children: Caleb, Allison. *Education:* Multnomah School of the Bible, bible certificate, 1974; Portland Community College, A.R.R.T. (X-ray technology), 1980. *Politics:* Republican. *Religion:* Christian-Protestant. *Hobbies and other interests:* Writing, reading, piano, camping, hiking.

■ Career

Portland Adventist Medical Center, Portland, OR, X-ray technologist, 1978-94; Questar Publishers, Sisters, OR, editor and writer, 1994-96.

■ Awards, Honors

C. S. Lewis Noteworthy Picture Books Series, 1990, for "Teach Me About ..." books; Final Nominee, Gold Medallion Book Award, Preschool Category, ECPA, 1995, for *When Stars Come Out: Bedtime Psalms for Little Ones.*

■ Writings

PICTURE BOOKS

My Very First Bible: New Testament Stories for Young Children (also see below), illustrated by Russ Flint, Harvest House Publishers, 1989.
God Made Me Most Wonderfully (poetry), illustrated by Julie Park, Chariot Books, 1992.
My Very First Bible: Old Testament Stories for Young Children (also see below), illustrated by Russ Flint, Harvest House Publishers, 1992.
When Stars Come Out: Bedtime Psalms for Little Ones (poetry), illustrated by Nancy Munger, Gold 'n' Honey, 1994.
My Little Promise Bible, illustrated by Nan Brooks, Gold 'n' Honey, 1994.
The First Step Bible Seek & Find Learning Book: A Building Block Book for Toddlers, illustrated by Joe Stites, Gold 'n' Honey, 1994.
Look What God Made! (poetry), illustrated by Janet McDonnell, Chariot Books, 1995.
The Nursery Bible Bedtime Book, illustrated by Tish Tenud, Gold 'n' Honey, 1995.
My Very First Bible (contains *My Very First Bible: New Testament Stories for Young Children* and *My Very First Bible: Old Testament Stories for Young Children*), illustrated by Russ Flint, Harvest House Publishers, 1995.
The Lost and Found Parables (board books, contains *Up & Over: The Story of the Lost Sheep, Counting: The Story of the Lost Coin,* and *Opposites: The Story of the Lost Son*), illustrated by Kathy Couri Bennett, Gold 'n' Honey, 1995.

LINDA J. SATTGAST

Good Morning, Jesus/Good Night, Jesus (poetry), illustrated by Janet Pietrobono, Chariot Books, 1996.
A Light on the Path: Proverbs for Growing Wise (poetry), illustrated by Nancy Munger, Gold 'n' Honey, 1996.
When the World Was New (poetry), illustrated by Steve Bjorkman, Gold 'n' Honey, 1996.
The Rhyme Bible (poetry), illustrated by Toni Goffe, Gold 'n' Honey, 1996.
My Little Book of Big Bible Promises, illustrated by Susan Reagan, Gold 'n' Honey, 1996.
Bible Heroes: Esther, illustrated by Nan Brooks, Questar, 1996.

PICTURE BOOKS; WITH CO-AUTHOR JAN ELKINS

Teach Me about Salvation (also see below), illustrated by Russ Flint, Multnomah Press, 1990.
Teach Me about Prayer (also see below), illustrated by Russ Flint, Multnomah Press, 1990.
Teach Me about the Bible (also see below), illustrated by Russ Flint, Multnomah Press, 1990.
Teach Me about the Holy Spirit (also see below), illustrated by Russ Flint, Multnomah Press, 1990.
Teach Me about God (includes *Teach Me about Salvation, Teach Me about Prayer, Teach Me about the Bible,* and *Teach Me about the Holy Spirit*), illustrated by Russ Flint, Gold 'n' Honey, 1993.
Teach Me about Jesus, illustrated by Russ Flint, Gold 'n' Honey, 1994.
The Rhyme Bible Book of Prayer, illustrated by Toni Goffe, Gold 'n' Honey, 1997.
The Rhyme Bible Activity Book, illustrated by Toni Goffe, Gold 'n' Honey, 1997.

■ Sidelights

Linda J. Sattgast told *SATA:* "I grew up in El Salvador, Central America, one of four children of missionary parents. At age six I went to an American boarding school and thus began many years of writing letters to my parents, a pen pal in the United States, and others. At the age of ten, I was given a diary that I faithfully kept every day until my senior year in high school. Since then I have kept a frequent journal.

"After high school and college in U.S. boarding schools, I traveled to Europe and the Middle East. More than one friend, after receiving a letter from me, told me that I should write a book, and I always knew that I would—someday.

"Two things pushed me into writing. After marriage and my first child, I could not find the quality of Bible storybook I wanted in the Christian bookstore, so I decided to write one. And secondly, I needed to either go back to work and leave my (by this time) two small children, or find another way to bring in some income. Oh, the innocence and expectations of beginning writers!

"Eight years later I am still writing and feel that I am just now coming 'of age' with my style and ability. Some of my books are specifically written to teach the basic tenets of the Christian faith in an understandable and enjoyable way, while others are simply 'just for fun.'

"My favorite book is my latest, *When the World Was New,* the story of the seven days of creation, illustrated by Steve Bjorkman. He did a magnificent job, better than I imagined it! I'm not always, however, that satisfied with the art. I have a secret dream of becoming an artist and illustrating my own book. And I'm going to do it—someday!"

*   *   *

SCHAEFER, Lola M. 1950-

■ Personal

Born July 23, 1950, in Fort Wayne, IN; daughter of Richard L. (in management) and Rosalyn M. (a home-maker; maiden name, Gale) Bennett; married Ted R. Schaefer (a woodworker), November 3, 1973; children: Adam R., Wyatt S. *Education:* Indiana University, B.S., 1972, M.S., 1984.

■ Addresses

Home and office—4924 CR 7, Garrett, IN 46738.

■ Career

St. Jude Elementary, Fort Wayne, IN, seventh grade teacher, 1973-76; J.E. Ober Elementary, Garrett, IN, kindergarten teacher, 1983-84; McKenney-Harrison, Auburn, IN, elementary teacher, 1984-88; McIntosh Elementary, Auburn, elementary teacher, 1988—. Educational consultant in reading, writing, and integrated language arts programs in Indiana elementary schools; speaker at Young Author Conferences in Indiana. *Member:* International Reading Association, Society of Children's Book Writers and Illustrators (regional advisor for Indiana), Pokagon Reading Council (president, 1986-87).

■ Awards, Honors

Maxine Huffman Excellence in Reading Education Award, Indiana University at Fort Wayne, 1991.

■ Writings

Out of the Night, illustrated by Robert Gilbert, Whispering Coyote Press (Danvers, MA), 1995.
Candlelight Service, illustrated by Michele Warner, Rigby, 1995.
Turtle Nest, illustrated by Neesa Becker, Richard C. Owen (Katonah, NY), 1996.

■ Sidelights

Lola M. Schaefer told *SATA:* "For years I have had the great pleasure of sharing the best of children's literature with students in my classroom. I have seen their joy of reading grow with each wonderful book. My love of

LOLA M. SCHAEFER

writing stems from a desire to contribute to the vast wealth of excellent literature.

"*Out of the Night* was first written as a model for students in an afternoon writing class. The children had such fun with it I decided to send the story out. After modest revision I mailed it. Whispering Coyote Press shared a vision for the story and chose Roby Gilbert as the illustrator. His use of fluorescent color has been a big attraction for the young reader. It has been fun to see this book come to life for children.

"I want to grow as a writer and be able to offer children stories that will tickle their funny bone, awaken a sense of wonder, or simply entertain. There are a lot of stories within all of us. I want to share many of mine with children through the power of written language."

*   *   *

SCHMIDT, Annie M. G. 1911-1995

OBITUARY NOTICE—See index for *SATA* sketch: Born May 20, 1911; died in 1995. Librarian and author. One of the most celebrated writers in Holland, Schmidt was the first from her country to win the Hans Christian Andersen Award, which she received in 1988 for her many contributions to children's literature. Schmidt contributed to a variety of genres, writing realistic and historical fiction, fantasy, musicals, and scripts for both radio and television. Many of these works, some of which are written for adults, are considered classics in the Netherlands. However, Schmidt is perhaps best known for her poetry, light verse which characteristically contrasts the imaginative world of childhood with the logical, conservative world of adults. Centering on both everyday life and fantastic subjects, many of her poems—which are noted for their lyricism, humor, liveliness, and happy endings—focus on the resistance of children to the regulations imposed on them by adults and the eventual triumph of youthful imagination and hope. Schmidt began her career as a librarian in 1932. In 1946, she joined the newspaper editorial staff of *Het Parool*, where she first published many of her stories and poems. Many of her children's works appear in English translation, including *Pink Lemonade: Poems for Children, Bob and Jilly are Friends, Dusty and Smudge Splash the Soup,* and *Grandpa's Glasses.*

OBITUARIES AND OTHER SOURCES:

PERIODICALS

Bookbird, fall-winter, 1995-1996, pp. 64-66.

*   *   *

SEBASTIAN, Lee
See SILVERBERG, Robert

SEGUIN, Marilyn W(eymouth) 1951-

■ Personal

Born July 14, 1951, in Hartland, ME; daughter of Lauriston and Erdene (Knight) Weymouth; married Roland Seguin (a chief financial officer), August 21, 1971; children: Scott, Kathryn. *Education:* University of Maine, B.S., 1973; University of Akron, M.A., 1977. *Politics:* Democrat. *Religion:* Protestant.

■ Addresses

Home—1830 Highbridge Rd., Cuyahoga Falls, OH 44223. *Office*—English Department, Kent State University, Kent, OH 44242.

■ Career

Department of English, Kent State University, Kent, Ohio, lecturer in writing program, 1989—. Freelance writer. *Member:* Society of Children's Book Writers and Illustrators, Women in Communications.

■ Writings

FOR CHILDREN

Song of Courage, Song of Freedom: The Story of Mary Campbell, Branden (Brookline Village, MA), 1993.

MARILYN W. SEGUIN

The Bell Keeper: The Story of Sophia and the Massacre of the Indians at Gnadenhutten, Ohio, in 1781 (historical fiction), Branden, 1995.

Silver Ribbon Skinny (historical fiction), Branden, 1996.

OTHER

The Perfect Portfolio, Career Press, 1990.

Teaching Middle Graders to Use Process Writing Skills: Strategies, Techniques, and Activities, Incentive, 1994.

■ Sidelights

"I began writing at the age of seven when I started to keep a diary," author Marilyn W. Seguin told *SATA*. "As an adult, I write on all kinds of topics and in many genres, including news and feature stories, book reviews, corporate annual reports, and fiction for young readers. Although my best writing is in the business and technical fields, my favorite writing is historical fiction. Quite often, readers will ask where I get the ideas for my historical stories. They are sometimes surprised when I tell them that I like to begin not with a plot, as they might expect, but with a character in crisis. Once I have found a character who piques my interest, then I begin the historical research that becomes the basis for the plot."

* * *

SHAW, Carolyn V. 1934-

■ Personal

Born August 23, 1934, in Fort Worth, TX; daughter of Floyd D. (an inventor) and Virginia (a music teacher; maiden name, Hardin) Roan; married G. David Shaw, May 27, 1954; children: Denise Kaiser, Diana, Howard, Suzanne Mathews, Mary Beth Oliver, Matthew. *Education:* Tomball College, B.A. (music); attended Texas Women's University. *Politics:* Independent. *Religion:* Christian.

■ Addresses

Home—7215 Root Rd., Spring, TX 77389.

■ Career

Writer. Teacher in elementary schools; private instructor in piano/organ. Director of youth choirs; has served as church organist.

■ Writings

The Adventures of Pudgie Duck, illustrated by Sherry Rampy, Dorrance (Pittsburgh, PA), 1995.

Also author of *On the Wing* (poetry), privately printed; author of narratives for choir and orchestra cantatas and of articles for church newsletter.

■ Work in Progress

A novel, *Portrait of Valor,* under the pseudonym Penelope; more adventures of Pudgie Duck.

* * *

SHRODE, Mary
See HOLLINGSWORTH, Mary

* * *

SILVERBERG, Robert 1935-
(Walker Chapman, Roy Cook, Walter Drummond, Dan Eliot, Don Elliott, Franklin Hamilton, Paul Hollander, Ivar Jorgenson, Calvin M. Knox, David Osborne, Lloyd Robinson, Lee Sebastian, Robert Randall)

■ Personal

Born January 15, 1935, in New York, NY; son of Michael (an accountant) and Helen (Baim) Silverberg; married Barbara H. Brown (an engineer), August 26, 1956 (separated, 1976; divorced, 1986); married Karen L. Haber, 1987. *Education:* Columbia University, B.A., 1956.

■ Addresses

Home—P.O. Box 13160, Station E, Oakland, CA 94661. *Agent*—Ralph Vicinanza, 111 Eighth Ave., No. 1501, New York, NY 10011.

■ Career

Writer, 1956—; president, Agberg Ltd., 1981—. *Member:* Science Fiction Writers of America (president, 1967-68), Hydra Club (chairman, 1958-61).

■ Awards, Honors

Hugo Award, World Science Fiction Convention, 1956, for best new author, 1969, for novella *Nightwings,* 1987, for novella *Gilgamesh in the Outback,* and 1990, for novelette *Enter a Soldier, Later: Enter Another; Lost Race of Mars* was chosen by the *New York Times* as one of the best hundred children's books of 1960; Spring Book Festival Award, *New York Herald Tribune,* 1962, for *Lost Cities and Vanished Civilizations,* and 1967, for *The Auk, the Dodo, and the Oryx: Vanished and Vanishing Creatures;* National Association of Independent Schools award, 1966, for *The Old Ones: Indians of the American Southwest;* Guest of Honor, World Science Fiction Convention, 1970; Nebula Award, Science Fiction Writers of America, 1970, for story "Passengers," 1972, for story "Good News from the Vatican," 1972, for novel *A Time of Changes,* 1975, for novella *Born with the Dead,* and 1986, for novella *Sailing to Byzantium;* John W. Campbell Memorial Award, 1973, for excellence in writing; Jupiter Award, 1973, for novella

ROBERT SILVERBERG

The Feast of St. Dionysus; Prix Apollo, 1976, for novel *Nightwings;* Milford Award, 1981, for editing; Locus Award, 1982, for fantasy novel *Lord Valentine's Castle;* Woodward Park Award, 1991, for *Letters from Atlantis.*

■ Writings

SCIENCE FICTION

Master of Life and Death (also see below), Ace Books, 1957.

The Thirteenth Immortal (bound with *This Fortress World* by J. E. Gunn), Ace Books, 1957.

Invaders from Earth (also see below; bound with *Across Time* by D. Grinnell), Ace Books, 1958, published separately, Avon, 1968, published as *We, the Marauders* (bound with *Giants in the Earth* by James Blish) under joint title *A Pair in Space,* Belmont, 1965.

Stepsons of Terra (bound with *A Man Called Destiny* by L. Wright), Ace Books, 1958, published separately, 1977.

The Planet Killers (bound with *We Claim These Stars!* by Poul Anderson), Ace Books, 1959.

Collision Course, Avalon, 1961.

Next Stop the Stars (story collection; bound with *The Seed of Earth* [novel] by Silverberg), Ace Books, 1962, each published separately, 1977.

Recalled to Life, Lancer Books, 1962.

The Silent Invaders (bound with *Battle on Venus* by William F. Temple), Ace Books, 1963, published separately, 1973.

Godling, Go Home! (story collection), Belmont, 1964.

Conquerors from the Darkness, Holt, 1965.

To Worlds Beyond: Stories of Science Fiction, Chilton, 1965.

Needle in a Timestack (story collection), Ballantine, 1966, revised edition, Ace Books, 1985.

Planet of Death, Holt, 1967.

Thorns, Ballantine, 1967.

Those Who Watch, New American Library, 1967.

The Time-Hoppers (also see below), Doubleday, 1967.

To Open the Sky (story collection), Ballantine, 1967.

Hawksbill Station, Doubleday, 1968 (published in England as *The Anvil of Time,* Sidgwick & Jackson, 1968).

The Masks of Time (also see below), Ballantine, 1968 (published in England as *Vornan-19,* Sidgwick & Jackson, 1970).

Dimension Thirteen (story collection), Ballantine, 1969.

The Man in the Maze (also see below), Avon, 1969.

Nightwings (also see below), Avon, 1969.

(Contributor) *Three for Tomorrow: Three Original Novellas of Science Fiction,* Meredith Press, 1969.

Three Survived, Holt, 1969.

To Live Again, Doubleday, 1969.

Up the Line, Ballantine, 1969, revised edition, 1978.

The Cube Root of Uncertainty (story collection), Macmillan, 1970.

Downward to the Earth (also see below), Doubleday, 1970.

Parsecs and Parables: Ten Science Fiction Stories, Doubleday, 1970.

A Robert Silverberg Omnibus (contains *Master of Life and Death, Invaders from Earth,* and *The Time-Hoppers*), Sidgwick & Jackson, 1970.

Tower of Glass, Scribner, 1970.

Moonferns and Starsongs (story collection), Ballantine, 1971.

Son of Man, Ballantine, 1971.

A Time of Changes, New American Library, 1971.

The World Inside, Doubleday, 1971.

The Book of Skulls, Scribner, 1972.

Dying Inside (also see below), Scribner, 1972.

The Reality Trip and Other Implausibilities (story collection), Ballantine, 1972.

The Second Trip, Doubleday, 1972.

(Contributor) *The Day the Sun Stood Still,* Thomas Nelson, 1972.

Earth's Other Shadow: Nine Science Fiction Stories, New American Library, 1973.

(Contributor) *An Exaltation of Stars: Transcendental Adventures in Science Fiction,* Simon & Schuster, 1973.

(Contributor) *No Mind of Man: Three Original Novellas of Science Fiction,* Hawthorn, 1973.

Unfamiliar Territory (story collection), Scribner, 1973.

Valley beyond Time (story collection), Dell, 1973.

Born with the Dead: Three Novellas about the Spirit of Man (also see below), Random House, 1974.

Sundance and Other Science Fiction Stories, Thomas Nelson, 1974.

The Feast of St. Dionysus: Five Science Fiction Stories, Scribner, 1975.

The Stochastic Man, Harper, 1975.

The Best of Robert Silverberg, Volume 1, Pocket Books, 1976, Volume 2, Gregg, 1978.

Capricorn Games (story collection), Random House, 1976.

Shadrach in the Furnace, Bobbs-Merrill, 1976.

The Shores of Tomorrow (story collection), Thomas Nelson, 1976.

The Songs of Summer and Other Stories, Gollancz, 1979.

Lord Valentine's Castle, Harper, 1980.

The Desert of Stolen Dreams, Underwood-Miller, 1981.

A Robert Silverberg Omnibus (contains *Downward to the Earth*, *The Man in the Maze*, and *Nightwings*), Harper, 1981.

Majipoor Chronicles, Arbor House, 1982.

World of a Thousand Colors (story collection), Arbor House, 1982.

Valentine Pontifex, Arbor House, 1983.

The Conglomeroid Cocktail Party (story collection), Arbor House, 1984.

Sailing to Byzantium, Underwood-Miller, 1985.

Tom O'Bedlam, Donald I. Fine, 1985.

Beyond the Safe Zone: Collected Short Fiction of Robert Silverberg, Donald I. Fine, 1986.

Star of Gypsies, Donald I. Fine, 1986.

(Editor) *Robert Silverberg's Worlds of Wonder*, Warner, 1987.

At Winter's End, Warner, 1988.

Born with the Dead (bound with *The Saliva Tree* by Brian W. Aldiss), Tor Books, 1988.

The Masks of Time, Born with the Dead, Dying Inside, Bantam, 1988.

To the Land of the Living, Gollancz, 1989.

(With Karen Haber) *The Mutant Season*, Foundation/Doubleday, 1989.

The New Springtime, Warner, 1990.

In Another Country: Vintage Season, Tor Books, 1990.

(With Isaac Asimov) *Nightfall*, Doubleday, 1990.

Time Gate II, Baen Books, 1990.

The Face of the Waters, Bantam, 1991.

The Queen of Springtime, Arrow Books, 1991.

(With Asimov) *Child of Time*, Gollancz, 1991.

The Collected Stories of Robert Silverberg, Bantam, 1992.

(With Asimov) *The Ugly Little Boy*, Doubleday, 1992.

(With Asimov) *The Positronic Man*, Doubleday, 1993.

Kingdoms of the Wall, Bantam, 1993.

Hot Sky at Midnight, Bantam, 1994.

The Mountains of Majipoor, Bantam, 1995.

Starborne, Bantam, 1996.

JUVENILE FICTION

Revolt on Alpha C, Crowell, 1955.

Starman's Quest, Gnome Press, 1959.

Lost Race of Mars, Winston, 1960.

Regan's Planet, Pyramid Books, 1964, revised edition published as *World's Fair, 1992*, Follett, 1970.

Time of the Great Freeze, Holt, 1964.

The Mask of Akhnaten, Macmillan, 1965.

The Gate of Worlds, Holt, 1967.

The Calibrated Alligator and Other Science Fiction Stories, Holt, 1969.

Across a Billion Years, Dial, 1969.

Sunrise on Mercury and Other Science Fiction Stories, Thomas Nelson, 1975.

(Editor with Charles G. Waugh and Martin H. Greenberg) *The Science Fictional Dinosaur*, Avon, 1982.

Project Pendulum, Walker & Co., 1987.

Letters from Atlantis, 1990.

NONFICTION

First American into Space, Monarch Books, 1961.

Lost Cities and Vanished Civilizations, Chilton, 1962.

Empires in the Dust: Ancient Civilizations Brought to Light, Chilton, 1963.

The Fabulous Rockefellers: A Compelling Personalized Account of One of America's First Families, Monarch Books, 1963.

Akhnaten: The Rebel Pharaoh, Chilton, 1964.

(Editor) *Great Adventures in Archaeology*, Dial, 1964.

Man before Adam: The Story of Man in Search of His Origins, Macrae Smith, 1964.

Scientists and Scoundrels: A Book of Hoaxes, Crowell, 1965.

The Great Wall of China, Chilton, 1965, published as *The Long Rampart: The Story of the Great Wall of China*, 1966.

Bridges, Macrae Smith, 1966.

Frontiers in Archaeology, Chilton, 1966.

The Auk, the Dodo, and the Oryx: Vanished and Vanishing Creatures, Crowell, 1967.

Light for the World: Edison and the Power Industry, Van Nostrand, 1967.

Men Against Time: Salvage Archaeology in the United States, Macmillan, 1967.

Mound Builders of Ancient America: The Archaeology of a Myth, New York Graphic Society, 1968.

The Challenge of Climate: Man and His Environment, Meredith Press, 1969.

The World of Space, Meredith Press, 1969.

If I Forget Thee, O Jerusalem: American Jews and the State of Israel, Morrow, 1970.

The Pueblo Revolt, Weybright & Talley, 1970.

Before the Sphinx: Early Egypt, Thomas Nelson, 1971.

Clocks for the Ages: How Scientists Date the Past, Macmillan, 1971.

To the Western Shore: Growth of the United States, 1776-1853, Doubleday, 1971.

The Longest Voyage: Circumnavigators in the Age of Discovery, Bobbs-Merrill, 1972.

The Realm of Prester John, Doubleday, 1972.

(Contributor) *Those Who Can*, New American Library, 1973.

Drug Themes in Science Fiction, National Institute on Drug Abuse, 1974.

(Contributor) *Hell's Cartographers: Some Personal Histories of Science Fiction Writers*, Harper, 1975.

(Editor with Byron Preiss) *The Ultimate Dinosaur: Past-Present-Future*, Bantam, 1992.

JUVENILE NONFICTION

Treasures beneath the Sea, Whitman Publishing, 1960.

Fifteen Battles That Changed the World, Putnam, 1963.

Home of the Red Man: Indian North America before Columbus, New York Graphic Society, 1963.

Sunken History: The Story of Underwater Archaeology, Chilton, 1963.

The Great Doctors, Putnam, 1964.

The Man Who Found Nineveh: The Story of Austen Henry Layard, Holt, 1964.

Men Who Mastered the Atom, Putnam, 1965.

Niels Bohr: The Man Who Mapped the Atom, Macrae Smith, 1965.

The Old Ones: Indians of the American Southwest, New York Graphic Society, 1965.

Socrates, Putnam, 1965.

The World of Coral, Duell, 1965.

Forgotten by Time: A Book of Living Fossils, Crowell, 1966.

To the Rock of Darius: The Story of Henry Rawlinson, Holt, 1966.

The Adventures of Nat Palmer: Antarctic Explorer and Clipper Ship Pioneer, McGraw, 1967.

The Dawn of Medicine, Putnam, 1967.

The World of the Rain Forest, Meredith Press, 1967.

Four Men Who Changed the Universe, Putnam, 1968.

Ghost Towns of the American West, Crowell, 1968.

Stormy Voyager: The Story of Charles Wilkes, Lippincott, 1968.

The World of the Ocean Depths, Meredith Press, 1968.

Bruce of the Blue Nile, Holt, 1969.

Vanishing Giants: The Story of the Sequoias, Simon & Schuster, 1969.

Wonders of Ancient Chinese Science, Hawthorn, 1969.

Mammoths, Mastodons, and Man, McGraw, 1970.

The Seven Wonders of the Ancient World, Crowell-Collier, 1970.

(With Arthur C. Clarke) *Into Space: A Young Person's Guide to Space*, Harper, revised edition (Silverberg not associated with earlier edition), 1971.

John Muir: Prophet Among the Glaciers, Putnam, 1972.

The World Within the Tide Pool, Weybright & Talley, 1972.

UNDER PSEUDONYM WALKER CHAPMAN

The Loneliest Continent: The Story of Antarctic Discovery, New York Graphic Society, 1964.

(Editor) *Antarctic Conquest: The Great Explorers in Their Own Words*, Bobbs-Merrill, 1966.

Kublai Khan: Lord of Xanadu, Bobbs-Merrill, 1966.

The Golden Dream: Seekers of El Dorado, Bobbs-Merrill, 1967, published as *The Search for El Dorado*, 1967.

Also author of one hundred other novels, 1959-73, under pseudonyms Dan Eliot or Don Elliott.

OTHER

(With Randall Garrett, under joint pseudonym Robert Randall) *The Shrouded Planet*, Gnome Press, 1957, published under names Robert Silverberg and Randall Garrett, Donning, 1980.

(Under pseudonym Calvin M. Knox) *Lest We Forget Thee, Earth*, Ace Books, 1958.

(Under pseudonym David Osborne) *Aliens from Space*, Avalon, 1958.

(Under pseudonym Ivar Jorgenson) *Starhaven*, Avalon, 1958.

(Under pseudonym David Osborne) *Invisible Barriers*, Avalon, 1958.

(With Garrett, under joint pseudonym Robert Randall) *The Dawning Light*, Gnome Press, 1959, published under names Robert Silverberg and Randall Garrett, Donning, 1981.

(Under pseudonym Calvin M. Knox) *The Plot against Earth*, Ace Books, 1959.

(Under pseudonym Walter Drummond) *Philosopher of Evil*, Regency Books, 1963.

(Under pseudonym Franklin Hamilton) *1066*, Dial, 1963.

(Under pseudonym Calvin M. Knox) *One of Our Asteroids Is Missing*, Ace Books, 1964.

(Under pseudonym Paul Hollander) *The Labors of Hercules*, Putnam, 1965.

(Under pseudonym Franklin Hamilton) *The Crusades*, Dial, 1965.

(Under pseudonym Lloyd Robinson) *The Hopefuls: Ten Presidential Candidates*, Doubleday, 1966.

(Under pseudonym Roy Cook) *Leaders of Labor*, Lippincott, 1966.

(Under pseudonym Lee Sebastian) *Rivers*, Holt, 1966.

(Under pseudonym Franklin Hamilton) *Challenge for a Throne: The War of the Roses*, Dial, 1967.

(Under pseudonym Lloyd Robinson) *The Stolen Election: Hayes versus Tilden*, Doubleday, 1968.

(Under pseudonym Paul Hollander) *Sam Houston*, Putnam, 1968.

(Under pseudonym Lee Sebastian) *The South Pole*, Holt, 1968.

Lord of Darkness (fiction), Arbor House, 1983.

Gilgamesh the King (fiction), Arbor House, 1984.

Contributor, sometimes under pseudonyms, to *Omni, Playboy, Amazing Stories Science Fiction, Fantastic Stories Science Fiction, Magazine of Science Fiction and Fantasy*, and other publications. Also editor of over 60 science fiction anthologies.

■ Sidelights

Winner of the prestigious Nebula and Hugo awards for his science fiction, Robert Silverberg is one of the most popular and prolific writers in the genre. His career falls into four chronological divisions which encompass several genres: early pulp science fiction of a more or less formulaic nature in the mid to late 1950s; nonfiction for both adult and juvenile readers during much of the 1960s; more experimental and quality science fiction from 1969 to 1976; and a blending of both science fiction and fantasy, including the Majipoor trilogy, that began in 1979 after his "retirement" and which continues to win new converts as well as keep the faithful pleased. "Most science-fiction authors and readers," according to George W. Tuma in *Dictionary of Literary Biography*, "consider Robert Silverberg to be one of the most important contemporary authors in the field. His contributions to science fiction, with respect to both influence and sheer literary output, are unparalleled."

Silverberg was born in 1935 in Brooklyn, New York, during the Great Depression. An only child, he was precocious and somewhat solitary. "I have no fond recollections of my childhood," Silverberg noted in his

Contemporary Authors Autobiography Series (*CAAS*) essay. "I was puny, sickly, plagued with allergies and freckles. I was too clever by at least half, which made for troubles with my playmates." His teacher mother and accountant father encouraged all intellectual endeavors by the young Silverberg, including his collection of coins and butterflies. At an early age he developed an intense interest in natural history, spending hours poring through the latest edition of *The National Geographic* and spending countless Sundays with his father at the American Museum of Natural History in New York. His love for the exotic first took the form of a fascination with dinosaurs; soon, however, he was visiting other times and worlds through the writings of Jules Verne and H. G. Wells. It was a short hop from these classics to the science-fiction magazines of the day and more contemporary writers such as Olaf Stapledon and H. P. Lovecraft.

Throughout high school, it was assumed Silverberg would pursue a career in the sciences, in botany or astronomy. He began writing for school newspapers and tried to sell pieces to the magazines he admired. Soon it became apparent to him that he wanted to pursue this course rather than a scientific career. "Writing science fiction would allow me to give free play to those fantasies of space and time and dinosaurs and supermen that were so gratifying to me," Silverberg recalled in *CAAS*. Entering Columbia University, Silverberg lived on his own and continued his writing. By 1953, at age 18, he had already sold some stories to science fiction magazines, and by January of 1954 his first novel was contracted. After several drafts, *Revolt on Alpha C* was published and his writing career was launched. Silverberg continued to attend Columbia, but at the same time began submitting more and more stories to a wide variety of magazines. His output, in fact, was so great that he had to write under a variety of pseudonyms. He had learned the ticket to success in science fiction writing: write to formula and know exactly what an editor's needs are.

"By the summer of 1956," Silverberg wrote, "—by which time I had graduated from college and had married—I was the compleat writing machine, turning out stories in all lengths at whatever quality the editor desired, from slam-bang adventure to cerebral pseudo-philosophy." He received a Hugo Award in 1956 as the most promising science fiction author of the previous year. His output in the late 1950s was phenomenal, logging over a million words per annum, most of them first draft as final draft. He made a handsome living; though, as Tuma noted, these early writings, "with a few exceptions, conform closely to the conventions of science fiction: alien beings, technological gadgetry, standard plot devices, confrontations between Terrans and extraterrestrial beings, and so forth."

This comfortable world of science fiction had collapsed by 1959, when many science fiction magazines went out of business due to distribution problems. Almost overnight, Silverberg's largest market simply vanished. He continued to write a limited amount of science fiction,

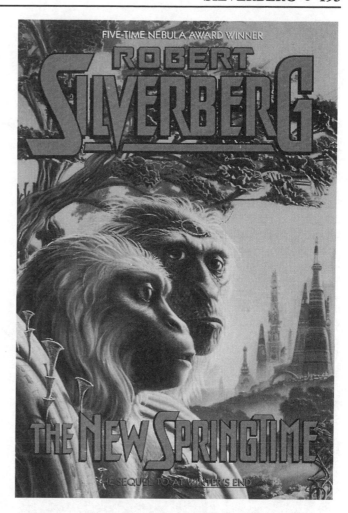

In this sequel to Silverberg's *At Winter's End*, Nialli, the young daughter of a chieftain, becomes the key figure in the struggle between her people and a group of highly evolved insectoids who believe that mastery of the earth is rightfully theirs. (Cover illustration by Michael Whelan.)

including a book for young readers, the award-winning *Lost Race of Mars*. Increasingly, however, Silverberg turned his hand to nonfiction, including many works for the juvenile market, such as *Lost Cities and Vanished Civilizations, Empires in the Dust: Ancient Civilizations Brought to Light, Man before Adam: The Story of Man in Search of His Origins,* and *The Old Ones: Indians of the American Southwest.* His nonfiction themes ranged from exploration to discovery in books about Antarctica, the American space program, archaeology and ancient Egypt, as well as biographies and medical and scientific histories. "I was considered one of the most skilled popularizers of the sciences in the United States," Silverberg noted in *CAAS*. One of his nonfiction books for adults, the 1968 *Mound Builders of Ancient America: The Archaeology of a Myth,* has become a standard reference book on the subject, remaining in print several decades after publication. Of his juvenile nonfiction book *Four Men Who Changed the Universe,* Harry C. Stubbs noted in *Horn Book* that Silverberg was able to blend the contrasting achievements of Copernicus, Galileo, Tycho Brahe, and Kepler, making the matter "clear and interesting, without losing sight of the main theme." Meanwhile, Silverberg was still able to write articles of all sorts and publish science fiction books and stories. He and his wife traveled widely and purchased the former New York mansion of Mayor Fiorello La Guardia. Silverberg's output increased to some two million words a year. Barry M. Malzberg, writing in the *Magazine of Fantasy and Science Fiction,* once commented that Silverberg "may be, in terms of accumulation of work per year, the most prolific writer who ever lived."

This all changed by the late 1960s, however, as Silverberg succumbed to an extended illness in 1966 brought on from overwork, a situation exacerbated by a fire in his home two years later. He was also beginning at this time to find his own voice in science fiction, with the dark and psychological *Thorns,* and with *Hawksbill Station,* both of which, according to Tuma, mark a break with his earlier formula writing. He began to explore more humanistic, psychological, and philosoph-

In this science fiction novel set in a post-apocalyptic world, a scientist, a spy, and a blind man with extrasensory vision struggle to ensure the future of humanity. (Cover illustration by Michael Whelan.)

ical themes in his science fiction, spurred on by a new generation of writers who were pushing the envelope of the genre. With *Thorns,* Silverberg explored the theme of alienation through his protagonist, the starman Minner Burris, whose body has been reconstructed by surgeons on a distant planet. Returning to earth, he becomes an outsider among his own because of his altered appearance. *Hawksbill Station* is another exploration on the theme of alienation, this time through political dissidents who have been banished into the past via a time machine. Such dissidents end up in the early Cambrian age, 500 million years ago.

Other notable novels of this time include *Nightwings,* which won a Hugo Award in 1969, and his 1979 novel *Downward to Earth,* "one of Silverberg's best novels," according to Tuma. This latter book was partly inspired by his travels in Africa and his own "growing sense of cosmic consciousness," as Silverberg reflected in *CAAS.* The book tells the story of Edmund Gundersen, a sector administrator for the planet Belzagor in the 24th century, who comes to realize that he has denied the main species of the planet, the Nildoror, any sense of dignity, and has behaved toward them as if they were subhuman because of their elephant-like appearance. With echoes of Conrad's *Heart of Darkness,* including a character named Kurtz, *Downward to Earth* is a powerful novel of transformation and redemption. Other well-known novels of the 1970s include *Tower of Glass, Son of Man, A Time of Changes,* and *The Book of Skulls,* several of which were award-winners and continued Silverberg's explorations of religious and philosophical themes.

However, just as the demand for the formula science fiction of the 1950s ended in 1959, so too did the exuberance of this experimental phase. "The s-f revolution of 1964-71 had been a fluke, an anomaly," Silverberg recalled in *CAAS.* "The bulk of the readers wanted the good old simple bang-bang adventure stuff." Silverberg, having moved to the San Francisco Bay Area, began to slow down even more. The frantic pace of million-word years was gone forever. In 1972 his output was 115,000 words, and he struggled for over a year with revisions on *The Stochastic Man,* after which he announced that he was retiring from writing. Investments had paid off and he was free to devote his time to gardening.

Silverberg's retirement lasted four years, during which he turned down book projects and advances. When his marriage dissolved, however, and his wife needed her own home, he returned to writing. The layoff had not hurt Silverberg's innate sense of market. He had noted the intervening shift in science fiction toward fantasy of the Tolkien variety, and with his comeback, he blended the two genres in *Lord Valentine's Castle,* a novel that was auctioned for the highest advance ever paid at that time for a science fiction novel—$127,500. The book, a story about a dispossessed as well as amnesiac ruler of the distant planet Majipoor, and his attempts to not only regain his throne but also his memory, was something of a throwback for Silverberg, in its heavy

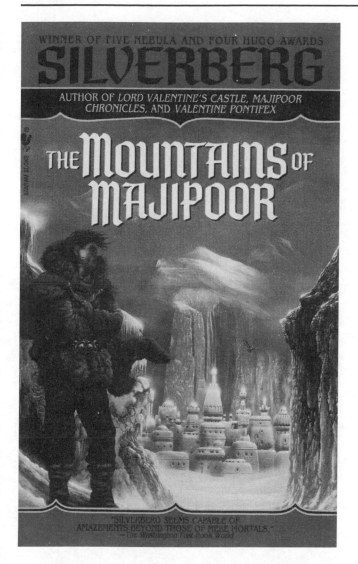

WINNER OF FIVE NEBULA AND FOUR HUGO AWARDS

SILVERBERG

AUTHOR OF *LORD VALENTINE'S CASTLE, MAJIPOOR CHRONICLES,* AND *VALENTINE PONTIFEX*

THE MOUNTAINS OF MAJIPOOR

"SILVERBERG SEEMS CAPABLE OF AMAZEMENTS BEYOND THOSE OF MERE MORTALS."
— The Washington Post Book World

The second volume in the "Majipoor Chronicles" trilogy describes the perilous journey of a young prince and his companions who encounter blizzards, ice storms, and barbarians in their quest to save a lost party of paleontologists searching for the fossils of a legendary species of dragon. (Cover illustration by Jim Burns.)

reliance on plot rather than the nuances of character. The novel ends with an upbeat resolution of Valentine managing to conquer his own personal demons and promising to right wrongs that he had committed earlier. While Jack Sullivan, reviewing the book in *New York Times Book Review,* found the plot to be "an imaginative fusion of action, sorcery and science fiction," he also noted that the language was "anything but imaginative," and concluded that the novel seemed "more like an overlong resume than a series of fantastic adventures." Claudia J. Morner commented in *School Library Journal* that *Lord Valentine's Castle* was "a good story, inventively told, which abounds with adventures and curious characters." Whatever the reviewers had to say about the book, readers gave it a thumbs up, and high sales influenced Silverberg to write several more short stories set on Majipoor which were collected

in *Majipoor Chronicles,* an "exciting and well written book," according to Morner in *School Library Journal.* Other reviewers, including a *Publishers Weekly* commentator, noted that *Majipoor Chronicles* was not a sequel, but "self-contained stories" which "give us a better picture than ever of magical Majipoor."

Valentine Pontifex was something Silverberg swore he would never write—a sequel. In this third volume of what became known as the Majipoor trilogy, Valentine battles a radical set on waging biological warfare, and also relinquishes his power to a successor, becoming a figurehead ruler of his world. Reviewers noted that this was not just *any* sequel. "Silverberg has truly done an excellent job of writing," John O. Christensen noted in *Voice of Youth Advocates.* "A masterpiece." A *Publishers Weekly* reviewer called the book an "expertly balanced novel," and noted that "Silverberg demonstrates that a trilogy *can* get better as it grows ... the best of its type since Zelazny's classic...."

The Majipoor novels brought Silverberg well out of retirement. Though his output since that time in no way rivals his earlier manic pace, he has published some 20 books since the mid-1980s, including science fiction and history, and has edited scores of science fiction short-story collections. His *Gilgamesh the King* was a retelling of the Sumerian epic, a book that would inspire "readers to return to the original translation on which it is based," according to a reviewer for *Booklist.* Other science fiction novels include *Star of Gypsies,* premised on an extraterrestrial past for the Romany people, and several ecological disaster stories, including *At Winter's End, The New Springtime,* and *Hot Sky at Midnight,* generally large, sprawling novels that rely more on plot than character. Silverberg also teamed up with Isaac Asimov on three novels, *Nightfall, The Ugly Little Boy,* and *The Positronic Man.* His 1990 juvenile novel, *Letters from Atlantis,* won a Woodward Park Award, and in 1995 he returned to the world of Majipoor with his *Mountains of Majipoor.* In this fourth installment, Silverberg revisits Majipoor five hundred years after the reign of Valentine and deals with the adventures of Prince Harpirias who, like Valentine before him, searches for redemption for past wrongs. Roland Green in *Booklist* found *Mountains of Majipoor* a "modest" story, but one that is swept along by Silverberg's "graceful prose." In 1996 Silverberg published *Starborne,* a novel of 23rd century Earth and its attempts to find new planets to colonize. This tale relates the experiences of passengers on the spaceship Wotan, traveling sixteen light years from Earth while maintaining contact with the home planet only through a telepathic crew member who communicates with her twin sister. Sue Hamburger, writing in *Library Journal,* commented that in this work Silverberg "deftly probes" why it is that humans need challenges, and indeed, what it means to be human. *Voice of Youth Advocates* contributor Christy Tyson, in her review of *Starborne,* asserted: "Silverberg has never been better than in this stunning combination of space adventure, psychological drama, and metaphysical speculation.... His experience comes through in the deft characterizations, the carefully paced plot and the sheer inventiveness of each new development."

Throughout this latest career phase, Silverberg has consciously attempted to write "commercially successful novels without forfeiting an integrity won in the hardest possible manner," as the author explained in *CAAS.* His works have taken him from ancient Egypt to the stars and back again, winning him four Hugos and five Nebulas, but he still responds to science fiction as he did as a boy, "for its capacity to open the gates of the universe, to show me the roots of time." And he continues to write, after giving it up twice in search of other modes of expression. As Silverberg concluded in *CAAS,* he plans to go on writing science fiction in his own fashion, "for it seems I have no choice but to continue."

■ Works Cited

Christensen, John O., review of *Valentine Pontifex, Voice of Youth Advocates,* June, 1984, p. 102.
Review of *Gilgamesh the King, Booklist,* September 1, 1984, p. 3.
Green, Roland, review of *The Mountains of Majipoor, Booklist,* February 1, 1995, p. 993.
Hamburger, Sue, review of *Starborne, Library Journal,* May 15, 1996, p. 86.
Review of *Majipoor Chronicles, Publishers Weekly,* January 22, 1982, p. 63.
Malzberg, Barry M., *Magazine of Fantasy and Science Fiction,* April, 1971.
Morner, Claudia J., review of *Lord Valentine's Castle, School Library Journal,* September, 1980, p. 93.
Morner, Claudia J., review of *Majipoor Chronicles, School Library Journal,* May, 1982, pp. 90-1.
Silverberg, Robert, essay in *Contemporary Authors Autobiography Series,* Volume 3, Gale, 1986, pp. 269-91.
Stubbs, Harry C., review of *Four Men Who Changed the Universe, Horn Book,* June, 1969, pp. 323-5.
Sullivan, Jack, "Ordinarily Fantastic," *New York Times Book Review,* August 3, 1980, p. 12.
Tuma, George W., "Robert Silverberg," *Dictionary of Literary Biography, Vol. 8: Twentieth-Century American Science-Fiction Writers,* Gale, 1981, pp. 106-19.
Tyson, Christy, review of *Starborne, Voice of Youth Advocates,* October, 1996, p. 221.
Review of *Valentine Pontifex, Publishers Weekly,* September 30, 1985, p. 112.

■ For More Information See

BOOKS

Aldiss, Brian and Harry Harrison, editors, *Hell's Cartographers: Some Personal Histories of Science Fiction Writers,* Harper, 1975.
Clareson, Thomas D., *Robert Silverberg: A Primary and Secondary Bibliography,* G. K. Hall, 1983.
Contemporary Literary Criticism, Volume 7, Gale, 1971.

Elkins, Charles L. and Martin Greenberg, editors, *Robert Silverberg's Many Trapdoors: Critical Essays on His Science Fiction,* Greenwood Press, 1992.
Rabkin, Eric S. and others, editors, *No Place Else,* Southern Illinois University Press, 1983.
Schweitzer, Darrell, editor, *Exploring Fantasy Worlds: Essays on Fantastic Literature,* Borgo Press, 1985.

PERIODICALS

Booklist, January 1, 1979; September 1, 1984; August 22, 1986; February 1, 1988; April 1, 1990; August, 1991.
Bulletin of the Center for Children's Books, June, 1969; September, 1969, p. 17; June, 1975, p. 167; November, 1976, p. 48; October, 1987, p. 37.
Extrapolation, December, 1975, pp. 18-28; summer, 1979, pp. 109-17.
The Junior Bookshelf, February, 1978, p. 49; August, 1989, p. 194.
Kirkus Reviews, August 1, 1979, p. 896; September 15, 1984, p. 874; February 15, 1992, p. 222.
New York Times Book Review, November 11, 1984, p. 13; December 15, 1991, pp. 20-1; May 3, 1992, p. 38; November 14, 1993, p. 74; March 13, 1994, p. 30.
Publishers Weekly, October 20, 1975, p. 74; July 2, 1979, p. 106; August 30, 1991, p. 71; November 1, 1993, p. 70; May 27, 1996, pp. 69-70.
School Library Journal, March, 1977, p. 153; November, 1979, p. 94; April, 1979, p. 72; March, 1987, p. 178; March, 1991, p. 218.
Voice of Youth Advocates, April, 1986, p. 42; June, 1988, p. 97; October, 1990, pp. 232-33; December, 1991, p. 322-23; August, 1993, pp. 170-71.*

—*Sketch by J. Sydney Jones*

*   *   *

SPINNER, Stephanie 1943-

■ Personal

Born November 16, 1943, in Davenport, IA; daughter of Ralph (a businessman) and Edna (Lowry) Spinner. *Education:* Bennington College, B.A., 1964. *Hobbies and other interests:* Horses, painting, travel.

■ Addresses

Home—Hickory Lane, Pawling, NY 12564.

■ Career

Children's book editor.

■ Awards, Honors

Texas Bluebonnet Award, 1991, for *Aliens for Breakfast.*

■ Writings

(Adaptor) *Popeye: The Storybook Based on the Movie,* Random House, 1980.

Dracula: A Step-Up Adventure, illustrated by Jim Spence, Random House, 1982.

(Adaptor) Carlo Collodi (under pseudonym Carlo Lorenzini) *The Adventures of Pinocchio,* illustrated by Diane Goode, Random House, 1983.

The Mummy's Tomb, Bantam, 1985.

(With Jonathan Etra) *Aliens for Breakfast,* illustrated by Steve Bjorkman, Random House, 1988.

(With Jonathan Etra) *Aliens for Lunch,* illustrated by Steve Bjorkman, Random House, 1991.

Little Sure Shot: The Story of Annie Oakley, illustrated by Jose Miralles, Random House, 1993.

Aliens for Dinner, Random House, 1994.

(With Ellen Weiss) *Gerbilitis,* illustrated by Steve Bjorkman, HarperCollins, 1996.

(With Ellen Weiss) *Sing, Elvis, Sing,* illustrated by Steve Bjorkman, HarperCollins, 1996.

EDITOR

Rock Is Beautiful: An Anthology of American Lyrics, 1953-1968, Dell, 1969.

Feminine Plural: Stories by Women about Growing Up, Macmillan, 1972.

Live and Learn: Stories about Students and Their Teachers, Macmillan, 1973.

Motherlove: Stories by Women about Motherhood, Dell, 1978.

■ Sidelights

Stephanie Spinner has written and edited a wide variety of works for both children and young adults. Her own books range from collections of essays on feminist topics to retellings of classic stories and humorous original chapter books. She has also edited the works of several prominent children's authors.

Spinner collaborated with Jonathan Etra on a series of three books about Richard Bickerstaff, a young science-fiction fan, and Aric, a tiny alien secret agent. The two characters meet for the first time in *Aliens for Breakfast,* published in 1988. In this story, Richard tries the new Alien Crisp cereal and finds Aric in his bowl. The alien soon informs his friend that they must work together to rid the world of a common enemy—a bad alien disguised as the cool new kid at Richard's school. The heroes soon embark on a frantic search to find the one earthling household object that will prevent the evil alien from replicating himself and taking over the world. A *Booklist* reviewer praised the book for its "clever plotting, right-on characterization, and ... jet-propelled pace."

In the first sequel, 1991's *Aliens for Lunch,* the greedy occupants of a distant planet have used up their resources of XTC-1000, the mysterious substance which makes desserts taste delicious. They threaten to steal the earth's supply and doom the planet to eating bland desserts unless Richard and Aric can stop them. By chance, Richard stumbles upon the secret weapon that can repel the evil invaders: the celery sticks he always carries in his pocket. A writer for *Kirkus Reviews* appreciated the book's "brisk, imaginatively conceived

In this humorous, fast-paced story by Stephanie Spinner and Jonathan Etra, young Richard Bickerstaff becomes involved in a mission to save the world after an alien emerges from his cereal bowl. (Cover illustration by Steve Bjorkman.)

action" and "rib-tickling dialogue," while Hazel Rochman noted in *Booklist* that "this is a story that will show smart new readers that books are fun." The intergalactic adventures of Richard and Aric continue in *Aliens for Dinner,* published in 1994, when they must save the earth from being turned into a toxic amusement park by aliens that thrive on pollution.

■ Works Cited

Review of *Aliens for Breakfast, Booklist,* January 15, 1989.

Review of *Aliens for Lunch, Kirkus Reviews,* May 1, 1991.

Rochman, Hazel, review of *Aliens for Lunch, Booklist,* June 1, 1991.

■ For More Information See

PERIODICALS

Booklist, May 15, 1978, p. 1478; February 15, 1984, p. 856; February 1, 1994, p. 98.

Bulletin of the Center for Children's Books, May 1973, p. 145; April 1984.

Kirkus Reviews, September 15, 1972, p. 1106.
Publishers Weekly, January 1, 1973, p. 57.
School Library Journal, August, 1982, p. 112; March, 1989; February 1994, p. 98.

*   *   *

SZYMANSKI, Lois 1957-

■ Personal

Born January 7, 1957, in Maryland; daughter of Donald (a county surveyor) and Elsie (a homemaker; maiden name, Schmitt) Knight; married Daniel Louis Szymanski, Jr. (a book binder), September 6, 1980; children: Shannon Anne, Ashley Marie. *Education:* Hagerstown Junior College, A.A., 1978. *Religion:* Lutheran.

■ Addresses

Home—3377 Littlestown Pike, Westminster, MD 21158.

■ Career

Author, journalist, teacher. *Carroll County Times,* Westminster, MD, correspondent, 1989-95; *Lancaster Farming* (newspaper), Lancaster, PA, correspondent, 1994—; *The Carroll Sun,* Westminster, MD, correspondent, 1995—. Freelance writer, 1990— . Instructor in continuing adult education at Carroll Community College, Westminster, MD. Carroll Co. 4-H leader, former Girl Scout leader, volunteer for Riding for the Handicapped Program and Women of the Moose #897. *Member:* Society of Children's Book Writers and Illustrators, Carroll Writer's Guild, Eastern Shore Writers Association.

■ Writings

Patches, Avon Books, 1993.
A New Kind of Magic, Avon Books, 1994.
Little Icicle, Avon Books, 1995.
A Pony Promise, Avon Books, 1996.
A Perfect Pony, Avon Books, 1996.

■ Work in Progress

"The Gettysburg Ghost Gang" series, stories written with coauthor Shelley Sykes that combine the history of the Civil War period with the supernatural; *Hugs and Kisses,* a true story about the survival of twin foals that have been marked for death; *Little Blue Eyes,* a fantasy about a unicorn.

■ Sidelights

Lois Szymanski told *SATA:* "It began simply enough. I was six years old and I wanted a horse. I asked for a horse. I begged for a horse. Each year I tried to bribe Santa into bringing one, too. Although that wish never came true, something magical happened instead. I discovered that I could live my dreams by immersing

LOIS SZYMANSKI

myself in every horse book I could get my hands on. I read Marguerite Henry's *Misty of Chincoteague* so many times that the cover fell off! When I read I *became* Maureen Beebe, chasing after a wisp of a pony named Misty. I believed so thoroughly that I began to look for wild pony tracks near my home. After all, a wild Assateague pony might escape and make it to where I lived!

"Back then I didn't know that readers often become writers. Writing began as a form of self-therapy, something that made me feel better. It wasn't until I had children of my own and was reading to them that I decided that I could write for publication. I began by writing for magazines. By the time I was brave enough to try my hand at a book I had sold stories to over fifty different publications, including *Highlights for Children, U*S* Kids,* and *Turtle,* magazines that I admired.

"When planning my first book I didn't have to think twice about the setting; I knew it would be those wild pony islands. After a 1988 surprise vacation there, planned by my husband Dan, the islands had become a second home. I remembered how I had scoured library shelves looking for more books about the wild ponies when I was young. Now, I would write them myself.

"Stories about the wild ponies come to me again and again. Local firemen Asa Hickman and Donald Leonard told me the true tale of little Icicle, which would become the book *Little Icicle.* Locals Paul Merritt and Jeanette Beebe, along with Michael Pryor, told me a true tale about the legendary Stormy and how she rejected her fifth foal only to have it adopted by a mare named Windy, who raised it with her own. That story would become *A Pony Promise.* With my knowledge of ponies and a little imagination, I created *Little Blue Eyes,* an upcoming book and the tale of Meg, whose new foal is born with a bump on its head. While she worries, the truth slowly reveals itself. The foal is a unicorn.

"Currently I am working with cowriter Shelley Sykes on a series to be titled 'The Gettysburg Ghost Gang.' The books will have accurate details about the Civil War ghosts our contemporary protagonists dig up, as well as the spine-tingling suspense readers demand in a ghost book.

"Everything about writing is fun; the research, the creation of characters, permission to use imagination to its fullest extent, having an excuse to read, and, most of all, seeing the satisfaction young readers get from my books, just as I did so many years ago when reading was an escape and pages in books took me to faraway places."

T

SUZANNE TATE

TATE, Suzanne 1930-

■ Personal

Born July 30, 1930, in Columbus, OH; daughter of Robert E. and Grace (Bateman) Rucker; married Everett D. Tate (a postmaster), January 11, 1954; children: Mark D., Frank E. (deceased). *Education:* Attended Muskingum College, 1948-50; University of New Mexico, B.A., 1952; graduate work at University of Tennes-

see, 1952-53. *Politics:* Democrat. *Religion:* United Methodist. *Hobbies and other interests:* Archeology, paleontology.

■ Addresses

Home—P.O. Box 88, 7734 Virginia Dare Tr., Nags Head, NC 27959.

■ Career

Children's writer, teacher, business executive. National Park Service, Manteo, NC, park ranger and interpreter, 1964-66; Dare County Board of Education, Manteo, NC, elementary teacher, 1967-70; Dare County Library, director, 1976-82; Dare County Arts Council, director, 1978-82; Nags Head Art, Inc. (wholesale art and book business), Nags Head, NC, president, 1980-96. North Carolina Aquarium, presenter. *Military service:* U.S. Naval Reserves, Lieutenant Junior Grade, 1952-54. *Member:* National Federation of Press Women.

■ Awards, Honors

Distinguished Service Award, Muskingum College, 1991; First Place, National Federation of Press Women, 1995, for *Ellie and Ollie Eel;* Children's Choice, International Reading Association, 1996, for *Katie K. Whale.*

■ Writings

"SUZANNE TATE'S NATURE SERIES"; ILLUSTRATED BY JAMES MELVIN; PUBLISHED BY NAGS HEAD ART (NAGS HEAD, NC)

Billy Bluefish: A Tale of Big Blues, 1988.
Crabby and Nabby: A Tale of Two Blue Crabs, 1988.
Flossie Flounder: A Tale of Flat Fish, 1989.
Lucky Lookdown: A Tale of a Funny Fish, 1989.
Pearlie Oyster: A Tale of an Amazing Oyster, 1989.
Spunky Spot: A Tale of One Smart Fish, 1989.
Mary Manatee: A Tale of Sea Cows, 1990.
Sammy Shrimp: A Tale of a Little Shrimp, 1990.
Crabby's Water Wish: A Tale of Saving Sea Life, 1991.
Harry Horseshoe Crab: A Tale of Crawly Creatures, 1991.

Tammy Turtle: A Tale of Saving Sea Turtles, 1991.
Danny and Daisy: A Tale of a Dolphin Duo, 1992.
Salty Seagull: A Tale of an Old Salt, 1992.
Old Reddy Drum: A Tale of Redfish, 1993.
Stevie B. Sea Horse: A Tale of a Proud Papa, 1993.
Ellie and Ollie Eel: A Tale of a Fantastic Voyage, 1994.
Katie K. Whale: A Whale of a Tale, 1995.
Perky Pelican: A Tale of a Lively Bird, 1996.

OTHER

(Compiler) Ruth Scarborough Tate, *Duck Tales: Folk Tales and Anecdotes: From Duck, a Fishing Village on the Outer Banks of North Carolina* (adult history), illustrated by James Melvin, Nags Head Art, 1986.
Bring Me Duck (revised edition), illustrated by James Melvin, Nags Head Art, 1986.
Whalehead, Tales of Corolla, N.C., Nags Head Art, 1987.
(Compiler) Cora Mae Basnight, *Memories of Manteo and Roanoke Island, N.C.* (adult history), illustrated by James Melvin, Nags Head Art, 1988.
A Teaching Guide for Suzanne Tate's Nature Series, Nags Head Art, 1994.

■ Work in Progress

Additional books for "Suzanne Tate's Nature Series," including *Oopsie Otter;* research on river otters and hot air ballooning.

■ Sidelights

Suzanne Tate commented: "I was born in Columbus, Ohio, but grew up on a farm near Westerville, Ohio. My ancestors have always been interested in nature and art. At an early age, my mother took me on long walks through our woods. She would identify and point out unusual species on our walks. My mother's father and grandfather were farmers and artists who were also appreciative of nature.

"I was educated at Muskingum College, New Concord, Ohio, and the University of New Mexico, where I received my B.A. degree in anthropology and biology.

"My favorite books when I was a child were the *Old Mother West Wind* tales. I liked any books about animals. I have written stories since childhood. My father always encouraged me to write and gave me a typewriter when I graduated from college.

"I live on Pond Island in Nags Head, North Carolina, and am married to Everett Tate, a retired postmaster. Everett was reared in the fishing village of Duck, North Carolina. He has had a varied background of commercial fishing, which he still pursues whenever time permits. Through the years, he has related to me many interesting facts about sea life, giving me wonderful material for my Nature Series. Our sons, Mark (born 1958) and Frank (born 1963, deceased 1982), also grew up with a love of fishing and interest in sea life.

"I often serve on advisory boards in art and education fields and have a special interest in women's issues,

particularly health. I also am especially interested in literacy programs.

"For seventeen years, I have owned and managed Nags Head Art, a wholesale firm. I have taught at the elementary level and served as LTJG in the U.S. Naval Reserves. For fun, I like to dance rock 'n roll!

"I feel certain that my life-long love of nature and interest in all scientific things has led me to write a nature series for children. I especially enjoy riding in a boat and watching my husband when he is fishing. It allows me the opportunity to do research and make first-hand observations. I like to do my writing while moving—in a boat or car!

"I enjoy incorporating real place names of North Carolina in my books. In addition to my nature series for children, I have written three oral history books— enjoying very much the preservation of local folk tales. My favorite, however, is writing tales for children.

"My advice to aspiring authors is to practice writing whenever one has the opportunity."

*   *   *

THOMAS, Jerry D. 1959-

■ Personal

Born October 30, 1959, in Quantico, VA; son of Hagar E. (a pastor) and Jean (a nurse; maiden name, Fletcher) Thomas; married Katherine Barron (an office manager), March 11, 1979; children: Jonathan, Jennifer, Jeremy. *Education:* Southwestern Adventist College, B.A., 1983; Andrews University, M.A., 1988. *Religion:* Seventh-day Adventist.

■ Addresses

Home—11294 Hall Dr., Nampa ID 83651; 22510 Ryan Dr., Wilder, ID 83676. *Office*—Pacific Press, P.O. Box 5353, Nampa, ID 83653.

■ Career

Highland View Academy, Hagerstown, MD, pastor/ chaplain, 1984-89, religion teacher, 1984-90; Pacific Press, Nampa, ID, book editor, 1991-96.

■ Writings

Great Stories for Kids, five volumes, Pacific Press (Nampa, ID), 1995.

Creator of the "Shoebox Kids" stories, which appear in *Primary Treasure.* Also creator and editor of the "Shoebox Kids Mysteries" series—books based on the "Shoebox Kids" stories.

"DETECTIVE ZACK" SERIES; PUBLISHED BY PACIFIC PRESS

Detective Zack and the Secret of Noah's Flood, 1992.
Detective Zack and the Red Hat Mystery, 1993.
Detective Zack and the Secrets in the Sand, 1993.

JERRY D. THOMAS

Detective Zack and the Mystery at Thunder Mountain, 1994.
Detective Zack and the Missing Manger Mystery, 1994.
Detective Zack and the Danger at Dinosaur Camp, 1995.
Detective Zack and the Secret in the Storm, 1995.
Detective Zack and the Mystery on the Midway, 1996.

Created *Detective Zack's Word Puzzle Safari,* a word puzzle book based on the "Detective Zack" series.

■ Sidelights

Jerry D. Thomas told *SATA:* "My approach to writing for kids is a reflection of this philosophy: truth must be discovered, not taught. By telling stories, especially mysteries, I can set kids up to discover important truths about themselves, about the world, or about God.

"*Great Stories for Kids* is the most massive project I've written so far. With five volumes and more than 130 stories, the set is beautifully illustrated. It is intended to help kids develop strong characters and learn how to deal with real problems. Many of the stories were based on events from my own childhood and from the experiences of my children."

TINGUM, Janice 1958-

■ Personal

Born October 29, 1958, in Mayville, ND; daughter of Leonard (a farmer) and Ida Mae (Vleck) Overmoe; married Kirk Tingum (a lawyer), August 20, 1983; children: Kathryn, Michael, Matthew. *Education:* University of North Dakota School of Law, J.D., 1983.

■ Addresses

Home—1317 Chestnut St., Grand Forks, ND 58201. *Office*—209 S. 3rd St., Grand Forks, ND 58206.

■ Career

Grand Forks Abstract, Grand Forks, ND, title examiner, 1984—; lawyer in private practice, beginning 1984; freelance writer. *Member:* Society of Children's Book Writers and Illustrators, American Judicature Society, North Dakota State Bar Association, Grand Forks County Bar Association.

■ Writings

E. B. White: The Elements of a Writer, Lerner Publications, 1995.

Also contributor to periodicals, including *Lady's Circle, Parents Magazine,* and *Turtle Magazine.*

■ Sidelights

"Researching the life of E. B. White proved to be the best writer's workshop that I could ever attend," Janice Tingum told *SATA.* "Thanks to the permission of White's son, Joel, and the courtesy of the Department of Rare Books and Manuscript Collections at Cornell University Library at Ithaca, New York, I was able to

Janice Tingum and family.

study White's original manuscripts, letters, sketches, and photographs. It was a thrill to hold the drafts of *Charlotte's Web, The Elements of Style,* and other manuscripts. White wrote and re-wrote. He self-edited even short thank-you notes. I learned a lot studying his works.

"I participate in a small but serious writers' group in my community. The group offers manuscript criticism, marketing suggestions, opportunities to share writing successes and experiences, and helps keep me updated on publishing news.

"I also credit the Children's Writers' Conference held annually at the University of North Dakota for bringing me into the field of children's literature. For a long time I had considered myself a sprinter in terms of writing—producing poems and articles. I began attending the conference for the fellowship of other writers and to strengthen my writing skills. Along the way, I developed a real interest in non-fiction writing for children and the desire to write a book. The result was a biography on White, my first book. I hope to continue writing for children."

■ For More Information See

PERIODICALS

Booklist, November 1, 1995, p. 464.
Kirkus Reviews, November 1, 1995.

*   *   *

TOWNSEND, Brad W. 1962-

■ Personal

Born January 1, 1962, in Waco, TX; son of G. P. Townsend, Jr. and Martha Jane Maly; married Sydney Stiles (in public relations), August 28, 1994. *Education:* University of Texas at Austin, B.J., 1984.

■ Addresses

Home—2224 Warrington, Flower Mound, TX 75028.

■ Career

San Antonio Light, San Antonio, TX, sports reporter, 1984-93; *Houston Chronicle,* Houston, TX, copy editor, 1993-94; *Dallas Morning News,* Dallas, TX, sports reporter, 1994—. *Member:* Professional Basketball Writers' Association.

■ Awards, Honors

Second place, Sports Feature Writing, Columbia Scholastic Press Association, 1985; Best Sports News Story award, 1991, and Best Sports Feature award, 1992, both from San Antonio Society of Professional Journalists; Southwest Region's Best Feature award, Associated Press Sports Editors, 1992.

BRAD W. TOWNSEND

■ Writings

Shaquille O'Neal: Center of Attention, Lerner (Minneapolis, MN), 1994.

■ Work in Progress

A children's book about Orlando Magic guard Anfernee Hardaway.

■ Sidelights

"I have worked in sports journalism since 1982," writer and sports reporter Brad Townsend told *SATA,* "when I joined the staff of the University of Texas student newspaper, the *Daily Texan.* My late grandfather, Fred Maly, was an outdoors editor and columnist in San Antonio for more than forty years, and definitely helped inspire my entry into the field.

"As for children's book writing, my start was part accident, part circumstances, part fate. The newspaper at which I had worked for nine years, the *San Antonio Light,* folded in February 1994. I went to the *Houston Chronicle* as a sports copy editor, a big change from having covered the NBA San Antonio Spurs from 1989 to 1994.

"A former lifestyles editor at the *Light,* Pat McMorrow King, heard through my editor at Lerner Publications, Julie Jensen, that Lerner needed someone to write a book about Shaquille O'Neal. Pat remembered that I had covered O'Neal's junior season at San Antonio Cole High before moving up to cover colleges, then the NBA.

"The opportunity to write *Shaquille O'Neal: Center of Attention* was extremely gratifying. I had flashbacks to my elementary and junior high days, when I read every sports biography I could get my hands on. While I have certainly learned there is much more to life than sports, there is no doubt that sports literature made me a voracious reader, and no doubt a better writer.

"I would like to think my book has encouraged young readers who otherwise might be reluctant to read, to acquire an interest in reading other works. I particularly have enjoyed reading comments about my book written by students and librarians. More than any NBA story I have broken, this book has given me a sense of importance and accomplishment. I hope I can carve the time to do several more."

■ For More Information See

PERIODICALS

Booklist, May 15, 1994, p. 1676.
School Library Journal, September, 1994, p. 236.

* * *

TROTT, Betty 1933-

■ Personal

Born October 7, 1933, in Bentonville, AR; daughter of Paul R. (a pianist) and Stella (a factory worker; maiden name, Williams) Rice; married B. Dale Trott (a research scientist), June 21, 1958; children: Cindy Lee Friel, Nancy Karen Deakins. *Education:* Pennsylvania State University, B.A., 1956; attended Syracuse University, 1956-57, and Fashion Academy, 1980. *Politics:* "Varies." *Religion:* Protestant. *Hobbies and other interests:* Theater, sailing, activities for children, writing plays for her grandchildren, and line, ballroom, and social dancing.

■ Addresses

Home and office—8808 Renfrew St., Powell, OH 43065.

■ Career

Teacher, writer. Bought Hills Grade School, Lathan, NY, third grade teacher, 1956-58; Merle Norman, Columbus, OH, beauty consultant, 1978-80; Fashion Academy, Columbus, OH, personal image consultant and teacher, 1980-90; freelance children's writer, 1990—. Director of children's sailing, 1970; director of children's television at the Center of Science and Industry (COSI), 1973; director of Grandview children's musical, 1994; director of Griswald Players play. Mem-

BETTY TROTT

ber of Griswald Players, 1995. *Member:* Theta Alpha Phi.

■ Awards, Honors

Sailor of the Year, Hoover Yacht Club, 1969.

■ Writings

Breathe On Me Butterflies, illustrated by Michelle McGrew, Winston Derek, 1994.

Also once wrote a newsletter on sailing.

■ Work in Progress

A children's chapter book about sailing, proposed title "Racing for the Championship," expected completion in 1996.

■ Sidelights

Betty Trott told *SATA:* "My grandmother, Ponyma, passed down to me the freedom to experience the ethereal part of my imagination. I would hope that my books would pass on to children of today and tomorrow that same freedom. I enjoy writing about precious moments in my own encounters with nature as well as writing about the secret yearnings of my grandchildren."

W

LAWRENCE WADDY

WADDY, Lawrence (Heber) 1914-

■ Personal

Born October 5, 1914, in Sydney, Australia; son of Percival S. (a minister) and Etheldred (Spittal) Waddy; married first wife, Natalie (deceased); married Laurie Hermanson, October 7, 1972; children: (first marriage) Helena Lepovitz, Nerissa Wilson, Joanna. *Education:* Balliol College, Oxford University, B.A., 1937, M.A., 1945. *Politics:* Republican. *Religion:* Episcopalian. *Hobbies and other interests:* Writing, directing, and acting for the theater.

■ Addresses

Home—5910 Camino de la Costa, La Jolla, CA 92034.

■ Career

Winchester College, Winchester, Hampshire, England, chaplain and teacher of classics, 1938-42, 1946-49; Tonbridge School, Tonbridge, Kent, England, headmaster, 1949-62; British Broadcasting Corporation, London, England, education officer, religious broadcaster, and writer, 1962-63; The Bishop's School, La Jolla, CA, chaplain, associate in administration, and teacher, 1963-67; University of California, San Diego, lecturer in classics, 1969-80. Lecturer in classics, University of California, Berkeley, 1961. Honorary canon, Diocese of Rochester, England, 1961-63; honorary chaplain to Bishop of Rochester, 1963-67; vicar, Church of the Good Samaritan, 1970-74. *Military service:* Royal Naval Volunteer Reserve, chaplain, 1942-46.

■ Awards, Honors

British Broadcasting Corporation production of his musical play, *Job,* was chosen as Britain's best religious program, 1963, and as a prize-winner at the Monte Carlo Film Festival, 1964.

■ Writings

FOR CHILDREN

First Bible Stories, Paulist Press, 1994.

PLAYS

The Prodigal Son (one-act; first produced in Coventry, England, at the Coventry Cathedral, 1963), Samuel French, 1963.

The Bible as Drama (includes *Job* [first produced on British Broadcasting Corporation (BBC) television, 1963], *Joseph, Good Friday, The Prodigal Son* [first produced on BBC television, 1963], and *The Wedding Feast* [first produced on BBC television, 1964]), Paulist/Newman, 1975.

Faith of Our Fathers, Morehouse, 1976.

Drama in Worship (includes *Jonah* [first produced on BBC television, 1964], *The Crafty Steward, Martin the Cobbler, God's Tumbler,* and *The Good Samaritan* [first produced on BBC television, 1963]), Paulist/Newman, 1978.

The Family of Man, first produced in La Jolla, CA, at Sherwood Auditorium, March, 1982.

Shakespeare Remembers, Players Press, 1994.

Florence Nightingale, Players Press, 1996.

Jonah, Players Press, 1996.

Musical scores for Waddy's plays are available from the author. Also author of thirteen radio plays for "The Witness" series of the Episcopal Church, 1964.

"EAGLE CITY" SERIES; NOVELS

Symphony, Lane & Associates, 1980.

Mayor's Race, Lane & Associates, 1980.

OTHER

Pax Romana and World Peace, Chapman & Hall, 1950.

A Parish by the Sea: A History of Saint James-by-the-Sea Episcopal Church, La Jolla, California, Saint James Bookshelf, 1988.

Contributor to periodicals, including *American Journal of Archaeology* and *Journal of Unconventional History.*

■ Work in Progress

Two plays: *Paul of Tarsus* and *Eleanor Roosevelt;* children's stories; a novel about the abolition of guns; a novel about organ transplants.

■ Sidelights

Lawrence Waddy told *SATA:* "I am a retired Episcopal minister and teacher. My interest in writing goes back a long way. I was an editor of my school magazine in England, and my education in the classics, history, and philosophy gave me a good deal of experience in writing papers, as well as Latin and Greek compositions.

"I began teaching in 1937 and was ordained deacon in 1940 (during the Battle of Britain), and priest in 1941. Early in 1942 I joined the British Navy as a chaplain and spent two years at sea. My first writing of any length occurred during four-hour watches in the cipher office of my cruiser, *HMS Jamaica.* I volunteered for this duty when we were at sea, and often it involved four uneventful hours in an office with a typewriter. On occasion, urgent signals came in, but usually they were routine, with gaps between them.

"For fun I began a novel about our situation, 'A Week in Iceland.' It was about two Navy officers who went ashore for an afternoon in Akureyri, the northernmost town in Iceland, and stumbled into a spy situation. A London publisher politely rejected it. Later I wrote another, 'Crime in a Cruiser,' about a murder which took place in a ship during one of the convoy operations.

"Writing these books gave me the feel of description and dialogue. When I came back from the war to teaching, to my surprise I was asked by Chapman and Hall to write a history of Rome, on the strength of my Oxford record. I said that I would do so if I could relate it to modern parallels. Result: *Pax Romana and World Peace,* which did quite well.

"In 1949 I became headmaster of a famous boarding school, Tonbridge, and for thirteen years I was too busy to write seriously; but in 1959, after a Greek cruise when I was a lecturer, I began to write songs which turned into a musical, *Isles of Greece.* It had one good amateur production in 1962. The text is horribly dated, but I still sing the songs in the shower.

"That led to a burst of song and play writing. A short musical, *The Prodigal Son,* written for my schoolboys, was accepted by the BBC for a TV play, and then published by Samuel French, all in 1963. In that year I moved to La Jolla, California, after one year of temporary work in the BBC's Schools department. During that year they accepted four more of my musicals.

"*Job* was very successful, being chosen as Britain's best religious program for 1963, and winning first prize in the Monte Carlo UNDA film festival. So I have been encouraged to write songs and plays ever since. Paulist Press later published two collections of plays.

"Apart from plays, I have written two published novels. This came about when my wife was president of the San Diego Symphony. I decided that a novel about a concert would be a good combination of fundraiser and publicity. It was, and I followed it with another novel published

"A Woman in a Crowded Street" from Waddy's collection of retellings from the Old and New Testaments, *First Bible Stories.* (Illustration by Mark Mitchell.)

locally. All the time I was very busy acting and directing plays as part of my ministry.

"Now I am in a burst of writing with my first computer to help. Players Press has published three plays. My first children's book is out (*First Bible Stories*), and I am trying to publish a bigger collection of children's stories, as well as two novels."

*   *   *

WAINWRIGHT, Richard M. 1935-

■ Personal

Born August 21, 1935, in Newton, MA; son of Edwin and Bertha Wainwright; married, 1962; wife's name, D'Ann (died, December 1995); children: (adopted sons) Fredy, Cesar, Pablo. *Education:* Boston University, B.A., 1961. *Hobbies and other interests:* Travel, backpacking, golf, tennis, fishing.

■ Addresses

Office—Family Life Publishing, Box 2010, Dennis, MA 02638; Box 353844, Palm Coast, FL 32135.

■ Career

Worked as a teacher, coach, and administrator in public and private schools; founder and headmaster, Charles River Academy (school for adolescent boys with learning disabilities), Cambridge, MA; Dennis-Yarmouth High School, Cape Cod, dean of students, beginning 1969. Creator and director of education and career programs, Barnstable House of Correction and Harwich Junior High School. Founder, Andean World (retail store), South Dennis, MA. Writer, beginning 1986. Lecturer to elementary schools through college, parent groups, and civic organizations. *Military service:* U.S. Army.

■ Writings

A Tiny Miracle, illustrated by Jack Crompton, Family Life Publishing (Dennis, MA), 1987.
Poofin: The Cloud that Cried on Christmas, illustrated by Jack Crompton, Family Life Publishing, 1988.
The Gift from Obadiah's Ghost, illustrated by Jack Crompton, Family Life Publishing, 1990.
Mountains to Climb, illustrated by Jack Crompton, Family Life Publishing, 1991.
A New Life for Sir Christopher, illustrated by Carolyn Sansone Dvorsack, Family Life Publishing, 1992.
Garden of Dreams, illustrated by Carolyn Sansone Dvorsack, Family Life Publishing, 1994.
The Crystal Palace of Adamas, illustrated by Ron Walotsky, Family Life Publishing, 1995.
Nana, Grampa and Tecumseh, Family Life Publishing, in press.

Author's works have been translated into Spanish.

RICHARD M. WAINWRIGHT

■ Work in Progress

More children's books.

■ Sidelights

"Frequently during a presentation on writing, I am asked how I would define a good writer," Richard M. Wainwright told *SATA.* "After ten years of responding to this question, I hope my answer has some merit. Education, life's experiences, genetic heritage, age or personality may contribute to one's ability, but basically a good writer is one who can string a few or thousands of words together and deeply touch the reader.

"Years ago a teacher showed me a single line written by one of her first grade students: 'Mommy and Daddy had a fight last week and Daddy hasn't come home.'

"Those few words brought a tear to my eyes. The writer certainly touched me deeply as I imagined the anguish the child was feeling. At that moment in time, that child was indeed a good writer.

"A writer's words may make the reader curious, fearful, sad, inspired and joyous, etc.—possibly at the same instant evoking several of the hundreds of human emotions we possess. An unheard laugh or unseen tear from the reader may be the greatest compliment the writer will ever receive.

"When a writer is told his or her story touched someone deeply, irrespective of the age of the reader, then the writer can feel that his or her literary effort was worth the hours, days, months, or years it took to create it.

"I write simply for the joy of writing. I do not write for an age but for people. If I do a good job readers will identify with the emotional aspect of the story on their intellectual level and with the totality of their life experiences, whether they be five or ninety-five.

"Just as we understood at the age of three or four in some way the meaning of the word love, at ages fourteen, twenty-five, forty-five, sixty-five, and eighty-five the meaning of the word love has changed and expanded tremendously.

"Remember, my writer friends, as the authors that we have read and admired have changed us, so our stories and poems too can touch the souls of our readers and will in a small way influence their lives."

■ For More Information See

PERIODICALS

Publishers Weekly, June 8, 1990, p. 54; October 26, 1992, p. 68.
School Library Journal, January 1992, p. 100.

* * *

WESTON, Allen
See HOGARTH, Grace (Weston) Allen

* * *

WESTON, Allen
See NORTON, Andre

* * *

WILKINSON, Brenda 1946-

■ Personal

Born January 1, 1946, in Moultrie, GA; daughter of Malcolm and Ethel (Anderson) Scott; children: Kim, Lori. *Education:* Attended Hunter College of the City University of New York.

■ Addresses

Home—123 West 104 St., New York, NY 10023.
Office—Board of Global Ministries, 475 Riverside Dr., Room 1524, New York, NY 10017.

■ Career

Poet and author of books for children. Gives poetry readings. *Member:* Authors Guild, Authors League of America.

■ Awards, Honors

National Book Award nomination, 1976, for *Ludell; Ludell and Willie* was named one of the outstanding children's books of the year by the *New York Times* and a Best Book for Young Adults by the American Library Association, both 1977.

■ Writings

Ludell (first book in trilogy), Harper, 1975.
Ludell and Willie (second book in trilogy), Harper, 1976.
Ludell's New York Time (third book in trilogy), Harper, 1980.
Not Separate, Not Equal, Harper, 1987.
Jesse Jackson: Still Fighting for the Dream, Silver Burdett (Morristown, NJ), 1990.
Definitely Cool, Scholastic, 1993.

Also contributor of poetry and short stories to periodicals.

■ Sidelights

Brenda Wilkinson's "Ludell" trilogy has been praised for its accurate yet sensitive and compassionate portrayal of rural black life. These books—*Ludell, Ludell and Willie,* and *Ludell's New York Time*—follow the life of a

BRENDA WILKINSON

All Roxanne wants is to be...

definitely COOL

Brenda Wilkinson

SCHOLASTIC

Roxanne faces a dilemma in her first year in junior high—should she follow the hip kids, who do some things she doesn't like, or go it alone?

poor black child growing up in Waycross, Georgia, in the late 1950s and early 1960s.

In the first volume of the trilogy, Ludell Wilson is left in the care of her grandmother after her mother moves to New York City in search of a better life. Leon W. Lindsay writes in the *Christian Science Monitor* that *Ludell* is a "beautiful little novel about a sensitive young girl whose individuality and talent blossom in spite of the abysmal circumstances under which she has to live and go to school." Addison Gayle notes in *Nation* that "the universe of this novel is alive with innocence, which emanates from the community ... and it is highlighted by the love and care that each black person exhibits toward the other—characteristics of black life from the days of slavery until the present time." "Unlike many novels of the South, 'Ludell' is not a tragedy in any sense, not an angry book, nor is it soft-centered," remarks Cynthia King in the *New York Times Book Review*. "By the end of the book I liked Ludell. I was glad to have known her and her friends."

Wilkinson's second book, *Ludell and Willie,* tells the story of Ludell's teenage years, when she falls in love, starts to plan for the future, and experiences the death of her grandmother. Ludell must leave her love, Willie, and her home in Georgia to live with her mother in New

York City. A critic in *Publishers Weekly* calls *Ludell and Willie* "a brilliant novel." In the *New York Times Book Review,* Georgess McHargue comments that "we should be grateful to Ludell and Willie, their families and friends, for living and talking like themselves, thus transcending weighty generalizations about black teenagers, Southern mores or social justice." Zena Sutherland of the *Bulletin of the Center for Children's Books* commented on the universality of Wilkinson's story, maintaining that while *Ludell and Willie* "is a story about a black adolescent, it is a story about problems all teenagers share: loving and being loved, moving toward independence, being concerned about the pattern of adult life that suddenly seems so close."

Ludell's New York Time, the last book in Wilkinson's trilogy, finds Ludell unhappily trying to cope with her separation from her love, while getting reacquainted with her mother and adjusting to her vastly different life in New York City. "Wilkinson has crafted a special kind of love story with wide ranging appeal," asserts *Christian Science Monitor* commentator Jerrie Norris, who adds: "The clash of Ludell's Waycross background with the Harlem of the '60s reveals the social fabric of both places. [Wilkinson writes] with a keen eye for detail and a carefully paced presentation of events to totally involve us with Ludell and her life."

Wilkinson followed her popular "Ludell" series with another novel about the difficulties young African Americans face growing up in the South. *Not Separate, Not Equal* chronicles the struggles six black students endure when integrating Georgia's all-white Pineridge High School in 1965. The central character in the story, Malene Freeman, finds every day a challenge, from fending off a bigot's dogs while walking to class, to being held at gunpoint in the same man's garage. While some of the racial conflicts are dramatic, Wilkinson also explores how anxieties common to teenagers of all races, such as being accepted by peer groups, become compounded when Malene and the other black students try to fit in at the new school. They soon find out that they are not wanted by either their new classmates in the integrated school, or by their old friends from the segregated school they previously attended.

Calling the work a "provocative and sobering story," a reviewer writing in *Publishers Weekly* applauded Wilkinson's deft handling of such a sensitive issue, especially her refusal to make the racial conflict "a simplistic battle between good and evil." Instead, the critic notes, Wilkinson shows how difficult the handling of racial differences can be and accurately "portrays the confusion and inner turmoil of even the well-intentioned." In *School Library Journal,* Gerry Larson describes *Not Separate, Not Equal* as "an action-packed account" of the Civil Rights Movement and praises "Malene's sensitive and intelligent perspective on the rights of all."

Definitely Cool, Wilkinson's 1993 work, features Roxanne, a young African-American girl who is entering junior high school. Although changing schools is an event many children encounter, Roxanne's experience is slightly different; she lives in a Bronx housing project, while her new school is located in an affluent suburb. Fitting in and making new friends are important to Roxanne, but when her new pals invite her to an unsupervised party during school hours and suggest she play hooky to attend, Roxanne decides being popular isn't worth getting in trouble. Reviewing *Definitely Cool,* a *Publishers Weekly* critic found Wilkinson's novel unsatisfying, saying she "tries too hard to dispel stereotypes about the African-American experience, and in doing so, trivializes potentially powerful themes." Other commentators, however, responded more favorably. Anxiety about attending a new school is a common theme, but according to a critic in *Kirkus Reviews,* Wilkinson brings new life to the subject by setting the action in a housing project, a setting often "ignored" by young adult writers, and by using "appealing, pell-mell narration peppered with exclamation marks." Janice Del Negro of *Booklist* similarly noted that *Definitely Cool* "is junior high formula fiction with a difference— its main characters are African-American urban kids."

■ Works Cited

Review of *Definitely Cool, Kirkus Reviews,* January 1, 1993, p. 69.
Review of *Definitely Cool, Publishers Weekly,* January 11, 1993, p. 64.
Del Negro, Janice, review of *Definitely Cool, Booklist,* February 15, 1993, p. 1062.
Gayle, Addison, review of *Ludell, Nation,* April 17, 1976, pp. 469-71.
King, Cynthia, review of *Ludell, New York Times Book Review,* February 22, 1976, pp. 16-18.
Lindsay, Leon W., review of *Ludell, Christian Science Monitor,* November 5, 1975, p. B10.
Review of *Ludell and Willie, Publishers Weekly,* February 7, 1977, p. 95.
McHargue, Georgess, review of *Ludell and Willie, New York Times Book Review,* May 22, 1977, p. 29.
Norris, Jerrie, review of *Ludell's New York Time, Christian Science Monitor,* April 14, 1980, p. B7.
Sutherland, Zena, review of *Ludell and Willie, Bulletin of the Center for Children's Books,* July-August, 1977, p. 184.

■ For More Information See

PERIODICALS

Booklist, December 15, 1990, p. 828.
Bulletin of the Center for Children's Books, July-August, 1977, p. 184; November, 1987, p. 59; March, 1993, p. 229.
Children's Book Review Service, January, 1988, p. 57; April, 1993, p. 108.
Christian Science Monitor, April 14, 1980, p. B7.
Horn Book, July, 1990, p. 140.
Ms., August, 1980.
Publishers Weekly, November 27, 1987, p. 83.
School Library Journal, April, 1988, p. 115; May, 1991, p. 101; March, 1993, p. 202.

Voice of Youth Advocates, October, 1991, p. 218; June, 1993, p. 97.

* * *

WINSLOW, Barbara 1947-

■ Personal

Born July 21, 1947, in Hartford, CT; daughter of Edward and Eleanor B. Tallmadge; married Paul (Skip) Winslow (an assistant principal), June 15, 1968; children: Hope, Sam, Stephen. *Education:* Yankon College, B.A. (education); attended University of Alaska, Oregon College of Education, and University of Maine. *Politics:* Democrat. *Religion:* Protestant. *Hobbies and other interests:* Hiking, cross-country skiing, travel.

■ Addresses

Home—R.F.D. 1, Box 2570, Norridgewock, ME 04957.

■ Career

Bureau of Indian Affairs, Bethel, AK, teacher, 1970-80; Maine School Administrative District 54, Skowhegan, ME, elementary school teacher, 1985—. Teacher of Sunday school classes, Norridgewock, ME. *Member:* Society of Children's Book Writers and Illustrators.

BARBARA WINSLOW

■ **Writings**

Dance on a Sealskin, Alaska Northwest Books (Portland, OR), 1995.

■ **Work in Progress**

A book about Russian Orthodox Christmas; a book about death and dying for children; an adult book about rural women.

■ **Sidelights**

"My husband and I lived and taught school in Western Alaska for ten years," Barbara Winslow told *SATA.* "We learned so much about Yu'pik customs and beliefs that eventually I felt moved to share them with children other than in my class. *Dance on a Sealskin* has brought me a great deal of pleasure by enabling me to share the important traditions of potlatch and the 'first dance.' My next book, illustrated by my dear friend Teri Sloat, is about a child's view of *Slavik,* Alaska's version of Russian Christmas.

"Perhaps because I am a full-time elementary teacher, and that uses up tremendous amounts of energy, I find I can only write well about subjects that are important to me. And I must 'teach' something. There is so much to be learned from a picture book, I hope that even high school teachers use that genre."

■ **For More Information See**

PERIODICALS

Booklist, August, 1995, p. 1958.
Kirkus Reviews, June 15, 1995, p. 866.
School Library Journal, December, 1995, p. 110.

*   *   *

WRIGHT, Leslie B(ailey) 1959-

■ **Personal**

Born October 23, 1959, in Richmond, VA; married Randy Wright (a teacher and writer); children: Austin, Jacquelyn, Courtney. *Education:* Virginia Commonwealth University, B.S.W., 1982, M.S.W., 1983.

■ **Addresses**

Home—11300 Edgewood Farm Ct., Richmond, VA 23233.

Leslie B. Wright with coauthor Mindy Loiselle

■ Career

Has held a variety of positions as a clinical social worker, primarily working with children, adolescents, and their families.

■ Writings

(With Mindy B. Loiselle) *Shining Through: Pulling It Together after Sexual Abuse,* Safer Society Press, 1994.

■ Work in Progress

A boys' book on sexual abuse, expected 1997.

■ Writings

Leslie B. Wright told *SATA:* "While working with sexually abused children, I was unable to find written materials that would be helpful to them. Sometimes seeing something in a book means more to a child than hearing it from an adult. Seeing the words—"You are not the only one who has had this problem. It was *not* your fault. Though it hurts now, it will get better'—can really help a child understand that other children have also needed and read this book, and this can help a child feel less alone, or bad, or helpless. Perhaps things *can* get better (it says so right here on this page).

"I love children's books, the hopeful perspective that we can find there. But, unfortunately, bad and sad things do happen to children. When adults can't talk about these things, children too often see themselves at fault. We must give children as much information, truth, *and* hope as we possibly can."

Z

ZAHN, Timothy 1951-

■ Personal

Born September 1, 1951, in Chicago, IL; son of Herbert William (an attorney) and Marilou (an attorney; maiden name, Webb) Zahn; married Anna L. Romo (a computer programmer), August 4, 1979; children: Corwin. *Education:* Michigan State University, B.A., 1973; University of Illinois at Urbana-Champaign, M.A., 1975, graduate study, 1975-80. *Hobbies and other interests:* Listening to classical music (particularly nineteenth-century Romantic era), crossword puzzles, and martial arts.

■ Addresses

Agent—Russell Galen, Scovil Chichak Galen Literary Agency Inc., 381 Park Avenue S., Suite 1020, New York, NY 10016-8806.

■ Career

Writer, 1980—. *Member:* Science Fiction Writers of America.

■ Awards, Honors

Hugo Award nomination for best short story, World Science Fiction Convention, 1983, for "Pawn's Gambit"; Hugo Award for best novella, 1984, for *Cascade Point;* Hugo Award nomination for best short story, 1985, for "Return to the Fold."

■ Writings

SCIENCE FICTION

The Blackcollar, DAW, 1983.
A Coming of Age, Bluejay Books, 1984.
Cobra, Baen, 1985.
Spinneret (first published serially in *Analog,* July-October, 1985), Bluejay Books, 1985.
Blackcollar: The Backlash Mission, DAW, 1986.
Cobra Strike, Baen, 1986.

Cascade Point and Other Stories, Bluejay Books, 1986, title novella published singly (bound with *Hardfought* by Greg Bear), Tor Books, 1988.
Triplet, Baen, 1987.
Cobra Bargain, Baen, 1988.
Deadman Switch, Baen, 1988.
Time Bomb and Zahndry Others (stories), Baen, 1988.
Warhorse, Baen, 1990.
Heir to the Empire (Star Wars Trilogy, Vol. 1), Bantam, 1991.
Distant Friends and Others (stories), Baen, 1992.
Cobras Two, Baen, 1992.
Dark Force Rising (Star Wars Trilogy, Vol. 2), Bantam, 1992.
The Last Command (Star Wars Trilogy, Vol. 3), Bantam, 1993.
Conquerors' Pride, Bantam, 1994.
Conquerors' Heritage, Bantam, 1995.
Conquerors' Legacy, Bantam, 1996.

Also author of *Starlord,* a three-part comic book, Marvel Comics, 1996-97. Zahn's work has been published in anthologies, including *The 1983 Annual World's Best SF,* edited by Donald A. Wollheim, DAW, 1983, and *Alien Stars,* edited by Elizabeth Mitchell, Baen, 1985. Also contributor of numerous stories and novelettes to magazines, including *Analog Science Fiction/Science Fact, Ares, Fantasy and Science Fiction, Fantasy Gamer, Isaac Asimov's Science Fiction Magazine, Rigel,* and *Space Gamer.*

■ Adaptations

Heir to the Empire, Conquerors' Pride, and *Conquerors' Heritage* have all been recorded on audio cassette for Bantam; *Heir to the Empire, Dark Force Rising,* and *The Last Command* have been recorded on audio cassette by BDD audio; *Conquerors' Pride* and *Conquerors' Heritage* have been recorded on audio cassette by the Brilliance Corp. A comic book version of *Heir to the Empire* was published by Dark Horse Comics, 1996, illustrated by Olivier Vatine.

■ Sidelights

Timothy Zahn is an award-winning author whose military and action science fiction stories and books often deal with topics of appeal to adolescents and feature youthful protagonists. But as his Star Wars series demonstrates, Zahn is much more than a young adult writer. An adaptation of the George Lucas films, Zahn's trilogy are all bestsellers, not only bringing him financial success but also establishing him as one of the foremost science fiction writers of the day. Yet it was a near miss for Zahn, who began writing science fiction only as a hobby while studying for his real career as a physicist.

Growing up in Chicago, Zahn earned his B.A. at Michigan State and M.A. at the University of Illinois, where he also continued on with graduate studies. During this time he began writing science fiction stories, but it wasn't until he sold his first story, "Ernie," to *Analog Science Fiction/Science Fact* in 1979 that he began to wonder if writing could be more than a hobby for him. He had resolved to take a year off from his studies and devote it to writing when his thesis advisor died in 1979, which would necessitate a new project under a new advisor. Instead of the latter course, Zahn decided to take his trial break, and published nine stories in one year. It was "enough to encourage me to continue," he once commented. In fact, there was no going back to academia for Zahn. Over the next few years, he published several dozen stories, becoming a regular contributor to *Analog Science Fiction/Science Fact,* and exploring the themes of militarism and the clash of cultures that would later inform his novels.

Zahn's first novel, *The Blackcollar,* was published in 1983, and posited an Earth dominated by an alien race, the Ryqril, who so oppress the remnant population of the planet that these humans rebel, with the help of a class of super-warriors who are not only trained in the martial arts, but who also have drug-enhanced reflexes. It is this same clash between Ryqrils and Blackcollar warriors that forms the centerpiece of a later Zahn book, *Blackcollar: The Backlash Mission.* Reviewing the first book in *Analog Science Fiction/Science Fact,* Tom Easton noted the "originality" in Zahn's debut novel, and also commented, regarding Zahn's style and use of detail, that "there is more realism here, and hence more satisfaction."

Psychic powers and a cautionary tale of generational competition inform Zahn's second novel, *A Coming of Age.* Mutational change among the children of the planet Tigris endows them with psychic powers between age five and the onset of puberty. At one point in Tigris's history, these supercharged children ruled the planet, though they largely misused their powers and proved violent. Now the adults, the Lost Generation, have developed new strategies to control them: child-rearing in large groups or hives, and deprivation of education among other restrictions. Out of this melange, Zahn creates a chase/detective story involving young Lisa, who does not want to lose her powers, a scientist who kidnaps his own son to experiment with a drug that

Zahn's novel revolves around a ring of moons called Solitaire, a place that contains mines filled with precious metals as well as a force field that keeps the moons inaccessible by exacting a heavy price from those who invade its sphere. (Cover illustration by David Mattingly.)

could prolong the life of such telekinetic powers, and Detective Stanford Tirrell and his young assistant Tonio, who are on the trail of the kidnapper. Reviewing the book for *School Library Journal,* Penny Parker noted that "the story will interest SF readers, as well as young adults interested in stories in which young adults outsmart the adult characters." A reviewer for *Kirkus Reviews* also found Zahn's idea appealing, though wondering at the execution: "Unfortunately ... Zahn turns this splendid notion into nothing more than a routine, kiddy-cops-and-baddies melodrama." Nancy Choice, however, writing in *Voice of Youth Advocates,* felt that *A Coming of Age* "successfully combines science fiction with a good detective story," and went on to say that the book should be recommended for the magazine's Best Books for Young Adults. A *Publishers Weekly* reviewer concurred: "Zahn has written an entertaining police procedural that should especially appeal to teenagers."

Zahn sets the first volume of his best-selling additions to the *Star Wars* saga—featuring Luke Skywalker as the first in a line of greatly anticipated Jedi knights and the expectant parents Princess Leia and Han Solo—five years after *Return of the Jedi.* (Cover illustration by Tom Jung.)

A serialized novel, *Spinneret* tells a story of Earth's first attempts at interstellar colonization. In a universe where aliens seemingly have snapped up all the good planets, Earthlings have to be content with Astra, a world so barren that no one else wants it. Astra, however, proves richer than anyone could imagine, yielding an ore that can be spun into a strong metallic thread. More of an old-fashioned space adventure than *A Coming of Age, Spinneret* was lauded by *Publishers Weekly* as one of "Zahn's best novels," and *Booklist* contributor Roland Green commented on the book's "excellent narrative technique, clear prose, and intelligent characterization." Hal Hoover, reviewing *Spinneret* in *Voice of Youth Advocates,* called the book "a first class sci-fi novel," and noted that Zahn "skillfully mixes espionage, archeology, human and alien psychology, and human rights psychology."

Zahn continued combining space adventures and militarism with a series of novels about more superhuman warriors, the Cobras, short for Computerized Body Reflex Armament. As with his Blackcollars, these Cobras are specially skilled soldiers with a technological edge: they have been programmed to react with deadly force to anything they sense as danger. Created to battle the Troft forces, they have no place in civilian society, and are banished to a far corner of the world where they can establish their own domain and protect settlers. The series is built around the Moreau clan, whose patriarch is Jonny Moreau, a young Cobra recruit in the first book, *Cobra.* Throughout the course of that book Jonny matures to become a leader of his people, and in the second of the series, *Cobra Strike,* he and his three sons must once again battle the Trofts and a strange group of humans who wish to use them as mercenaries. By the third book in the series, *Cobra Bargain,* a granddaugh-

In the short novel *Distant Friends,* one of seven tales in this collection, telepathic lovers Dale Ravenhall and Colleen Isaac are forced to develop a shield that blocks their powers when they, and all telepaths, become victimized because of their gift. (Cover illustration by David Mattingly.)

ter, Justine, has decided to enter this all-male domain of action hero. While mentioning that Zahn's Cobra series provides "plenty of heart-stopping action," Diane G. Yates in *Voice of Youth Advocates* also noted that Zahn manages to avoid all-out war in these books, coming up with other more creative solutions to carnage. "The moral questions that [the Moreaus] struggle with are those that concern us all," Yates commented, "and to find a character in a military SF novel who agonizes over ethical questions is a refreshing change, and a welcome one."

In 1984 Zahn won a Hugo Award for his novella *Cascade Point,* about a spaceship that winds up in an alternate universe. This work was gathered with other published short stories for the 1986 publication, *Cascade Point and Other Stories.* Reviewing the collection for *Washington Post Book World,* Gregory Frost noted that "every story of Zahn's contains a novel idea," and *Booklist* reviewer Green remarked that the collection is "certainly high-quality work," though rather traditional in nature. Writing in *Voice of Youth Advocates,* Joni Bodart described the collection as "well-written, with believable situations, witty dialogue and engaging characters." Other short story collections include 1988's *Time Bomb and Zahndry Others,* and *Distant Friends and Others,* published in 1992.

Three other of Zahn's works of the late 1980s also rely less on militarism and adventure and more on psychological analysis of characters. *Triplet* is, according to Green in *Booklist,* "an intelligent, literate exploration of how science and magic coexist on three planets," while *Deadman Switch* is an examination of possible negative consequences of the death penalty. Death row is in the pilot's cabin on commercial ships bound for the world of Solitaire, whose territory can only be entered or exited by a spaceship navigated by a corpse—hence the use of convict pilots who will be executed upon entry to Solitaire. The 1990 work *Warhorse* is more of a return to Zahn's favorite theme of conflict between alien cultures, in this case an alien species who are biological engineers, Tampies, who think that all life is valuable. This belief structure comes into conflict with the rough and ready human colonists, and the Tampies' biologically-engineered spaceships—warhorses—act like updated Blackcollars or Cobras in the drama. "Zahn at his best," is how Roland Green described *Warhorse* in *Booklist.*

Zahn's career, already successful by most standards, went interstellar in 1991 with the introduction of his Star Wars series. Picking up the story five years after the point where George Lucas had left it with his final movie, *The Return of the Jedi,* Zahn has Han Solo and Princess Leia married and expecting twins. The evil Empire of Darth Vader has been defeated and Luke Skywalker continues to study the secrets of the Jedi. Trouble soon brews, however, when Grand Admiral Thrawn, a former Empire warlord, attacks the Republic in the first book in the trilogy, *Heir to the Empire.* The adventures and escapades continue in volume two, *Dark Force Rising,* "a thundering melodrama with a satisfy-

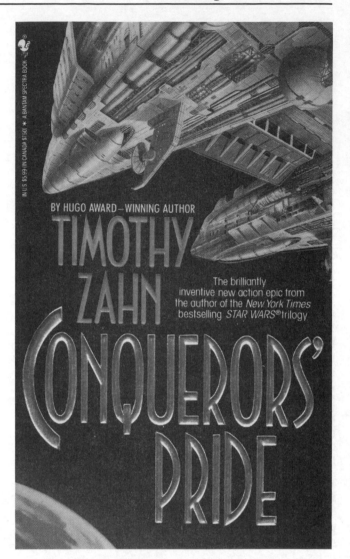

Zahn's futuristic action/adventure epic outlines the quest of Lord Stewart Cavanaugh to rescue his son, Commander Pheylon Cavanaugh, from the aliens who have attacked their home. (Cover illustration by Paul Youll.)

ingly complicated plot," according to *Kirkus Reviews.* A commentator reviewing this second book in *Publishers Weekly* noted that Zahn "adroitly" juggles plot twists and plot lines "to produce skillfully paced entertainment," while *Booklist* reviewer Green concluded that Zahn's adaptation was "one of the more remarkable pastiches of recent years." The trilogy was completed by *The Last Command,* with the ultimate vanquishing of Thrawn's forces by a small group led by Luke Skywalker who infiltrate the Grand Admiral's stronghold. Lisa Prolman commented in *Voice of Youth Advocates* that "Zahn's handling of the characters and plot create a work that readers will enjoy and is a joy to read," and noted that this final installment is a "thoroughly mesmerizing and satisfying continuation of the Star Wars saga." Each volume of the trilogy spent weeks on the *New York Times* bestseller list, with *Heir to the Empire* reaching number one.

Zahn, however, has not been resting on his laurels. The 1994 *Conquerors' Pride* initiated another trilogy, continued in *Conquerors' Heritage* and *Conquerors' Legacy*. Combining the theme of clashing cultures with a militaristic flavor, Zahn sets the first novel in the far future when humanity is facing difficulties and tensions both externally and from within. A new militaristic enemy attacks, and the son of an important statesman is captured after a space battle. *Booklist* reviewer Green commended Zahn for his "usual knack for swift pacing, plausible technology and characters, and a lived-in setting," all of which, Green commented, combine to make *Conquerors' Pride* both realistic and a page-turner. Interstellar war erupts in the second novel of the trilogy, *Conquerors' Heritage*, another "finely wrought space adventure," according to Green. The Zhirrzh, or alien race of conquerors of the title, battle the humans and their super-weapons in this installment. The trilogy is completed with *Conquerors' Legacy*.

Despite his successful exploration of thought-provoking themes, Zahn is wary of dubbing himself anything more than a teller of tales. "I consider myself primarily a storyteller," he once remarked, "and as such have no major pulpit-thumping 'message' that I always try to insert in each story or book. If any theme crops up more than any other, it is my strong belief that there is no prison—whether physical, social, or emotional—that can permanently trap a person who truly wishes to break free of the bonds."

■ Works Cited

Bodart, Joni, review of *Cascade Point and Other Stories, Voice of Youth Advocates,* June, 1986, pp. 91-92.

Choice, Nancy, review of *A Coming of Age, Voice of Youth Advocates,* August, 1985, p. 196.

Review of *A Coming of Age, Kirkus Reviews,* November 1, 1984, p. 1025.

Review of *A Coming of Age, Publishers Weekly,* December 14, 1984, pp. 41-42.

Review of *Dark Force Rising, Kirkus Reviews,* April 1, 1992, p. 434.

Review of *Dark Force Rising, Publishers Weekly,* March 23, 1992, p. 64.

Easton, Tom, review of *The Blackcollars, Analog Science Fiction/Science Fact,* February, 1984, pp. 167-68.

Frost, Gregory, "Hard Tech," *Washington Post Book World,* May 25, 1986, p. 8.

Green, Roland, review of *Spinneret, Booklist,* January 1, 1986, p. 662.

Green, Roland, review of *Cascade Point and Other Stories, Booklist,* May 1, 1986, p. 1288.

Green, Roland, review of *Triplet, Booklist,* August, 1987, p. 1722.

Green, Roland, review of *Warhorse, Booklist,* March 15, 1990, p. 1420.

Green, Roland, review of *Dark Force Rising, Booklist,* April 1, 1992, p. 1413.

Green, Roland, review of *Conquerors' Pride, Booklist,* September 1, 1994, p. 28.

Green, Roland, review of *Conquerors' Heritage, Booklist,* September 1, 1995, p. 48.

Hoover, Hal, review of *Spinneret, Voice of Youth Advocates,* June, 1986, p. 92.

Parker, Penny, review of *A Coming of Age, School Library Journal,* September, 1985, p. 155.

Prolman, Lisa, review of *The Last Command, Voice of Youth Advocates,* October, 1993, p. 237.

Review of *Spinneret, Publishers Weekly,* October 25, 1985, p. 61.

Yates, Diane G., review of *Cobra* and *Cobra Strikes, Voice of Youth Advocates,* June, 1986, p. 92.

■ For More Information See

BOOKS

Chute, John, and Peter Nicholls, *The Encyclopedia of Science Fiction,* St. Martin's, 1993.

Twentieth-Century Science Fiction Writers, 3rd edition, St. James Press, 1992.

PERIODICALS

Analog Science Fiction/Science Fact, October, 1985, p. 182; November, 1985, pp. 182-83; August, 1986, pp. 178-79; November, 1986, p. 182; April, 1988, pp. 181-82.

Christian Science Monitor, January 3, 1986, p. 18.

Fantasy Review, April, 1985, p. 31; May, 1985, p. 22; December, 1985, p. 26; March, 1986, p. 25.

Library Journal, April 15, 1992, p. 125.

Publishers Weekly, March 21, 1987, p. 77; July 3, 1987, p. 58.

School Library Journal, February, 1992, p. 122.

—*Sketch by J. Sydney Jones*

*   *   *

ZHANG, Christopher Zhong-Yuan 1954-

■ Personal

Born February 16, 1954, in Shanghai, China; son of Zhi Bang (a high school teacher) and Pei Yu (a high school teacher) Zhang; married Wen Ying Yan (a doctor); children: Xing Xing. *Education:* East China University, B.F.A., 1988; Rhode Island College, M.F.A., 1992.

■ Addresses

Home and office—66 Berkeley Ave., New London, CT 06320. *Agent*—Karen Klockner, 23825 Stanford Rd., Shaker Heights, OH 44122.

■ Career

Artist and illustrator, New London, CT, 1967—. Has also worked as an art teacher. *Member:* Mystic Art Association, Lyme Academy of Fine Arts, Copley Society of Boston.

CHRISTOPHER ZHONG-YUAN ZHANG

■ Awards, Honors

Has won numerous exhibition awards and prizes in both the United States and China.

■ Writings

(With Yong Ping Li; self-illustrated) *The Silk Route,* Shanghai People's Fine Art Press, 1989.

ILLUSTRATOR

He Ling, *Glory of the Truth,* Shanghai People's Fine Art Press (Shanghai, China), 1988.
Ching Yeung Russell, *First Apple,* Boyds Mills Press, 1994.
Ching Yeung Russell, *Water Ghost,* Boyds Mills Press, 1995.
Ching Yeung Russell, *Lichee Tree,* Boyds Mills Press, 1996.

■ Work in Progress

Thirty-two full-color illustrations for *Moon Festival,* a poem by Ching Yeung Russell.

■ Sidelights

"Born in an intellectual family in Shanghai, I was deeply influenced by traditional Chinese education, and loved art when I was a child," illustrator Christopher Zhong-Yuan Zhang told *SATA.* "Fascinated by the Western arts, I chose to be an artist, thus starting my painting career. As a Chinese artist living in the United States, I was able to see lots of cultural conflicts between the West and the East on one hand, and much more significantly, the inter-cultural tolerance, interaction, and harmony between the two, on the other hand. My obsession with this whole new world of arts, an exceptionally beautiful combination of Western and Oriental arts, highly motivates me to pursue its artistic truth, developing a painting style of my own for both Western and Oriental peoples. This has become the focus of my career: I apply the Western painting and drawing techniques to the lives and social customs of the Chinese people, trying to create a cultural unity as a symbol of our common humanity. Over thirty years of relentless effort, I have successfully displayed my oil paintings, watercolors, and drawings across the United States. Many exhibits have been collected privately by individuals and institutions. The success suggests people's appreciation and recognition of my artistic contribution.

"At a one-man show in Charleston, South Carolina, I met Christina (Ching Yeung) Russell, a Chinese American writer who loved my works and invited me to do the illustrations for her first novel, *First Apple.* In 1995 her second novel, *Water Ghost,* was published with my illustrations and became one of that year's recommended books." Lauren Peterson noted in her review of *Water Ghost* for *Booklist,* "Delicate illustrations in washes of gray tones are nicely interspersed throughout the compelling drama." "Shortly after *Water Ghost,*" Zhang explained to *SATA,* "I accepted another commission for her third children's book, *Moon Festival.* As it needed thirty-two full-color illustrations, I decided to work in all oils. I spent three months travelling in China, tracing and collecting bits and pieces of cultural information. The research helped me a great deal with a whole lot of good ideas.

"Illustrations strengthen the flavor and impression of a novel. A story with illustrations is told vividly, not only by words, but by pictures as well. To do such a good illustration, however, requires both a good idea and good skills, like oil painting. More importantly, the illustrator must understand the story extremely well; not only literally, but also culturally. When American readers are puzzled by the Chinese culture in the novel, the illustrations will definitely provide the keys. In this sense, my illustrations will bridge the cultural gap. I can't stop loving this tough but meaningful job."

■ Works Cited

Peterson, Lauren, review of *Water Ghost, Booklist,* October 15, 1995, p. 405.

■ For More Information See

PERIODICALS

Booklist, November 1, 1994.
School Library Journal, September, 1994; December, 1995, p. 108.

Cumulative Indexes

Illustrations Index

(In the following index, the number of the volume in which an illustrator's work appears is given *before* the colon, and the page number on which it appears is given *after* the colon. For example, a drawing by Adams, Adrienne appears in Volume 2 on page 6, another drawing by her appears in Volume 3 on page 80, another drawing in Volume 8 on page 1, another drawing in Volume 15 on page 107, and so on and so on....)

YABC

Index citations including this abbreviation refer to listings appearing in
Yesterday's Authors of Books for Children, also published by Gale Research
Inc., which covers authors who died prior to 1960.

A

Aas, Ulf *5:* 174
Abbé, S. van
  See van Abbé, S.
Abel, Raymond *6:* 122; *7:* 195; *12:* 3;
  21: 86; *25:* 119
Abelliera, Aldo *71:* 120
Abolafia, Yossi *60:* 2
Abrahams, Hilary *26:* 205; *29:* 24-25;
  53: 61
Abrams, Kathie *36:* 170
Abrams, Lester *49:* 26
Accorsi, William *11:* 198
Acs, Laszlo *14:* 156; *42:* 22
Adams, Adrienne *2:* 6; *3:* 80; *8:* 1; *15:*
  107; *16:* 180; *20:* 65; *22:* 134-135;
  33: 75; *36:* 103, 112; *39:* 74; *86:* 54;
  90: 2, 3
Adams, John Wolcott *17:* 162
Adams, Norman *55:* 82
Adamson, George *30:* 23, 24; *69:* 64
Addams, Charles *55:* 5
Ade, Rene *76:* 198
Adkins, Alta *22:* 250
Adkins, Jan *8:* 3; *69:* 4
Adler, Peggy *22:* 6; *29:* 31
Adler, Ruth *29:* 29
Adragna, Robert *47:* 145
Agard, Nadema *18:* 1
Agre, Patricia *47:* 195
Ahl, Anna Maria *32:* 24
Ahlberg, Allan *68:* 6-7, 9
Ahlberg, Janet *68:* 6-7, 9
Aicher-Scholl, Inge *63:* 127
Aichinger, Helga *4:* 5, 45
Aitken, Amy *31:* 34
Akaba, Suekichi *46:* 23; *53:* 127
Akasaka, Miyoshi *YABC 2:* 261
Akino, Fuku *6:* 144
Alain *40:* 41
Alajalov *2:* 226
Alborough, Jez *86:* 1, 2, 3
Albrecht, Jan *37:* 176
Albright, Donn *1:* 91
Alcala, Alfredo *91:* 128
Alcorn, John *3:* 159; *7:* 165; *31:* 22; *44:*
  127; *46:* 23, 170
Alda, Arlene *44:* 24
Alden, Albert *11:* 103
Aldridge, Andy *27:* 131
Alex, Ben *45:* 25, 26
Alexander, Ellen *91:* 3
Alexander, Lloyd *49:* 34
Alexander, Martha *3:* 206; *11:* 103; *13:*
  109; *25:* 100; *36:* 131; *70:* 6, 7
Alexander, Paul *85:* 57; *90:* 9
Alexeieff, Alexander *14:* 6; *26:* 199
Alfano, Wayne *80:* 69
Aliki

See Brandenberg, Aliki
Allamand, Pascale *12:* 9
Allan, Judith *38:* 166
Alland, Alexandra *16:* 255
Allen, Gertrude *9:* 6
Allen, Graham *31:* 145
Allen, Pamela *50:* 25, 26-27, 28; *81:* 9,
  10
Allen, Rowena *47:* 75
Allen, Thomas B. *81:* 101; *82:* 248; *89:*
  37
Allen, Tom *85:* 176
Allender, David *73:* 223
Alley, R. W. *80:* 183
Allison, Linda *43:* 27
Allport, Mike *71:* 55
Almquist, Don *11:* 8; *12:* 128; *17:* 46;
  22: 110
Aloise, Frank *5:* 38; *10:* 133; *30:* 92
Althea
  See Braithwaite, Althea
Altschuler, Franz *11:* 185; *23:* 141; *40:*
  48; *45:* 29; *57:* 181
Ambrus, Victor G. *1:* 6-7, 194; *3:* 69; *5:*
  15; *6:* 44; *7:* 36; *8:* 210; *12:* 227; *14:*
  213; *15:* 213; *22:* 209; *24:* 36; *28:*
  179; *30:* 178; *32:* 44, 46; *38:* 143; *41:*
  25, 26, 27, 28, 29, 30, 31, 32; *42:* 87;
  44: 190; *55:* 172; *62:* 30, 144, 145,
  148; *86:* 99, 100, 101; *87:* 66, 137;
  89: 162
Ames, Lee J. *3:* 12; *9:* 130; *10:* 69; *17:*
  214; *22:* 124
Amon, Aline *9:* 9
Amoss, Berthe *5:* 5
Amundsen, Dick *7:* 77
Amundsen, Richard E. *5:* 10; *24:* 122
Ancona, George *12:* 11; *55:* 144
Anderson, Alasdair *18:* 122
Anderson, Brad *33:* 28
Anderson, C. W. *11:* 10
Anderson, Carl *7:* 4
Anderson, Catherine Corley *72:* 2
Anderson, Doug *40:* 111
Anderson, Erica *23:* 65
Anderson, Laurie *12:* 153, 155
Anderson, Susan *90:* 12
Anderson, Wayne *23:* 119; *41:* 239; *56:*
  7; *62:* 26
Andreasen, Daniel *86:* 157; *87:* 104
Andrew, John *22:* 4
Andrews, Benny *14:* 251; *31:* 24; *57:* 6,
  7
Anelay, Henry *57:* 173
Angel, Marie *47:* 22
Angelo, Valenti *14:* 8; *18:* 100; *20:* 232;
  32: 70
Anglund, Joan Walsh *2:* 7, 250-251; *37:*
  198, 199, 200
Anholt, Catherine *74:* 8
Anno, Mitsumasa *5:* 7; *38:* 25, 26-27,
  28, 29, 30, 31, 32; *77:* 3, 4

Antal, Andrew *1:* 124; *30:* 145
Apple, Margot *33:* 25; *35:* 206; *46:* 81;
  53: 8; *61:* 109; *64:* 21, 22, 24, 25, 27;
  71: 176; *77:* 53; *82:* 245
Appleyard, Dev *2:* 192
Aragonés, Sergio *48:* 23, 24, 25, 26, 27
Araneus *40:* 29
Archambault, Matthew *85:* 173
Archer, Janet *16:* 69
Ardizzone, Edward *1:* 11, 12; *2:* 105; *3:*
  258; *4:* 78; *7:* 79; *10:* 100; *15:* 232;
  20: 69, 178; *23:* 223; *24:* 125; *28:* 25,
  26, 27, 28, 29, 30, 31, 33, 34, 35, 36,
  37; *31:* 192, 193; *34:* 215, 217; *60:*
  173; *64:* 145; *87:* 176; *YABC 2:* 25
Arenella, Roy *14:* 9
Armer, Austin *13:* 3
Armer, Laura Adams *13:* 3
Armer, Sidney *13:* 3
Armitage, David *47:* 23
Armitage, Eileen *4:* 16
Armstrong, George *10:* 6; *21:* 72
Arno, Enrico *1:* 217; *2:* 22, 210; *4:* 9; *5:*
  43; *6:* 52; *29:* 217, 219; *33:* 152; *35:*
  99; *43:* 31, 32, 33; *45:* 212, 213, 214;
  72: 72; *74:* 166
Arnold, Emily *76:* 7, 9, 10
Arnosky, Jim *22:* 20; *70:* 9, 10, 11
Arrowood, Clinton *12:* 193; *19:* 11; *65:*
  210
Artell, Mike *89:* 8
Arting, Fred J. *41:* 63
Artzybasheff, Boris *13:* 143; *14:* 15; *40:*
  152, 155
Aruego, Ariane *6:* 4
Aruego, Jose *4:* 140; *6:* 4; *7:* 64; *33:*
  195; *35:* 208; *68:* 16, 17; *75:* 46
Asare, Meshack *86:* 9
Asch, Frank *5:* 9; *66:* 2, 4, 6, 7, 9, 10
Ashby, Gail *11:* 135
Ashby, Gwynneth *44:* 26
Ashley, C. W. *19:* 197
Ashmead, Hal *8:* 70
Aska, Warabe *56:* 10
Assel, Steven *44:* 153; *77:* 22, 97
Astrop, John *32:* 56
Atene, Ann *12:* 18
Atherton, Lisa *38:* 198
Atkinson, Allen *60:* 5
Atkinson, J. Priestman *17:* 275
Atkinson, Janet *86:* 147
Atkinson, Wayne *40:* 46
Attebery, Charles *38:* 170
Atwood, Ann *7:* 9
Aubrey, Meg Kelleher *77:* 159
Augarde, Steve *25:* 22
Austerman, Miriam *23:* 107
Austin, Margot *11:* 16
Austin, Robert *3:* 44
Austin, Virginia *81:* 205
Auth, Tony *51:* 5
Avedon, Richard *57:* 140

Author Index

The following index gives the number of the volume in which an author's biographical sketch, Brief Entry, or Obituary appears.

This index includes references to all entries in the following series, which are also published by Gale Research Inc.

YABC—*Yesterday's Authors of Books for Children: Facts and Pictures about Authors and Illustrators of Books for Young People from Early Times to 1960*
CLR—*Children's Literature Review: Excerpts from Reviews, Criticism, and Commentary on Books for Children*
SAAS—*Something about the Author Autobiography Series*

Anderson, Mary 1939- 82
  Earlier sketch in SATA 7
  See also SAAS 23
Anderson, Mona 1910- 40
Anderson, Mrs. Melvin
  See Anderson, Catherine Corley
Anderson, Norman D(ean) 1928- 22
Anderson, Peggy Perry 1953- 84
Anderson, Poul (William) 1926- 90
  Brief entry 39
Anderson, Rachel 1943- 86
  Earlier sketch in SATA 34
  See also SAAS 18
Anderson, Susan 1952- 90
Anderson, Wayne 1946- 56
Andre, Evelyn M(arie) 1924- 27
Andree, Louise
  See Coury, Louise Andree
Andrew, Prudence (Hastings) 1924- 87
Andrews, Benny 1930- 31
Andrews, F(rank) Emerson
  1902-1978 22
Andrews, J(ames) S(ydney) 1934- 4
Andrews, Jan 1942- 58
  Brief entry 49
Andrews, Julie 1935- 7
Andrews, Laura
  See Coury, Louise Andree
Andrews, Roy Chapman 1884-1960 19
Andrews, V(irginia) C(leo) (?)-1986
  Obituary 50
Andrews, Wendy
  See Sharmat, Marjorie Weinman
Andrews, William G. 1930- 74
Andrezel, Pierre
  See Blixen, Karen (Christentze Dinesen)
Andriola, Alfred J. 1912-1983
  Obituary 34
Andrist, Ralph K. 1914- 45
Andryszewski, Tricia 1956- 88
Anfousse, Ginette 1944-
  Brief entry 48
Angel, Marie (Felicity) 1923- 47
Angeles, Peter A. 1931- 40
Angell, Judie 1937- 78
  Earlier sketch in SATA 22
  See also CLR 33
Angell, Madeline 1919- 18
Angelo, Valenti 1897- 14
Angelou, Maya 1928- 49
Angier, Bradford 12
Angle, Paul M(cClelland) 1900-1975
  Obituary 20
Anglund, Joan Walsh 1926- 2
  See also CLR 1
Angrist, Stanley W(olff) 1933- 4
Anholt, Catherine 1958- 74
Anholt, Laurence 1959- 74
Anita
  See Daniel, Anita
Annett, Cora
  See Scott, Cora Annett (Pipitone)
Annixter, Jane
  See Sturtzel, Jane Levington
Annixter, Paul
  See Sturtzel, Howard A(llison)
Anno, Mitsumasa 1926- 77
  Earlier sketches in SATA 5, 38
  See also CLR 14
Anrooy, Frans van
  See Van Anrooy, Francine
Anstey, Caroline 1958- 81
Antell, Will D. 1935- 31
Anthony, Barbara 1932- 29
Anthony, C. L.
  See Smith, Dorothy Gladys
Anthony, Edward 1895-1971 21
Anthony, John
  See Ciardi, John (Anthony)
Anthony, Piers 1934- 84
  See also SAAS 22
Anthony, Susan C(arol) 1953- 87
Anticaglia, Elizabeth 1939- 12
Antolini, Margaret Fishback 1904-1985
  Obituary 45
Anton, Michael (James) 1940- 12

Antonacci, Robert J(oseph) 1916- 45
  Brief entry 37
Aoki, Hisako 1942- 45
Apfel, Necia H(alpern) 1930- 51
  Brief entry 41
Aphrodite, J.
  See Livingston, Carole
Apostolou, Christine Hale 1955- 82
Appel, Benjamin 1907-1977 39
  Obituary 21
Appel, Martin E(liot) 1948- 45
Appel, Marty
  See Appel, Martin E(liot)
Appelt, Kathi 1954- 83
Appiah, Peggy 1921- 84
  Earlier sketch in SATA 15
  See also SAAS 19
Apple, Margot 64
  Brief entry 42
Applebaum, Stan 1929- 45
Appleton, Victor
  See Macdonald, James D.
Appleton, Victor [Collective
  pseudonym] 67
  Earlier sketch in SATA 1
Appleton, Victor II [Collective
  pseudonym] 67
  Earlier sketch in SATA 1
Apsler, Alfred 1907- 10
Aquillo, Don
  See Prince, J(ack) H(arvey)
Aragones, Sergio 1937- 48
  Brief entry 39
Araujo, Frank P. 1937- 86
Arbuckle, Dorothy Fry 1910-1982
  Obituary 33
Arbuthnot, May Hill 1884-1969 2
Archambault, John 67
Archer, Frank
  See O'Connor, Richard
Archer, Jules 1915- 85
  Earlier sketch in SATA 4
  See also SAAS 5
Archer, Marion Fuller 1917- 11
Archibald, Joe
  See Archibald, Joseph S(topford)
Archibald, Joseph S(topford)
  1898-1986 3
  Obituary 47
Ardai, Charles 1969- 85
Arden, Barbie
  See Stoutenburg, Adrien
Arden, William
  See Lynds, Dennis
Ardizzone, Edward 1900-1979 28
  Obituary 21
  Earlier sketch in SATA 1
  See also CLR 3
Ardley, Neil (Richard) 1937- 43
Arehart-Treichel, Joan 1942- 22
Arenella, Roy 1939- 14
Arkin, Alan (Wolf) 1934- 59
  Brief entry 32
Arley, Robert
  See Jackson, Mike
Armer, Alberta (Roller) 1904- 9
Armer, Laura Adams 1874-1963 13
Armitage, David 1943-
  Brief entry 38
Armitage, Ronda (Jacqueline)
  1943- 47
  Brief entry 38
Armour, Richard (Willard)
  1906-1989 14
  Obituary 61
Armstrong, George D. 1927- 10
Armstrong, Gerry (Breen) 1929- 10
Armstrong, Jennifer 1961- 77
Armstrong, Louise 43
  Brief entry 33
Armstrong, Richard 1903- 11
Armstrong, William H. 1914- 4
  See also CLR 1
  See also SAAS 7
Arndt, Ursula (Martha H.) 56
  Brief entry 39
Arneson, D(on) J(on) 1935- 37

Arnett, Carolyn
  See Cole, Lois Dwight
Arno, Enrico 1913-1981 43
  Obituary 28
Arnold, Caroline 1944- 85
  Brief entry 34
  Earlier sketch in SATA 36
  See also SAAS 23
Arnold, Elliott 1912-1980 5
  Obituary 22
Arnold, Emily 1939- 76
  Earlier sketch in SATA 50
Arnold, Katya 1947- 82
Arnold, Oren 1900- 4
Arnold, Susan (Riser) 1951- 58
Arnold, Tedd 1949- 69
Arnoldy, Julie
  See Bischoff, Julia Bristol
Arnosky, Jim 1946- 70
  Earlier sketch in SATA 22
  See also CLR 15
Arnott, Kathleen 1914- 20
Arnov, Boris, Jr. 1926- 12
Arnow, Harriette (Louisa) Simpson
  1908-1986 42
  Obituary 47
Arnsteen, Katy Keck 1934- 68
Arnstein, Helene S(olomon) 1915- 12
Arntson, Herbert E(dward) 1911- 12
Aroner, Miriam 82
Aronin, Ben 1904-1980
  Obituary 25
Arora, Shirley (Lease) 1930- 2
Arquette, Lois S(teinmetz) 1934- 1
  See Duncan, Lois S(teinmetz)
Arrick, Fran
  See Angell, Judie
Arrowood, (McKendrick Lee) Clinton
  1939- 19
Arrowsmith, Pat
  See Barton, Pat
Artell, Mike 1948- 89
Arthur, Robert
  See Feder, Robert Arthur
Arthur, Ruth M(abel) 1905-1979 7
  Obituary 26
Artis, Vicki Kimmel 1945- 12
Artzybasheff, Boris (Miklailovich)
  1899-1965 14
Aruego, Ariane
  See Dewey, Ariane
Aruego, Jose 1932- 68
  Earlier sketch in SATA 6
  See also CLR 5
Arundel, Honor (Morfydd)
  1919-1973 4
  Obituary 24
  See also CLR 35
Arundel, Jocelyn
  See Alexander, Jocelyn (Anne) Arundel
Arvey, Michael 1948- 79
Asare, Meshack (Yaw) 1945- 86
Asbjoernsen, Peter Christen
  1812-1885 15
Asch, Frank 1946- 66
  Earlier sketch in SATA 5
Ash, Jutta 1942- 38
Ashabranner, Brent (Kenneth)
  1921- 67
  Earlier sketch in SATA 1
  See also CLR 28
  See also SAAS 14
Ashby, Gwynneth 1922- 44
Ashe, Arthur (Robert, Jr.), Jr.
  1943-1993 65
  Obituary 87
Ashe, Geoffrey (Thomas) 1923- 17
Ashe, Mary Ann
  See Lewis, Mary (Christianna)
Asher, Sandy (Fenichel) 1942- 71
  Brief entry 34
  Earlier sketch in SATA 36
  See also SAAS 13
Ashey, Bella
  See Breinburg, Petronella
Ashford, Daisy
  See Ashford, Margaret Mary